C. Steinberg

LATIN AMERICAN CULTURE

LATIN AMERICAN CULTURE

AN ANTHROPOLOGICAL SYNTHESIS

EMILIO WILLEMS
Vanderbilt University

HARPER & ROW, PUBLISHERS
New York, Evanston, San Francisco, London

Sponsoring Editor: Walter H. Lippincott, Jr.
Project Editor: Elizabeth Dilernia
Designer: Frances Torbert Tilley
Production Supervisor: Will C. Jomarrón

LATIN AMERICAN CULTURE: An Anthropological Synthesis

Library of Congress Cataloging in Publication Data

Willems, Emilio.
    Latin American culture.
    Bibliography: p.
    1. Latin America.   I. Title.
F1408.W7   309.1′8′003   74-11651
ISBN 0-06-047118-2

Contents

v

Preface

This book is the outcome of a lifelong involvement in Latin America. In 1949 when I began to teach American students about contemporary Latin America, I could look back on eighteen years of continuous residence in Brazil, not as a visiting scholar, but as an immigrant who had been facing the difficult task of earning a living and raising a family on the meager income of a teacher. Although frustrating at times, adaptation to Brazilian small-town life proved not only inevitable but invaluable, and eventually I found myself to be a member of the Brazilian middle class. Instead of being an abstraction its culture became my own. I was "going native," but without ceasing to be an anthropologist. The experience certainly afforded ample opportunity for me to understand the culture from within and strictly in its own terms.

Years of residence in three different states—Santa Catarina, Paraná, and São Paulo—gradually expanded and deepened my familiarity with the country. In 1937 I joined the faculty of the University of São Paulo, and during the following ten years I was able to carry out a series of research projects that took me to different regions and strongly contrasting ethnic groups. In 1949 I decided to accept an invitation to join the faculty of Vanderbilt University and its newly established Institute for Brazilian Studies.

In the 1950s and 1960s I concentrated on Spanish America. I spent one year in Chile and another in Colombia teaching and doing research. During the same period I was able to renew my contact with Brazil. In 1960 I studied the development of Protestantism in that country, and in 1967 I spent four months in northern Paraná to gather data on social mobility in a frontier society. To complete preparation for this book I embarked on another field trip in 1970–1971 that took me to Mexico, Brazil, Argentina, Chile, Peru, Ecuador, and Colombia. During six months I managed to gather a substantial amount of data on urbanization and urban culture.

Admitting that our knowledge of complex cultures such as those of modern Latin America can never be as deep as that of a small community, I am nevertheless convinced that there is no substitute for continuous first-hand contact with the people under scrutiny. Not only does one develop a growing sensitivity to the many disguises under which complacency and ethnocentric slants creep into the ways American and European scholars interpret Latin Americans, but one also learns to detect preconceptions and biases in the way Latin American scholars approach their own societies.

I would like to express my gratitude to Peter Marzahl, Ronald Spores, and Werner Baer, whose constructive criticism did much to improve the quality of the book. I also wish to acknowledge my debt to the Center for Latin American Studies of Vanderbilt University, which funded my field trip to Latin America in 1970–1971.

E. W.

Introduction

Our approach to Latin American culture

Latin America, as understood here, encompasses all the lands south of the Rio Grande that were originally conquered and settled by "Latin" peoples, namely, the Spaniards, the Portuguese, and the French. Obviously this area does not include the English-speaking West Indies and the Guyanas. Also excluded are all territories remaining under the sovereignty of France, Great Britain, the Netherlands, and the United States. A strong case could be made for including Puerto Rico and the French Antilles, but allegiance to other nations and dependence on their economic systems seem to create conditions that substantially reduce the comparability of such territories to the Latin American republics.

1

This book deviates from the conventional approach to the study of complex culture areas. Usually the area under scrutiny is divided according to a combination of geographical and cultural criteria into distinct regions, and the societies of each region, whether tribal or national, are submitted to separate inquiries.

No such a priori division is proposed here. Whatever regional variants emerged were *effects* of an evolutionary process that was unitary rather than differential. The conception of Latin American culture as a single or monistic process was inspired by the observation that many diverse native societies living in sharply contrasting habitats were exposed to the highly homogeneous cultural pressures of Iberian society, which was determined to impose feudal dependency and medieval Christianity. This is not to imply that the impact of Iberian culture generated identical effects everywhere; however, the Iberian imprint or common denominator appears to be unmistakable, ubiquitous, and capable of surviving adverse conditions.

It will be shown how the component forces of the cultural process— the patrimonial state, the Catholic Church, the landed estate, the kinship group, the colonial city, and peasantry—interacted with native societies, with each other, and with the habitat to create a traditional culture whose foundations had been transferred from Europe. The culture was traditional in that behavior was modeled on patterns imparted with little change by each generation to the next, mainly through the mechanisms of *patria potestas*, an autocratic state, an authoritarian church, and church-controlled educational institutions.

It will also be shown that tradition did not imply stagnancy. Continuous expansion of the settled regions of Latin America, the discovery of new mining areas, and the founding of numerous cities resulted in a massive influx of settlers from Iberia and slaves from Africa, as well as the dislocation of human and technological resources from established areas into newly settled ones. Although there were many advancing frontiers throughout the colonial period and the nineteenth century, the new cities, villages, and landed estates tended to fall in with established structural patterns once the initial struggle over land ownership had been settled. As we shall see, the occupation of new lands often generated subcultures without causing a major break with Iberian traditions.

The second part of the book begins with a discussion of the impact of the industrial revolution in Europe on the national societies of Latin America. Substantial expansion of international trade followed by industrialization brought a series of changes that eventually affected all aspects of the traditional culture.

Increasing differentiation and specialization of component units are believed to be inherent in cultural evolution. This raises the question of whether the evolution of Latin American culture ever reached the point of obliterating the common Iberian roots. To provide answers, a considerable amount of comparison was necessary. Brazil had to be compared with Spanish America, and the independent republics with one another. Thus a comparative line of inquiry runs parallel to the study of evolution. And to complete the anthropological perspective, the dominant aspects of the culture had to be viewed in relation to one another.

This book is no substitute for monographic studies of single countries. The emphasis is decidedly on Latin America, not on any of its component nations. Furthermore, since the book is an overview, detailed attention to particular countries or cultural aspects was out of the question. A few republics are hardly mentioned at all; such neglect does not imply unimportance, however, but sometimes lack of relevant data. Whenever it was possible to choose from a number of equally relevant factual accounts, the choice became, almost inevitably, a matter of subjective judgment. If equal attention had been paid to the whole range of specific events occurring in various countries and in different sectors of the culture, the book would exceed, by far, the limits of a synopsis.

There are more references to Brazil than to any other country. This merely reflects the relative size and complexity of Portuguese America. Brazil covers 49 percent of the total area of all 20 republics, and its population represents about 35 percent of all inhabitants of those countries. Internally, Brazil mirrors all the levels or stages of development occurring anywhere in Spanish America; thus the country appears to be a subcontinent, and it is dealt with as such.

No attempt has been made to include a description, analysis, or classification of the indigenous societies *as such*, past or present. The Amerindian cultures are taken into account only to the extent that they had or have a definite bearing on the cultural process commencing with the Iberian conquest and the permanent occupation of the continent.

Far from being taken for granted here, the assumption of a common Iberian heritage raises several initial questions. Is the idea of a Latin American culture to be taken literally, as a way of life common to all the peoples south of the Rio Grande, or is it merely a shorthand expression referring to a collection of national societies, each adhering to its way of life? The problem of cultural similarities and differences between two or more distinct societies is, of course, as old as anthropology, and in time emphasis has shifted back and forth from what is historically unique or particular in a given society to what that society may share with others. Turning away from the excesses of historical particularism, cultural anthropology again has focused its attention on the comparative approach and the search for cross-cultural regularities.

Nowadays no one would seriously question the uniqueness of any particular culture. Indeed, one may argue that so many traits and trait complexes are combined in a single culture that the uniqueness of the whole becomes a matter of probability, perhaps as much as the association of genes in the chromosomes of the human individual. There are so many modes of acting, thinking, and feeling—so many methods of coping with a vast array of environmental conditions, so many possible ways of organizing the various aspects of a society and reacting to the presence of other societies, and so many approaches to and conceptions of the supernatural—that the combination of patterns of behavior chosen from the arsenal of available options, is bound to be unique. For clearly, coincidence with combinations found in other societies is sufficiently improbable to permit us to discard the idea of one culture being the exact replica of any other culture.

However, uniqueness does not rule out or contradict the existence of similarities. Comparisons of societies located in widely separated parts of the world shows that a number of them share, for example, agricultural techniques, patterns of family and kinship organization, ways of allocating resources, distribution of political power, and institutional approaches to what is believed to be the supernatural world. It can also be shown that combinations of such elements are consistent rather than haphazard. Among the features allegedly common to all Latin American societies, the landed estate has attracted a great deal of attention. To keep comparison free from confusion, terms like plantation, latifundio, hacienda, fazenda, finca, fundo, rancho, and hato ought to be avoided. Not only do these terms convey distinct meanings in different regions, they have variously been chosen by different authors to signify either a general type of landholding or several distinct subtypes.

A cursory look at the large estate reveals many differentiating features. Crops range from sugar cane, tobacco, henequen, coffee, cotton, cocoa, bananas, and African palm, to wheat, rice, potatoes, and grapes. The annual round of activities related to each crop varies in rhythm and technique, in labor requirements, and in the way labor is used. Many of the estates are only partially cultivated; soil erosion is rampant, and technology follows the time-honored patterns that have been decried so often as sources of economic stagnation. On the other hand, more than a few large agricultural holdings have been modernized: All arable land is under cultivation, and fertilizers, hybrid seeds, and modern machinery are being used to increase production and improve the product. As one might expect, numerous large estates are neither extremely modern nor hopelessly archaic; they lie between the two extremes.

Most landed estates are family owned and have been since the first occupation of the land, but not always by successive generations of the same family. On the contrary, many of the large estates have changed owners quite often. Moreover, many holdings are owned by corporations, and modernization is often related to the shareholders' expectations of returns from their investments. In many regions the resident and transient labor force is composed of unassimilated or partially assimilated Indians; elsewhere the workers are Negroes, mestizoes, or descendents of European or Asian immigrants. Housing provided by the owners is often poor by anybody's standards; wages or payment in kind are close to the starvation level, and services such as schools, clinics, and hospitals are nonexistent. The opposite extreme is represented by individual owners and corporations that provide adequate housing, schools, and medical and sometimes social services to resident laborers. Labor shortage and a high degree of labor mobility can cause wages and other forms of compensation to rise at least to the subsistence level.

Let this incomplete account of differentiating features suffice to indicate for now, the complexity of the comparative approach. Is there really a common denominator in all those versions of the large agricultural estate? And provided it can be identified, is it significant enough to be used in the characterization of Latin America as a single cultural area?

Much as working conditions, housing, wages, and other factors vary, the structural ties relating labor to owner or manager are very much the same all over Latin America. The relationship between employer and worker (day laborer, sharecropper, tenant farmer) is marked by a highly unequal distribution of power that keeps the chances of the labor force to influence the owner's decisions to a minimum. Traditionally, and accurately, the social structure of the rural estate has been defined in terms of authoritarian paternalism; however, its persistence remains unexplained as long as one fails to perceive (1) the structural isolation of the labor force, its lack of organization, and its consequent inability to fight for changes, and (2) the way the power of the landowners is anchored in the political and economic institutions of the larger society. Even where the large landowners are no longer able to monopolize political power, they are united in political parties or party coalitions influential enough to prevent radical changes in the existing agrarian structure or to render ineffective legal innovations designed to improve the socioeconomic conditions of the workers. Thus attempts to unionize rural labor have met little or no success, and such measures as minimum wages and family wages have failed for various reasons—the wages were too low, the plan was not enforced, or the currency did not maintain purchasing power in a highly inflationary monetary system.

These conditions prevail in virtually all countries of Latin America regardless of the differentiating traits mentioned before. The social structure of the large estate has remained rigid, and there are few, if any, opportunities to change existing conditions except by migrating to urban centers; labor productivity remains relatively low and, to the extent that the estate is cultivated by sharecroppers and tenant farmers, the productivity of the soil deteriorates rapidly.

We can clarify the significance of this common denominator by noting that in every country of Latin America, the number of people working on or for the large agricultural estate constitutes a very large proportion, usually the majority, of the total rural population.

The social structure of the landed estate as outlined here is hardly confined to Latin America. Its significance as a characteristic of Latin American culture does not lie in its (questionable) uniqueness, but rather in the way it is associated with other common traits, discussed later. Reliance on a single feature to characterize a whole culture borders on naïveté or irresponsibility, particularly in dealing with highly complex cultures of heterogeneous origin.

Sources of cultural parity and disparity

Three factors, especially their manner of interaction, seem to account for most of the cultural differences and similarities within Latin America. The physical environment is one factor, the term being synonymous with what geographers call habitat. The presence of indigenous societies is another variable in the development of Latin American culture. Many of these societies differed from one another as much as they did from the Iberian conquerors; but whatever their level of development, interaction with the invaders, whether sporadic or continuous, was bound to affect the way of life of the new society.

The third major variable is the conquering society itself. If it is compared with the indigenous people, two basic differences strike the observer. First, although the native societies represent a broad spectrum of levels of cultural evolution, from nomadic hunters and gatherers to horticultural village communities to the "higher" civilizations of Incas, Aztecs, and Mayas, the cultural heritage of the conquering Spaniards and Portuguese was uniformly Iberian. Furthermore, whether primitive or civilized, the indigenous societies had developed ways of life that were autonomous and "complete" in the sense of being fully self-sustaining cultural systems. The Spaniards and the Portuguese brought with them no more than *samples* of Iberian culture. The selection of Iberian elements was random in that it was determined by regional origin, social class, occupation, and education of the people who happened to go to America; it was deliberate to the extent that it obeyed guidelines and policies established by civil and religious authorities.

Cultural development in Latin America reflects a highly complex interplay of these three factors or variables. Adding to the complexity, moreover, was the forced transfer of large numbers of Africans and, since the arrival of political emancipation, immigration of Europeans and Asians, each group with its baggage of distinct traditions and ethnic aspirations.

There is little need to emphasize the extraordinary variety of environmental conditions. Physical contrasts, such as those between the Andean highland and the Pacific coast, between the pampas and the Amazon Basin, between the desertlike interior of northeastern Brazil and the lush massapé regions of the coast, between the Paraguayan Chaco and Patagonia may be interpreted in terms of widely differing adaptive demands on potential and actual inhabitants. This is not an obsolete "geographic determinism," but merely an acknowledgment that no known mode of cultural adaptation is wholly intelligible without taking into account a variable array of environmental conditions.

Whatever the impact of environmental variables on Ibero-America, it would be difficult to maintain that political boundaries, past or present, reflect the differentiating effects of these variables. On the contrary, the unity suggested by political borderlines is more often than not at variance with the differentiating effects of the physical environment. The contrasts appear to be particularly sharp in Bolivia, Peru, Ecuador, Colombia, and Mexico—all sharply divided into highland and lowland regions—but few are the republics that are not internally differentiated by regional adaptations to peculiar environmental conditions. Frequently these regional cultures cut across national boundaries. For example, the predominant forms of Amazonian culture are fairly homogeneous regardless of whether they are located in Brazil, Venezuela, Colombia, Peru, or Bolivia. Colombia and Venezuela share the Llanos Orientales, but culturally the region is one and the same. Traditional gaucho culture emerged in an area that is now divided among three countries: Argentina, Uruguay, and Brazil. The Quechua-speaking communities of the Peruvian Andes resemble more those of Bolivia and Ecuador than any of the other regional cultures of either country. There are other instances of cross-national cultural areas, from Mesoamerica down to the Gran Chaco. Some of these regions are pre-Columbian in origin, others developed before definite borderlines existed.

That the Spaniards left a relatively uniform and ubiquitous imprint on the regions they once controlled has never been doubted. But there has been considerable doubt about Brazil. Can we assume a common Iberian culture and say that Portuguese America is close enough to Spanish-speaking America to bear out the hypothesis of a common Latin American culture? And if so, close as the cultural affinities may be between Portugal and Spain, were the Portuguese conquerors and settlers as effective as the Spaniards in achieving cultural penetration and assimilation? Brazil is so much vaster than Portugal that it is hard to imagine how a people of one million, diverted by the multiple problems of its African and Asian possessions, could possibly have remade Brazil in its own cultural image.

Spain and Portugal:
offshoots of the same cultural tree

By the time the Iberian peninsula became Roman territory it had already been the scene of intensive cultural amalgamation of Celtic, Phoenician, Greek, and other less known elements. The fifth century A.D. brought a variety of German invaders, and eventually the Visigoth monarchy assumed the Roman heritage modified by Christianity. "It was not until the middle of the seventh century that the assimilation of Goths and Hispano-Romans was completed, to such an extent that all traces of invasion and conquest had vanished." (Oliveira Martins, 1930:68)

This historical background is relevant insofar as it contributed to the development of a patterned mode of behavior that enabled Iberians to deal with cultures different from their own by resistance, accommodation, or absorption. Thus when the peninsula was conquered by the Moors in the eighth century, the Iberians were prepared, so to speak, to cope with their Islamic rulers in a fashion that combined opposition with accomodation and acculturation. On the one hand, military resistance began a few decades after the Moorish invasion had taken place and was carried to a successful conclusion over a period of 800 years. On the other hand, the Iberian peoples absorbed Arabic culture to such a degree that a mixed or "Mozarab" population emerged which, in a different context, might have signified the first step to a complete cultural fusion. "It was not only in internal habits that the Christians became Arabs; they even forgot their native language to such an extent that the bishops admitted the necessity of translating the Scriptures into the language of the Koran." (Oliveira Martins, 1930:112) As the reconquest neared completion, the cultural process was reversed and the remaining Moorish population was gradually absorbed by the Iberians. The peninsula withstood eight centuries of Islamic domination without losing its cultural identity; but Moorish customs and institutions had profoundly affected the Iberian way of life.

The reconquest failed to weld the Iberians into a single political structure. In that territory, during the Middle Ages a varying number of Christian kingdoms—sometimes as many as 13—preceded Spain, which did not exist as a political entity until the end of the fifteenth century. Portugal gained independence in 1140. Linguistically, the peninsula was divided into a large number of dialects including Galician, Catalan, and Portuguese. They all derived from the same brand of the Romance family and differed from one another much less than they do now. As a matter of fact, "between the Spanish and Portuguese literature no real separation occurs until the middle of the sixteenth century. The writers of medieval Spain prefer Galician-Portuguese in their lyric compositions. . . . In the fifteenth and sixteenth century, however, the Portuguese writers are the ones that alternately use Spanish and their own language." (Criado de Val, 1954:225)

It may be argued that a separate national existence widened the gap between Portuguese and Spanish, but it seems questionable whether Portuguese now differs from Spanish more than, for example, Galician or Catalan, even though Galicia and Catalonia have been Spanish provinces for centuries.

Nothing in the cultural history of the peninsula prior to the discovery of America invalidates the interpretation of Portugal as a regional subculture of Iberia. In fact, the reconquest further contributed to the development of relevant cultural similarities. Difficult as a judicious evaluation of the reconquest may be, the following facts are significant enough to demand attention:

1. The gradual occupation of territories under Moorish control led to an increasing concentration of power in the monarchy. The conquering kings effectively prevented the establishment of a full-fledged feudal system in the newly occupied territories of the peninsula. It thus became feasible to transfer an absolutist regime to America at a time when most European monarchs were still engaged in breaking the power of a feudal aristocracy. Whatever feudal concessions were initially made to the Spanish conquistadores and the Portuguese donatarios, they were soon abolished, and Iberian America came under the undivided control of the Portuguese and Spanish kings. The tradition of a centralized and authoritarian political structure was established. As we know, it survived the colonial period, and so did most of its ramifications in nonpolitical aspects of the social structure.

2. Eight hundred years of intermittent but relentless warfare could not fail to have specializing effects on Iberian culture. The reconquest originated a warlike and expansionist tradition that eventually carried Portuguese and Spaniards alike well beyond the confines of the Peninsula.

3. The reconquest was not just warfare, but war against infidels, enemies of the true faith to which the Iberians clung with medieval fervor. It was a succession of crusades in which religion provided the basis for strong and continuing emotional involvement. However, religious zeal did not develop as a separate force superimposed on or competing with what could be termed, with some qualifications, "nationalism." Religious fervor and national feelings were identical, that is, inseparable in a person's thought and in his action. In the conquest of America and the formation of colonial empires, this pairing of motivations generated the zealous determination that has bewildered and fascinated the Western world.

Portugal and Spain in America:
a comparison

Our initial assumption that Latin America might be regarded as a single culture area hardly implies that Brazil is culturally undistinguishable from Spanish America. There is no intent to deny or even to minimize cultural differences between the two areas. What we are trying to demonstrate is exemplified by the relationships between the Spanish and Portuguese languages: The similarities are obvious and incontestable; single words and idiomatic expressions may be mutually unintelligible, but there is no linguistic barrier impeding communication. No literate Brazilian needs to learn Spanish to read books, magazines, and journals published in Mexico or Argentina. Spanish Americans comprehend Brazilian Portuguese almost as easily as Brazilians understand Spanish, as long as standard versions of either language are spoken. Much as one wishes to stress the differences between the two idioms, they are nevertheless mutually intelligible. There is an underlying design or pattern that is meaningful, thus comprehensible to people brought up in Mexico, Colombia, or Brazil.

The foregoing statement suggests that comparison of two or more cultures requires more than a compilation of elements that may or may not be present in the cultures under scrutiny. Any kind and any number of elements can be included in such a checklist, from chaperoned courtship, swidden agriculture, polygamy, belief in the evil, and cult of the saints, to peonage, shamanism, cousin marriage, and caudillism. According to the checklist approach, the presence of an element in culture A and its absence in culture B would mean "difference"; its presence in both cultures would mean "similarity."

Much depends, of course, on the conceptualization of cultural elements. The more general or inclusive a concept, the more frequent the occurrence of the conceptualized element tends to be. Indeed, a number of culture elements can be conceptualized in such a general fashion that their occurrence is virtually universal. In 1945 George P. Murdock published a partial list of 72 such "cultural universals" or traits to be found in any human society. Included in this list are community organization, cooperative labor, courtship, ethics, food taboos, funeral rites, greetings, marriage, medicine, music, religious ritual, soul concepts, toolmaking, and language. Obviously, the degree of generality of each concept is so high that none can be used to characterize *specific* cultures. For example, the existence of the family in two particular cultures is no basis for arguing specific similarities, but if the narrower concept of the bilineal, patripotestal, neolocal, and extended family is used instead, the chances for meaningful comparisons improve considerably.

Several objections may be raised against the checklist approach. For example, it presents cultural traits out of context, thus preventing the observer from fully understanding them. The implications of such a sweeping indictment call for a careful definition of "full understanding" of a culture element. The notion that a trait is part of a context refers to its location in a particular sector of a culture and to the way it is related to that sector. It has been said, for instance, that the patripotestal extended family is part and parcel of the traditional agrarian structure of Latin America. But since agrarian society in Latin America is highly stratified, one may ask whether it occurs in *all* the different strata or only in some. The discovery that it does not exist among landless rural workers suggests that it may be related to the ownership of land. In view of numerous historical data, it is reasonable to assume that the larger the estate, the more cohesive and extended the family. A large and tightly knit kinship group gave protection the state was often unable to provide; moreover, it afforded a political potential that could be used against predatory colonial authorities or to establish political control in alliance or competition with other kinship groups powerful enough to manipulate national legislation.

Furthermore, the large estate exercises a strong centripetal force on the members of the owner's extended family, for in purely agrarian societies the economic future of the younger generation lies in land resources controlled by families.

Not much imagination is needed to understand that this kind of family structure would be rather out of step with the lifeways of the rural working class. Family cohesion provides no protection against economic exploitation, nor does it afford political leverage or economic opportunities, because the supporting factor of landownership is absent. And in the case of dismissal or ejection—a rather frequent occurrence—a large dependent family would be a liability rather than an asset. Small wonder, then, that the working class family tends to be nuclear and relatively unstable.

Aside from indicating the context of the patripotestal extended family, the aforementioned observations afford partial answers to other questions relevant to a full understanding of the institution under scrutiny. First of all, among the landowning strata, particularly the big landowners, the family had and still has an immense *functional* importance, not only with regard to its own members but in the society at large. Another chapter explores its multiple functions in greater detail and the extent to which it was allowed to encroach on other institutions is taken as an index of its functional dominance. Furthermore, the relative position of the patripotestal extended family in the social structure appears to be a clear expression of the rank it holds in the general value system of Latin American society. Actually, its dominant positions in the social structure *and* in the value system may be regarded as two sides of the same coin.

Previously, cultural affinity between Portuguese and Spanish America was compared to linguistic affinity. Mutual intelligibility of the two languages was assumed to parallel mutual intelligibility and meaningfulness of other aspects of the culture. In the extended patripotestal family, for example, the functions performed by the unit provide clues to its meaning. If the functions are alike, the meanings cannot be different. The family *means* protection, security, and furtherance of economic and political interests because it has demonstrated that it is capable of providing these things. And since no institution can exist without appropriate reciprocity arrangements, the privilege of availing oneself of family "services" has to be repaid in terms of loyalty and subordination to the norms inherent in its structure. A detailed account of the implications of this statement is given later. At this juncture it is important only to grasp the general idea of mutual intelligibility of culture traits. So far as the family of the landowning strata is concerned, we assume that to Latin Americans—regardless of whether they are Brazilians, Mexicans, Chileans, or Peruvians—references to the family carry essentially the same implications. These individuals of different nationalities do not have to interpret the family institution to one another to understand its significance.

Similarities and differences:
the Spanish and Portuguese conquests

The formidable thrust of the Spanish conquest has often been contrasted with the hesitations, failures, and lack of commitment characterizing early attempts of the Portuguese to bring their American territory under control. By the middle of the sixteenth century the shape of the Spanish colonial empire had already emerged. It extended contiguously from California to Chile and the Plata region, and an estimated 100,000 Spaniards had established residence there. At the same time, the Portuguese had gained hardly more than a few isolated footholds along the coastline of the Atlantic, and the total number of colonists, according to João Ribeiro, was less than 3000. (J. Ribeiro, 1935:75)

The contrast is impressive, but the thrust of Portuguese expansion went in another direction. Since 1433 Portuguese seafarers had been systematically exploring the coast of West Africa, establishing trading posts and military bases. By the end of the century they had rounded the Cape of Good Hope and begun to establish themselves on the eastern coast of Africa. They reached India, gained control of the Indian Ocean, and founded strongholds and trading posts in Malaya, Indochina, and Indonesia. Eventually, Portuguese traders and missionaries reached

China and Japan, where their establishments enjoyed extraterritorial rights. The attraction of the Far East was primarily the lucrative spice trade, but like the Spanish conquest, Portuguese colonial expansion was motivated by a combination of economic interests and missionary zeal. Considering the limited resources of the tiny homeland, the impetus of the Portuguese conquest seems even more astonishing than the accomplishments of the Spaniards in America.

During the sixteenth century, Portugal was so deeply involved in Africa and Asia that relatively little was done about Brazil. It has often been said that the Portuguese merely stuck to the littoral of America, all important settlements being located on or very close to the Atlantic coast, whereas the Spaniards penetrated the interior and settled in the heartlands of the geographical outline of Chile and Peru. The image of the Portuguese clinging to the coast "like crabs to a rock" gained currency and became a kind of stereotype. Translated into political terms, it could mean that Brazil's national territory might have developed into something resembling Chile. This did not happen, however. It is Brazil rather than Spanish America which now controls most of the central area of the continent.

The role of the bandeirantes

The conquest of Brazil commenced a century after the Spaniards had first set foot on American soil. It all started in Sao Paulo, a tiny settlement founded by Jesuits in 1554. Fighting for control of the surrounding area, the people of São Paulo (*Paulistas*) gradually developed a set of attitudes and values which Brazilians call *bandeirismo*. Bandeiras were groups of experienced *sertanejos,* or individuals familiar with the conditions and resources of the vast hinterland (sertão), who would embark on expeditions into uncharted regions to capture and enslave Indians or to prospect for mineral wealth. Throughout the seventeenth and part of the eighteenth century, bandeiras from São Paulo traversed the continent in almost every conceivable direction. Overland routes were established to Paraguay, Bolivia, and Peru, to the Plata and Amazon regions. Paulistas were the first permanent settlers in many areas east, south, and north. They supplied slave labor to sugar plantations and discovered gold in various parts of the sertão; but the most outstanding and lasting effect of bandeirismo was the tremendous territorial expansion of Brazil, which was eventually sanctioned in the treaties of Madrid (1750) and

San Ildefonso (1777). Actually, the bandeirante conquest tripled the territory that had been apportioned to Portugal by the treaty of Tordesilhas (1494). In other words, the bandeirantes did for Portugal what the conquistadores had done for Spain.

Whereas the conquistadores were Spaniards relying on metropolitan support, the bandeirantes were predominantly Brazilian-born mestizoes (mamelucos), and allied Indians depending on their own resourcefulness and adaptive abilities. Perhaps the bandeira is lineally related to the Iberian *cabalgada*, as Mario Góngora suggested (1960), but the possible correctness of this hypothesis hardly precludes the need to readapt the Iberian pattern of the cabalgada to very different environmental demands and, particularly, to a field of action whose extension by far exceeded the total area of Spain and Portugal. If the expansionist vigor and geographical scope of the bandeiras are quite comparable to those of the Spanish conquest, there remains the question of the effectiveness of bandeirismo in disseminating Iberian culture. The bandeirantes were primarily slave-hunters, prospectors, and "pathfinders," to use a term suggested by Richard M. Morse (1965). Yet they laid the foundations of permanent settlements in many interior regions of Brazil. Thus São Paulo became a focus of cultural diffusion of a pervasiveness that seems to be incommensurate with its size. How could a borough with a population estimated at about 6000 in the late seventeenth century become a center of migration and cultural irradiation? Indeed, the bandeiras became a constant and severe drain on São Paulo's human resources, and when gold was discovered in Minas Gerais, Goiás, and Mato Grosso, depopulation set in at a disquieting rate. Bandeirismo certainly did not contribute to the development of São Paulo, which remained one of the less developed regions of colonial Brazil. In fact, lack of known resources was one of the factors that motivated the paulistas to seek their fortunes elsewhere.

There is no doubt about the extraordinary spatial mobility of the paulistas, but exactly what are the cultural implications of bandeirismo? What kind of culture did the paulistas disseminate throughout hitherto unexplored areas of the continent? Since the bandeiras initiated only one of many spontaneous migratory movements that populated, to some extent at least, considerable portions of Latin America, the question goes beyond the scope of bandeirismo proper. What happened in São Paulo was repeated time and again in many regions where anonymous breeds of settlers, of common birth, without capital and official support, and often against the will of colonial authorities or without their knowledge, ventured into unexplored areas to establish shifting agricultural settlements or cattle ranches. More often than not, these men took Indian women, and before long there were mestizo populations whose way of life was as hybrid as their genetic makeup. Adaptive demands of the environment forced them to accept Indian crops and Indian agricultural techniques. They learned the processing of the manioc root from the Indians, and their ways of trapping, fishing, and collecting wild nuts, fruits, and tubers were more indigenous than European. Iberian folk Catholicism was part of their cultural heritage, but unhampered by church control they added beliefs in Indian spirits and demons, and their ways of coping with sickness became a mixture of Iberian and indigenous medicine. The mamelucos who so conspicuously participated in the bandeiras were such biological and cultural hybrids, and such was the culture they imparted to settlements throughout the sertão. But in contrast to many anonymous migratory movements, the bandeiras acquired a distinct historic identity through their leaders, whose personality was not unlike that of Spanish conquistadores. Although involved mostly in the private enterprises of slave hunting and prospecting, they were sometimes used by the colonial government for political missions. Comparing the role of the bandeirantes and Spanish conquistadores as disseminators of Iberian culture, at least one difference is fairly obvious. The conquistadores worked, so to speak, from the top down to the bottom; the bandeirantes acted at the folk level and only occasionally worked within the domain of officialdom. The conquistadores were Spanish-born, acting as representatives of the Spanish crown and the Catholic Church; they formally established the rule of Spain and then began to work their way down to the level of the subjugated Indian masses. The paulistas began by developing a biologically and culturally hybrid society adapted to the rigors of the *sertão* and in opposition to the official Portuguese order. A Brazilian scholar wrote,

> The official order was to scratch along the coast like crabs, in the picturesque phrase of Frei Vincente do Salvador. The charters of the captaincies made the same stipulation, that no one should slip inland to the sertão. It was the Brazilian of the plateau (São Paulo) who, independently and at his own risk, disobeyed the order of the crown and tore up—devil take it—the famous treaty of Tordesilhas. The work of geographic expansion then, is an achievement exclusively ours, since the crown took cognizance of the conquest only after it was completed. (Ricardo, 1965:205)

Not content with being confined to the coast, the Portuguese settlers of the north and northeast sustained a long series of forays into the interior, mostly to enslave or drive back Indians and to prospect for mineral wealth. In contrast to the bandeiras, many of these expeditions departing from Rio de Janeiro, Bahia (Salvador), Recife, and towns farther north, were organized and carried out by colonial authorities. To distinguish them from the bandeiras, they have been labeled *entradas*, but the line of demarcation is not always easy to recognize. At any rate, the pioneer conquest of the entradas was mainly responsible for opening the northern sertão to the cattle breeders who established themselves in the São Francisco River Basin and in the vast transitional zone between the fertile coastal belt and the arid *caatinga* (a region of thorny, stunted vegetation). Of course, the entradas were never more than a sideline of the plantation and urban society of the coast, whereas the bandeiras had a highly specializing influence on the paulista culture of the sixteenth and seventeenth century.

The spiritual conquest

The conquest of America was not accomplished entirely by military means. The papal mandate to Christianize the indigenous societies was interpreted by the Iberian monarchies as a legal title authorizing the appropriation of the American territories. (Konetzke 1965:220). To live up to the terms of the mandate, the Spanish and Portuguese kings developed missionary initiatives sufficiently effective to leave a profound imprint on the conquest and its aftermath.

Taken literally, spiritual conquest is the inducing of people to surrender and become subordinate through persuasion and indoctrination rather than through the actual or threatened use of force. Since resistance to Christian doctrine could and often enough was met with punishment, including execution, the spiritual nature of the missionary conquest is open to doubt.

The close alliance between the sword and the cross in the conquest of America was a reflection of "the indissoluble union of the altar and the throne [which] mutually supported one another. The Church defended the divine sanctity of kings; the crown upheld the ecumenical authority of the Roman Catholic Church." (Haring, 1947:179)

Mutual support of crown and missions in Portugal and Spanish America does not mean that the friars moved only in the wake of the military. Often missionary endeavor converged on areas and peoples outside the orbit of actual government control. It is more significant, however, that

the religious orders (mainly Franciscans, Dominicans, and Jesuits), entrusted with the task of christianization, were expected not merely to
"convert the heathen" but to transform his way of life in terms of Iberian
humanism of the sixteenth century. Carried away by a sort of scholarly
idealism, some friars attempted to model Indian communities of New
Spain on Thomas More's *Utopia* "with communally owned property,
communally performed labor, representative government, and a variety
of other features of More's ideal Society." (Gibson, 1966:74)

Such elaborate experiments, as well as the opposite approach of mass
baptisms without the benefit of religious instruction, reflected the lack
of missionary experience of the medieval church. Yet even a more realistic
understanding of the mechanisms of cultural change would not necessarily have led to successful conversion. Christianity is inherently
exclusive and intolerant of what is perceived as non-Christian. The neo-
phyte is required to relinquish all his former beliefs and practices, but
such intolerance is difficult to grasp by people whose societies interpret
acceptance of a new religion as an enrichment of or addition to their
arsenal of alternate beliefs and ways of dealing with supernatural powers.
If the missionaries were successful in implanting Christianity, they failed
to eliminate all traces of indigenous religions. These were there to stay,
and they remain up to the present day, not only in Indian communities,
but also, though to a lesser extent and in more diffuse forms, in the world
of the mestizo.

Perhaps the most thorough and consistent experiment of spiritual
conquest and guided culture change was carried out by the Jesuit fathers.
Of course, any reference to the Society of Jesus calls to mind the Jesuit
"state" of Paraguay, which was neither a state nor originally an initiative
of the Jesuits. "The state authorities utilized the missionary zeal of the
Jesuits to subjugate savage Indian tribes through christianization and
effectively to appropriate distant domains." (Konetzke, 1965: 270) Land
for Indian reductions or reservations was assigned rather than usurped,
and nowhere did the Jesuit reductions acquire the legal attributes of
sovereign states. If one wishes to emphasize the *actual* power position
of the Jesuit order vis-à-vis their Indian subjects, the expression "state
within the state" may be appropriate, but the Jesuit missions shared this
quality with many large colonial estates in which the owning family had
virtually absolute control of the resident labor force, whether slaves or
peons.

Jesuit participation in the Spanish conquest was closely paralleled by
the role the Society of Jesus played in Portuguese America. The Indian

reductions of Paraguay were not unique; they merely followed a model that spread all over the continent, and its performance as an organized distributor of Iberian culture varied only insofar as the Jesuits were dealing with extremely heterogeneous Indian cultures. One factor has often been overlooked in considering organized culture change on the scale adopted by the Jesuits: It is one thing when attempted among surplus-producing agricultural communities with a sedentary tradition anchored in pre-Spanish market systems and politics; it becomes a different proposition when tried among nomadic or seminomadic Indians who, must first be induced to accept sedentariness in the midst of surrounding tribes preferring their own independent traditions. Such was the situation of the Jesuit reductions in many regions east of the Andes. The cultural experiment of the Jesuit reduction has often been criticized for neglecting to prepare the Indians for political and economic emancipation. In fact, when the Jesuits were expelled, the Indians were totally unprepared to withstand the pressures of the Spanish and Portuguese who jumped at the opportunity to enslave or kill them and to appropriate their land. None of the remaining religious orders could fill the gap left by the Jesuits. The reductions thus collapsed, and the Indians who were fortunate enough to escape, went back to a way of life characteristic of the tropical forest tribes. Incidentally, the expulsion of the Jesuits from Spanish America (1767) closely followed their banishment from Brazil in 1759.

Although crown and church were allies in the common enterprise of the conquest, their humanistic and humane policies toward the indigenous peoples were at variance with the attitudes of the Portuguese and Spanish settlers, who immediately proceeded to reduce the Indians, wherever economically desirable and politically possible, to the condition of slavery or serfdom. There were some inconsistencies in the policies of the royal governments toward Indian slavery, but on the whole the state, and more consistently, the church, endeavored to root out not only Indian slavery, but other systems of forced labor imposed on indigenous populations. The settlers, particularly the owners of large estates requiring abundant supplies of labor, resisted the combined attempts of church and state by requesting legislative changes or by simply ignoring the law. The most spectacular case of defiance and consistent flaunting of the law may be seen in the slave-hunting bandeiras. They were designed not just to capture tribal Indians but to conquer Indian reductions under Jesuit control with the intent to enslave the Indian populations, which had already been assimilated to a labor regime consistent with the demands of the plantation economy.

Indian slavery eventually disappeared, but Indian serfdom did not. Conflict between state and estate owners about the rights of the Indian lasted throughout the colonial era. Except for a few modest victories, neither the Spanish nor the Portuguese government proved capable of enforcing laws intended to prevent Indians from becoming serfs. In the emergent power structure of the colonial society, the interests of the landowning upper class prevailed against the state and the religious orders. Since neither the law nor the attitude of defiance showed signs of basic change, the conflict became a permanent fixture of Latin American culture.

Inconsistencies are, of course, inherent in all cultures. Actual behavior never comes up to the level of moral and legal precepts, but in our case the issue involved was of such magnitude that it could not fail to affect the major sectors of the social structure. Persistent nonenforcement of laws intended to define and protect the status of indigenous peoples had direct effects on the process of social stratification: It forced the Indians to the bottom of the social pyramid, and it failed to curb the power of the large landowners. Respect for the law is not furthered when violation with impunity by some becomes a tradition. In fact, the irreconcilability of legal order and social structure that has plagued the Latin American republics up to the present time, seems to have its roots in the colonial heritage. Failure to enforce political decisions of the crown was not confined to legislation on Indians. "The difference between enacted legislation at a distance and interpreted legislation on the scene was manifested again and again. *Obedezco pero no cumplo*— I obey but I do not fulfill—was the viceregal response to legislation that would not be enforced." (Gibson 1966:94) The situation was very much the same in Portuguese America.

Conquest culture

The conquest can be presented as a chain of historical events such as military campaigns, the establishment of administrative and ecclesiastic structures, the founding of towns, the concession of land grants and commercial monopolies, and the introduction of Spanish and Portuguese laws. It is also possible to view the conquest as a cultural process—a massive intrusion of cultural forms on a number of indigenous societies and the ensuing changes in both the donor culture and the recipient cultures. This is not to say that the cultural process is "ahistorical" or "nonhistorical." Historians and anthropologists are, of course, dealing with the same chain of events, but their points of emphasis differ. As a rule, historians do not stress the informal mechanisms by which culture traits were selected and diffused to America; however, these processes were especially evident in such areas as food, family life, the life cycle, music, folklore, medical beliefs and practices, magic, and superstitions. (Foster, 1960:14) By "informal mechanisms" we mean those not intended, pursued, oriented, or guided by state or church. They "just occurred," whether foreseen or unforeseen, producing effects that were deemed desirable or undesirable by some or perhaps all the people involved. More is said later about the details of this cultural process. Here only two of its many aspects demand attention—the reduction of the Iberian heritage and the "crystallization" of Iberian culture brought to America during the conquest period. George M. Foster, who suggested these concepts, referred only to Spanish culture; but since the Portuguese heritage went through exactly the same process, it seems safe to speak of Iberian culture.

Reduction

Spain presents a bewildering variety of regional subcultures. Andalusia, Aragon, the Castiles, Catalonia, Estremadura, and Galicia, for example, have distinct ways of life manifest in urban as well as rural areas; and Portugal in spite of its small size, appears to be rich in regional differences, many of which have been described by ethnographers and folklorists. However, the cultural spectrum of Spanish and Portuguese America never was, and is not now, a replica of the cultural differentiation of Iberia, the multiple regional origins of the settlers who migrated to the New World notwithstanding. Adaptation to a vastly different environment imposed a *reduction* or stripping-down process serving to remove many elements of the donor culture and to simplify the complexity and variety of many configurations. (Foster, 1960:12) The principles of selection and removal asserted themselves during the conquest period, and they have not ceased to perform their sifting or screening role. The term "principle" should not suggest any kind of rule formally adopted and deliberately carried out, but merely criteria that spontaneously emerged out of the experience of living and gaining a livelihood. But the process of stripping down has also its formal aspects.

Formal processes, for example, produced standard municipal organizations, as contrasted to the variety of local Iberian forms, and it produced the gridplan town in place of the loosely planned or completely unplanned Spanish community of the sixteenth century. Formal processes likewise congregated Indians in villages, governed commerce and trade, and introduced an ideal or theologically justified Catholic dogma and ritual to America. (Foster, 1960:14)

Formal and informal processes of reduction resulted in a culture whose Iberian ingredients were far more homogeneous than either Spanish or Portuguese culture. Whatever cultural differention took place in America is *not* due to diversifying influences of regional factors *within* the two Iberian countries.

Crystallization

Reduction of Iberian culture was accompanied by the crystallization of elements that were transferred to America by settlers moving in the wake of the conquest. Among the first groups of Spaniards, those from Andalusia and Estramadura constituted a majority large enough to impose their regional way of life in a variety of adaptive situations requiring immediate response. Once a *modus vivendi* had been established, succeeding waves of immigrants from other parts of Spain found little receptivity to their own distinct regional cultures. Thus contemporary Spanish America's agricultural and fishing techniques, arts and crafts, social patterns, and funeral practices reflect a preponderance of forms imported from southern and western Spain rather than from the central and northern portions.

No predominance of any one of Portugal's regional cultures has ever been noted in Brazil, possibly because no region was strongly enough represented to control the adaptive responses of the early settlers. Nevertheless, out of a vast repertory of regional elements, comparatively few transfers took roots in Brazil, and, as in Spanish America, legislative and administrative processes formally helped make the political structure uniform. But Portugal never attempted to introduce a single master plan designed to control urbanization in Brazil. This does not mean, as we shall see later, that there is a fundamental difference between Spanish American and Brazilian cities.

Crystallization of early Portuguese transfers played a role quite comparable to that which Foster observed in Spanish America. Agricultural and fishing techniques, crafts, rituals characterizing the individual life cycle, and folk festivals, such as the feast of the Holy Ghost, have changed little since they were first reported by writers of the fifteenth and sixteenth centuries. These early forms were adopted by successive generations of immigrants, not only from Portugal but from other European countries as well.

The concept of crystallization may profitably be extended from the Iberian cultural ingredients alone to colonial culture in general. In fact, it would be misleading to view the ingredients as frozen particles in an otherwise dynamic picture of cultural forms tried out, selected, or rejected by Europeans as well as natives. Out of the conquest emerged a seigneurial social order of great stability. Its component parts, whether Iberian or otherwise, settled around a few major complexes that remained *essentially* unchanged up to the nineteenth century. This does *not* mean that no changes were attempted or that the seigneurial order did not have to readapt to changing conditions to preserve its continuity. Certain aspects of the seigneurial order were permeated with unsolved conflicts— for example, there was basic disagreement between the big landowners and the state–church coalition over the use of Indian labor. These and other power contests are reflected in a long chain of conspiracies and insurgencies that more than once threatened to tear apart the fabric of colonial society. Throughout three centuries of colonial rule there were at least 76 rebellions and uprisings: 15 were revolts of Negro slaves, 31 were major Indian uprisings, and 30 were insurgencies of Creoles and mestizoes against Spanish and Portuguese authorities. (Rama, 1967) They all were directed against particular aspects of the existing seigneurial order: against institutionalized exploitation of serf and slave labor by the owners of agricultural estates and mines, against the encroachment of the hacienda on Indian land, and against predatory taxes, commercial monopolies, and the rising cost of living. The frequency of these rebellions, the considerable extent and duration of some, and their distribution over all regions of Ibero-America including Brazil, suggest a pattern or set of attitudes that was clearly distinguishable when political independence came and could not have been unrelated to the revolutionary tradition of the nineteenth and twentieth centuries. The somewhat casual attention most historians have paid to this aspect of colonial Latin America has perhaps contributed to the stereotype of the "apathetic" masses, patiently carrying the burden of an oppressive and exploitative economic and political system.

It makes little sense to characterize as stable a social order that was almost continuously exposed to internal conflict. The paradox is apparent rather than real. All rebellions were local or regional uprisings, and the objectives of most were limited to the interests and vindications of certain groups. Only toward the end of the colonial period were there some who sought independence from Spain and Portugal. Not even the wars of independence were concerned with subversion of the seigneurial order. Yet the insurgencies of the colonial period were relevant insofar as they contributed to the "marginalization" of a large proportion of the people in Brazil and in Spanish America.

Crystallization occurred in all major facets of colonial culture, which will be presented here in the form of complexes. The term "complex" suggests a number of functionally interrelated elements integrated around a matrix or core element that provides meaning and direction. The cultural complexes to be analyzed here are the following: (1) the landed estate; (2) sex, miscegenation, the family, and kinship; (3) the patrimonial state; (4) the religious system; (5) the town; and (6) the peasantry. Each of these complexes is to be understood as a particular manifestation of the seigneurial order, a term that should not be taken as a mere synonym of political structure.

A culture complex comprises physical structures and objects, techniques or ways of creating and using such objects, forms of social organization, and a system of beliefs, attitudes, and norms designed to keep the complex alive and to regulate its relationships with other complexes. Too much insistence on "functional integration" has occasionally led to romantic distortions of cultural realities. Not only are there tensions, antagonisms, frictions, inconsistencies, and conflicts in each complex, but these seemingly "dysfunctional" vicissitudes are the normal accompaniment of social life and sometimes harbingers of change.

Genesis of
the cultural traditions

The landed estate

The Iberian kings had a feudal way of rewarding loyal and meritorious subjects by granting them pieces of real estate in America. They were called *mercedes de tierra* in Spanish America and *sesmarias* in Brazil. As one might expect, much land was usurped by early settlers, but soon a convenient pattern developed to legalize ownership of occupied land. For a consideration, the process (the *composición*) institutionalized legal approval of an illegal act that greatly benefited settlers and the royal treasury alike. The illegal practice of selling titles of land grants or of acquiring them through a dummy contributed to increase the size of the estates. Furthermore, the institution of primogeniture, whereby a man's entire estate automatically went to his eldest son, prevented their division through inheritance. It seems that in Brazil much land was officially granted that had already been under control of the grantee.

The desirability of large land holdings had its roots in a value system that rewards the owner of land with status benefits. Imbued with feudal ideas about land, the Iberian settlers acquired estates not only to increase their income, but also or even primarily to *"señorear"*—to perform the role of the lord of the manor. (Chevalier, 1963:176) Feudal valuation of the landed estate appears to be an extreme case of cultural crystallization, because up to the present time, the acquisition of large holdings has been widely used as a means of status validation.

The economic function of the system is clear enough: It made land ownership possible with little or no capital, in times when capital was scarce and its flow cumbersome and irregular. Scarcity of capital affected almost every aspect of the operation of the landed estate. It kept technology on a relatively low level and impeded costly innovations. It contributed to the practice of paying labor totally or partly in kind rather than in cash. Furthermore, it imposed subsistence agriculture at two different levels: Resident laborers were assigned small plots for cultivation; they were allowed to extract firewood from forest tracts and to hold a few animals on grazing land belonging to the estate. Specialization in a major cash crop rarely prevented the estate from raising food to pay the laborers and to feed the owner's family. The estate owner had little or no access to capital resources to tide him over periods of ruinous price fluctuations, but he at least could switch to commercially viable minor crops and livestock raising in times of crisis. Unencumbered by heavy debts, he was generally able to survive slumps in the market.

To view the landed estate as a modern business enterprise bent on maximizing profits would be out of step with the general tenor of Latin American traditions. Maximization of profit, as we know it nowadays, requires a degree of technological and organizational efficiency alien to the mind of seigneurial landlords. The operation of the estate was primarily geared to the maintenance of what was regarded as an aristocratic style of life. Whether the big landowners were actually aristocrats seems to be beside the point: They considered themselves to be such, and the costs of their seigneurial style of life had to be borne by the estate. Thus emphasis was on conspicuous consumption rather than on reinvestment of profits for technical innovation and expansion of production, and the system had a built-in tendency toward the routine, crystallizing around a set of time-honored, rigid patterns.

Closely associated with control over land is the control of labor.

Slavery and serfdom were well-developed institutions in the Iberian peninsula, and both were transferred to America. The availability of numerous populations of sedentary Indians with a pre-Columbian tradition of servile labor invited compulsory recruitment and bondage of several kinds. In the eastern parts of South America the Indians, who were totally alien to the tributary labor regimes of the Andes and Mesoamerica, were far less amenable to the conditions of bondage. The Portuguese tried hard to enslave them, but they did not begin to satisfy the labor demand of the plantations. Even if they had adapted to the hardships of slavery, their numbers would not have been sufficient. Thus those in need of laborers came to rely on imported Africans, and before long the African slave trade also began to flourish in many parts of Spanish America.

Along with slavery of Indians and Africans, a tributary labor system was instituted under the name of *encomienda*. Estate owners were legally appointed trustees of Indians who were forced to pay tribute in the form of menial services to the *encomenderos* or trustees. Attempts to abolish the abuse-ridden practice were only partially successful.

Debt peonage was another variety of bondage that has been traced to the sixteenth century. By advancing money wages to impecunious laborers, a condition of indebtedness was created which was maintained by keeping the wage level low and forcing the peon to buy everything he needed in the commissary of the estate at exorbitant prices. Often such debts could only be paid with labor; but since there was always a balance in favor of the employer, and the indebted peon was not allowed to leave the estate, the relationship resulted in lifelong bondage. Frequently, families were held collectively responsible for the debts of one of their deceased members, thus bondage was perpetuated from generation to generation. Not only was debt peonage the most durable of all colonial labor forms, as noted by Gibson, it survived throughout the nineteenth and twentieth century, in spite of numerous legislative attempts to curb the most blatant abuses or to abolish it altogether. (Gibson, 1966:147) Sometimes the institution is discussed as if it had been inflicted only on the Indian, whereas actually it victimized all those who happened to be at the bottom of the social pyramid and was quite as common in Brazil as it was in Spanish America. Only the encomienda was unknown in Brazil because the relative scarcity and nomadism of its aboriginal populations would have thwarted the adoption of this institution in Portuguese America.

Although emphasis on compulsory labor systems may convey the impression that the recruitment of a dependent labor force was based entirely on coercion, labor relations were often established voluntarily within the complex of the landed estate. To call this "free" labor would, perhaps, be euphemistic, but at least it was neither slavery nor serfdom if we take the latter term to mean a permanent tributary relationship. Much remains to be done in the way of historical research, but available data clearly indicate that many estates entered contractual relationships with renters and sharecroppers. In colonial Brazil they were usually called *foreiros*, in Argentina *agregados*. Writing about the Chilean hacienda, Mario Góngora clearly distinguishes three different institutions: slavery, peonage, and *arrendamiento*. He refers to "the nomadic, unruly and unreliable element" composed of poor Spaniards and mestizoes who roamed the Chilean countryside during the sixteenth century but "gradually began to stabilize and to adapt themselves to the institutions" during the seventeenth century. (Góngora, 1960:115) They developed into what much later was termed *inquilinos* or resident laborers. The *inquilinaje* is not related to the encomienda or other institutions of the conquest. (Góngora, 1960:116)

Control over labor, whatever its composition and characteristics, never was based entirely on coercion. In most rural areas of colonial Latin America the landed estate was the only institution that could provide economic and political security. In the course of time, a type of feudal relationship developed between the landlord and his laborers. It was feudal only insofar as it was based on mutual loyalty—a willingness of the landlord to take care of his laborers in exchange for services rendered according to traditional standards. Mutual expectations were not confined to specified, contractual terms.

The patron-peon relationship has often been called "paternalistic," imputing fatherly feelings and responsibilities to the landlord and filial deference and obedience to the laborer. As a term, paternalism seems adequate enough as long as it is taken in the patriarchal or patripotestal sense implying a "father image" in which the autocrat and stern disciplinarian prevails over any of the more benevolent associated roles. One manifestation of paternalism appears in the traditional *compadrazgo* relationship between a landlord and any number of his resident- laborers. It was (and still is) customary for a landlord to accede to the request of a laborer to become the baptismal godfather of one of his children. The compadrazgo established a reciprocal bond not only with the child but also his biological father.

Such personal affective relationships paid off in terms of loyalty and flexibility of demands for services. On the other hand, it was important to reciprocate loyalty with special favors and perquisites. The Spanish hacienda and the Brazilian fazenda were scenes not only of unmitigated drudgery and harsh treatment, but also of annual fiestas honoring saints or celebrating the completion of the harvest season. Laborers could be depended on to fight for their lords if the lords became embroiled in private wars or blood feuds. If lives were taken, the killer could rely on the protection of his landlord, who would not surrender him to the authorities. Whereas nowadays a progressive *hacendado* sometimes employs a trained social worker to look after the welfare of his workers, his forefathers provided similar services informally, usually through members of their own household. These statements are not meant to minimize the stark rigors of bondage and exploitation; they are merely intended to help explain the stability of the landed estate, which would not have lasted as long as it did if it had rested on the use of the whip and the stock.

The absorption of renters and sharecroppers by the landed estate suggests its interrelationships with another cultural complex—namely, the peasantry. It is one of our fundamental assumptions that the viability of any cultural complex depends on its functional connections with other complexes. There are various ways in which the landed estate is related to the peasantry. Usurpation of land and the recruitment of labor seem to be the main links between these two complexes. But this is the theme of Chapter 7.

The landed estate was not just an agricultural establishment bent on economic pursuits. A number of circumstances contributed to develop it into a structure of many facets and multiple purposes. During the conquest, considerable power was at first delegated to the representatives of the Iberian kings. Particularly the Portuguese donatarios, or recipients of huge land grants, were almost absolute rulers of their territories. The metropolitan governments never completely succeeded in their determined endeavors to recapture these powers and to regain control from their delegates, and feudal residues became solidly embedded in the structure of the landed estate. In Portuguese America, for example, territorial immunity—the power to grant asylum to criminals and the usurpation of judicial functions—caused the Brazilian landed estate to become almost a little state within the state. "Authorities and the police respect the *engenhos* (sugar cane plantations), sometimes sanctuaries of criminals, defended and inaccessible like sacred taboos. Certain arrogant lords did not permit the most reasonable visits of the police on their properties. They regard them as insults requiring retaliation no matter how." (Bello, 1948:183)

The accumulation of political power in the landed estate, in competition with and opposition to legitimate authority, is not to be interpreted merely as a victory of feudal ambitions or of a whimsical desire to build private empires; rather, it was an adaptive process, better understood by trying to visualize the circumstances under which it occurred. Spatial isolation, lack of communication, and a weak or distant government left little choice to those who wished to convert a tract of "untamed wilderness" into a cattle ranch or a sugar cane plantation. Complete control over a recalcitrant labor force was essential; hostile Indians had to be fought off, and roving bands of marauders, deserters, and runaway slaves required much vigilance. Assistance from public authorities could not be relied on and was not even expected, unless major uprisings of Indians or slaves directly threatened the colonial establishment. In Brazil, governmental power was centralized in capital cities and district towns, and hundreds of miles of territory had no government at all. (Prado, 1963:300)

Numerous reports on the political power of the large estate in Spanish America are similar to those referring to Brazil. Writing about Mexico, Chevalier remarked that "with the exception of the Bajio plains, close to Mexico City, the northern zone was therefore to be the zone of powerful individuals, large family circles, housefuls of dependents, and huge estates. . . . [North of Zacatecas public authorities were] hardly ever obeyed." (Chevalier, 1963:149–150) Private armies seem to have been fairly common in the continual fighting against nomadic Indians and bandits. (Chevalier, 1963:149)

To the extent that local government existed at all, it tended almost inevitably to be taken over by powerful land-owning families, often in competition with rival families. In Spanish America the offices of *alcalde* (mayor) and *regidor* (councilman) were often sold by the crown to the highest bidder, or, quite in accord with the rules of patrimonialism, they were considered to be the private property of their holders, who were allowed to sell them, providing a percentage of the proceeds was turned over to the royal treasury as tax. Not infrequently, such offices became hereditary or could be leased by the holder to someone willing to pay the fee, the crown always collecting taxes on such transactions. In colonial Brazil, local offices were not for sale, but access to the municipal councils was confined to those who were not engaged in menial occupations. At any rate, the effects of such practices and restrictions were almost everywhere identical: They opened the door to an oligarchical rule of powerful landowners and shut off everyone else, except in the larger cities, where well-to-do merchants were able successfuly to compete with the fazendeiros. Reflecting the patrimonial stance of the political structure, the local potentates invariably showed great reluctance to be bound by laws. Often there was no clear distinction between private and public sources of income, and expenditures for public services and facilities, such as they were, tended to become manifestations of seigneurial munificence.

The encroachment of the landed estate on the political structure seems to contradict the meaning of the term "adaptive," which was proposed to interpret the emergence of large landholdings in Latin America. Doubtless the landed estate used all conceivable means at its command to survive, to consolidate its power, and to expand its territorial range. Under the circumstances it is difficult to see how it could have survived without assuming political functions the state was unwilling or unable to perform. This does not mean, of course, that it made a substantial contribution to the "orderly" development of the general political process. What appears to be adaptive on one level or in one sector may cause malfunctioning elsewhere. And there are, of course, temporal limits to the adaptive value of cultural patterns. As we shall see later, the traditional form of the landed estate gradually lost its adaptive functions to become the kind of social problem it is nowadays.

However closely the landed estate was interwoven with the political structure, it was even more intimately related to the kinship complex. Indeed, the landed estate was a kinship enterprise in the broadest possible sense. Here emphasis is on kinship rather than family because the conjugal or nuclear family of the landholder was hardly more than one component of a larger web of kin, both consanguine and affinal.

The words of the chief constable of New Galicia's capital, a town of 160 *vecinos* (citizens) in 1602, easily apply not only to any number of localities in Mexico but to many other regions of South America, whether Spanish or Portuguese. In this tiny, wretched town,

the aforementioned President [of new Galicia Audiencia] has 37 relatives and in-laws, counting his own and his sons' and nephews', plus 9 sons, sons-in-law, or grandsons, not to mention cousins' cousins and a host of Spanish friends and dependents of all these people. Said sons, sons-in-law, and nephews, all married if old enough, are constantly in his company; they all live under his roof and in one building; they take their meals around a common board. (Chevalier, 1963:161)

The Iberian model of kinship structure set the pace for American developments, but these were obviously influenced by the needs to fill social voids and to overcome lack of cohesiveness in an emergent and turbulent society. In other words, there was a definite requirement for a tightly knit, dependable structure, whose effectiveness did not depend on any single individual and whose temporal dimensions were not confined to the lifespan of an individual. To keep the estate undivided, the Iberian institution of the *majorazgo* (or *morgadio* in Portuguese) was introduced. If only the oldest son qualified for inheritance, the others were not abandoned to the uncertain and often precarious conditions of their Iberian counterparts. These sons, as well as married daughters and their children, were granted contiguous or nearby territories; thus in time a huge area would be ruled by a single strongly solidary kinship group. (Oliveira Vianna 1949:246ff.) Consanguine marriages within the group served to reinforce its solidarity and to hold the land together. According to Vianna, in Brazil the index of consanguine connubiality was 23.3 percent in the seventeenth century and 42.8 percent in the subsequent century. (Vianna, 1949:260). Obviously, the forces of such conglomerate holdings kept the kinship group together, and the structure of the group kept the holdings together.

Race, sex,
and miscegenation

The paradox of Iberian attitudes toward race

The act of conquest—the initial contact beween victorious armies and pioneering settlers on the one hand, and the surrendering native societies on the other—almost inevitably produces a collapse of traditional sexual mores. As a rule, women are scarce among the invaders, and it may be years or even decades before the sex ratio can be normalized. Meanwhile, only native women are available for sexual intercourse. The breakdown of indigenous institutions, and the difficulty of establishing effective controls among the conquerors, lead to widespread sexual anomie and to the emergence of a mestizo population. To judge from numerous historically known contact situations both interbreeding and the breakdown of sexual

mores seem to be universal; but the nature of the relationships beyond
the physiological level and the social position assigned to those of
mixed birth depend not only on the cultural traditions of either society
but also on the exigencies of the contact situation. To establish a permanent relationship with an individual from a biologically and culturally
different society may be a novel experience. Existing value orientations
and established ways of behavior may bear on the scale of sexual contact
and, more significantly, on the nature and duration of the attachment
acceptable or desirable from the standpoint of either society. Aside from
casual promiscuity, concubinage or even intermarriage may become recognized forms of relationship. Of course, people of different social classes
may feel and act differently about the acceptability of any such relationship. Members of the nobility may be inclined to take native concubines,
but intermarriage would be out of the question, except perhaps with
members of a recognized indigenous nobility.

The sexual mores of the Iberian conquerors were most definitely con-
ducive to an open and rather uninhibited acceptance of Indian or African
women as concubines and sometimes as wives. Most aspects of Iberian
sexual mores were familiar in other regions of Europe, but the cultural
heritage of the Moors strongly emphasized behavior that was less pronounced, barely tolerated, or frowned on as deviant in most areas of
Europe. A double standard of sexual morals existed everywhere, but
the Spaniards and Portuguese followed Islamic norms and carried it
much farther. Far from accepting the prevalent Christian notion that sex
was synonymous with sin, the male code of behavior unabashedly en-
dorsed unrestricted enjoyment of sex. The Christian precept of premarital chastity was flouted, and the sexual restrictions imposed by the
marriage vows were seldom taken seriously. In fact, manhood and self-
esteem were largely measured in terms of sexual prowess.

Diametrically opposed to the male code, the female code so heavily
stresses premarital chastity and conjugal fidelity that known violations
entailed the most drastic penalties. Since women were not believed to be
strong enough to resist sexual temptation, their life was rigidly controlled
by a complex set of rules proscribing most activities outside the home.
This kind of family structure was viable only among the middle and upper
strata of the society, where the women did not have to face the harsh
economic conditions endured by agricultural laborers and peasants.

Of course, seclusion of women is inconsistent with an exaggerated
emphasis on male sexuality, which seeks outlets and finds them among
the Indian servants and Negro slaves of the household or among lower-

class women generally, who cannot afford to ignore the economic advantages of becoming concubines of wealthy men. As captive women become scarce and eventually disappear, prostitution grows into a highly differentiated institution, and the need for it is tacitly recognized but never publicly admitted. Thus a variety of relationships somewhat arbitrarily classified as polygyny, common-law marriage, concubinage, and prostitution can be considered to be structural complements of the Moorish–Iberian family systems. These practices were known in Spain and Portugal, but all gained momentum in America.

Other aspects of the Moorish–Iberian heritage are more difficult to gauge. Miscegenation with the African conquerors left its imprint on the somatic makeup of many Spaniards and Portuguese, yet without shaking their belief in their own whiteness. Now the assumption of being white Europeans could be maintained only by stretching the criteria far enough to allow the somewhat darker individuals to be perceived as white, too. It is not likely that this had much bearing on the relationships with American Indians and Africans, but it almost certainly influenced the Iberian attitudes towards mixed-breds. Hoetink's remark that "the Latin whites simply accept 'coloureds' in their midst because by their physical criteria they are not 'coloured' " refers to the present-day situation (1967: 168). But considering the racial history of the Iberians, is is unlikely that such a flexible self-image would be wholly an American development. This possibility becomes even less credible if we consider that since the first half of the sixteenth century, numerous African slaves were imported into the Iberian peninsula. Lisbon, for example, had 9950 African slaves in 1551, close to 10 percent of its total population (Rebello da Silva, 1868:60); and in 1565 there were 6327 Negro slaves in Seville alone. (Mörner, 1967:16) Biological absorption of a continuous flow of Africans must have further stretched the racial criteria the Portuguese and Spaniards brought to the New World. They came prepared to perceive individuals of mixed parentage as white, provided that they were of legitimate birth.

Undoubtedly, a high degree of intermingling and racial tolerance had become a cultural tradition at the time of the conquest. However, this pattern seemingly stands in sharp contrast to the Iberian concern about purity of blood (limpieza de sangre), which inspired legal sanctions, prejudice, and widespread discrimination against racial hybrids, not to mention Indians and Negroes. It has often been said that in contrast to the bigotry of the Spaniards, the Portuguese assumed a more tolerant attitude and even encouraged mixed marriages. Actually, marriages between white Portuguese and Negroes and Indians were prohibited (Azevedo, 1963:129), and official encouragement came rather late, with a ministerial order of 1755 exempting Portuguese married to Indians from "infamy." But official encouragement did not extend to marriages with people of unmixed African descent. (Mörner, 1967:49–50) Both Spaniards and Portuguese showed concern with *limpieza de sangre,* but on the whole the Portuguese were more relaxed about miscegenation, and unlike the Spaniards, they never became entangled in futile attempts to create a society of racial "castes."

To gain a realistic view of the situation, one should realize that the gusto and abandon with which Portuguese and Spaniards alike embraced Indian and African women could scarcely have been intensified by official encouragement, nor could the rate of miscegenation have been reduced by attempts to apply legal and social sanctions to a society that had reached a tacit consensus about the desirability of the practice. Neither the preachings of the friars nor the social disgrace invited by spurious origin had any noticeable influence on the scale of miscegenation through-out the colonial period. Toward the end if the eighteenth century the mixed population of Mexico, Central America, and the West Indies amounted to 23.91 percent of the total population. (Rosenblat, 1954, 2: 36ff) Perhaps more significant than global figures are references to spe-cific regions. For example, in 1778 the mixed-bred groups under the jurisdiction of Nueva Granada amounted to 44.5 percent of the total population, whereas only 15 percent were Indians and 5 percent Negro slaves. (Jaramillo Uribe, 1965:25) According to the census of 1803–1804, 30.7 percent of the population of Guatemala were mestizoes, and in 1807 the mestizo population of El Salvador totaled 43.1 percent. (Rosenblat, 1954, 2:69–70) At the beginning of the nineteenth century, mixed-breds already numbered slightly more than 50 percent of all Venezuelans. (Rosenblat, 1954, 2:77) Although in most countries the mestizoes far outnumbered the Indians, the indigenous peoples of Peru, Bolivia, Guatemala, and Mexico were numerous enough to constitute significant majorities. In Peru in 1791, for example, the mestizoes did not exceed 24.4 percent of the total population, of which the Spaniards, both Euro-pean and American-born, represented no more than 13.7 percent. (Rosen-blat, 1954, 2:96)

Chile and Argentina, usually thought of as European in ethnic compo-sition, were well within the Latin American pattern of miscegenation. Estimates of Chile's mestizo population in 1810 vary between 60 and 80 percent. One of the sources lumps together whites and those showing hardly noticeable traces of miscegenation, thus expressing the tendency to ignore the less obtrusive signs of cross-breeding. (Rosenblat, 1954, 2:126) Argentine censuses rarely separated mixed-breds from Indians and Negroes, but miscegenation proceeded at the same pace as elsewhere. For example, of the 71,357 inhabitants of Cuyo province in 1778, 9,834 were white, 15,417 mestizoes, 20,558 Indians, and 25,548 Negroes and mulattoes. (Rosenblat, 1954, 2:131) In Brazil too, early estimates failed to distinguish mixed-breds from the supposedly unmixed white, Negro, and Indian population; but by 1818 there was a colored majority of about 66 percent, of which at least one-third was of mixed (mostly Portuguese-Negro) descent. (Ramos, 1951:151)

Population figures bearing on miscegenation in colonial Latin America should not be taken literally. Even when presented as census data, their accuracy is questionable on various grounds. One reads, for example, that mestizoes born in legitimate marriage were accepted and consequently counted as "Spaniards." Marriages between Iberians and Indians were "rare," we are told by historians, but there can be no doubt that the mixed offspring of such marriages further contributed to miscegenation among the American-born Spaniards (*criollos* or *Creoles*). It seems fairly safe to assume that the majority of the mixed-bred criollos would not forego their high status in colonial society by marrying Indians or Negroes; but whatever an individual's choice of marriage partner, with each succeeding generation miscegenation would spread further, although the visibility of the family's mixed ancestry might progressively diminish.

The overwhelming majority of the mixed-bred population in all regions of Latin America sprang from "free" sexual associations between Iberians and Indians or Africans. Many such associations were free only in the sense that they were not sanctioned by church or state, but they were not necessarily manifestations of sexual license as many contemporaries seemed to think. The Middle Ages knew a form of concubinage or common-law marriage (*barragania*) that transferred to the New World, was particularly viable in situations of cross-cultural and interracial contact. If marriage to an Indian or Negro woman was judged "infamous," concubinage was not. Most peasant settlers, who owned neither plantations nor mines, pioneered in remote and isolated areas where European women were unavailable and reliance on associations with Indian women might be essential to economic survival. Such unions were not necessarily permanent or monogamous, but often enough they were; and most of the time assumption of mutual responsibilities tended to stabilize the association. It would be the height of ethnocentric complacency to classify the occurrence of barragania in Latin America as deviant behavior. Based on cultural precedent in Europe, it was sanctioned by custom and has remained so to the present day, regardless of whether differences of culture or race are involved. There was, of course, a great deal of sexual deviance insofar as behavior did not conform to *any* recognized set of rules. Absolute control of large numbers of slaves or serfs inevitably invites sexual use and abuse of easily available females. But sexual promiscuity was by no means contingent on servitude. An increasingly numerous population of mixed origin was disfranchised by the fact of illegitimate birth. Like Indians and Negroes they were excluded from public office; they were not even allowed to vote for white candidates. The few educational facilities were closed to them, and whenever they ran afoul of the law, public flogging was the humiliating penalty; Creoles and Spaniards, on the other hand, could only be fined or incarcerated. There were many other attempts to discriminate against the *castas*, as mestizoes, mulattoes, and Indians were called. Frequently, they were not allowed to join military bodies, craft guilds, and "white" religious brotherhoods; they could not be ordained to the Catholic priesthood, and in some places the castas did not attend mass in some churches frequented by Spaniards.

In Brazil some religious brotherhoods split into several branches, each representing a different degree of pigmentation, and ecclesiastical authorities probed the racial purity of candidates to the priesthood. (R. Ribeiro, 1956:64–65)

Often enough such discriminating practices fell short of their objectives, and enforcement of rules designed to keep colored people out of secular and religious corporations was neither consistent nor uniform in different parts of the Spanish and Portuguese colonies. At any rate, prejudice and discrimination against the castas ran deep, contributing to an increasing marginalization of the colored population stigmatized by illegitimacy. Unable to find a niche in the economic order, thousands of mestizoes and mulattoes roamed the countryside, desperately struggling to survive in an environment whose hostility increased as the social structure grew more rigid toward the end of the colonial period.

Delinquency and sexual promiscuity seem to have been rampant among the castas. Their "vices" and "shiftlessness" were believed to be consequences of their spurious origin. Unable or unwilling correctly to diagnose this major social problem, colonial society applied the screws of repression and savage punishment, forcing this segment of the population to adopt a way of life that conflicted with the mores and laws of the land.

The nature of the Iberian prejudice against the castas has been an object of controversy. Several facts contradict the assumption that it was *racial* prejudice as we understand it nowadays. Its origin has been correctly traced back to the medieval concern with *limpieza de sangre* and *linaje* (lineage), which was directed against Moorish and Jewish admixture. Family lines allegedly containing Moorish or Jewish ancestors were discriminated against by those who claimed unmixed descent, and a presumably "pure" family line was considered a necessary ingredient of nobility. Of course, there was no way of recognizing individuals of mixed descent as physically distinct from those of "pure" lineage. Throughout the Middle Ages, miscegenation had been so widespread on all social levels that the genetic contribution of Moorish or Jewish ancestors could seldom be ascertained by the presence or absence of bodily traits. Neither Moors nor Jews constituted racial types of clear-cut somatic visibility comparable to those of American Indians, African Negroes, or their mixed-bred offspring. It has been suggested that this prejudice was religious rather than racial, that it was the infidel or the crucifier of Christ who was discriminated against, rather than the bearer of distinct somatic characteristics. Such an explanation, of course, would imply belief in some mysterious or mystic link between religious affiliation and purity (or impurity) of blood. At any rate, the problem of *limpieza de sangre* was perceived at the family level; its major manifestation was a pervasive obsession with genealogy, which in turn could not fail to affect family structure. Once a family had succeeded in establishing its *limpieza de sangre*, the only conceivable connubial association was to be with lineages of equal distinction. Thus *limpieza de sangre* came to determine—and usually to narrow down—the permissible choice of mates to relatively few families believed to be above suspicion. Celibacy was preferable to contamination, and many young women were confined to convents to prevent marriages that would have disgraced the family name.

In America, prejudice and discrimination based on the concept of *limpieza de sangre* proved to be a convenient tool of political domination and economic exploitation. *Limpieza* was supposed to be the distinguishing mark of all Iberian settlers. It fully justified the claim to nobility, but the Spaniards took the idea far more seriously than the Portuguese. In contrast to Iberia, however, the reality of somatic differences between the contacting groups cannot be denied, and the hypothesis that prejudice and discrimination reposed on the assumption that Indians, Negroes, and their mixed offspring were *biologically* inferior to white conquerors seems to gain credibility. Biological inferiority, as understood by racists, encompasses the *whole* person—his physical makeup as well as his mental equipment and "moral character." And being biological, this inferiority cannot be altered. Thus genuine racial prejudice is uncompromising; but compromise is exactly what we find in traditional Latin America. In fact, the fabric of colonial society was shot through with compromises and glaring inconsistencies concerning race.

Interracial marriage, although relatively rare, was tolerated, and the mixed offspring of such marriages were considered Spaniards or criollos. Furthermore, a Spaniard or criollo could legitimatize his illegitimate children. A formal petition had to be submitted to the king, who had the exclusive right to grant legitimization. The outcome of such processes seemed to depend mainly on the payment of a stiff fee. A tariff was established according to the specific conditions of the case. To receive legitimization of a son or a daughter of unmarried parents, 5500 reales had to be paid. Contingent on a fee of 33,000 reales were extraordinary legitimizations by means of which the sons of clerics or noblemen who belonged to a military order became entitled to inherit and acquire the nobility of the natural parents. And legitimization of sons had by married fathers and single women could be had for 25,800 reales. (Konetzke, 1965:185–186) The institution was used to such an extent that Konetzke refers to a "torrent of such gracious acts which provided a considerable income for the Crown." (Konetzke, 1967:185)

Toleration of interracial marriages and legitimization of mixed offspring, born out of wedlock, would be difficult to explain if genuine racial prejudice had been prevalent in Latin America. Biological inferiority cannot be removed by legal process, but the social handicaps of spurious birth can. Nobility can be conferred by investiture; but if the recipient were believed to belong to a lower biological order, the act would be as futile as an attempt to cure blindness by judicial decree.

A third institution incompatible with true racial prejudice was a process by which the taint of mixed origin could be removed by royal decree (the cedula de gracias al sacar). According to James King, the intention was "to compensate individual merits among the subjects of color, to drain the possible leader force from the colored masses by creating, at the same time, partisans grateful to the Crown who added to the white minority and undermined the pretensions of the criollo aristocracy." (King, 1951: 644) The institution was widely used during the eighteenth century and, like legitimization, it was contingent on a fee payable to the royal treasury. Obviously neither recourse was open to the poor. Thus wealth regardless of color was well on the way to becoming instrumental in the process of social ascent.

Finally, true racial prejudice ignores social differentiation among those considered to be biologically inferior. This was definitely *not* the case in areas in which indigenous society was stratified and topped by a hereditary aristocracy. The Spaniards recognized Inca nobility, and marriages between them and native women of "royal blood," the so-called *goyas*, were not unusual. Some of the old Peruvian families can be traced back to such mixed marriages. (Descola, 1962:31) Even local chieftains (*caciques*) ranked high in the politically inspired social scale of the Spaniards: "The Spanish rule used the authority of the caciques in the local administration of the Indian villages, and it distinguished these caciques by bestowing upon them privileges of nobility and by raising them to the level of Spanish hidalgos." (Konetzke, 1967:61) There are indications that in some regions Spaniards were encouraged to marry into the families of caciques. (Mörner, 1967:37)

Prejudice and discrimination were no less injurious to the colored population of Latin America for not being genuinely racial. Those who had neither the wealth nor the protection of a powerful father by which to secure redemption from the stigma of mixed origin were forced to live as outcasts. Discrimination was directed primarily against colored people of illegitimate birth belonging to the lower strata of the society. Since different or mixed racial origin did not constitute an insurmountable barrier, however, there were institutionalized as well as informal processes allowing a person to attain the social level supposedly reserved to Spaniards, Portuguese, and criollos, and these practices prevented Latin American society from freezing into a social structure divided into castes.

The two levels of miscegenation

As indicated earlier, miscegenation occurred (and continues to occur) on two social levels. There were numerous sexual associations in which one partner, usually the male, belonged to a social class superior to that of the other partner. But frequently there was little or no social difference between the partners of a sexual union, even though they belonged to diverse racial groups. Differential as well as egalitarian unions might be ephemeral or stable, and to the extent that they were stable they were common-law marriages or unions sanctioned by ecclesiastical and civil law.

Most egalitarian associations occurred among the "common people," whose lives and deeds were not recorded by chroniclers and travelers; thus our knowledge about the type of miscegenation they practiced is full of gaps. However, there is a wealth of information about differential sexual contacts involving people of high status. Aside from mere prostitution, most differential associations were between the landowners and the native or African women under their control. There we find a remarkable consistency of sexual behavior, which begins with the conquerors and encomenderos and continues through the centuries up to the contemporary plantation owner or administrator, who often enough has one or more concubines. From descriptive studies, such as these by Gilberto Freyre, it appears that the Iberian male realized the opportunity to play out his culturally induced role of a potent *macho* to the highest possible degree. So far as sexual prowess is concerned, Spanish encomenderos successfully competed with the plantation owners of the Brazilian northeast. Spaniards in what is now Colombia, for example, held 15 or 20 Indian women for domestic as well as sexual services. (Gutierrez de Pineda, 1963:185) Although the turnover of women in some of these households was probably rather high, many Spaniards and Portuguese were known to live in fairly stable unions with lower-class women, most of whom probably were mulattoes or mestizoes. In fact, mulatto girls were believed to be highly "aphrodisiac," and their sexual desirability has remained virtually uncontested up to the present day. Jaramillo Uribe wrote that "the attraction which Negro and mulatto women held for the white man was one of the most powerful factors of miscegenation in the [Colombian] society of the seventeenth and eighteenth century" (1963:36). The remark applies to any part of Latin America where African slavery existed, and the lore that developed around the beauty and sexuality of the mulatto woman is exemplified by a folk poem encountered in areas of Minas Gerais and Goiás (Brazil) in the early nineteenth century. (von Spix and von Martius, 1824; 2:298)

Huma Mulata bonita	A pretty mulatto
Basta o mimo que tem	need not pray
Para sua alma salvar	her loveliness suffices
Mulata se eu podia	to save her soul
Formar altar	Mulatto if I could
N'elle te collocaria	build an altar
Para o povo te adorar.	I would place you on it
	for the people to worship you.

A traveler, Le Gentil de la Barbinais, was among many to notice in the middle of the nineteenth century "the preference of the Brazilian-born Portuguese for the Negro or mulatto woman whom they would not exchange for the most beautiful European woman, an inclination which they themselves were unable to explain and which the visitor thought they acquired with the milk of the black mammies who had raised and nursed them." (Azevedo, 1963:123)

Aside from satisfying the sexuality of the adult males of the big estate, Indian and Negro women sexually initiated the adolescent males of the household, a function that in many regions of Latin America has remained until recently a tacit privilege of colored women. When slaves or serfs were no longer available, this function was assumed by professional prostitutes and colored maids.

Differential associations also occurred between Indians and Negro slaves. The Guajiro Indians of Colombia and Venezuela, for example, profusely interbred with Negro slaves they acquired in exchange for smuggled merchandise. (Gutierrez de Pineda, 1963:191–192) One of the most massive and thoroughgoing processes of miscegenation occurred in Paraguay between 1500 and 1600. After spending many years exploring the area for mineral wealth and suffering heavy casualties inflicted by hostile Indians, the Spaniards—about 600—had to settle for an extremely modest life of subsistence farming. They probably would not have been able to achieve even this without the cooperation of the Guaraní Indians. Almost completely isolated, deprived of European women and of the influence of additional migrants, the Spaniards depended on the Indians for almost everything. *Encomiendas* were established, but since the economy was based on barter rather than money, the Indians paid their tribute exclusively in labor. In a subsistence economy the demands for labor, thus the possibilities of exploiting Indian labor, were of course very limited. Large-scale miscegenation with the Guaraní began immediately with the arrival of the first Spanish settlers, and the mixed offspring soon outnumbered the Spaniards in Paraguay. (Service, 1954: 24) Typically, the mestizo sons—whether legitimate or spurious, we are not told— were legally "Spaniards" and could succeed their fathers as encomenderos of Indians.

Of the original Spaniards, only about 300 were left by 1566. Ten years later, Asunción alone had a population of 4000 mestizoes, and in 1585 nine-tenths of the non-Indian population of Paraguay were mestizo. (Service, 1954:54) "Proud and ambitious men, they were instrumental in founding new colonial towns in eastern Paraguay and in Argentina, for Asunción no longer offered them the possibility of becoming encomenderos of large numbers of Indians. Eventually, Asunción itself was dominated by mestizoes as the peninsular Spaniards died out." (Service, 1954:41)

In spite of the encomienda, the economic structure of the colony had a strong equalizing influence on relations between Spaniards and Indians. Without a monetary system, without commercial crops, import trade, mining, or other sources of wealth, class differentiation remained rudimentary and very unlike that of Mexico, Peru, or northeastern Brazil. "The Spaniards living here," we are told, "are so poor that their only clothes are of cotton and they wear palm-leaf hats, for no Spanish merchandise ever gets here, and they have nothing with which to buy any." (Vasquez de Espinosa, 1942:687) The leveling influence of poverty and cultural isolation is manifest in the way Spaniards and Indians had to adapt to each other. Of course, nothing in the Guaraní culture could match the patterns of Spanish political organization, and the Spaniards were able to introduce new tools, European crops, and European techniques. On the other hand, native crops, especially manioc, were accepted by the Spaniards, and the language of the mestizo population became Guaraní instead of Spanish. The family structure was polygynous, but we do not know whether or to what extent native polygyny was instrumental in the adoption of this pattern. In view of events elsewhere in Latin America, we can assume that even without indigenous encouragement, polygyny would have become the preferred form of marital life. Most Spaniards were said to have 15, 20, 30, or even 70 wives, and only a poor man would have to make do with only a half-dozen. (Service, 1954:34) Excessive as these figures may be, polygyny was the prevailing pattern; the moral indignation of occasional critics was of no avail, and the Catholic church was far too weak in Paraguay to curtail the practice, which so clearly conflicted with Christian doctrine.

Further evidence of the equalizing effects of Spanish–Guaraní culture contact is to be seen in the status of the mestizo, who did not have to labor under the social handicaps characteristic of mestizo populations elsewhere in Latin America. Of course once the original settlers from Spain had died out, there was no one left to contest the power position of the mestizoes. If this seems quite unusual within the context of traditional Latin American culture, the acculturative process that is represented is not. The way Iberian and Indian culture traits were welded into a viable whole was quite typical of immense areas of Ibero-America. More about this is said in the chapter on the peasantry.

The scale of egalitarian sexual contact is extremely difficult to estimate, but it must have been extensive—probably more so than interbreeding between individuals of different social status. Most migrants from Portugal and Spain were peasants, artisans, former sailors and soldiers and other people without capital to invest in extensive landholdings or in mercantile enterprises. Contrary to the traditional stereotype, in which the Iberian migrant is cast in the role of city dweller, a very large proportion of these people moved into remote and sparsely populated areas, often in search of mineral wealth, but usually finishing as they did in Paraguay and the Plata region as cattle ranchers or subsistence farmers. Thus, for example, extensive regions of Colombia (Savana de Bogotá, Antioquia, Boyacá, Llanos Orientales), some river valleys of the Amazon Basin, the São Franisco River system in Brazil, much of southern Brazil, the pampas, northern Argentina, and considerable portions of Central America, were opened and partially settled by Spaniards or Portuguese. The land they occupied lay outside the mining and plantation areas already controlled by the ruling class. Some of it became economically important later, and a considerable portion has remained of marginal interest up to the present day.

Circumstances forced the nonaristocratic Iberian settlers to compromise their aristocratic aspirations and to associate with Indians and mestizoes in conditions of near equality. They were not numerous enough to establish their own communities or systematically to exploit Indian labor. Nor were the nomadic or seminomadic Indians amenable to institutionalized exploitation. But the settlers took Indian women, and before long there was a rapidly growing mestizo population, available for further miscegenation. Of course, Iberian colonists must have found unions with mestizo women preferable to those with Indians. Culturally as well as physically, mestizoes resembled Iberians as much as Indians; within a few generations they tended to outnumber the Indians, and eventually no unmixed natives were left. If under the circumstances just described sexual associations with Indian women tended to be egalitarian, those with mestizoes were even more so. Often enough the process of miscegenation gained in complexity as Negroes—frequently runaway slaves—interbred with Indian women, and their offspring (*zambos, cafusos*) entered the gene pool characterizing a given population. Once the original ethnic boundaries were blurred and miscegenation among the components of the three major racial stocks had become a cultural pattern, there was no way of turning back the clock, and the quixotic attempts of the Spaniards to establish a society of castes was bound to fail. The Portuguese did not even consider such a policy. Generalized miscegenation among the "common people" affected the future development of race relations in Latin America in a highly significant way: It prevented the formation of a white lower class whose economic interests might have conflicted with those of the colored population.

The "common people" living outside the cities and the rural areas controlled by the land-holding aristocracy were not, as some historical sources seem to suggest, exclusively vagrants, paupers, and bandits. Genuine pioneering in the vast backlands, yet untouched by economic development, generated an anonymous peasantry whose way of life was both indigenous and European. The selective processes at work among the peasant farmers and ranchers are almost totally unknown, but a combination of ecological, economic, and political factors probably accounts for the social ascent of a significant number of the people, particularly during the nineteenth century. The first step was the acquisition of wealth on which further claims could be based. Of course legitimacy of marriage and birth had to be established and *limpieza de sangre* had to be proven, either by judicial process or informally by gaining acceptance in the social circles whose judgment was respected. Social ascent of this sort used to take more than one generation. An individual was relatively safe if he was believed to be descended from legally married parents and grandparents and if it was thought that none of these immediate lineal ascendants was of Indian or African extraction. Often enough, particularly in Brazil, demonstrations of economic or political power were more convincing than genealogical evidence. As the Brazilians say, a rich Negro is white, and a poor white is Negro. Interesting in this connection is the criminal process initiated in 1792 by a certain Pedro Lucas Zárate, citizen of La Rioja (Argentina), against Antonio Oviedo, of Córdoba (Argentina) who had called him publicly a "thieving Indian dog." In his presentation, Zárate admitted to being a *moreno*, a catchall adjective covering every conceivable shade of pigmentation, from sallow to dark brown. Of course he claimed *limpieza de sangre*, but his remarks convey an unusual sense of realism:

> I frankly confess that I ignore my ascendance because in these regions of *estancias* we only know who our grandparents were; but I do affirm that in my (region) we are known as Spaniards, and as such we serve the King Our Lord. And if Oviedo did not lack veracity as he usually does, he would either have to admit the same or show the genealogy of his family and his noble ancestry whence he descends. One is tempted to laugh if he hears one of those who do not know their third or fourth ascending generation, bragging about nobility, there being certainty that if one shook the tree of their genealogy, 'acorns' would come down all around its circumference. (Endrek, 1966:97)

The morenos of dubious ancestry were legion, and everywhere they were considered and considered themselves to be white. They certainly were not included among the mixed-bred population reported by census takers.

Attempts to summarize the salient aspects of miscegenation should take into account the following facts:

1. A high degree of racial miscibility characterized both the Spaniards and the Portuguese, regardless of status and class. On the higher social levels, miscegenation appears to be a socially undesirable (i.e. nonadaptive) by-product of slavery and serfdom. On the lower social levels, particularly among the peasantry, miscegenation seems to be adaptive insofar as it ensures economic survival and the selective absorption of indigenous cultural traits.

2. Attitudes toward the mixed-bred population are highly inconsistent. On the one hand, mestizoes and mulattoes are discriminated against in virtually all sectors of colonial society. On the other hand, informal and formal channels permit escape from the stigma of "infamy" attached to mixed ancestry. The mixed-bred was not merely perceived as a biological hybrid; his image was a rather complex association of somatic traits and cultural attributes, such as illegitimate or legitimate birth, occupation, and economic achievements. In spite of widespread prejudice and discrimination, the status of the mixed-bred was fluid. There was always a possibility of being accepted as white, because "the mixing of the races had reached a state which made it difficult to ascertain, at least by external characteristics, who was white and who was mestizo. Many mestizoes publicly declared to be white and of pure blood although they admitted having an indigenous ancestor." (Jarmillo Uribe, 1965:36) Of course, such claims to whiteness had to be backed up by economic wealth to be accepted socially.

Political emancipation in Latin America failed to produce startling changes in the social structure, but it did open channels of social ascent to the population of mixed ancestry. Legal handicaps intended to freeze the social position of the mixed-breds in castelike rigidity were removed. Although prejudice did not disappear with the stroke of a pen, upward social mobility of mulattoes and mestizoes was common during the nineteenth century, particularly as acquired through the channels of higher education. As a matter of fact, once a mestizo or mulatto had graduated from a university, often with the financial assistance of his natural white father, he found marriage to a white woman well within his reach. (Azevedo, 1963:127) Furthermore, the status value of a college degree, especially in law, was such that it opened career possibilities in politics and the civil service, regardless of a candidate's ancestry.

Nowhere did the mixed-bred population of Latin America rise as a group. Social ascent was individual, and individual acceptance of mestizo and mulatto is understandable only within the context of a cultural pattern that has been called "individualism" or "personalism." Since political and economic connotations tend to prevail in the use of these terms, another concept or conceptual dichotomy may be more appropriate to encompass the full extent of the behavioral pattern under scrutiny. According to a traditional classification, social contacts may be categorical or sympathetic. In categorical contacts, the relationship established between two or more individuals is based on the mutual perception of traits pertaining to the groups (or categories) of which they are members, regardless of differentiating personal attributes. The opposite is true of sympathetic contacts. Here people trying to establish relationships are oriented predominantly by the perception of differentiating personal attributes, regardless of group differences. Thus in spite of existing cleavages, the prevalence of sympathetic over categorical contacts in a society divided by racial antagonisms makes it possible for members of one racial category to recognize, and to accept as equal, individuals of the opposing category. In traditional North American race relations, personal qualities and achievements of individual Negroes were totally ignored by whites, who treated Negroes as if they constituted a homogeneous aggregate. In Latin America precisely the opposite is true. In spite of categorical antagonism, individual Indians, mestizoes, or mulattoes were accepted by whites (or pseudo-whites) because they were known to be descendants of Indian nobles or caciques, or white men of wealth and high status. During the nineteenth century, wealth or a college degree became attributes required to climb to the higher rungs of the social ladder controlled by the "white" upper class. It would be difficult to overrate the functional significance of this selective process, which *prevented the large colored sector of Latin American society from developing into a caste.*

The kinship complex

The Latin American family in cross-cultural perspective

In the preceding chapters we have found it necessary more than once to touch on family structure. There is a rather obvious relationship between ownership of land and structural-functional aspects of the family and kinship groups. Family structure, particularly its Moorish-Iberian antecedents, had to be considered to explain the extraordinary scale of miscegenation, as well as some of its particular aspects. Inevitably, these references raise a series of questions. What is meant, for example, by "patriopotestal extended family"? Or, how could the widespread occurrence of polygyny be reconciled with the official institution and sacramental character of monogamy? Was the term polygyny used loosely, perhaps as a synonym for any kind of extramarital relationship, or was it meant to have more consequential implications?

Since it is not our task to moralize about the Latin American family, but to understand it, the notion of what the family is or ought to be according to the Anglo-Saxon or any other model, is irrelevant. Often enough, ethnocentric preconceptions have produced distorted views of Latin American institutions. The case of the family is particularly complicated because there is a chasm between ideal and real pattern, between Christian precepts and actual behavior. To some, the patripotestal family is the only existing family type in traditional Latin American society. Consensual unions are glossed over or merely seen as deviations from "normal" marriage, and references to the mating habits of the lower classes are often referred to in terms of sexual "chaos," "anarchy," or "promiscuity." Needless to say, such views reflect prejudice that not surprisingly is often shared by urbanized Latin Americans who know little about the lower-class subculture of their own nations.

In a general cross-cultural perspective, an institution should be conceived in terms of its invariant aspects only. In this sense, marriage—the act by which a family is established—can be comprehensively defined as "socially sanctioned mating entered into with the assumption of permanency." (Herskovits, 1948:296)

The least variable structural element of the family is the mother–child relationship. Everything else—the role of the husband and those of other consanguine and affinal relatives—vary so widely and so thoroughly that any generalization would have to lack validity.

Since the three major ethnic components of Latin American society—Iberians, Indians, and Africans—bore widely different cultures, we may ask whether or to what extent family and kinship organization were influenced by these groups. With regard to Iberian influences it should be emphasized that in medieval Portugal and Spain, marriage was not noted for institutional homogeneity. In fact, there were three types of marriage: *ad benedictionem*, by *publica forma*, and *de jure in manu clerici*. Marriage *ad benedictionem* was no more than a public and religious consecration, at the entrance of a church, of a consensual union that had been recognized by the respective families and usually consummated by the marriage partners long before the public ceremony. Marriage by *publica forma* was merely recognized by public opinion, whereas the third form, *de jure in manu clerici*, was contracted in the presence of witnesses and a priest, but not in church. It has been argued that the three forms are legally equivalent on the ground that according to any of the three versions a married man could not be punished for killing his adulterous wife and her accomplice, and the family of the killed person had no right to blood revenge. (Cabral de Moncada, 1922:17; also Gutierrez de Pineda, 1963:164) The difference between *publica forma* marriage and barragania is not entirely clear, but the common denominator of all these forms is the implicit recognition that marriage was a *private act* whose legality lay in the consensus of the spouses and in the absence of impediments. In other words, marriage was fundamentally a consensual union, and its validity might or might not be reinforced by religious or legal ritual. Although the Catholic church tightened control over the marriage act and outlawed "clandestine" forms of matrimony, it has never succeeded in completely eliminating consensual unions, either in Iberia or in Latin America.

All this means of course that the consensual union, whatever its specific form, was a deep-rooted cultural pattern rather than a deviation; it was certainly transplanted to America, where it found a receptive environment, particularly among the peasantry and the rural laborers.

The tolerant attitude toward natural children, usually mixed-bred, was also part of the Iberian heritage.

> As is known, the Iberian peoples, from their prolonged contact with the Moors, viewed the illegitimate child with a complacency which astonished the rest of Europe. At the beginning of the eighteenth century Saint Simon marveled at the facility with which among the highest Spanish nobility illegitimate sons automatically inherited money, land and titles. At a time when in France, and especially in the Nordic countries, illegitimacy awakened profound horror . . . in Spain and Portugal the illegitimate child suffered little in comparison with the legitimate in prestige and social status, everything depending upon the disposition of the father. (Candido, 1951:300–301)

As described in the preceding chapter, formal legitimation, was only one way of raising the status of illegitimate offspring in Latin America, and probably it was not the most common approach. A child born of a slave mother was often manumitted and helped along economically. Education and jobs frequently were provided for by the natural father according to his wealth, political influence, and emotional involvement: Figures are unavailable of course, but the process was common enough to be considered a major channel of social ascent, particularly for the numerous population of mestizoes and mulattoes. (See, e.g., Gutierrez de Pineda, 1963:182ff.)

The possible influence of the many different Indian cultures on family and kinship is most difficult to assess. Some indigenous elements, such as various forms of polyygyny, trial marriage (*sirvinacuy*), and sexual mores ignoring the rules of premarital chastity and female virginity probably affected the local customs; because of the almost total lack of precise documentation, however, the extent and frequency of such influences remain a matter of conjecture. Native kinship systems were fully or partly preserved only in corporate Indian communities or in isolated tribal groups. In mixed groups, some indigenous elements concerning family and marriage may have been imparted by Indian mothers to their mestizo offspring. Polygynous arrangements, favored by Indian caciques, were found to be economically and politically expedient because the ties of kinship thus established bound a large number of Indians to a few Spaniards or Portuguese. For example, prior to the introduction of encomiendas in Paraguay

> the Spaniards acquired a number of Guaraní women as wives or concubines, but also as servants and food providers. The relatives of these women also helped to provide food and labor for the Spaniards in the same manner in which they customarily provided for the heads of their own lineages. The Guaraní apparently considered this situation a normal consequence of the alliance. (Service, 1954:20)

Undoubtedly, polygyny proved to be highly adaptive insofar as it solved basic problems the Iberian settlers had to face in situations such as those described by Service. Furthermore, polygyny accelerated the rhythm of miscegenation, and the following generation of mestizoes could draw on a selection of mixed cultural resources that enabled them to play a crucial role in the opening and colonization of immense areas of Latin America. The bandeirantes, for example, would not have been able to conquer the vast hinterland of Brazil without the assistance of the mamelucos, or Indian-Portuguese mestizoes.

Trial marriage is definitely a tradition of the Andean cultural complex, particularly of the Quechua Indians. (Mishkin, 1946:455) Institutionalized under the name of *amaño*, it was and to some extent still is very common in many regions of Colombia. The probability of the amaño being related to indigenous traditions is very high, but definite evidence of direct cultural linkage is hard to come by. (Gutierrez de Pineda, 1968:57–60)

Equally difficult to assess are conceivable African influences on Latin American family structure. Both polygyny and matripotestal or matricentric family have been attributed to Negro influences, but whether the occurrence of these phenomena is due to the conditions of slavery or to a genuine transfer from different African cultures remains a matter of conjecture. The matripotestal family consisting of a woman, her off-spring from one or several (absent) men, and perhaps her mother and unmarried sisters, has been observed among most Negro populations of America, but it appears to be common also in areas where Negro influences are negligible. Gutierrez de Pineda calls this type of family *madresolterismo* and attributes its currency in Colombia to indigenous influences. (Gutierrez de Pineda, 1968:60–66)

Family structure and social class

Whatever the role of Indian and African culture influences may have been, it seems to be safer to interpret variations of family and kinship structure *primarily* as functions of social class. This does not mean that we should disregard possible ethnic influences, it is merely to suggest that the social classes exhibit differing degrees of receptivity to Indian and African influences.

Among the highest strata of traditional Latin American society, particularly among the landholding aristocracy, the family is characterized by its large size, stability or continuity in time, structural complexity, high degree of solidarity, and multiplicity of functions. As one moves down in the social structure, these traits gradually loose some of their saliency. Among the lower strata the family tends to be smaller, somewhat unstable, relatively simple, and limited to the performance of fewer functions.

On the higher social levels, marriage is heavily ritualized and sanctioned by religious and civil authorities. On the lower levels, marriage is often or even predominantly based on consensus alone. If outside pressures are strong enough, a religious or civil marriage ceremony may occur years after children have been born to a couple.

In traditional Iberian law the definition of the *patria potestas* played a central role. Although the law almost invariably represents an ideal rather than the real pattern, it is remarkable how close the structure of the Latin American family came to the legal norms established in the *Las Siete Partidas*, the laws of Castile compiled by King Alphonso X. Here *patria potestas* is defined as the authority of fathers "over their children and grandchildren and all others descended from them in the direct line who are born in lawful wedlock." (*Las Siete Partidas*, 1931: 960) The status of women vis-à-vis their fathers, husband, older brothers, and other male relations was clearly subordinate.

> An unmarried woman always lived under the authority of her father, or under the tutelage exercised by the oldest of her brothers, or by the closest of her other relatives. Marriage, the sole cause of familial emancipation, liberated her from this tight network, but made her fall into the orbit of a new power (that of her husband) as pronounced as the first one. Only widowhood allowed a woman to exercise full civil capacity. (Ots Capdequi, 1941:84)

The double standard of sexual mores was sanctioned by Spanish and Portuguese law. Adultery was an offense only if committed by a woman. Spanish law stipulated that "a woman who had committed adultery was to be turned over with her lover, to the offended husband in order that he might satiate his thirst for revenge on the guilty. The only requirement was that the insulted husband might not kill one of the adulterers without killing the other too." (Ots Capdequi, 1941:99) Although men owed marital fidelity to their wives, there was no penalty for male adultery.

A possible class difference is suggested by the distinction between Spaniards and "mulattoes, Negroes, coyotes [natives] and individuals of similar castes." (Ots Capdequi, 1941:63) No Spaniard was allowed to marry without paternal consent, but people of the second category did not have to fulfill this legal requirement.

Paternal consent was likely to be given only to marriages that conformed to family interest, as opposed to individual choice. Thus such a union was typically a transaction between family groups establishing or reinforcing economic or political alliances through intermarriage. Yet this description should not be taken to indicate the violation of individual freedom or "emotional cruelty," because sexual and affectional satisfaction were not within the legal orbit of the patriarchal family. (Candido, 1951:300) Women were not brought up in the tradition of "romantic love"; they learned to obey and respect their husbands. Expectations of deep emotional attachment between spouses were alien to both Islamic and Iberian culture. Under such conditions, a male's sexual adventures outside marriage were not felt to be an intolerable burden; the emotional crises characterizing modern companionship marriage were unlikely to occur, and if they did, they could not affect the structure of the family because the nuclear or conjugal unit was solidly embedded in the wider structure of the extended family. The conjugal or nuclear unit was not sufficiently autonomous to make decisions that might imperil its own continuity. The head of an extended family who authorized a marriage held also the power to prevent its dissolution. The *patria potestes* of the male did not terminate with the marriage of his offspring, it terminated only with the death of the former. The structure of the society at large provided no niches for unattached females, except in convents and brothels. The idea of divorcées or single women gaining their livelihood or pursuing a career was not only unthinkable but structurally impossible in societies as androcentric and agrarian as traditional Latin American society.

The term "extended family," which is sometimes misunderstood, does not necessarily mean joint residence. Of course, some or all component units might live under the same roof, but rather than coresidence it was solidarity, cohesion, or *esprit de corps* that characterized the Latin American family. It was a kind of moral bond that enabled a number of consanguine and affinal relatives, as well as any number of retainers to act *in corpore*. To say that there was a tight network of interrelations implies reciprocal expectations, responsibilities, and privileges that kept the group alive and prevented its component parts from breaking away

The patripotestal extended family was a highly centralized group because control of its economic and political resources was vested in the leading male. He used his power, often ruthlessly, to maintain discipline among his dependent kin and retainers. The chroniclers of colonial Brazil recorded a number of cases in which patriarchal potentates killed wives or daughters for having violated the sexual mores. Or sons were put to death for acts of disloyalty. (Candido, 1951:295; also Costa Pinto, 1949, passim) Punishment without resort to outside institutions was the result of infractions of work discipline or rules stipulating obligations of any kind, not only by slaves but by anyone who lived and worked under the protection of the estate. Thus the patripotestal extended family developed its own private judicial system in contraposition to the state. "Such a private system of law and order can exist only where the state is either too weak to exert control on the local level, or where it supports the delegation of judicial functions to local entrepreneurs. Mexican haciendas used to maintain their own police, judges and jails." (Wolf and Mintz, 1957:395) It may be argued that tight discipline was necessary to defend the estate against its foes, such as fugitive slaves, hostile Indians, or litigious neighbors, who might take advantage of organizational weaknesses to translate their claims into overt aggression. Obviously, a private judicial system easily becomes an instrument of vendetta when external conflict occurs, and this is exactly what happened in a number of cases, particularly in Brazil. (Costa Pinto, 1949)

The ways in which political organization and the kinship complex are interrelated in traditional Latin America are clearly revealed by the observation that the patripotestal extended family was powerful enough to assume political functions usually monopolized by the state and to resist attempts of the state to reclaim these functions. Indeed, a meaningful discussion of one is almost impossible without reference to the other. The landowning extended family or coalitions of interrelated families (kinship groups) became political subdivisions, as we shall see in Chapter 5.

Continuity and coherence of the extended family were considerably enhanced by linkages between landownership and family lines rather than the individual proprietors. Writing about Mexico, Chevalier pointed out that

> in the seventeenth century, the true owners of haciendas were families and lineages, rather than individuals. Some estates were owned jointly by a number of relatives and, therefore, could not be divided; many others were entailed, so that individual owners could not dispose of their property, which remained indissolubly linked to a family name, a pedigree, or, sometimes, to a title. (Chevalier, 1963:295)

Usually associated with primogeniture, entailment was probably as common in Spanish America as it was in Brazil, where it was known as *morgadio*. Not only did this practice prevent the landed estate from being divided among several heirs, it forced the family to branch out in various directions. Family members who were not entitled to inheritance often settled new land or entered urban professions or enterprises, always with the support of the family. Either way, the power domain of the extended family expanded.

Little information is available about the role of the extended family in nonagricultural sectors of the society, but as interest in social history grows, more evidence is unearthed suggesting that family ties were crucially important in mercantile enterprise.

> Family ties, and secondarily regional origin, were important in the formation of companies. Peru was the most distant and wealthiest part of the Indies, where governmental authority was weakest. Without the family bond, merchants of Seville could not begin to trust their factors in Peru, whose records, even when they were

relatives, was not good. The ideal, rarely achieved, was to have the father in Seville, and sons in Panama, Lima, and elsewhere in Peru. When it was necessary to trust someone from outside the family, every effort was made to marry him into it; his new wife's dowry could be left in Spain as additional security for his good behavior. The extrafamilial partner could have some young member of the family with him, partly to gain experience and partly to keep watch over the family interests. (Lockhart, 1968:81)

It has been suggested that the family took on new significance in what has been called the "contracting economy of the seventeenth century." From the level of the ruling dynasty to that of the most humble bureaucrat, family relationship were matters of economic survival. "Alliance and kindred" are key words to Spanish society of this period for upon such relationships depended in great measure access to livelihood and wealth and status. (Stein and Stein, 1970:19) It may be added that structural encroachment of the extended family on newly emerging cultural forms became a tradition in itself, attesting to the amazing vitality of the kinship principle, almost up to the present time.

Polygyny and the double standard of sexual behavior

However we approach the question of polygyny in Latin American society, we cannot ignore a basic cultural inconsistency pitting deep-rooted customary behavior against the moral, legal, and religious sanctions protecting the monogamous and sacramental character of marriage. The double standard of sexual mores allows the male to engage in extramarital relationships, of which many are transient and do not involve lasting commitments. But there is another kind of consensual union in which both parties assume definite responsibilities. The male, already legally married, becomes emotionally attached to a young woman, usually of a social class inferior to his own, and sets her up in a separate household. He takes full financial responsibility for all her needs, and if she bears children, his obligations extend to their upbringing and education. Such unions may not last a lifetime, but they are established with the assumption of *relative* permanency. Before committing himself, the male often seeks the consent of the girl's family. If, as it often happens, the family is economically dependent on the suitor, refusal is unlikely, particularly in view of the relatively disadvantageous prospect of a marriage or consensual union with a man of the girl's own social class.

Sometimes a man would establish more than one secondary household, but of course the extent to which he was able to allocate resources to his various families depended on his income. In the lower classes, such multiple unions do not always imply serious economic commitments by the male.

The concept of polygyny seems applicable to these arrangements because they involve mutual responsibilities, they are relatively stable, and they are not sanctioned as deviant behavior by the society at large. As a matter of fact, males among males tend to encourage and admire polygynous behavior, which is part and parcel of what we may call the *virility complex* in Latin American culture. Originally we suggest the term in connection with Brazilian sex patterns, but there is enough evidence to extend it to Spanish America. Indeed, there is no significant difference between Brazilian and Spanish American sexual mores. The virility complex is a cluster of interrelated values and attitudes, all centered around what is conventionally believed to be proper sexual behavior of the male. According to this pattern, the male is expected to become sexually active at the age of puberty. He learns that frequent sexual intercourse is not only believed to be physiologically healthy, it is also an essential attribute of manhood. Marriage is not expected to impose limitations on a man's sexual activities, and most males feel free to have intercourse with as many different women as may be available.

Hard as the Catholic Church has tried to impose its teachings on premarital chastity and extramarital sex, it has never been able to control more than a small minority of Latin American men. Male chastity is ridiculed and looked on as possible evidence of sexual impotence. Early in life the Latin American male learns to build his self-esteem largely in terms of sexual prowess. Erotic adventures perform the function of bolstering his ego, and considerable attention is paid to the presumed aphrodisiac effects of certain food, beverages, and drugs, with food items and drugs believed to reduce sexual potency carefully avoided. In other words, the virility complex is virtually synonymous with *machismo* if this term is divested of its nonsexual implications.

We propose to label the cluster of interrelated values and attitudes intended to control female sexual behavior the *virginity complex*. It is centered around the idea that the virginity of unmarried females should be preserved at any cost. Such institutional arrangements as segregation of the sexes, chaperonage, and closely controlled courtship are component parts of the virginity complex. Most men feel that to marry a girl who had been "deflowered" (*deflorada*) would be to make fools of them-selves. Men either avoid girls suspected of premarital sexual exposure or, if they unknowingly marry a nonvirgin, they probably seek annulment or divorce on the ground of the physical condition of the bride. This sanction is supported by some of the civil codes of Latin America.

Marriage does not bring relief from most premarital restrictions. Exactly as before marriage, the woman's behavior is strictly controlled. She must refrain from any activity that could be interpreted by a jealous husband as interference, actual or imagined, with his sexual monopoly. In other words, she must avoid all situations in which a man could find an opportunity to make advances to her if he wanted to. Sanctions inflicted on unfaithful women are comparable to those punishing premarital sexual experiences. If discovered, the lovers may be put to death by the injured husband, who is relieved of legal responsibility because he is assumed to have succumbed to uncontrollable rage. If the wife survives being caught with her lover, legal separation or divorce follows almost inevitably. A man who does not make use of such radical sanctions is likely to lose his standing in male society. To be cuckolded is almost the worst fate that can befall a man.

Like female adultery, premarital sex relations are felt to be an un-bearable insult and stain on the family honor. Here, the deflowered girl's brothers are the primary ones expected to take action against the perpetrator, but the girl herself may be expelled by the irate father. (Willems, 1953:340–341)

Although the virility complex cuts across class lines, the lifestyles of the lower class, both rural and urban, are obviously incompatible with the elaborate system of control that is assumed to prevent middle- and upper-class women from having illicit sexual experiences. Lower-class women work in the fields and sell produce in the market, they hire themselves out as domestic servants and often peddle wares in the streets of towns and cities. Sexual mores are generally more relaxed, and lower class men are unlikely to attribute such exaggerated importance to female virginity as do men of higher class levels.

Since the virility complex encourages unrestricted sex for males, and the virginity complex allows no socially acceptable alternatives to marriage and spinsterhood, prostitution becomes a structural corollary to the pre-vailing mores. Few reliable data on prostitution are available, but we can safely make the following assumptions: that the practice is a tra-ditional component of virtually all urbanized localities, regardless of size;

that it is stratified in larger urban centers; and that the society at large tacitly recognizes its functional relevance, occasional outbursts of reformist fervor notwithstanding.

Ritual kinship

Godparenthood or ritual kinship is an institution designed either to extend a family beyond the confines of consanguinity and affinity or to reinforce existing kinship ties. It carries the sanction of the Catholic Church, which requires a man and a woman to assume moral responsibility for the religious upbringing of a newly baptized child. These sponsors are freely chosen by the biological parents of the child, and the bond established between godparents and child is one of "spiritual kinship." Actually, the structural and functional elaborations of ritual kinship went far beyond the responsibilities prescribed by the Church.

In addition to establishing mutual obligations between baptismal godparents and child, a very close relationship is set up between biological parents and godparents. In Latin America emphasis seems to be on ritual coparenthood (*compadrazgo, compadrio*) rather than on godparenthood. Three sets of ritual kinship terms are used, representing the relational triangle between biological parents, godparents, and godchildren. *Compadre* (masculine) and *comadre* (feminine) are terms by which biological parents and ritual parents address one another. A godfather is called *padrinho* (Portuguese) or *padrino* (Spanish) by his *ahijado* or *afilhado* (Spanish and Portuguese for "male godchild"). The corresponding female terms are *madrina* and *madrinha, ahijada* and *afilhada.*

References to social relationships are meaningless if the inherent reciprocal obligations and privileges are not spelled out. Compadrazgo often reinforces or "intensifies" existing kinship ties, rather than extending them. This means that the biological parents choose consanguine or affinal relatives as baptismal godparents of a child, a choice that further defines and perhaps expands existing obligations.

The selection of ritual coparents may fall on persons belonging to the same social class as the biological parents; in this case the new set of relationships is structured horizontally. (Mintz and Wolf, 1950:352ff.) Or, persons of a higher class are requested to assume compadrazgo responsibilities. Such vertically structured relationships are always one-way streets; that is, an Indian may ask a ladino in a Guatemalan community to be the godfather of his child, but a ladino would never approach an Indian for the same purpose.

Whether horizontal or vertical, the compadrazgo system is expected to function as a kind of "social insurance." Compadres help each other by performing various services or by lending money, tools, draft animals, or any other object. It is a relationship of mutual trust and respect. (Foster, 1948:264)

Vertical compadrazgo relationships cut across class lines and sometimes help stabilize productive relations between large and small landholders, or between landholders and their sharecropping employees and laborers. (Mintz and Wolf, 1950:363) Godparents are expected to assist their godchildren whenever need arises. They may assume parental responsibilities if the biological parents of the godchild die or are handicapped by sickness or excessive poverty.

In urban society, individuals holding high-ranking positions in the civil service, in business, or in industry are often beseeched by their numerous compadres and godchildren to provide jobs or promotions. In politics, ritual relatives are of course expected to support a compadre running for office, and if elected, a compadre in turn will prefer his ritual relatives in dispensing patronage.

The religious complex
and its ramifications

Medieval traits in Iberian Catholicism

Iberian Catholicism had at least two distinguishing qualities that were transferred to the New World, where they exerted profound influence on the emergent culture of Latin America. Confrontation with Islam accounts for much of the religious zeal and extraordinary vigor that inspired the spiritual conquest and determined the prevailing attitudes toward heterodoxy for centuries to come. Furthermore, Iberian society was not exposed to the religious and political vicissitudes of the Reformation. Medieval forms of Catholicism remained essentially intact and became entrenched in Spanish and Portuguese America. The cult of the saints, monasticism, mysticism, religious fiestas, and a proliferation of religious brotherhoods are usually cited to characterize Latin American Catholicism. These phenomena did not cease to exist in Europe, outside the Iberian peninsula; the emphasis the medieval church had placed on them was merely perpetuated in Spain and Portugal. In fact, the cult of the saints, the fiesta complex, and the religious sodalities encountered fertile soil in America and eventually assumed forms and functions that stood in open or latent conflict with dogma and ecclesiastical discipline. On the folk level the saints were frequently deified, and the religious fiesta developed into an elaborate mechanism promoting the circulation of wealth and controlling social ascent within the community. In colonial towns, religious sodalities, particularly those with upper-class membership, often became powerful and wealthy enough to defy the authority of the clergy.

More indicative of medieval religiosity perhaps was the unconditional and spontaneous acceptance of doctrine and sacraments. Religious conviction was not arrived at after weighing possible alternatives and overcoming nagging doubts. It was simply there, unquestioned and unchallenged by dissent or unbelief. Impiety, atheism, or agnosticism, in the sense of attitudes or forms of militancy, were simply inconceivable within the context of colonial culture. The few deviants "carefully hide their unbelief, worse than criminals, they would appear to be fearfully insane in the eyes of the surrounding world" (Prado Junior, 1963:327)

This complex of unquestioning faith, intensive participation in religious ceremonies, and devotional practices contrasts sharply to the persistent refusal to obey certain Catholic moral precepts. The male code of behavior as we have seen involved an almost contemptuous disregard for the rules of premarital chastity and marital fidelity. Apparently, few people were aware of or disturbed by such contradictions. Attempts to explain these inconsistencies have not been very successful. To some critics, traditional Iberian Catholicism is hardly more than colorful pageantry, devoid of true religiosity and moral conduct. Others find fault with religious instruction in colonial times, deficiencies resulting "in a very sincere but ignorant religiosity, in faith mixed with superstitions, sentimentality without substance; a religiosity which failed to prevent moral deviations; one invoked the Virgin, but lived in concubinage." (Pin, 1963:31)

The recurrent explanation that religious instruction was deficient in colonial Latin America touches only the surface of the phenomenon. In comparison with other religious systems, Roman Catholicism seems to require an unusually high degree of indoctrination and regimentation to keep it on the level of strict orthodoxy. There is perhaps little awareness that such a high level of ecclesiastical discipline has seldom been achieved. "Ignorant religiosity," "superstitions," and illiterate priests were quite common throughout the Middle Ages. One can hardly expect the Church to accomplish in colonial Latin America what it failed to do in Europe. The problem is one of enculturation rather than mere instruction. Formal teaching of the doctrine has little chance to succeed if it must compete with the massive inculcation of "ignorant religiosity" performed by the groups that closely control the individual from infancy to adulthood. There is abundant evidence that even at the present time heterodox and —by church standards—almost sacrilegious practices have a way of surviving in spite of relatively high levels of religious instruction.

Social class, ethnicity, and religion

Superficial impressions of Latin American Catholicism, especially when mediated by census figures about religious "affiliation," easily convey the idea of monolithic homogeneity. Nothing could be farther from reality: There is a very high degree of internal differentiation or variation, and sometimes the variations are so great that it is difficult to discover the common theme. Among other things, social class and ethnicity must be taken into account to understand the bewildering complexity of religious belief and practice. To avoid confusion or misunderstandings, religion is defined here as the belief in, and dealings with, forces believed to be supernatural. These dealings are intended to secure benefits, or to prevent harm expected to result from the intervention of the supernatural in human affairs. Beliefs and practices may or may not develop into formalized theology, priesthood, and temple cult, but whenever they do, a "church" is born, and the priesthood often tends to monopolize the knowledge and skills held to be indispensable to cope with the supernatural.

Of course the social scientist has no way to distinguish between "true" and "false" religions. A religious system is merely taken as an assembly of facts. A belief is a fact, not because it is true, but because it affects people in a number of ways; it makes them feel, think, or act, and these feelings, thoughts, and actions are the anthropologist's business. If different religious systems begin to interfere with one another, as in Latin America, we face a complex situation. The Catholic missionaries, endeavoring to convert the Indians, were not the only bearers of differing beliefs. Moreover, although soldiers and settlers did not preach, instruct, or baptize, they were carriers of beliefs, some of them handed down from pre-Christian times. The belief in witchcraft, in the evil eye, and in werewolves are examples in point. And transactions with the supernatural had a way of assuming magical or coercive forms.*

Many elements of Iberian folk religion gained ample currency in Latin America (Ribeiro, 1956:49), but more numerous and significant were the survivals of indigenous and African religious systems that could not be eradicated by the missionaries and their successors, the parish priests. Wherever Indian communities succeeded in preserving their corporate character, a pantheon of major and minor deities, of spirits and demons, survived. Elsewhere the disappearance of distinct Indian societies due to epidemics, warfare, and miscegenation was not accompanied by the obliteration of all indigenous religion. Throughout the Amazon region Indian shamanism and beliefs in spirits of the forest were taken over by mestizo society. Almost everywhere rural mestizo culture exhibited a varying assortment of magical usages that can be traced back to indigenous or Iberian traditions. There is no single answer to the question of why so much indigenous religion and magic became embedded in Latin American folk culture. As indicated earlier, most Indians regarded the Catholic religion as a welcome accretion to, rather than substitution for, their own beliefs. Very often conversion consisted in administering the sacrament of baptism to the largest possible number of Indians; the act was neither preceded nor followed by indoctrination. If possible at all, indoctrination tended to be superficial and intermittent. Only in rare instances was the Catholic church able to establish controls effective enough to purge the neophytes of the remnants of their former beliefs.

Furthermore, the low-ranking clergy were seldom prepared to cope successfully with the implantation of a religious system as complex as Roman Catholicism.

Especially the lower clergy, both secular and regular, are accused of faults commonly attributed to the clergy in general, particularly immorality, ignorance, and lack of vocation. Stemming almost totally

---

* Any religious act—a prayer or a sacrifice, for example—becomes magical if the expected effect is believed to be the mechanical consequence of the act regardless of the motivations, intentions, and the state of mind of the performer. Failure to produce results is attributed to faulty performance, rather than to the "inscrutable wisdom of God" or to the lack of piety or humility of the petitioner. Since correct performance of a magical act cannot fail to produce the desired effect, an element of coercion is involved in all magic, and coercion is often directly applied to the effigy of a supernatural being.

> from the least educated social classes and lacking a regular system
> of instruction, the low clergy was composed, to a very large extent
> of ignorant priests. (Tormo, 1962:20)

In other words, a large proportion of the peninsular priests entrusted with
the task of indoctrination had never fully absorbed the culture complex it
was supposed to transmit. Small wonder that the Jesuits complained that
such priests "were singularly complacent about polygynous unions and
indeed often indulged in concubinage themselves." (Boxer, 1963:89)

Lack of continuity also helped thwart the implantation of Catholicism
in Spanish and Portuguese America. The Church never had the manpower to keep abreast of the highly dispersive process of colonization.
Under these conditions, selective retention of indigenous elements of
religion and magic was to be expected.

In regions of Latin America in which much of the population is
descended from African slaves, religion was strongly influenced by various
African cultures. This is the case in coastal Brazil, in Haiti, and in the
West Indies where folk religion appears to be primarily Catholic-African
syncretism. In fact, Catholic-African syncretism may be taken as a differentiating rather than a unifying feature in a comparison of Spanish and
Portuguese America. The African component of Brazilian folk religion,
which has shown an amazing staying power, as well as the capacity to
adapt to a changing sociocultural environment without losing its identity,
is discussed within the evolutionary context of Part II.

In the context of traditional Latin American culture folk Catholicism has always been a religious system in its own right. Ours is not
the perspective of the theologian who perceives it as an aberration or
a jumble of superstitions and distortions. We try to understand it in
terms of what it means and does to the peasants and townspeople who
practice it. Several of its component parts are ubiquitous regardless of
country and region. Above all, there is what may be called the "healing
complex"—that part of folk medicine which endeavors to harness supernatural resources of various kinds. Healers are specialists, of course
(often shamans, as in the Amazon region), who are believed to be powerful enough to enlist the help of spirits to perform cures. To the extent
that healers (*curanderos, curandeiros*) do not exclusively rely on herbs,
they use approaches that are at least implicitly shamanistic. Outside
the major urban centers, Latin American society survived without the
benefit of what was held to be scientific medicine. Later, medical progress
remained unavailable to most rural people, and even today little scientific
medicine reaches the immense backlands of the continent. Whatever its

particular aspects and resources, folk medicine has meant a great deal to the people. No clear distinctions are made between natural and supernatural healing techniques; the herbalist is not pitted against the witch doctor; on the contrary, most healers are well acquainted with herbs and incantations, with prayers, and with some rudiments of pharmacology.

The cult of the saints is as much emphasized in Spanish America as in Brazil. Without close supervision by the Church, it tended to become quite unorthodox in belief and practice. In folk usage, probably transferred from Iberia, the saints often are approached as if they were deities rather than mediators. Saints are supplicated, worshipped, coaxed, coerced, and sometimes punished. Perhaps the most common approach to a saint is the *promesa* or compact. To obtain a particular benefit one promises a candle, a novena, a pig, a heifer, a certain amount of corn, a pilgrimage, and so forth. To many devotees, communal celebrations in honor of a saint are occasions to fulfill a promesa. Three major problem areas are felt to be in need of saintly succor: the individual life cycle (mainly birth, marriage, illness, and death); natural forces related to success and failure in agriculture and livestock raising; and supernatural beings and forces generally believed to be harmful to man. Illness and accidents play a particular conspicuous role in the cult of certain saints famed for their miraculous powers. Each year hundreds of thousands undertake pilgrimages to the many shrines to seek cures from crippling maladies or injuries. Aside from the great national centers of pilgrimage such as Guadalupe in Mexico or Aparecida in Brazil, there are hundreds of local churches where statues of thaumaturgic saints are continuously supplicated through various kinds of compact. The search for miracles is not confined to the lower classes, of course; but the social background of most miracle seekers, as well as the rather unorthodox ways the saints are usually approached (e.g., through bodily contact with their effigies) suggest the folk character of the phenomenon.

Crops and cattle may be protected through a compact with a saint. It is believed that draughts or floods can be averted by performing supplicatory processions, in which the statue of a saint is carried through the fields. Sometimes, as in Yucatan, a particularly powerful saint, St. Michael, is thought to control the raingods. (Redfield, 1941:140) Maya Indians believe in deities of rain, cornfield, bush, and village, and special ceremonies are carried out in their honor to assure good crops. (Redfield, 1941:95) Elsewhere, crops and animals must be protected from the evil eye or from destructive magic inflicted by human enemies or evil spirits. Not only are domestic animals, crops, and dwelling sites threatened by supernatural forces, man himself feels exposed to the malevolent actions of bush spirits (e.g., the *sacy-pererê* in Brazil), werewolves, errant souls of the dead, and a host of "mythological" beings. The signal of the cross, an ejaculatory invocation of a saint, a *promesa* on the spur of the moment may save one's life or sanity.

Latin American folk religion has been described and analyzed in numerous monographs dealing with communities located in Mexico, Central America, Columbia, Ecuador, Peru, Paraguay, Brazil, Venezuela, and various Caribbean islands. The religious system found in one community is never an exact replica of any other system. Each has its own set of saints, although some saints are revered and worshipped almost everywhere; the number and relative importance of non-Christian elements blended into the various aspects of belief and cult differ, but some elements are always present. The religious specialists and officials of one community tend to carry more or less authority or prestige than those of other places; their functions vary, and so does their position vis-à-vis the legitimate representatives of the church hierarchy. But there always is a structure of such specialists and functionaries, often native priests, home-grown miracle workers, witch doctors, prayer leaders, and the like. Thus there are differences among individual communities and sets of communities, but no overall difference has ever been discovered between Spanish America and Brazil, with respect to the nature and the structure of folk religion.

Doubtless most aspects of Latin American folk Catholicism resulted from early crystallization processes. Later developments were probably adaptations to previous options of content or structure. On the whole, local systems have great staying power, and many that have been studied recently were traced back several hundred years. In describing them, one may use present or past tense almost interchangeably as we have done. But in some regions (not whole countries), folk religion has ceased to exist as a *system*. Change in this area is not related to a tightening of church controls, alone, or to a general decline of religious beliefs. The situation is far more complex, as we shall see later.

Religion at the upper-class levels

In the towns and plantation areas of colonial Latin America, the Iberian church, such as it was, proved capable of asserting a certain degree of authority against the intrusions and encroachments of Indian and

African elements. However, it was not so much a matter of urban sophistication prevailing over peasant naïveté as of class diversities reflecting different degrees of indoctrination and theological literacy. Apparently the supernatural world of the Indian and African did not automatically succumb to the Catholic officialdom of the colonial city. After all, it was in the cities rather than in the countryside that African deities and African cult forms survived. There are many indications that in the cities of Spanish America, too, the lower classes retained forms of witchcraft and magic of mixed Iberian, indigenous, and sometimes African origin. At least the well-documented case of Brazil suggests that the anonymity of the city provided an effective cover for unorthodox dealings with the supernatural.

Among the middle and upper classes religious belief and practice were closely associated with the cult of the saints, religious sodalities, and monasticism. In the larger cities, each of the many churches developed its own cycle of annual fiestas with spectacular services and processions in which the effigies of patron saints, of the Virgin Mary, and of Christ were carried around in the streets. In the numerous local adaptations, a particular saint was attributed with the power to prevent or solve problems related to the immediate environment. For example, earthquakes constantly threatened the survival of the Andean cities, and since earthquakes cannot be physically controlled, recourse to supernatural powers seems to offer the only chance to the faithful. Thus Lima as well as Cuzco developed a special cult designed to propitiate the Lord of the Earthquakes (*El Señor de los Temblores*), one of the many localized versions or facets of Christ. These cults emerged in the wake of major seismic catastrophes in 1654 in Lima and in 1650 in Cuzco.

The wealthy willed much of their money and property to the Church and to the brotherhoods of which they had been members. Donation of wealth to religious institutions became an established way of atoning for sins, thus ensuring salvation in the afterworld. This pattern of generous giving enabled the religious orders and brotherhoods to build the many sumptuous temples that constitute major esthethic attractions of such cities as Lima, Quito, Bahia, Mexico, Bogotá, Recife, Ouro Prêto, and Cuzco. Sodalities with upper-class membership often became rich and powerful enough to defy clerical authority.

Brotherhoods, like other voluntary associations sponsored by the Church, are institutional devices intended to link the people and the ecclesiastical hierarchy. They are integrating devices, as well, defining responsibilities by sex and age, and carrying out specialized activities related to the cult and to charitable enterprises. Funds for the construction and maintenance of hospitals, for example, came from certain sodalities. This is one of the many medieval patterns that in some cities at least, have been preserved up to the present time. Membership in upper-class brotherhoods was very much sought after, perhaps for the same reasons social climbers nowadays anxiously try to join exclusive country clubs. Owing to the lack of empirical studies, generalizations are difficult to sustain, but the carefully researched case of the *Misericordia de Salvador* reveals the mechanism of social mobility built into the structure of the brotherhood that had assumed responsibility for the hospital of the capital of colonial Brazil. Beginning with a change of its charter in 1618, the *confraria* assumed the functions of a boundary-maintaining institution by establishing definite social criteria for the admission of members. Not only had the aspirant to be literate and well-to-do; he and his wife were also required to be of "pure blood," without Moorish or Jewish admixture. (Russell-Wood, 1969: 177–178) If the aspirant did menial· work he could only be allowed to join to the lower rank of a brother of minor condition (*menor condição*); admission to the upper rank, a kind of brotherhood "nobility" was contingent on the exercise of nonmenial occupations. The upper stratum was further divided into members of the "hermetically closed" landed aristocracy and the representatives of what Russell-Wood calls *haute bourgeoisie*: high-ranking members of the executive and judiciary, members of the clergy, university graduates (*bachareis*), and wealthy merchants. Those allowed to join the lower ranks of the brotherhood, the *petite bourgeoisie*, were mostly shopkeepers and artisans. (Russell-Wood, 1969:182ff.)

Between 1676 and 1802, 74 brothers of "inferior condition" rose to the upper stratum. The figure does not seem impressive, but the total membership of the brotherhood was never higher than 600, and, according to the census of 1775, Bahia had a free population of only 20,557. Apparently, there was no lack of aspirants, and the social ambitions of some were not satisfied with the condition of a "minor brother." Elected to the lower ranks, they refused to swear allegiance to the association.

Through the brotherhood the religious complex of the city was linked not only to the class structure but to the kinship system and to the municipal government. The traditional upper class families, related to one another by kinship, continuously held leading positions in the brotherhood, and all the councilmen of the municipal legislature were also brothers of the confraria. Either one of these institutions made a person eligible for membership in the other. However, lower officials of the municipal bureaucracy were eligible only for minor positions in the confraria. (Russell-Wood, 1969:182ff.)

Although the internal stratification of the Bahian brotherhood was not common at all, the upper-class sodalities probably served as channels of social ascent in many, perhaps most cities of colonial Latin America.

A free burial was and still is one of the services the upper-class brotherhoods provided for their members. Burial inside a church was probably the most socially distinguished form of interment. Many brotherhoods had their own walled cemeteries or maintained a section of the common cemetery for their deceased members. The walls were divided into layers of niches where the bodies were entombed sideways, each tomb bearing a biographic inscription on a stone slab. Transferred from the Iberian peninsula, church and wall burials show a high degree of uniformity throughout Latin America. During the nineteenth century, when French culture patterns began to dominate the lifestyle of the upper strata, the graveyards became urbanized and developed into veritable necropolises—wide open spaces densely covered with mausoleums and similar imposing tombs, always following the pattern of Père Lachaise cemetery in Paris. Formerly determined by a common Iberian background, cultural homogeneity was now the unintended result of cultural diffusion from France.

Although differing from one another in scope and in structure, the religious sodalities can be considered to be extensions of monasticism. Indeed, many were so-called third orders of such full-fledged clerical orders as the Franciscans, Capuchins, Augustinians, Dominicans, Carmelites, Benedictines, and Mercedarians. Without the strictures of monastic life, they afforded opportunities for the laity to strive for "Christian perfection." The members had to undergo initiation, and they wore the habit consisting of scapula and cord under their everyday clothes. In Brazil as well as in Spanish America, the members of such lay orders, particularly those who took their devotional obligations seriously, were frequently called *beatos* (masculine) and *beatas* (feminine), although in the course of time the term acquired the derogatory connotation of religious bigotry.

The other major type of religious sodalities was represented by the confraternities (*hermandades* or *cofradria* in Spanish; *irmandades* or *confraria* in Portuguese). Of their original (medieval) functions—fraternization through prayer and devotional services rendered to the souls of the dead—the latter became one of the major concerns of many Latin American confraternities. However, the most common specialization was (and still is) corporate participation in and promotion of public worship.

Sometimes, the sodality encompassed lay members *and* clerics. The *Hermandad de San Pedro*, which existed in Buenos Aires from 1691 until 1805, was composed of priests and high-ranking military men (*hombres de sotana* and *hombres de espada*), thus symbolizing the close alliance of state and church. The annual celebration of the fiesta in honor of Saint Peter, and the burial of deceased brothers and religious services in benefit of their souls, were the group's two main responsibilities. Typically, its dead were entombed in the cathedral. (Fasolino, 1938:342ff.)

The importance of the monastic orders proper cannot be gauged in terms of sheer numbers, impressive as these may be. In 1775 Lima, one of the largest and most magnificent centers of traditional Latin American Catholicism, had 19 monasteries with a total of 1306 friars and novices, and 14 convents housing 822 nuns and novices. (Descola, 1962:205) Of the 8000 clerics reported to live in Mexico City in the late eighteenth century, a large percentage, perhaps the majority, belonged to the regular clergy.

Internally, the monastic orders were as stratified as the society of which they formed part. The upper stratum consisted of ordained priests, often related to high-ranking Creole families; the lower stratum was composed of illiterate lay brothers, often Indians or mestizoes of lower-class extraction, who were in charge of menial jobs in the workshops and fields of the monastery. The activities of the monastic orders, in addition to their various rather specialized approaches to the supernatural, left no aspect of the culture unaffected. Their churches and monasteries were by far the most impressive pieces of colonial architecture. Most of the resources to build and to lavishly decorate these temples came from the huge landed estates, and ownership of such property put the monastic orders in the same social category as the seigneurial estate owners. Like the former, the monastic orders often employed African slave labor, but at the same time they were outspoken critics of the encomienda system, and especially of Indian slavery. Their mission villages became centers of diffusion of European crafts and agricultural techniques, but also of capitalistic enterprise. The surplus derived from the employment of Indian labor on the Jesuit reductions, for example, made it possible for the order to build a profitable system of international trade. Missionary zeal induced the friars to use Indian languages as instruments of conversion, thus contributing to the preservation of such languages as Nahuatl, Quechua, and Tupí.

Of course, intentional and systematic diffusion of knowledge and skills is synonymous with education, and it was the educational role of the monastic orders which had the most far-reaching and unifying effects upon Ibero-American culture.

No order was more deeply committed to formal education than the Society of Jesus. The Jesuits worked simultaneously at the bottom of the emergent society and at its top level. The Indian reduction and the city colleges were established concomitantly as the order was admitted to the New World. The Indian reductions were intended to convert and civilize the Indian masses; the city colleges served the elites of Ibero-American society. The significance and scope of the Jesuit establishment can be measured by the gaps in the educational system of Latin America that appeared following the expulsion of the order. The other monastic orders were unable to fill these gaps, and expressions of dismay and criticism were heard in all parts of Spanish America, particularly in Mexico City, in Guadalajara, and in Campeche, where no grammar schools opened for 30 years after the Jesuits had to close theirs, and in Ecuador, where the educational system collapsed except for a single school in Cuenca. In Buenos Aires and Córdoba, in Asunción and Santa Fé—everywhere formal education had been dealt a "staggering blow" from which it took decades to recover. (Eguia Ruiz, 1953:584–596) In Portuguese America, where schools on all levels were almost entirely in the hands of the Jesuits, the disaster was even worse. (Azevedo, 1943: 314ff.)

The significance of Jesuit education did not lie in its ubiquitousness alone. Founded to inject new life into the decadent system of medieval education, to restore the purity of Catholic doctrine, and to stem the tide of the Protestant Reformation, the Society of Jesus was an institution designed to pursue education in the widest possible sense. Not only did the Jesuits select and delimit the body of substantive knowledge to be transmitted, in Claudio Aquaviva's *Ratio Studiorum* they defined and adopted a system of principles and methods to carry out the process of cultural implantation. In the present context, we are less concerned with the techniques of transmission than with the principle of catholicity or universality, which represented one of the distinctive marks of the Jesuit value system at a time when medieval Europe was breaking up under the stress of religious dissent and incipient nationalism. Jesuit education established its own identity, overriding regional and national boundaries. Whether administered in Rome, Madrid, Mexico, Córdoba, Quito, or Bahia, Jesuit education was uniformly geared to transmit a body of literary knowledge essentially defined as the study of Greek and Latin and Greco-Roman literature. Greek was dropped in the colonies, but Latin was taught regardless of whether the recipients were of Iberian, Indian, or African extraction. It was basically a *humanistic* orientation, which was firmly implanted wherever the Jesuits opened a college. The small intellectual elite who wished to rise to the level of higher education would embark in a study of philosophy or arts, encompassing logic, general metaphysics, mathematics, ethics, theology, and sciences, all defined in a strictly Aristotelian sense. Thus all learning was predicated on the assumption that knowledge was to be accepted *as it was*. There was nothing to be investigated; all material was merely to be assimilated and to be commented on. This thoroughly authoritarian system of learning was likely to produce a high degree of intellectual homogeneity. Furthermore, it had the makings of a self-perpetuating system, and its authoritarian character fitted the existing social structure almost to perfection.

Humanistic education, as conceived by the Jesuits, became the predominant if not the only type of secondary and higher education in Europe as well as in Latin America. Increasing secularization of some European educational systems released humanistic education from its dependency on the Jesuits or any other religious order, moving it, in the wake of the French Revolution, into the orbit of state-sponsored public education.

Jesuit education deliberately converged on the small elites of Spanish and Portuguese America. It succeeded in turning out a highly homogeneous and artificial product, almost in the botanical sense of "cultivated" as opposed to native or spontaneous.

The recipients of the Jesuit donor culture, the high-ranking functionaries and ecclesiastical dignitaries, the rare professionals and the literate sector of the landholding aristocracy, were of course the only ones capable of translating their ideas and knowledge, their intellectual skills and esthetic propensities into tangible links to the Old World, comprehensible as such by observers from other lands. There were magnificent baroque churches, palaces, and mansions; there were the paintings of the Cuzco and Quito schools, the sculpture of Alejadinho in Ouro Prêto; the works of chroniclers and poets, sacred orators and theologians, jurists and philologists. Eventually this humanistic universe came to be identified as Latin American culture, although it reflected no more than the lifestyle of a small minority. Political emancipation added political philosophy to its repertory, and secularization freed it from theology and church control; but whatever the accretions, they were European transfers, intelligible and meaningful only to the elites. Jesuit education was what nowadays is called "elitist," and elitist it remained long after the Society of Jesus had been expelled from Spanish and Portuguese America. Jesuit education, with its strong emphasis on classic literature, logic, dialectics, verbalization, and verbal manipulations, laid the foundations for a value system in which empiricism, pragmatism, thus genuine scientific investigation, would be given short shrift. In other words, it produced an intellectual elite ill prepared for the Industrial Revolution. (See Gillin, 1946–1947: 243–248.) In the early nineteenth century, when the Latin American elites switched to the French cultural model, traditional humanism revived under the stimulating influence of French literature and art.

Church and state

Linkages among the different sectors or aspects of a culture vary from hidden to manifest, from formal to informal, from direct to indirect, and from close to distant. The connection between church and state in Latin America was manifest, formal, direct, and close. It was sanctioned by the papal bulls of 1501 and 1508 investing the Iberian kings with

> basic power to appoint churchmen in the colonies, and the additional power to administer ecclesiastical jurisdictions and revenues and to veto papal bulls. With this the crown could decide which clerics would be appointed, where they should go, what the limits of their jurisdictions were to be, and what they should be paid." (Gibson, 1966:76)

Appointments by the crown, Spanish or Portuguese, were subject to confirmation by the Vatican, but this was merely a formality; often enough Church dignitaries appointed by the king assumed office prior to approval by the pope. (Konetzke, 1965:229) Before a royal appointment could become effective, the appointee, a bishop or archbishop, had to swear allegiance to the king, an act which made him a functionary of the state. Clerics of all echelons being appointed to secular offices became an established pattern. The church hierarchy was drawn into and partially absorbed by the political structure. Fusion of temporal and spiritual power was hardly incompatible with current ideas about the role of the Church in the world; but in Latin America this alliance favored the state rather than the church, which was reduced to the role of satellite within the power domain of the state.

The alliance of church and state remained viable as long as both institutions adhered to the role that had been agreed on. The revolutionary wars and eventual political emancipation brought about two abrupt and almost traumatic changes in Spanish America. The dependency relationship between church and crown was suddenly severed, and the clergy was drawn into a kind of power struggle that spelled disaster for the Church. Emphasis on historical conflict situations easily conveys the impression that all was peace and harmony prior to the eruption of the struggle. Far from being a monolithic structure, the Catholic hierarchy was split by antagonisms, tensions, open conflict, and even violence among its ranks. The secular clergy was usually at odds with the religious orders, the orders were consistently embroiled in quarrels with one another, and a sharp antagonism divided the American-born priests from the peninsular clergy. (Pike, 1964:9)

Not surprisingly, the native-born priests identified themselves with Creole interests and incipient Creole nationalism, whereas the peninsulars viewed themselves as Spaniards and Portuguese and as such tended to look down on the colonials. The wars of independenece deepened the conflict between native and Iberian clergy. Most Spanish priests "tended to regard favorable attitudes toward independence as impious if not downright heretical." (Pike, 1964:12) And all over Spanish America the majority of the native-born clergy, among them a good many mestizoes, sided with the independence movement, with quite a few political activists taking leading positions in the struggle against Spanish domination.

The next steps in the process of political involvement were almost inevitable. Instead of bringing peace and consolidation to the new republics, emancipation led everywhere in Spanish America to serious internal disorders, often to a violent contest for power. Gradually, clerical participation in the struggle for independence became participation in partisan politics. Obviously the role of the cleric, whether diocesan bishop or parish priest, is incompatible with that of a party politician. Participation, particularly leadership in political parties, tends to impair the effectiveness of the pastoral role of the priest. Within the context of Latin American culture, party politics are often divisive to the point of splitting communities into hostile factions, relentlessly opposing each other and frequently engaging in violence. By assuming the role of a politician, or merely by committing himself to the cause of a particular faction, the curate automatically becomes a personal enemy of all those who happen to belong to opposite factions. Thus role incompatibility on a personal level escalates into disorganization on a structural level.

The situation was further complicated because the Church, particularly the religious orders, often engaged in agricultural and commercial enterprises. In Spanish and Portuguese America the orders owned immense latifundios and much urban real estate. Anticlerical factions viewed these holdings with confiscatory intentions and actively promoted the secularization of church property. The wish to protect their sources of income caused individual and corporate owners to side with political factions opposing confiscation, thus to enter dependency relationships that tended to be at variance with the institutional role of the Church.

Even more destructive effects on the institutional structure of the church derived from the prolonged conflict between the new nations and the Vatican which, in deference to Spain, refused to transfer patronage privileges to the republican governments. Papal appointees to ecclesiastical positions were unacceptable to the governments, and government appointees were refused approval and consecration by the pope.

> With the exile or flight of most of thirty-five bishops and archbishops, and the major religious superiors of the Orders (most of whom were Spanish and were presumed to be royalists, which often they were not), the leadership of the Church came to an abrupt end. Religious communities lost their superiors, and their property was nationalized. The morale of each community was wrecked by the inevitable political division of royalists or republicans, *peninsulares* or *Americanos*. The secular clergy was equally affected and reduced by at least fifty percent of its strength. There was no chance of replacing them, since seminaries were nationalized as part of the universities, and entrance requirements of an impossible nature were imposed by the civil government. (Coleman, 1958:15)

To stem "the impending ruin of the Church in America and the demoralization of the clergy," the conflict was eventually accommodated by mutual compromise. (Mecham, 1934:102)

Events took another course in Brazil. The differences appear to be consistent with long-established patterns according to which conflict seemed to lack the fierceness and irreconcilability characteristic of Spanish America. Military victory over the Portuguese was accomplished swiftly and without much bloodshed, but the country did not become a republic like the Spanish colonies. Prince Pedro, regent of Brazil and heir to the Portuguese throne, took the initiative in the emancipation movement and became emperor of independent Brazil. The monarchic tradition was preserved with a minimum of disruption, and since the Vatican decided to "tolerate" patronage privileges which the emperor assumed as a matter of course, the clergy was not caught in dilemma of conflicting loyalties as in Spanish America.

Significant as these differences are, particularly in a broader cultural context, they did not rule out some rather close parallel developments in other aspects. In the first place, the movement toward independence politicalized the Brazilian clergy as much as it did the Spanish American clergy. Catholic priests had a leading role in the conspiracy of 1789, the *Inconfidencia Mineira*, and the revolt of 1817 in Pernambuco was a "revolution of the padres." A total of 57 priests were imprisoned after the suppression of the revolt. (Mecham, 1934:306) Among the politicians of independent Brazil, many liberal-minded prelates held positions of parliamentary leadership, and out of the political disturbances accompanying the abdication of the first emperor (in 1832) emerged a priest, Diogo Antonio Feijó, as elected regent of Brazil. He actually governed the country from 1835 to 1840.

Second, the antagonism between secular and regular clergy was as strong in Brazil as it was elsewhere in Spanish America. The secular clergy lined up with the imperial government against the religious orders, whose wealth stood in sharp contrast to the relative poverty of the seculars and who "were ultramontane in sympathy and foreign in compositions and control." (Mecham, 1934:312) Already under the reign of Dom Pedro I, the creation of new religious orders was prohibited, and drastic restrictions were imposed on the existing ones. Entry and residence of foreign friars were no longer permitted, and those who obeyed authorities residing outside Brazil were expelled. Two orders, the Benedictines and the Carmelites, were forbidden to accept new members. Whenever a religious order became extinct, its property was confiscated by the state. (Mecham, 1934:313)

Finally, the smooth relation between Church and state was suddenly disturbed by the so-called religious problem (*questão religiosa*), which pushed Brazil to the brink of a religious war (1872–1873). Since the beginning of the century a good many Brazilian priests had joined Freemasonry, and it was quite customary to admit Masons to the ranks of religious sodalities. Regalists and liberals, the masonic priests and lay members of the brotherhoods saw no conflict between their roles of Catholics and Masons. In a papal encyclical, however, Freemasonry had been branded as inimical to the Catholic faith and incompatible with communicant membership in the Church. The papal anathema was ignored by Emperor Pedro II, but a few zealous prelates, determined to obey Rome and to reestablish papal control over the Brazilian Church, prohibited clerical participation in Masonic rites and ordered the sodalities to expel brothers who were also members of masonic lodges. The brotherhoods disobeyed, approaching the emperor for arbitration, but without support from the Vatican the cause of the two American bishops was lost. They were tried and convicted to imprisonment but later were granted amnesty. (Mecham, 1934:321) These events were accompanied by severe public disturbances showing the degree to which the masses were still emotionally involved in religious issues.

Both Spain and Portugal used their institutional power to safeguard the colonies from the schismatic movements that were destroying the unity of the established Church in Europe. In Spanish as well as in Portuguese America the Tribunal of the Holy Office of the Inquisition was instrumental in establishing and maintaining censorship and in prosecuting individuals suspected of heresy or apostasy. Again, the Portuguese inquisitors took a far more conciliatory attitude than their Spanish counterparts. In contrast to Spanish America, few people were prosecuted and all were shipped to Portugal to stand trial.

In view of the liberal climate characterizing the Church of independent Brazil, we might expect a more relaxed attitude regarding religious faiths other than Catholicism. As early as 1810 British Protestants residing in Rio de Janeiro were allowed to have their own place of worship. The Bishop of Rio, José Castano, was said to strongly favor this concession to Protestant believers. (Pike, 1964:19) It is difficult to imagine a similar response from a Spanish prelate in the same year. Religious freedom was assured, "although with limitations, in the Constituent Assembly of 1823 and in the Constitution of 1824 [and] evangelical churches took root in Brazil, with their form of worship carried on in houses with the appearance of residences and without the external form of a church." (Azevedo, 1943:157)

Thus in Brazil, earlier than anywhere in Spanish America, the foundations were laid for a system of religious pluralism.

The political system

The political process

The foregoing study of three major institutions—the landed estate, kinship, and the Catholic Church—yielded some information about the political system prevalent in Portuguese and Spanish America. In fact, an understanding of any of these institutions was impossible without frequent reference to political organization. Almost all these references stressed the struggle for power in its multiple aspects: the Iberian monarchies attempting to regain the power they had delegated to the conquistadores and donatarios; the landed estates, the encomenderos and the bandeirantes defying the power of the monarchies and their representatives in America; oligarchies of big landowners usurping municipal power; landowning kinship groups invading one another's power domains; the state imposing its power on the Church, and so forth.

As the foregoing examples show, the exercise of power is predicated on the existence of a social relationship involving people and institutions. It is also clear that a person or group of persons participating in such a power relationship has a reasonably good "chance to carry out his own will even against resistance, regardless of the basis on which that chance rests." This is Weber's classic definition of power, and since he set no conceptual restrictions on the source or basis of power, far more than "government" or "established authority" is implied. Power is as necessary to exercise authority as it is to overthrow established authority.

We can object to defining political organization as the way in which power is distributed and exercised in a social aggregate on the grounds that power, as previously defined, is found in all human groups, that it is always somehow distributed among and exercised by the members of such groups, that it must be considered to be part and parcel of any organizational process, and that consequently it fails to define the *specific* features of political organization. To state these features in terms of the activities "more or less directly related to the making of binding decisions for a society and its major subdivisions" (Easton, 1959:227) is to require a definition of "major subdivisions." Of course, the making of binding decisions implies the exercise of power, and nobody would argue about the political nature of decision-making processes affecting a society as a whole. For the sake of clarity, we can distinguish between territorial subdivisions and segmentary subdivisions, but not without being aware of considerable overlapping. Furthermore, either category may exist de jure or de facto.

Viceroyalties, audiencias, capitanias, municipios, cities, provinces, departamentos, and estados are examples of territorial subdivisions, whereas political parties are considered to be segmentary subdivisions. Both categories are established de jure; that is, their organization is formally recognized by the state. If a party acquires, by whatever means, enough support to monopolize political power within a territory, the party becomes a territorial rather than a segmentary subdivision, at least with regard to the region it controls.

De facto subdivisions, both territorial and segmentary, have played an extremely important role in the political tradition of Latin America, perhaps more so in Portuguese- than in Spanish-dominated areas. They have no legal existence, of course; they may even be outlawed, but often enough their power is such that official territorial subdivision seek to enlist their political support.

The extended family as a political subdivision

Those who assume a legalistic attitude tend to discard de facto political subdivisions as encroachments on or temporary deviations from the "normal" political process. For example, many would reject out of hand the suggestion that the family be included among the political subdivisions of a society. Yet, if, as it often happens in Latin America, entire municipios, states, or provinces were run by a single extended family, not temporarily but continuously for years or even decades, would this not make the family part of the political system? Especially if the family were structurally geared to performing such a complex task. Indeed, families are up to the undertaking if they control enough natural resources and people to outbid competitors and to marshal further support available in the form of ballots, bribery, coercion, patronage, purchase of office, or a combination of several such devices. Furthermore, the power-seeking family would have to display internal solidarity and it would have to be large enough to man all strategically relevant posts with consanguine, affinal, or ceremonial kinsmen.

Within the context of traditional Latin American society, only extended, wealthy, landowning families of upper-class standing could fulfill the foregoing prerequisites and become permanent fixtures of the political system. They could take over a local or provincial government *as* family groups and run it like a family enterprise. Often it was not a single extended family but a coalition of interrelated families that ruled municipios or larger territorial units. Still, kinship provided the bonds of solidarity and the mutual trust required to engage in concerted action.

It would seem that the power and persistence of the extended landowning family derived from the fact that it was simultaneously a territorial *and* a segmentary subdivision; because of this dualism, moreover, it was able to establish control over the de jure territorial subdivision within reach and to manipulate its institutional apparatus to maintain or expand its own power domain. The landed state takes on a political quality because the owner has the power to develop all the organizational devices required to maintain internal order without recourse to outside authority. Even conflict with "external enemies," rival kinship groups or marauding bands of fugitive slaves, Indians, or pirates could be settled through the use of private armies. Thus the landed estate with its hundreds or sometimes thousands of inhabitants constituted a de facto territorial division headed by a single extended family or part of it.

At the same time, transcending the orbit of the landed estate, the extended family functioned as a de facto segmentary subdivision striving to establish or maintain power within the municipal structure or some larger territorial unit. At this point a fusion of de facto and de jure subdivisions was extremely common, and heads of extended families (or coalitions of interrelated families) exercising the authority of gobernadores, alcaldes, and regidores (in Spanish America) and of capitães, presidentes, vereadores (in Portuguese America) constituted the rule rather than the exception.

Political developments in the nineteenth century reinforced the power of the family and kinship group (often incorrectly called "clan"). Following political emancipation, the political party provided a new device by means of which large landowning families could marshal political support at the local level. The picture stands in obvious contrast to the strenuous efforts of the Iberian monarchies to keep political power centralized; but as historians have frequently pointed out, the state was too weak to effectively challenge the power of the big landowners. Unfortunately, it has been little noted that the power of the wealthy landowners reposed on the combination of strong kinship solidarity *and* almost absolute control of natural and human resources.

Although the system was basically the same in all plantation areas of Latin America, the Brazilian planters were more successful in securing privileges than their Spanish American counterparts.

> Gubernatorial and royal decrees exempted their sugar mills, technical equipment and slaves, from being seized or distrained for outstanding debts. Their creditors were only allowed to take a portion of the cane ground at harvest time. These privileges were later extended to the *lavradores* or copyholders who cultivated smaller fields and had their cane ground by the planters. (Boxer, 1969:150)

The military as a political subdivision

Some may hesitate to consider the military to be another segmentary subdivision of the political structure on the grounds that the military are not, or should not be, involved in the process of making binding decisions on any level and that they are not expected to participate in decision making or merely to carry out decisions made by "civil" authority. Now the question of whether a given group or institution takes part in the political process cannot be answered by the constitution or statute law, nor by recourse to extraneous models referring to the actual or ideal patterns of other societies. Only an objective scrutiny of the *functions* the group *actually* performs can provide the answer we are looking for. By "function" we mean *all the intended or unintended effects of the action of an individual or group of individuals on a particular social structure.* The action is political if it tends either to perpetuate or to alter the distribution of power in a society at a given time. Such an action may be successful or not, desirable or undesirable from the standpoint of any sector of the society concerned; it may conform to established patterns or it may constitute a novelty. In fact, it covers conspiracies, revolutions, coups d'etat, and reforms, as well as any action designed to maintain the political status quo.

Radcliffe-Brown has said that as a process, political organization consists to a variable extent in the exercise of coercive authority through the use, or possibility of use of physical force. Such a possibility exists only if the government effectively controls a body of men prepared to use physical force if necessary. Any government, whatever its nature or claim to legitimacy, attempts to maintain or to consolidate its power through the use of physical force or at least by threatening to use physical coercion if and when its authority is challenged by demands that cannot be met within the existing regime. Often a demonstration of available means of physical coercion or "power capabilities" is sufficient to determine the outcome of a power contest, (Anderson, 1964). Whatever the situation, however, a government has little chance to survive without armed force. There is little point in distinguishing here between "police" and "military," the former being in charge of the internal order, and the latter exercising physical force against external foes. In Latin America the military have constantly been deployed in internal power contests along with police forces, and the police often are under direct control of military officers and organized in a way that makes them virtually undistinguishable from the military forces.

Professional armies became the rule later in the second half of the nineteenth century, and professional armies are inherently capable of rendering effective control by civil authority very difficult. First of all, the military are highly specialized in the techniques of coercion by violence, and more than any other sector of a society, they control the instruments of physical coercion. Second, the social structure of the armed forces is usually different from that of the general society. The "hierarchical command structure" is designed to exact maximal performance in war and to shield its strategic, tactical, and technological complexities from the rank and file, as well as from the institutions expected to keep the military under control. (Wildenmann, 1968:61) In other words, an element of secrecy is almost always necessary to ensure military superiority over potential or actual enemies. Thus effective exclusion of the military from political decision making is at best fraught with uncertainties and liabilities.

As soon as political dissent and competition for power are intensified to the point of creating a climate of unrest, agitation, and insecurity, the chances of military intervention in the political process tend to increase. This exactly was the situation following political independence in Spanish America. Of course the long drawn-out revolutionary wars had expanded the power domain of the military sufficiently to make a return to civil government problematic at least. Two sets of facts had particularly aggravating effects on the attempts to achieve political reorganization and on the role of the military:

1. Following the defeat and withdrawal of the Spanish civil and ecclesiastical authorities, there was a total collapse of the existing government structure (in contrast to the situation in Brazil, as indicated before).

2. The colonial power structure had been so authoritarian that forms of self-government were stifled that conceivably could have served as models for political reorganization. However, an immediate qualification of this statement is in order: A model was not only available but widely put into practice—namely, the very authoritarian rule imposed by Spain but eroded by centuries of faulty enforcement, defiance by and compromise with local powerholders, and outright rebellion. Nothing could be farther from the truth than the stereotype of "unquestioning obedience" of either the "masses" or the Creole elites. Prior to political emancipation there were 77 minor or major revolts and insurrections. (Rama, 1967) They were originated by Indians, Negro slaves, mestizoes, or Creoles in almost every part of Latin America. Forty-eight (62.4 percent) of the revolts took place in the eighteenth and early nineteenth centuries, and 32 (66.6 percent) of these occurred between 1750 and 1809. Countless urban riots, innumerable acts of banditry, and many local slave revolts and family feuds were not included in these figures. The data strongly suggest that an increasing amount of anomie and violence had become deeply embedded in Latin American culture long before the wars of independence

gave free rein to the interplay between authoritarian rule and revolutionary response. Alienated from the function feeble attempts at constitutional government had assigned to them, the military became freewheeling political factions assuming every available role in the struggle for power. Generals took over governments by force or by default, only to be dislodged by rival generals. Military factions sided with or fought against any political party, and direct intervention in the political process alternated with authoritative arbitration.

In some parts of Spanish America political anomie rendered distinctions between de jure and de facto military subdivisions almost useless. There was of course the patrimonial heritage of the "private army" usually consisting of retainers and familiars of big landowners who might or might not hold a military title. (Chevalier, 1963:302) Private armies were used in family feuds (Costa Pinto, 1949) and against pirates, rebelling Indians, settlements of fugitive Negro slaves, and bandits; with the advent of political independence, they participated in all kinds of revolutionary and counterrevolutionary uprisings.

But throughout most of the nineteenth century the dividing lines between private and public armies, between professional and nonprofessional military, were so blurred that it was virtually impossible to make clear distinctions. At this juncture we wish only to call attention to three conditions.

1. Under certain circumstances, the very nature of the military and their unique position in *any* political system are factors that may induce the officer corps to assume an autonomous political role comparable to that of a party or faction.

2. In a long series of revolts, insurrections, and feuds preceding political emancipation, the use of physical coercion or violence had become a customary way of solving conflicts.

3. The revolutionary wars and the ensuing civil strife fully released these forces and transformed the military into major political factions in Spanish America.

Comparisons with Brazil never fail to point out the relatively peaceful transition from colonial status to independence. However, the implication that Brazil constitutes an altogether different political species seems to be incompatible with certain facts. The imperial government had to repress a number of revolutions, the most serious being the so-called *Farroupilha*, which threw the province of Rio Grande do Sul into civil war. Moreover, the two principal leaders were military, and most of the officers and troops stationed in the region joined the revolution eventually, to proclaim the independence of the province. The civil war lasted 10 years, and at one time (1838) the entire province was under separatist control. The military were also thoroughly involved in the São Paulo revolution of 1842. In fact, the revolutionary appointed military commanders for all towns of the province. (Rocha Pombo, 8:434, 587, 630)

These occurrences suggest a difference in degree rather than in kind, in comparison with the Spanish American republics. Military factionalism and participation in the political power struggle came to the fore with the advent of the republic. Indeed, the army was instrumental in the overthrow of the empire.

The model of patrimonialism
and its applicability to Latin America

A copious vocabulary has been used to define political organization in Latin America. Feudalism, absolutism, despotism, tyranny, caudillism, coronelism, personalism, militarism, oligarchy, democracy, dictatorship, paternalism, patrimonialism, praetorianism, and other concepts refer to basic ways political power was or is distributed and exercised. Although a few of these words are more suitable for literary hyperbole than for objective analysis, most correspond to empirical realities. In a general interpretive treatment of political organization designed to capture baseline trends that will serve to gauge more recent developments, preference should be given to the concept that combines explanatory potential with broad coverage. We suggest that patrimonialism, as defined by Max Weber, possesses these attributes more than any other concept. It sits well with absolutism, oligarchy, dictatorship, caudillism, coronelism, personalism, paternalism, and patriarchalism, but its explanatory power transcends any one of these terms. Weber called it "fluid," or flexible enough to cover a variety of political structures or structural components.

Particularly relevant in the present context is the patriarchal origin attributed to the patrimonial regime. The patriarchal *oikos* or household including an extended family, slaves, serfs, tenants, and other dependents, tends to evolve into a patrimonial dominion if and when it becomes so operationally complex that kinship alone no longer suffices as an integrating factor. An "administrative staff" is added to act as a *personal* extension of the discretionary power of the patrimonial ruler.

Patrimonial structures of varying degrees of complexity intervene between the *oikos* and the full-fledged patrimonial state. The single patriarchal household expands by assigning new holdings to kinsmen, tenants, serfs, thereby gaining control over a larger territory and an increasing number of households. Conquest may of course become an additional means of patrimonial expansion. As seen against the background of the patriarchal *oikos*, the process is tantamount to decentralization, at least in the economic and socio-ecological sense of the word.

In a patrimonial system, all political and administrative decisions remain personal acts of the ruler, and the bonds between him and his functionaries are those of personal loyalty. There is absolutely no conception of "public" service, nor is there a distinction between "official" and "private" spheres of politico-administrative action. The patrimonial army is likewise a personal instrument of seigneurial power. Fees, tributes, taxes, tithes, and levies are components of the ruler's personal income. The job of collecting taxes or fees may be leased to functionaries, but such concessions are not attached to or inherent in any "office." In fact, the notion of "office" as an objective construct with definable tasks or functions, independent of any particular office holder, is alien to the patrimonial regime. Any position in the politico-administrative structure of the patrimonial state is conceived of as a personal privilege granted by the ruler. Indeed, people are subjects rather than citizens—they may claim no rights. If they enter petitions, these are decided on personal grounds, and a favorable decision constitutes no legal precedent for identical or similar cases. The idea that the ruler or his functionaries fulfill obligations to tax-paying citizens is thoroughly alien to the patrimonial regime. The public seeks favors rather than services, and favors are granted on a personal basis.

On the other hand, the ruler may exact services from his subjects or particular segments of them. Trade and industry are typically monopolized by the ruler, but in more complex patrimonial structures sharing of economic assets with a privileged seigneurial stratum (estates or *stände*, in Weber's terminology) may become inevitable. These privileged *stände* are allowed to "appropriate" various sources of income, especially land, on a temporary or permanent basis, always as a form of remuneration for services rendered to the ruler. Here a fusion of feudalism and patrimonialism becomes apparent, yet highly centralized patrimonial structures fit the model of absolutism. One of the implications of the more decentralized forms is that there are patrimonial structures *within* the patrimonial state proper.

Max Weber considered tradition to be the source of patrimonial authority. More accurately, this means that the discretionary power of the ruler is defined and limited by traditional expectations and consensus. (Weber, 1925, 1:133–137; 2:679–723)

There seems to be a high degree of congruence between the patrimonial model and the Iberian monarchies. The Portuguese monarchy was an "immense organism represented by the king who was head, chief, father, representative of God on earth, supreme dispensator of all graces and born regulator of all activities, and still more, of all personal and individual expressions of his subjects and vassals, down to the most lowly of these . . . ." (Prado Junior, 1963:297)

The same description applies to the Spanish monarchy. The discretionary power of the king carried supernatural sanction; it was bestowed by God and to God alone he was responsible. The colonies were *reinos patrimoniales* —patrimonial property of the crown. (Konetzke, 1965:113) Colonization and administration of the overseas territories were functions of the state, and the acts of granting mercedes de tierra, capitanias, sesmarias, and encomiendas were typical exhibitions of patrimonial power. In strict conformity with the model, such grants created a privileged stratum of aristocratic standing owing personal allegiance to the monarch. The selection and appointment of high-ranking functionaries in charge of the colonial administration also met the requisites of patrimonialism. In addition, their authority of such functionaries was carefully circumscribed to fit the principles of a monocratic regime. Neither viceroys in Spanish America nor governors or captains general in Brazil were authorized to appoint their own subordinates; thus no loyalty or even dependency relationship was allowed to arise within the bureaucratic hierarchy. Neither Spanish nor Portuguese America constituted a single administrative unit: First two, later four, viceroyalties divided Spanish America into territories directly administered by the crown, and independent of one another. Similarly, Brazil was sliced up into a number of major and minor *capitanias*, the latter being subordinated to the principal ones, but these were under the immediate authority of the crown and independent of one another. The viceroy of Rio de Janeiro had not jurisdiction beyond the border if his *capitania*, and the so-called *Estado do Pará e Maranhão*, encompassing the northern capitanias, was a verbal frill without practical consequence. (Prado Junior, 1963:302)

The titles bestowed on those whom the king appointed to the highest offices suggest a degree of authority that the holders of the positions did not possess. The rulers of complex patrimonial states are always torn between the inevitable need for a measure of decentralization and the desire to preserve the principles of absolutism. The distance between the peninsular seats of authority and Ibero-America was as immense as the distance within the enormous landmasses of the colonies. The problem was compounded by the primitive state of communications. It took several months for royal decisions to reach Mexico, Lima, or Bahia and, given the extremely poor road conditions, it took almost as long to convey such decisions to the outlying seats of subordinate authority. Distances and slow communication suggested political decentralization, but delegation of power invited a measure of local autonomy incompatible with the monocratic structure of the regime. And the fear of Creole rebellion always was in the back of the king's mind, generating distrust and suspicion of his own overseas delegates.

Consistent with the rules of patrimonialism, Spain and Portugal chose a form of centralized political control that reduced the viceroys and governors to mere executors of decisions made by the Spanish king and his Council of the Indies or the Portuguese king and his Overseas Council. From the most momentous to the most trivial matters, everything was decided in Madrid and Lisbon. Not surprisingly, the system soon became inextricably tangled in red tape. The work load of the councils was such that delays of several years were not uncommon, and many cases were left to "eternal rest in the drawers of the archives." (Prado Junior, 1963: 303)

The system of rigid political centralization had a counterproductive effect on the societies it was supposed to control. The translation of laws and decrees into social reality is precarious under the most favorable conditions, but legislation at a distance that is spatial and cultural at the same time involves the hazards of incompatibility with established modes of behavior, with vested interests, or with the *actual* distribution of power. Under the circumstances, new legislation tended to be unenforceable, which induced the royal administrators to reinterpret the law and to adapt it to the context. This is merely an example of the same universal process of cultural reinterpretation that accompanies transplants from one society to another, subjecting them to a series of adaptive changes. As a rule, such changes are designed to circumvent the upsetting effects the new transplant might exercise if adopted without alterations. In the case of legal transplants, interpretive adaptation usually meant that the law would not be enforced. In other words, the royal administrator exercised far more power than his institutional position warranted, and, what seems more important, noncompliance was forced on him by the political system. The principle of *obedezco pero no cumplo* (I obey but I do not fulfill) *was equivalent to the institutionalization of noncompliance.*

Noncompliance of course extended to everyone supposedly covered by the steady flow of laws and decrees. As indicated in an earlier chapter, noncompliance with legal norms became a cultural tradition that outlasted 300 years of colonial rule and remained one of the most troubling facets of contemporary Latin American culture.

In colonial times the problem of noncompliance was compounded by the refusal of the Iberian kings to create the infrastructure and the institutional prerequisites indispensable to effective law enforcement. Institutions of this kind could have been available only at great cost to the royal treasury. Expenditures of such magnitude, however, were inconsistent with the patrimonial rule that subjects are first of all producers of royal revenues. Maximal returns were expected from minimal investments. The maintenance of a costly law enforcement apparatus would have seriously interfered with the enormously increasing financial needs of the royal treasuries.

The problem of internal inconsistencies of the patrimonial regime was further aggravated by the practice of selling or renting out municipal offices to the highest bidder. The practice by itself was quite compatible with patrimonialism: The crown felt free to use its discretionary power to fill vacancies in any way that served royalty's private purpose. The very transaction entitled the buyer to regard the office as his private possession, which was equally consistent with patrimonial principles. It merely legitimized these precepts on the level of local government, thus contributing to the centrifugal or decentralizing tendencies that contradicted the very essence of absolutism. (Sarfatti 1966:37, 52) By selling or leasing offices, particularly by making them hereditary (at a price, of course) the crown relinquished power and, in fact, legitimized local patrimonialism.

Although no instances of the sale of municipal offices have been discovered in Portuguese America, "private ownership of public office became widespread in colonial Brazil, where virtually all posts except those of governors and senior magistrates could be obtained from the Crown by concession or by purchase." (Alden, 1968:295–296) Alden also reports that proprietorship of offices could be inherited from father to son and sometimes remained in the possession of the same family for a century or longer.

In Spanish America, the sale of offices was merely a contributing factor to the implantation of municipal patrimonialism. The decisive factor in *both* areas was the emergence of a privileged stratum of aristocratic landowners who met little resistance when extending their power domain to encompass municipal government, which they proceeded to run like a family enterprise. Here, the relationship between patriarchalism and patrimonialism is clearly visible. The patriarchal rule of the big landed estate with its numerous familiars, slaves, serfs, and tenants, and its private army, was transplanted to the municipal realm, becoming a patrimonial dominion by adding the artisans, merchants, and low-ranking local functionaries to the multitude of retainers who were economically and politically dependent on the landed estate. Sometimes a single extended family was powerful enough to gain municipal hegemony; sometimes a coalition of such families bound by marriage, consanguinity, and compadrazgo took over the reins of municipal government, not infrequently on a hereditary basis.

Although conclusive evidence is lacking, municipal patrimonialism seems to have been more pronounced in Brazil than in Spanish America. Colonial Brazil was less urbanized, and until the nineteenth century the locus of power was the latifundio rather than the town, except for a few larger coastal cities. Most towns were mere dependencies of the surrounding landed estates, not urban centers.

One of the salient characteristics of patrimonialism is the absence of clear lines between private and public spheres of action, between administration as a public service and as a source of private gains. The Iberian kings never renounced the traditional right to exert discretionary power in financial matters, but they tried to introduce a distinction between public and private domain in the colonial bureaucracy. The royal administrators were forbidden to use their official positions to accumulate wealth; but the practices of selling or renting offices and leasing tax collectorships to private entrepreneurs (also in Brazil) reinforced rather than abolished the patrimonial tradition. This should be kept in mind if one wishes to criticize such practices in terms of venality, embezzling, graft, bribery, and the like. It was clearly a case of attempting to change established custom by legal measures. The maneuvers were futile, of course, because they lacked moral consensus among those whom they were supposed to affect. "The situation was not one in which a normal and expectable integrity in officeholding was occasionally violated by a dishonest administrator. The situation was rather of normal and expectable corruption, within which an occasional figure stood out for resisting corruption." (Gibson, 1966:108)

Three forms of corruption became customary in colonial Latin America: direct appropriation of public funds by office holders; bribery or acceptance of remuneration for services, both legal and illegal; and involvement in commercial, industrial, or agricultural enterprise in clear violation of the law prohibiting such activities to office holders. Actually, the salary scales were inadequate most of the time and for most ranks; furthermore, they lagged behind the rising cost of living, and payments were chronically in arrears. (Konetzke, 1965:152–153) Malfunctioning of the system thus contributed to the very abuses it tried to prevent.

Attempts to transplant the Iberian tradition of municipal self-government to America clashed of course with the principle of patrimonial absolutism. The rather unsettled conditions of the conquest favored a measure of municipal autonomy (Konetzke, 1965:142–143), but in the course of time municipal power withered away, at least in Spanish America. By the end of the colonial period, the structure of municipal government was hardly more than an empty shell.

In Spanish as well as in Portuguese America municipal government consisted essentially of a council (*cabildo* in Spanish and *senado da camara* in Portuguese). The Spanish American officials were *regidores* and *alcaldes*, and in Brazilian councils there were *vereadores, juizes,* and a *procurador. Regidores* and *vereadores* were councilors, *alcaldes* and *juizes* were councilors and judges. Other functionaries could be added, but there was no mayor, although the Brazilian council was presided over by a judge. On important occasions the people could be called to an open meeting, called *cabildo abierto* in Spanish America and *junta geral* in Brazil.

The resemblances of the municipal structures were more than formal. Writing about the municipal council of Bahia, Boxer remarked that

the seats of *vereador* and *regidor*, respectively, were valued chiefly for the social status which they conferred and for the patronage which their occupants could wield, rather than for the usually modest stipends which were attached to them, or even for their more considerable perquisites and pickings. Camaras and cabildos alike, though often heavily indebted and with their public works unfinished or in disrepair, would borrow large sums to lavish on the celebration of their patron saint's feast-day. (Boxer, 1969:149)

Along with these resemblances, rather striking differences are to be seen, not only in the proprietary and hereditary rights attached to most municipal office holders in Spanish America, but also in the close financial and administrative supervision of the cabildos by superior authorities. The Portuguese senados da camara were neither closed corporations nor were they as tightly controlled as their Spanish counterparts. (Boxer, 1969:148) The Brazilian municipal councils were elected every three years, not democratically by the people at large, but by the individuals of high status within the administrative district of which the town was the political center. In some urban centers, voting rights and membership in the municipal council became the bone of contention between rival factions, the Creole planters lining up against the merchant class, usually Portuguese. (Prado Junior, 1963:313)

Toward the end of the sixteenth century the King of Portugal granted permission to include three representatives of six craft guilds in the camara of Salvador (Bahia). Although their participation was restricted to the concerns of the guilds, the presence of such lowly councilors was not agreeable to the aristocratic members, and the six seats were abolished in 1713. (Boxer, 1969:76–77)

In early colonial times the power of the senados da camara was considerable. Some camaras, especially those of São Luis de Maranhão, Rio de Janeiro, and also São Paulo, became at times, the principal authorities in their respective captaincies, overriding the governor and even removing him from office. (Prado Junior, 1963:314) The power of the municipal councils eventually diminished, but never quite as much in Brazil as in Spanish America.

In a patrimonial system the economy revolves in the orbit of the royal *oikos*, and if there are colonies they exist exclusively for the benefit of the ruler and his privileged retainers. On the whole, policies are established to drain off economic surplus rather than to further development. The elementary rule that surplus production depends on resource development was never consistently followed in colonial Latin America. To the contrary, until the late eighteenth century, predatory fiscal policy associated with economic monopolies strangled economic development, thus defeating the continuous attempts to augment revenues and to meet the steadily rising level of royal expenditures. The successful combination of a predatory fiscal system and trade monopolies requires constant exercise of coercive authority, and many of the local revolts occurring in Spanish and Portuguese America were directly related to fiscal inequities and trade monopolies. The export and import monopoly of the Companhia do Comercio do Maranhão, for example, was so inept and abusive that it was responsible for a popular uprising in Belém do Pará in 1684. Quito was twice the scene of popular rebellion (1592 and 1765) directed against the sales tax and the tobacco monopoly. The second revolt was part of the comunero uprising that pushed the viceroyalty of New Granada to the brink of civil war.

The monopolies of the Spanish and Portuguese governments meant not only tight controls of trade relations between the motherland and the colonies, they were also intended to exclude other nations from trading with the American territories. However, like most aspects of the Iberian patrimonial system, fiscal laws and trade monopolies were difficult or impossible to enforce.

In Brazil it was very common to farm out tax collection to private entrepreneurs who assumed contractual responsibility for a certain amount, stipulated prior to collection. In spite of ruthless and extortionary collection practices, the tax contractors often failed to raise the amount owed to the fiscal authorities. Tithes and other levies were payable in currency only, an obligation that had disastrous effects in an economy suffering from chronic shortage of currency and credit. Except for a few profitable commercial crops, agricultural production was kept down to the subsistence level to avoid ruinous tax debts. Tithe collectors normally made only one trip to raise the amount of the tax corresponding to the entire period of the contract, usually three years. Of course to generate the highest possible profit for the contractor, the tax was calculated on the basis of the largest production figures and the highest prices prevailing during that period. Numerous farmers, unable to pay, had all or most of their properties confiscated on the spot by the tithe contractors, who were legally empowered to use such harsh procedures. Confiscation not only paralyzed agriculture but tended to scatter the peasantry into the most inaccessible regions, where at least they were safe from the tax collectors. (Prado Junior, 1963:321)

Although evidence is scanty, it seems that tithe collection and compulsory military recruiting were major factors of dispersion and marginalization of the rural population, certainly in Brazil, but probably in Spanish America, too. (Prado Junior, 1963:309)

If the predatory tax system led to withdrawal, evasion, and rebellion, the trade monopolies and extremely high customs barriers generated contraband on so large a scale that it could be called a way of life, or an occupational career open to many of those involved in commerce. Large-scale contraband was not restricted to any particular period or area; it appeared throughout colonial and republican history of Spanish and Portuguese America alike, always going strong and always satisfying a variety of pressing needs. In fact, without the illegal importation of certain types of merchandise, the economic systems of many colonial cities would probably have collapsed. The situation was clearly diagnosed by Sergio Villalobos, who referred to the "enthronement of contraband" by Iberian patrimonialism.

> Clandestine commerce came to be an activity which employed an infinity of people and extended to all regions without anybody being capable of stopping it, for it obeyed a necessity of the colonies. The penetration of foreign commodities was so active and seemingly so justifiable to many that not only the merchants used it to their advantage, but the authorities too. (Villalobos, 1968:58)

Apparently contraband was protected and trafficked in even by Catholic clerics.

> The ease with which this trade developed was the consequence of measures taken by the Crown which stimulated both internal and external trade of the empire. The latter transformations were important enough to justify the assertion that the American colonies found themselves to be linked to foreign markets and that therefore the monopoly of the metropolis was virtually nonexistent. (Villalobos, 1968:259)

The roles of contraband in Brazil and in the Spanish empire were similar, and complicity of customs officers was reported in both places. (Alden, 1968:396–417) There were reasons to believe that around 1780 nearly 10 percent of the population of Lisbon lived on illicit trade.

The tremendous proportion and the matter-of-course attitude implicit in illicit trade relations suggest that contraband had become an accepted way of adapting patrimonial fiscal policies to economic realities. The fact that illicit trade was taken for granted may also be interpreted as a manifestation of the patrimonial value system and its typical confusion of public and private interests. Nevertheless, the Portuguese and Spanish governments never ceased to apply repressive sanctions to illicit trade, thus emphasizing its criminal nature. The cultural tradition of maintaining a rigid though unenforceable legal structure on the one hand, and customary and equally persistent noncompliance with the law on the other, haunts the Latin American nations to the present day.

The authoritarian heritage in independent Latin America: caudillism and its variants

The conventional stereotype of the caudillo is that of a "man on horseback," most likely in a general's uniform, wielding great personal power, utterly ruthless in the use of violence, a notorious lecher, and a master of pilferage and plunder. This image is roughly accurate except for the possible implication of militarism. More often than not, caudillos were merely self-styled generals, and the political system they introduced in postrevolutionary Spanish America bore no resemblance to genuine militarism. True enough, the caudillo arose out of the political chaos accompanying the long wars of independence, but all the cultural ingredients were there already: authoritarianism in values and attitudes and anchored in the social structure; the use of discretionary power for personal ends, a predatory tax system allowed to be exploited for the benefit of private entrepreneurs; the use of violence by those rebelling against established authority, as well as by that authority to suppress popular uprisings; the availability of a large mestizo class (i.e., persons dispossessed); Indians forced out of their communities, manumitted and runaway slaves; illegitimate and unclaimed offspring of Creoles and non-Creole women, and the descendants of impoverished colonists. (Wolf, 1967:172)

Forced into illegal activities by colonial society and eking out a marginal living, the dispossessed constituted a formidable force available for recruitment. The "rule of law" proposed by well-meaning intellectuals under the sway of political ideals borrowed from Europe, held no appeal for the dispossessed. Nor was respect for the law characteristic of the ruling classes, accustomed as they were to noncompliance. Finally, the colonial "rule of the law" did not invite either respect or compliance. Adding up all these circumstances and established modes of behavior, one cannot escape the conclusion that the political climate was ripe for something like caudillism.

Precedents for caudillolike attitudes and actions abounded in the political posture of the landed estate owners, which reveals at least two of the four "salient characteristics" of caudillism suggested by Wolf and Hansen: a large group of retainers, who were (1) armed and (2) bound to the landowner "by personal ties of dominance and submission and the use of violence in political competition." (Wolf and Hansen, 1967:169)

Violence was directed mainly against rival kin groups, one of several factors severely curtailing the integrative functions of the kinship group. Once the props of Spanish political institutions had been withdrawn or had collapsed, there was little left to hold the various societies together. In view of the actual distribution of power, attempts at setting up constitutional government could not have more than passing success.

All over the countryside, self-styled leaders recruited bands of followers with the intention of gaining wealth by force of arms. Such leaders came from the most disparate backgrounds. Many had been dispossessed mestizoes, some had been military officers, and others were big landowners themselves. Whatever his origin, the caudillo tended to identify with the interests of the landowning class. Most caudillos never rose above the local level and consequently merited no more than passing references in historical studies. The ones who played for higher stakes had to demonstrate their abililty to reciprocate the loyalty of the band with booty and, at the same time, to keep abreast of rival caudillos.

Much has been written about the "personal magnetism" or "charisma" of the caudillo and about his machismo or sexual prowess. Since caudillism is a form of highly personal leadership, such attributes certainly played a significant role in the success of outstanding chieftains. But, according to Wolf and Hansen's perceptive analysis, much more was required of the successful caudillo.

> This aim of the caudillo band is to gain wealth; the tactic employed is essentially pillage. For the retainers, correct selection of a leader is paramount. No retainer can guarantee that he will receive recompense from his leader in advance, because the band seeks to obtain wealth which is not yet in its possession. All know that the wealth sought after is finite, only certain resources are "safe game." The band cannot attack with impunity the basic sources of *criollo* wealth, such as land; and it cannot sequester without international complications, the property of foreign firms operating in the area. Hence there is not only intense competition for movable resources, but great skill is required in diagnosing which resources are currently "available" and which taboo. The exercise of power therefore gives rise to a code which regulates the mode of access to resources. The code refers to two basic attitudes of leadership: first the interpersonal skills needed to keep the band together; second the acumen required to cement these relationships through the correct distribution of wealth. Possession of interpersonal skills is the initial prerequisite; it suggests to the retainers that the second attribute will also be fulfilled. (Wolf and Hansen, 1967:173–174)

The caudillo who, after mobilizing the total resources of his country, attempted to appropriate land belonging to Brazil, Uruguay, and Argentina, was Solano Lopez of Paraguay. Probably the most colossal blunder ever committed by a caudillo, this strategy led to the Paraguayan war (1864–1870) and almost annihilated the male population of Paraguay.

It would be difficult to overrate the role of the landed estate in the development of caudillism. Many outstanding caudillos owned large haciendas or cattle ranches. Supported by their kin and close retainers, and drawing on the resources of their estates, they were able to prepare their campaigns. The hacienda provided a base of action and replenishment where the caudillo-owner was able to weather political and economic adversities without disbanding his forces. Economically, the hacienda remained a safe island because it could always be used for subsistence agriculture and self-sufficiency. (Wolf and Hansen, 1967:170) José A. Paez in Venezuela and Juan Manual Rosas in Argentina were two of the most successful hacienda-born caudillos. Venezuela saw caudillos who

> were chiefs, heads of clans, great landowners, like Diego Colina who could at a word call out the cane cutters of the southern sierra in the Coro area, or like General Ramon Castillo who could draft a thousand men from his family properties, or like the Tellerias who through family occupancy of most of the higher and many of the middle and lower posts of state government could use the resources of the State of Falcón. (Gilmore, 1964:52–53)

Not unexpectedly, these and many similar cases show the close relationship between caudillism and kinship structure. In contrast to hacienda-born Creole caudillos, however, there were mestizo caudillos who had no rural properties; hence their success was contingent on "continuing abundance" of resources that could be appropriated by force of arms. (Wolf and Hansen, 1967:176)

Inevitably the staying power of the caudillo depended on the amount of wealth available for appropriation. Poorer countries, such as Bolivia, might average one or more overthrows of government every year, whereas Rosas controlled Argentina for two decades (1829–1831; 1835–1852) and the rule of Paez in Venezuela lasted 33 years (1830–1863). Lacking the land resources of the Creole, the mestizo caudillo's span of success tended to be considerably shorter.

Yet even under optimal condition, the caudillo had to fight almost constantly for survival, and in the end he was defeated by the very system which had brought him to power. Indeed, this is one of the characteristics of caudillism: Usurpation and subversion are built into the system. Usurpation substitutes for orderly succession, and subversion prevents unlimited tenure.

The term "anarchy" has often been used to describe the social conditions accompanying caudillism. If anarchy is meant to be synonymous with "disorder and violence," it would seem to exclude any adaptive functions that caudillism could conceivably perform in a society. For example, Venezuelan caudillism, rampant for almost a century, has been pictured as a force so destructive and devastating that one might expect a measure of depopulation to follow famine and fighting. Actually,

Venezuela's population increased from approximately 800,000 in 1810 (Vallenilla Lanz, 1961:17) to 1.2 million in 1842–1943. (Gilmore, 1964: 141) Thus in terms of sheer survival at least, caudillism was far from producing the destructive effects implied by some of, its critics.

Some Latin American historians, such as Sanchez Viamonte, took a more realistic view, interpreting Argentine caudillism as a form of regional integration. "Without the caudillo the rural population of the provinces . . . counted for nothing. . . . The Caudillo gave it personality by personifying it." (In Gilmore, 964:38). Vallenilla Lanz sees the caudillo as "the only force of social preservation," and in Venezuela, he says, "Paez, Bermudez, Monagas, Urdeneta had to fulfill the supreme obligation of protecting, with their authority, the renascent social order, from those bands which devastated the countryside, plundered and burned the villages, vexed the authorities and *killed the whites.*" (Vallenilla Lanz, 1961:127) Apparently, the writer refers to the many small bands of mestizo caudillos who, blinded by their hatred for the Creole land-owners, ignored the difference between "available" and "unavailable" resources and consequently died before a firing squad. The integrative function of the maximal bands headed by outstanding chieftains appeared to consist, at least in certain phases of the power contest, of the absorption or elimination of the smaller bands under minor caudillos who often were mestizos rather than Creoles.

If the nineteenth century was an era of caudillism, it was also a period of constitution making. Constitutions were thought to provide protection against usurpation and arbitrary government, but constitutions were also used by caudillos and their intellectual advisers "to facilitate and dignify the exercise of power." (Gilmore, 1964:57) Whenever such documents ceased to fit the designs and ambitions of the caudillo, they were changed or suspended with the greatest ease. They supplied no more than convenient ideological trappings of what was essentially arbitrary government. The reluctance to be bound by law may be interpreted as part of the patrimonial heritage, with the difference that the restraining influence of tradition had ceased to check the exercise of discretionary power.

Caudillism did not affect all Spanish-American countries to the same degree. It was dominant in Mexico, Venezuela, Bolivia, and Argentina, relatively weak in Colombia, and even weaker in Chile. However, caudillism is historically perceived as such only when it acts on a national level (i.e., when chieftains of maximal bands struggle to gain control of the national government). Minimal bands under local chieftains, especially if these are mestizos of dubious origin, are customarily relegated to the ranks of "bandits," "cattle rustlers," or other categories of local trouble-maker. Local chieftains do not command the resources and skills to compete for national prominence, but they possess all the characteristics of genuine caudillos. If they are accorded caudillo status too, the afore-mentioned differences among the various Latin American countries, *including Brazil*, can no longer be maintained. Brazil was certainly spared the phenomenon of national caudillism, but on the local level caudillism has been rampant almost up to the present time.

Formal variance of local chieftainship is reflected perhaps in the words used to characterize such self-styled leadership: *mandón, cacique,* and *gamonal* are the most common terms in Spanish America. *Mandão,* the Portuguese version of *mandón,* is quite common in Brazil too, but a more precise meaning is attached to *coronel* and *coronelismo.* Particularly in northeastern Brazil, the coronel possesses all the attributes of the genuine caudillo: indomitable machismo; use of violence at the slighest provoca-tion; command of a loyal and submissive band of retainers and familiars, who can be mobilized on the spur of the moment; elimination of rivals and adversaries, including those in local office; control of municipal gov-ernment and local resources; readiness to take the law in his own hands, to manipulate, or to disregard it according to personal designs; and the habit of rewarding retainers, relatives, and compadres with gifts, municipal offices, and other spoils. Like the true caudillo, the coronel eventually suffers the fate of his weaker adversaries: He is gunned down by a foe or a traitor in his own band. Often he has one or several followers in the state legislature, and candidates to political office are forced to make deals with him if they want to win elections. The electoral process itself is no more than a convenient means to reinforce the power position of the coronel. Defunct or moribund in most regions of Brazil, coronelism managed to survive in northeastern Brazil, at least until the early 1960s. (See Vilaça and Albuquerque, 1965 passim) Occasionally, caudillo-led bands of north-eastern Brazil expanded their range of action to the point of becoming a threat to the state government. (See della Cava, 1970:155ff.)

The southernmost part of Brazil, particularly the pastoral region of Rio Grande do Sul, which is culturally a branch of the gaucho complex and influenced by its Spanish American neighbors, was deeply involved in caudillism throughout the nineteenth century.

The Spanish-American version of *coronelismo* is *caciquismo* (Lambert, 1967:153), but one should remember that any term referring to caudillo-like behavior, especially on the local or regional level may not meet the realities of a particular region or time. Coronelismo, caciquismo, and gamonalismo blend into the economic and political landscape; from open violence and undisguised pillage they change into more or less institutionalized devices to manipulate elections by economic pressure, veiled threats, occasional assassinations and, increasingly, by purchasing votes. A typical development seems to be the change from *voto-de-cabresto* or captive ballots, to *voto-mercadoria* or negotiable ballots (Vilaça and Albuquerque 1965:40). Of course, these stages were preceded by one in which local caudillism was merely a power contest among rival bands represented by feuding landowners, and elections did not enter the picture at all. But as the power domain of the state gained ground against the rural potentates, elections became increasingly important, imposing a new technique of political control. The dependent mass of voters, mostly rural laborers, were herded to the ballot boxes to vote for the individual or individuals indicated by the coronel or cacique. Voting was a command performance. "Unreliable" voters, especially in the smaller towns, were frequently prevented from balloting by armed bands acting at the order of the coronel or cacique. However, in the less isolated regions, where effective protection of the political system could be provided and the people lost some of their submissiveness; elections became "expensive"; votes had to be purchased with gifts in clothes, shoes, food, or money. This of course did not happen all at once, or simultaneously in all regions of the same country. But where it took place it presaged the end of genuine coronelismo and caciquismo.

Caudillism is often used synonymously with dictatorship. Undoubtedly, a caudillo is a dictator in the broad sense of the word, but not all dictators are caudillos of the kind outlined in the preceding pages. Today, men like Rosas, Paez, or Monagas would be completely incompatible with the complex socioeconomic structure of the least-developed Latin American country. Modern dictators rule vast government machinery; they are confronted with the problems of industrialization, rapid urban growth, a rebellious working class, an impatient peasantry, and a powerful foreign capitalism. These forces cannot be controlled and exploited in the primitive ways in which the man on horseback, with a few thousand improvised soldiers, drained off "available" resources of a simple agrarian economy. Wolf and Hansen consider Porfirio Diaz of Mexico (1876–1911) to be the prototype of the modern dictator:

His expressive slogan *pan o palo* (bread or club) symbolizes the twin functions of his government: wealth (*pan*) to the beneficiaries of the alliance (between foreign interests and native criollo oligarchies of landowners and merchants), the use of force (*palo*) against potential challengers. Thus while harbors were dredged, industry built, commerce expanded and foreign capital poured into the country, Mexico's prisons were filled to capacity. (Wolf and Hansen, 1967:178)

Although caudillism was characteristic of traditional Latin American culture, dictatorship was not, and the more dictatorship evolved, the less it stands for traditional values. But both are different branches of the same root, which is authoritarian government.

Urbanization
and urban culture

The urban tradition in America and Iberia

Following an ancient Mediterranean tradition, the Spaniards founded
numerous cities in freshly conquered America. Toward the end of the
sixteenth century, 200 urban centers had been formally established in
Hispaniola, Cuba, Mexico, Central America, the Andean area, and the
Plata region. But what at first seems to be an amazing accomplishment
looks quite different if population figures are considered. In 1575 no more
than 26,500 Spanish households existed in the New World, the total
Spanish population not exceeding 160,000. (Wilhelmy, 1952:47) Even
if all the Spaniards had resided in those 200 cities (which they did not),
few of the new cities could have been very large in terms of sheer popu-

lation. In fact, more than half of these localities had fewer than 50 Spanish households. In 27 so-called cities the number of peninsular families varied between 200 and 1000. Mexico had 3,000 and Lima 2,000 households, composed of 18,000 and 12,000 individuals, respectively. Adding the resident Indian population, Mexico City had about 60,000 and Lima close to 40,000 inhabitants. (Wilhelmy, 1952:48) However, the largest city by far was San Luis Potosí, Bolivia, whose reported population was 120,000 in 1573. It was larger than Lisbon, Madrid, London, Paris, or Rome. (Wilhelmy, 1952:48) Silver mining provided the economic basis for such unusual growth.

Population size is only one of several criteria to distinguish between urban and rural settlements. A few hard facts account for the structure of an urban, as opposed to a rural, society. They may not cover all essential traits of city life; but they are to be regarded as necessary prerequisites to the emergence of an urban way of life. A fundamental division of labor into producers of food and producers of services and artifacts is at the very root of city life. This process has economic and political aspects. The technology of food production (i.e., agriculture and livestock raising) must be sufficiently advanced to allow at least some people—administrators and clerics, merchants and artisans, lawyers, doctors, and architects, servants, mendicants, gamblers, and prostitutes—to live off the surplus produced by the peasantry. These individuals eat the food produced by the agriculturists; but to drain off food resources into the channels of urban consumption, the city must be able to exert coercive authority on the food producers.

In other words, to become a city, a settlement must exercise effective political control over a rural area large enough and sufficiently populated to feed the citizenry. Several options are open to accomplish this. Urban residents may own rural establishments, worked by slaves or serfs, whose production goes totally or in part to the urban market. Or, agricultural production is left to peasants, who may or may not own the land they cultivate. The obligation to pay taxes, tributes, or rent forces them to take part of their produce to the urban market, even at the risk of being unable to feed their own families properly. Where agricultural techniques are rudimentary and productivity is low, bondage essential to the survival of the city. In Spanish America the institution of the encomienda provided the necessary agricultural labor force to feed the city. In Brazil slaves were used by fazendeiros and small holders to supply the urban markets with necessary staples. Where high profits induced agriculturalists to specialize in commercial crops, the production of food staples suffered, and scarcity caused disarrays in the urban market. In Portuguese and Spanish America alike, the cities were surrounded by *quintas* and *chacaras*, or small farms producing for urban landlords. (Wilhelmy 1952:86) Thus urban residents often had their own chacaras in the immediate vicinity of the city. (Reis Filho, 1970:95) Even within the cities, orchards and vegetable gardens were quite common. Apparently, quintas and chacaras served also as alternative places of residence, reflecting a taste for rural living that seems to be at odds with the Spanish preference for city life. Of the Chilean capital we are told that in the early nineteenth century

> the characteristics of country living continued to dominate the habits of its residents. . . . [who] lived more in the country, on their *fundos* or *haciendas* than in the city. . . . Already in November or December the families emigrated to the *haciendas* where they remained until the month of April or May. And country houses surrounded by extensive orchards abounded in the environs of Santiago. There rich proprietors and merchants relaxed from the fatigues of the capital. The soil was very fertile and produced abundantly everything that was necessary for life. (Cruz, 1970:44–45)

Until the middle of the eighteenth century, Lima was "a bucolic country town surrounded by orchard bearing pomegranates, citrons and grapefruits, more like a forest than a city." Outside the city, wrote Cieza de León, "there are many *estancias* and landed estates where the Spaniards have their cattle and pigeon houses and many vineyards and fresh, delectable gardens full of native fruits. . . ." (Descola, 1962: 80)

The extent to which the colonial cities of Latin America were involved in horticultural pursuits may have been sufficient to justify Wilhelmy's proposal to classify them as *Ackerbürgerstädte*, Max Weber's term for medieval towns whose citizenry produced part of their own food supply inside or in the immediate vicinity of the city. Wilhelmy did not wish to extend his classification to the mining towns of Latin America. (Wilhelmy, 1952:49) Indeed, this seems to mark a major difference that ought to be kept in mind. In the mining towns and perhaps in some port cities, Iberian urbanism was allowed to develop without the bucolic distractions of cities like Lima, Santiago, or Rio de Janeiro. To be sure, the manifestations of a genuinely urban style of life, in terms of a pre-industrial culture, was limited to the core of the city and to the central plaza and its vicinity, where sumptuous churches and palatial homes dominated the landscape and the rich displayed their wealth; here religious fiestas, bull fights, processions, and masquerades were held, and men of high standing enjoyed their leisure in *tertulias*, gambling and amorous adventures. Outside the core area, most colonial cities looked like no more than villages. (Hardoy, 1969:52)

In Portuguese America urbanization followed an orientation that is often believed to differ from that of Spanish America. Deeply engaged in Africa and India, the Portuguese took little interest in Brazil, and almost all the "cities" founded during the sixteenth century were cities in name only. Salvador (Bahia), with a population of about 8000 toward the end of the century, was the only locality that had come close to developing urban forms of living. The Spaniards asserted themselves politically by founding several hundred cities, which then served as bases for the conquest of the land. The Portuguese established their rural domains mostly without the benefit of urban rallying points. Towns and cities tended to be secondary developments depending on and reflecting the prosperity of the surrounding agricultural estates. Until the nineteenth century the Brazilian landowners lived on their estates most of the time. In some regions they spent the winter months in their urban residence, but everywhere it was customary to spend Sundays and holidays (or rather, holy days) in the city. In the smaller towns life came almost to a standstill during the week.

Typical of Brazil, in contrast to Spanish America, was the so-called patrimonial town, a private project of one or several landowners who staked out a plaza where they built a church, had it consecrated to a saint, and turned it over to the Church, with the only stipulation that from time to time masses be celebrated for the builders' souls. Often enough these religious assembly points attracted merchants and artisans, and the area gradually acquired urban characteristics. Not infrequently such private urbanization projects were quite profitable for the landowners, who divided the land around the church into small lots and sold them to newcomers. During the nineteenth century, as cultural values took an increasingly secular turn, the interpolation of the Church was judged unnecessary. (Wilhelmy, 1952:284; Rios, 1951:200–201) Politically, the patrimonial town tended to remain within the power domain of the surrounding fazendas. Unfortunately, little attention has been paid so far to this most interesting relationship between urbanization and the landed estate.

Much of the difference in the early rhythm and nature of urbanization of Spanish and Portuguese America occurred because the wealth of sixteenth-century Spanish America derived primarily from mining, which allowed for a much higher degree of urbanization than commercial agriculture based on a medieval technology. When the Portuguese discovered gold and diamonds at the end of the seventeenth century, urbanization in the vast mining area took forms similar to those of Spanish America.

It has often been pointed out that the Spaniards selected the sites of their cities in the interior, where a dense and sedentary indigenous population supplied the necessary labor force, whereas the Portuguese preferred coastal locations for their cities. As it happens, the interior location of the Mesoamerican and Andean cities was determined by pre-Spanish urbanization. Mexico City, Cuzco, and Quito were erected on the sites of indigenous urban centers, and Bogotá and Tunja were located in the core area of the Chibcha civilization. The labor potential of these areas and the wealth accumulated there held the economic attention of the conquerors, requiring in addition political and ecclesiastic decisions determining the location of political, religious, and economic institutions in or nearby sites inherited from native societies.

None of these attractions existed either in Brazil or in the Plata region. As long as the mineral wealth of Portuguese America remained undiscovered, there was no reason to urbanize immense jungle areas, thinly populated by nomadic Indians living in paleolithic cultures. It made some economic sense to capture as many Indians as possible and to take them to the coastal plantations, or to concentrate them, for the purpose of religious conversion, in villages controlled by Catholic orders. Indeed, coastal cities were as comon in Spanish America as they were in Brazil. The Spaniards founded Santo Domingo, Havana, Veracruz, Portobelo, Cartagena, Callao (Lima), Valparaiso, Buenos Aires and others for the same reasons the Portuguese established Belém, São Luis de Maranhão, Recife, Salvador, Vitória, Rio de Janeiro, and Santos: They were commercial ports, fortresses, and naval bases. The discovery of mineral wealth radically altered the alleged tendency of the Portuguese to cling to the coast. During the eighteenth century numerous mining towns emerged in what is now the state of Minas Gerais. The examples of Mariana, Ouro Prêto, São João del Rei, and Sabará are outstanding illustrations of the urbanizing effects of the mining of gold and diamonds on colonial Brazil. In fact, cities like Cuiabá and Goiás (Vila Boa) bear witness to the impact of mining even on some of the remotest parts of central Brazil.

On the whole, however, up to the late nineteenth century, Brazil remained far more rural than Spanish America. At the end of the colonial period, Brazil had only five cities with more than 10,000 inhabitants, adding up to 5.7 percent of a total population of about 2,850,000. The cities were Rio de Janeiro (50,000), Salvador (Bahia) (45,600), Recife (30,000), São Luis de Maranhão (22,000), and São Paulo (16,000). (Pinchas

Table 1 *Population of selected Latin American cities*

City	Population	Year	Source
Buenos Aires	40,000	1801	Azara, 1923
Santiago	50,000	1818	Wilhelmy, 1952
Valparaiso	25,000	1818	Wilhelmy, 1952
La Paz	21,120	1796	Wilhelmy, 1952
Lima	52,627	1791	Viceregal Census, 1791
Quito	70,000	1816	Wilhelmy, 1952
Bogotá	21,394	1801	Martinez, 1968
Caracas	40,000	1800	Wilhelmy, 1952
Guatemala	25,000	1821	Wilhelmy, 1952
Mexico	130,602	1793	Viceregal Census, 1793
Puebla	56,859	1793	Viceregal Census, 1793
Guanajuato	28,963	1793	Viceregal Census, 1793
Zacatecas	25,495	1794	Humboldt, 1811
Oaxaca	19,069	1794	Humboldt, 1811
Valladolid	32,098	1794	Humboldt, 1811
Durango	11,027	1793	Viceregal Census, 1793

Geiger, 1963:70) The others were "big villages," in the orbit of the landed estate.

Table 1 shows the population of a number of Spanish American cities in the late eighteenth century or the early nineteenth century. Recent research on the population of the viceroyalty of Peru at the end of the eighteenth century produced some significant data extracted from the censuses of 1786 and 1792. Of the total population of 1,150,000, 70 percent lived in settlements having fewer than 5,000 inhabitants; 140,000 (12 percent) lived in middle towns whose population lay between 5,000 and 10,000; and 210,000 (18 percent) of the people were concentrated in four cities with more than 10,000 inhabitants (Lima, Arequipa, Huamanga, and Cuzco). (Vollmer, 1967:345)

Doubtless an urbanization index of 18 percent seems high in comparison to Brazil's, 5.7 percent. To qualify what has been written about urban orientation of Spanish colonization, however, keep in mind that toward the end of the colonial period, more Spaniards and their descendants were living in the country on haciendas and ranchos than in the cities. (Konetzke, 1965:47) Other data justify considerable doubt about the alleged preference of the Spanish settlers for urban life. In Chile so many Spaniards lived in the countryside against the will of the king that the royal cedula of 1703 was deemed necessary to compel them to take up residence in a city or Spanish town. The penalty for those who disobeyed was exile and confiscation of property. (Guarda, 1968:20) On the other hand, the economic structure of the colonial city offered extremely limited possibilities of gaining a livelihood except for the functionaries of the crown, the merchants, artisans, and the big landowners.

The physical structure of the colonial city

Numerous traits of medieval culture were transplanted to America, but the medieval city was not one of them. Instead, the grid pattern was introduced, first by royal instruction in 1513, and later by decree in 1573. Rooted in classic Greek and Roman models, the grid design was never entirely superseded by "medieval spontaneity." In fact, medieval Spanish cities, such as Briviesca (Burgos), Santa Fé, and Puerto Real, already show the pattern the Spanish crown attempted to impose on its colonies. (Konetzke, 1965:47; Foster, 1960:40ff.)

The Spanish colonial city was supposed to be built around a single center of dominance, a rectangular plaza devoid of constructions and designed for the presentation of military parades and other spectacles. Facing the plaza, the metropolitan church, the government buildings, and the residences of the leading families were aligned. At right angles to the plaza, a number of streets, equidistant from each other, ran straight in all four directions. At regular intervals the streets were crossed by transverse avenues forming a checkerboard pattern of symmetrical blocks. The important people in town tended to live and work as close to the center as possible, and the blocks adjacent to the plaza were choice locations for residences and businesses. The famous patrician residence of Torre-Tagle in Lima occupies part of a city block next to the Plaza de Armas, for example. This building, like so many others near the center, has two stories, more often than not, however, buildings on the plaza had only a ground floor.

Smaller stores and the workshops of the artisans lay farther away from the center, and peripherally to the "Spanish" town proper there were the barrios of the Indians. Often the colonial city was walled in.

In urban residences of the upper strata, depth made up for height. Behind the main body of the house, comprising parlor and living rooms, there was a patio around which bedrooms and dining room were located. The remaining facilities were built around a second patio leading into orchard and garden. Patios were less common in colonial Brazil, but kitchen and servants' quarters often occupied detached or semidetached dependencies in the back, and extensive gardens completed the family's living compound.

Many but by no means all Spanish American cities conformed rather rigidly to the grid pattern. Since Portugal did not attempt to impose a universal master plan on its city builders, one may expect to encounter greater diversity in Brazilian cities. This is indeed the case, but greater diversity does not imply, as has been claimed, "picturesque confusion" (R. S. Smith, 1966:289) or "medieval spontaneity." On close scrutiny of Brazilian coastal cities, none appears to be a replica of the Portuguese medieval town, with its maze of narrow, crooked streets running in every direction. Salvador, the colonial capital, sometimes cited as an example of medieval urbanization, had its clearly defined central square (Tomé de Souza), where the governmental palace, the senado da camara, and other public buildings were located. This site is not in the geometrical center of the old town, being perched instead on the edge of a high escarpment overlooking the bay and the lower town. At a short distance from the Praça Tomé de Souza there is a second square, the Largo da Sé. The cathedral, three more churches, and two convents occupied three sides of the plaza almost entirely. Obviously, one square was secular and the other was religious, a functional specialization not uncommon in Brazilian cities. A similar division characterizes Belém do Pará where the Praça do Carmo constitutes the civic center, and the Largo da Sé the religious center. In Recife the civic-religious dualism is suggested by the Praça da Independencia, with one of the older churches, and the nearby Praça da República, with government palace, courthouse, and municipal theater.

The central plaza pattern is found in virtually every coastal city of Brazil. The center of São Luis do Maranhão is a long rectangular plaza dominated by the cathedral and flanked by the Palacia do Governo on the south and the courthouse and other public edifices on the north. "The city of S. Luis do Maranhão, founded in 1615, was the first one to have . . . a completely regular layout, but without the monotony of the perfect checkerboard common in the cities of Spanish America." (Santos, 1963:154) In Natal Praça André Albuquerque constitutes the center, and Florianópolis is laid out around the Praça Quinze de Novembro. Rio de Janeiro's colonial past is almost entirely obliterated, but the historical Palace Square, as it was in 1808, could easily be taken as a perfect example of a Spanish town plaza. Even the thoroughly modern cities of southern Brazil, such as São Paulo, Curitiba, and Pôrto Alegre are to a considerable degree still oriented toward a central plaza. Here the persistence of the colonial pattern is as obvious as it is in the relatively modern cities of the Argentine Pampa Humeda. (Randle, 1969)

The street design of Brazilian cities like Belém, Natal, São Luis, and Salvador is a far cry from the labyrinth of crooked streets typical of the medieval town. On the contrary, most streets run at right angles from the central square, and they are crossed by equally straight streets forming fairly regular blocks. But others are either curved or not strictly parallel to each other, following the contours of the terrain or the irregularities of a waterfront. There is certainly less concern with geometry than in comparable Spanish American cities; but the basic design and its functional implications are close enough to those of Spanish America to suggest a rather impressive similarity. The perfectly geometrical layouts of Brazilian cities located near the continental borderline may be due to Spanish influence. Pelotas in Rio Grande do Sul has been cited as the "most Spanish" of all Brazilian cities. (Santos, 1963:154)

On the other hand, the grid pattern was not always rigidly adhered to by the Spanish city builders. The oldest section of Callao (Peru), contiguous to the irregularly shaped Plaza Real Felipe, bears no resemblance to a checkerboard. Nor is the street design of Cartagena in the orthodox grid model. Far from being a Brazilian peculiarity, the dual plaza pattern exists in a number of Spanish American cities. Cuzco (Peru), whose center was erected on the foundations of Inca temples and palaces, appears to be a compromise between the grid pattern and local topography. There is the classic Plaza de Armas dominated by the cathedral and the Jesuit church, but the government building is located on the nearby Plaza de Recocijo. As one moves away from the plazas, the symmetry of the central city blocks gives way to narrow streets climbing hills and winding around their irregular contours.

In Quito (Ecuador) the non-Spanish traits are even more conspicuous than in Cuzco. There are three major plazas in the colonial center, two surrounded by churches and monasteries, and the third (Plaza de la Independencia) dominated by the Palacio de Gobierno. La Ronda, supposedly the oldest street in Quito and certainly the most picturesque, runs in an arch—it neither begins nor ends in a plaza, and it is only one of many crooked streets in the vicinity of the old city core. With their whitewashed ancient residences, the old streets remind the observer of the Moorish barrios of certain Iberian towns.

These rather extensive sections of Cuzco and Quito closely resemble a group of Latin American cities whose physical structure fails to reflect concern with checkerboard symmetry. Guanajuato, Zacatecas, and Taxco in Mexico, and Ouro Prêto, Mariana, and São João del Rei in Brazil, are outstanding examples of this type of colonial urbanization. They emerged as local centers of a flourishing mining industry, and their location in highly mountainous terrain, unsuitable for urban development would be implausible except in terms of the economic implications of that industry. The topography of the sites left little choice to the founders, who had to adapt to the exigencies of rugged, steep slopes and narrow valleys. They developed labyrinthine street plans with steep inclines and small plazas of irreguar shape offering vistas on baroque churches and palaces. Guanajuato, Taxco, and Ouro Prêto resemble one another more closely than the more conventional colonial cities of either Spanish or Portuguese America.

The variability of the Spanish American cities has been fully recognized by Chueca Goitia and Torres Balbas, who closely scrutinized hundreds of colonial town plans (1951). In fact, the classification proposed by these authors is based on the extent to which the cities conform to or deviate from the grid pattern. They distinguish irregular, semi-irregular, and regular cities, fortified cities of regular design, and "unique cases." Santo Domingo (prior to 1608), Ixmiquilpan (Mexico), Loja (Ecuador), and the mining towns were included among cities of "irregular design." In semiirregular cities the streets are not parallel but run in convergent or divergent lines, exactly like the streets in most colonial cities of Brazil. Besides, the plaza is often trapezoid instead of rectangular. Havana, Santiago de Cuba, Veracruz, Cartagena, Valladolid, Baracoa, Guanabacoa, San Agustin de la Florida, and San Salvador del Bagamo are mentioned as examples of semiirregular cities. (Chueca Goitia and Torres Balbas, 1951:XII–XVIII)

Thus our comparative scrutiny does not support the theory that Spanish American and Portuguese American cities constitute two distinct categories of physical structure. It seems that the colonial cities of Brazil were either "irregular" or "semiirregular"; and the classification proposed by Chueca Goitia and Torres Balbas appears to be applicable to all of Latin America rather than to Spanish America alone.*

The preservation of the colonial core of many Latin American cities

---

* Contrary to common belief, the Portuguese government did concern itself with the details of town planning. In connection with the transplantation of several thousand families from the Azores to southern Brazil, a resolution of the Conselho Ultramarino, issued in 1747, established the guidelines for towns to be founded on the Island of Santa Catarina: On the site intended for the locality a square will be assigned for a plaza measuring five hundred palmos on each side, and on one side a church will be built, a street or streets will be demarked having a width of no less than forty palmos, and in these and on the side of the plaza the residences are to be erected in good order. (Ferreira Rodrigues, 1915:213)

easily conveys the impression of generalized wealth and splendor, high esthetic achievement, and an aristocratic style of life. Actually, these attributes were restricted to the small upper class. The less splendid and more perishable buildings have long since given way to modern urban constructions. A very large proportion of the Spaniards and Creoles lived in unprepossessing, whitewashed adobe houses, often covered with thatch rather than tiles, and much smaller than the ample structures gracing the central plaza or adjacent streets. The mass of Indians and poor mestizoes lived on the very periphery of the urban grid in marginal settlements of *bohios* or huts which, in some cases at least, can be regarded as ancestral forms of modern shantytowns. There is no evidence of Indian influences on architecture and art forms of the colonial city (Kubler, 1964:55), but native influences must have been present in the bohios of the Indians. The grading of urban into rural architecture can be observed even in many contemporary cities, and this usually means a blending of Indian and Iberian elements in the rustic settlements of the urban periphery.

Urban structure and social structure

The physical structure of the colonial city was an unambiguous reflection of its social structure. The buildings of the center housed the spiritual and temporal powers, as well as wealthy families of encomenderos, sesmeiros and import and export merchants. Shopkeepers and artisans occupied blocks farther removed from the central plaza and its vicinity, and the peripheral sections sheltered the poor, including the Indians. Although in many Spanish American cities the Indians were segregated in their own barrios, this pattern was not always strictly adhered to. In Mexico City, for example, segregation proved impossible, and by 1570 it had already given way to a mixed residence pattern. (Schwartz, 1969:627) Nor was there abrupt and rigid grading along class or ethnic boundaries within the urban area proper. On the whole, however, the sense of hierarchy was expressed in the ordering of the different classes within the urban area. Hierarchical arrangement was combined with centralism, the dominance of the urban core was undisputed, and economic and political dependence increased toward the outskirts, reaching its maximum in the Indian barrios. In this limited sense the colonial city was a highly integrated structure, but the outer areas of many cities, especially toward the end of the eighteenth century, developed into a twilight zone, where

a marginal population of mixed ethnic origin lived a life of what contemporaries called "vice and corruption."

Initially the republican pattern of urbanization was hardly different
from that of the colonial period. On the contrary, "the centralized
orientation of Hispanic urbanization pales when compared to the one
imposed by the Republic and manifest in the spirit and form of the cities,
particularly in the plains where not even a topographic accident could
deviate the implacable intentions of official conformity." (Randle, 1969:39)
In nineteenth-century Brazil, the Iberian heritage persisted with the same
tenacity. It is particularly visible in the cities founded in the state of
São Paulo during the last century and a half.

Virtually all students of colonial Latin America agree that society everywhere was highly stratified, and they recognize the sharpness of the
contrasts between the wealthy and the poor, between proprietors of landed
estates, mines, and wholesale businesses on the one hand, and slaves,
serfs, and free laborers on the other. However, the nature of these strata,
their continuity and, particularly, the existence, numerical importance, and
composition of the middle strata, have been objects of considerable
controversy. Some authors have taken the extreme view that the strata
were castes rather than classes and that there was no middle class at all.

Enough historical evidence has been amassed to reject such extreme
views. Incontrovertibly, many poor Iberian settlers prospered in agriculture,
mining, and commerce, and they succeeded in obtaining the status privileges
necessary to validate their claims to an aristocratic way of life. It is equally
true that many mestizoes of dubious origin overcame the social barriers
of *limpieza de sangre* and *linaje*. Intermarriages between families of
aristocratic landowners and the new rich who had amassed fortunes in
the "ignoble" (by medieval criteria) pursuits of commerce and money
lending were rather common, and the practice further blurred the boundaries that Iberian prejudice and pride sought to maintain. But success
was no guarantee of stability, and upward mobility alternated with downward mobility. "In Peru, while the encomenderos became poor because
of the abolition of the encomiendas in the eighteenth century, a commercial bourgeoisie ascended, and many of its members hastened to acquire titles of nobility, to join the most privileged circles." (Bagú, 1952:95)

Writing about Chile, Alberto Edwards remarked:

Long before 1810 the old families of the conquistadores and encomenderos, ruined by luxury and otiosity, or extinguished in wars or
convents, found themselves in full decadence. New breeds of merchants
and working men with only three or four generations of opulence and

social distinction had slowly absorbed or replaced them. Thus a mixed aristocracy, bourgeois by origin, came to control the country economically and socially due to the triumph of money through its mercantilistic spirit, sensible, frugal, of regular and orderly habits, but having in its veins the blood of some of the old feudal families. (Edwards, 1928:95)

Where there is social mobility there can be no caste in the strict sense of the word, although on a local level castelike structures may be viable for limited periods of time, as we shall see later.

In the cities upward mobility was typically a function of being among the founders or first families to participate in the free distribution of land, via grants, which was often the first step on the social ladder. If the initiative took hold and the city developed, the founding families owning most of the land in and around the urban centers were naturally in an advantageous position vis-à-vis the newcomers. They set themselves up as the upper class, although there was seldom anything in the family genealogies to justify the usual status claims. Both in Spanish America and Brazil, this process was common enough to constitute a cultural pattern. (Morse, 1965:38)

The tendency to dichotomize the social structure of the colonial city in terms of a two-class (or caste) system must be rejected in view of available evidence. Describing Lima at the beginning of the seventeenth century, Father Barnabé Cobo focused on the people who did not belong either to the local aristocracy or to the mass of unskilled laborers, paupers, serfs and slaves.

It is an amazing thing to see the great number of stores and workshops existing all over the city, particularly in the streets near the principal plaza, for only the merchants' shops exceed one hundred and fifty not including many stores located in private houses; and the silversmiths alone occupy one of the principal streets of the city; there is only one corner where there is not a wine tavern or eating place which here we call *pulperia*, so that there are more than two hundred and seventy in the entire city. (Bagú, 1952:89)

More precise information about the urban social structure can be gleaned from the 1775 census of a single parish forming part of Salvador (Bahia). Recognition of 83 different activities suggests a degree of social differentiation that does not bear out the idea of a highly polarized society.

The census (da Costa, 1965) listed 523 heads of households, of whom 51 were self-supporting proprietors. The professions were represented by

18 priests, 6 judges, 3 physicians, 3 surgeons, 2 lawyers, 1 notary, 10 registrars, and 4 musicians. Six merchants were prosperous enough to rank high in the social scale. In fact, one of them owned 46 slaves, the highest number recorded in the whole census. One hundred or 19.1 percent of all householders of the parish of São Pedro probably composed the upper strata of the parochial society.

A relatively large population of 985 slaves could be regarded as the bottom layer of the local society. But the census also recorded 79 paupers, 15 beggars, 10 blind, and 1 insane person, who together represented 20.1 percent of all householders. The rest of the recorded heads of households (40.7 percent of the total) did not belong to either the lowest or highest stratum of the society. To call them "middle class" would be rash and unwarranted, but a fairly reliable criterion of differentiating them socially is slave ownership (for its economic advantages as well as for the prestige associated with it). Of those 40.7 percent, 133 or 25.4 percent were craftsmen, vendors, and day laborers who did not own slaves. Since they all did menial work, they would fall into the lower ranks of the social structure. However, 80 or 15.3 percent of the householders did own slaves, suggesting that many or most of them did no menial work themselves. Of these persons, 67.6 percent owned from one to three slaves, 23.7 percent had from four to six slaves, and 8.7 percent owned seven or more. A shoemaker who owned five slaves, or a baker (a 35-year-old mulatto woman by the way) owning 24 slaves, or a carpenter with 9 slaves seem to be in the category of small-scale entrepreneurs, perhaps equidistant from the lower and the higher levels of the society. The case of São Pedro is further complicated by the recorded number of 403 *agregados*—persons of various age, background, social level, and occupation, attached to the families of the 523 recorded heads of households. Many had families of their own, and occupations as contrasting as cleric, cobbler, colonel, and beggar, suggest considerable internal differentiation, as does the fact that 78 slaves were owned by these agregados. All this is a far cry from the dichotomized society that appears in oversimplified schemes.

Similar census data are available for 10 towns located in the province of São Paulo. In contrast to Bahia, they were all small and functionally related to agricultural regions. In 1823, Sorocaba, the largest, listed 1788 heads of households, 510 agregados, and 2034 slaves. Cananéia, the smallest, recorded 268 householders, 160 agregados, and 586 slaves. The remaining towns—Areias, Taubaté, Iguape, Piracicaba, Itú, Itapetininga, Bragança, and Franca—stood closer to Sorocaba than to Cananéia, as far as size is concerned. All censuses were carried out between 1822 and

1824. Not unexpectedly, in all towns except one, the majority of the house-holders were agriculturists, but a sizable proportion (between 59.2 and 14.3 percent) were craftsmen, day laborers, merchants, fishermen, professionals, and administrators. Occupational differentiation varied between 14 and 43 designations listed by the censuses, the average being 26.5, a relatively high figure in view of the small size of the towns. As in Bahia, slave ownership can be used to distinguish between traders and craftsmen who did their own work and those who had slaves to do all or most of the menial work. (Willems, 1970a) The sample suggests that even in the smaller colonial towns, society cannot be interpreted as a two-class system.

The phenomenon of urban development in Spanish America differed from its Brazilian counterpart in three rather sigificant aspects. Universities were established in a number of major Spanish cities, but not in Brazil. The European tradition of craft and merchant guilds found a receptive environment in Spanish America, but not in Brazil. Furthermore, industrial forms of production could be transplanted to certain areas of Spanish America, but not to Brazil, except in the late eighteenth century and then only temporarily.

"By 1560 Mexico City could boast of a university, a flourishing printing press, impressive public buildings, and inspiring gothic churches and monasteries." (Schwartz, 1969:617) In Spanish America, four universities were founded during the sixteenth century; in Santo Domingo (1538), Mexico City (1551), Lima (1551) and Bogotá (1563). The sixteenth century also saw the establishment of five Jesuit institutions of higher learning: in Córdoba (1613), Bogotá (1622), Sucre (1624), Santiago de Guatemala (1676), and Cuzco (1692). Between 1701 and 1809 five more universities were established: in Caracas (1729), Havana (1728), Santiago de Chile (1738), Quito (1769), and Guadalajara (1791) (Steger, 1965: 45–47). Of course, these 14 universities, all under clerical control and strictly within either the medieval or the Jesuit tradition, did not promote scientific research or critical thought. They were institutions of theological, philosophical, and literary learning, humanistic rather than scientific. However, they launched an intellectual tradition powerful enough to leave unmistakable vestiges in present-day university education.

There were no universities in Portuguese America. Young Brazilians wishing to acquire a degree in the fine arts, law, or medicine had to enroll in the University of Coimbra. Fearing that a colonial university might easily develop into a seedbed of political subversion, Portugal preferred to keep the intellectual elite of its colonies under close surveillance. At any rate, cultural continuity was not disrupted by the transfer from Brazilian preparatory schools to a Portuguese university: the students were all under the intellectual tutorship of the Jesuits.

The transplantation of the Spanish guild pattern to the major colonial cities was quite successful. Craft guilds as well as merchant guilds flourished in Mexico City, Lima, Bogotá, Quito, Havana, Santo Domingo, and other cities. In Brazil, similar attempts met with little success. Craft guilds existed, but their functions were curtailed, Buarque de Holanda thinks, by the preponderance of slave labor, the self-sufficiency of the landed estate, the scarcity of specialists, the failure to enforce guild regulations, and occupational instability. (Buarque de Holanda, (1948:62–63) Two causes may be added to these. The Indian cultures of Mesoamerica and the Andes had a craft tradition of their own, and the urban markets in Spanish America were much larger and more diversified than those of Brazil, at least during the sixteenth and seventeenth centuries. In the late eighteenth century, Mexico City, which produced a great variety of goods, had more than 50 craft guilds employing some 18,000 people. (Gibson, 1969:236) No Brazilian city could match such figures at any point of colonial history.

At the time when the Iberian guilds were transplanted to the New World, however, they had already been exposed to the disintegrating influences of industrial competition. Not surprisingly, the same kind of competition threatened the Spanish guild artisans in America. The *obrajes* —industrial establishments producing wool and cotton textiles with Spanish equipment—were designed for an expanding market, whereas guild-regulated production was static and noncompetitive. Furthermore, exactly as in Europe, the obrajes could rely on cheap forced labor. (Wolf, 1959:184–185)

Mercantilism was less consistent in Spain than in Portugal. As the system was supposed to work, colonies mainly were to provide raw materials and to consume manufactured goods produced by the homeland. After initially performing this subordinate role of economic production, however, the Spanish colonies were allowed to compete so heavily with metropolitan industry that the mercantilistic relationship was in danger of being thwarted. (Gibson, 1966:106)

Portuguese mercantilism proved rather inflexible. Only the crudest industries were allowed to exist in Brazil. In the second half of the eighteenth century Portuguese vigilance temporarily relaxed, and textile mills and forges sprang up in Minas Gerais and Rio de Janeiro, only to be extinguished again by royal decree in 1785. (Prado Junior, 1963:222–223)

Finally, three more structural features were shared by Spanish American and Brazilian cities alike. "In Brazil and much of Spanish America continuity of municipal institutions and processes was threatened by the displacement of city elders to their rural domains. Having radiated energies centrifugally to the land, all but the large commercial or bureaucratic cities tended to become appendages of the country." (Morse, 1965:38) Since urban "centrifugalism" took different forms, some clarifications are necessary at this point. The ordinary "displacement of city elders" occurred at more or less regular intervals involving what may be called *residential bilocalism*. The large landowners and their families alternated between two places of residence, the *casa grande* of the hacienda and the town house. But there was also a tendency that induced urban dwellers to abandon the city, usually in search of mineral wealth or new rural domains. Such moves might eventually lead to the establishment of new towns in the hinterland. The city of São Paulo during the seventeenth and early eighteenth centuries provides an extreme case of flight from an urban area. It is true that many bandeirantes returned to the city after several years of absence, but others did not. At any rate, the almost constant exodus of people seriously interfered with the growth of the city. Whether or to what extent this condition produced depopulation is largely a matter of controversy. The previously mentioned census of 1775 refers to "the great desertion the inhabitants (of Bahia) undertook to the interior of the sertão." Moreover, in the parish of São Pedro da Bahia 180 houses stood vacant. (da Costa, 1965:56–57) Thus we have one more indication that not even the largest city of colonial Brazil escaped the effects of such "desertion."

The practice of having two residences seems to be directly related to the familistic urban social structure of colonial Latin America. Urban structure remained familistic in contrast to Europe. The families of the big landowners "commuted" between town and country. "The substitution of locality groups for kin group which Weber felt to be so characteristic of medieval European towns often failed to occur in Latin America." (Morse, 1965:38) Urban social structure, at least at the higher levels, was no more than an extension of the kinship system that controlled the country. And by kinship system we mean a group of families held together by consanguineal and affinal relationships capable of concerted action in the countryside as well as the city.

It is probable that the integration of city and surrounding countryside into a single political structure, the Latin American municipality, occurred because rural and urban social structures alike were controlled by the same bilocal kinship groups. It would be difficult to overrate this structural characteristic and its role in the process of urban development. Among other things, it enabled the city directly to appropriate—through taxes, fees, fines, compulsory labor, and market organization—surpluses generated by the peasantry under its jurisdiction. It also enables holders of municipal power to redistribute these surpluses in a way that best fitted the interests of their respective rural domains.

The urban ethos

Cities are supposedly founded to serve certain purposes or functions. Administration, military defense, organized worship, marketing, manufacturing, and import and export trade are some purposes determining the choice of a given location and its development into an urban agglomeration. Colonial cities may be expected to make sense in terms of socioecological system whose center of gravity is a distant metropolis. Yet such a purely pragmatic approach fails to capture some of the essence of Latin American urbanism. With reference to the cities of New Spain, Gibson thinks that "only in the mining cities and the ports was there a close connection between urbanism and the main economic purposes of empire. An economic determinist would have difficulty in explaining what the other cities of New Spain were for." (Gibson, 1969:239) According to the same author, Spanish urbanism is not primarily explainable in terms of other institutions: "Again and again other institutions assumed or were subordinated to urbanism, which therefore appears in an independent role." (Gibson, 1969:239)

This means that living in cities ranked very high in the hierarchy of cultural values, as indeed it did, not only in New Spain but all over Spanish and Portuguese America. Like any other cultural complex, urbanism can be understood as an assemblage or cluster of symbols. That is, within a given society certain things and forms of behavior *mean* city or city life. Most of these meanings were part and parcel of the cultural baggage of the Iberian settlers brought from their homelands. Predictably, the essence of urban life was associated with the central sector of the city, which projected the conventional idea what a city should look like. Urban edifices had to stand close together, presenting unbroken rows of facades in exact alignment. Detached or semidetached houses, separated from the street by gardens, were considered incompatible with genuine urban life. Gardens were located behind the residence, where they could be enjoyed in complete privacy.

Menial work was anathema to the residents of the most urbanized sectors of the city. Apparel and deportment were intended to symbolize breeding and wealth, refinement and dignity. The women lived a rather secluded life, but the men spent much time together. *Tertulia* was the term designating these informal gatherings in private homes, in the streets or, toward the end of the eighteenth century, in cafes. To some extent at least, the tertulias reflected the intellectual interests of the participants.

There was a rather strong emphasis on the strictly nonutilitarian aspects of the culture. Literature, fine arts, oratory, music, and the theater had many highly educated devotees, at least in the larger cities. In spite of the censorship of the Holy Inquisition, forbidden books entered and were widely read and discussed in the major colonial cities of the eighteenth century. The pageantry of religious and civil ceremonies provided another extremely elaborate component of nonutilitarian urban culture. Religious processions, particularly those associated with Holy Week and with the fiestas in honor of the patron saints of the various churches and parishes, strongly appealed to everyone, regardless of class. Religious pageantry, leisurely sociability, ostentatious display of wealth, and cultivation of esthetic and intellectual values, taken together, constituted the cultural focus of the colonial city. In economic terms, all this means consumption rather than production. And the wealth consumed was produced in mining and agriculture by a labor force of serfs and slaves, tenant farmers, and heavily taxed small holders. Obviously, in an urban culture of this type the ruling class must identify its interests with those of the city, thus permitting a large proportion of available resources to be channeled into the city and used for conspicuous consumption in the widest possible sense.

Fundamental to Latin American urbanism is the fact that the inflow of resources controlled by the city always stood in the sharpest possible contrast to the meager outflow of resources, in the form of services and facilities, provided to the politically and economically dependent countryside. The pattern emerged in colonial times and clearly reflected the social structure. To this day the Latin American city is accused of social parasitism, of waxing fat and being useless at the expense of the rural areas.

The peasantry

Are there peasants in Latin America?

Somehow the term "peasant" does not seem to describe the rural population of Latin America. Emphasis on the large agricultural estate, the wealth and power of the owners pointing up the poverty and impotence of the labor force, seems to have led us to discard the possibility of encountering agriculturalists who are neither feudal barons nor wretched fieldhands.

Since the days of the conquest there has been a class of people in Latin America who worked the soil with their own hands and were neither dependent laborers nor members of the rural aristocracy. With the assistance of their families and perhaps a few slaves or serfs, they worked a tract of land that was not necessarily smaller than many of the aristocratic holdings. (Candido, 1964:59) However, the forms of agricultural exploitation differed from those used in operating the hacienda or fazenda. Whereas marked preponderance of commercial crops and relatively heavy investment in slave labor characterized the hacienda, emphasis in this other class usually was on subsistence crops and self-sufficiency. In accordance with anthropological usage we propose to call those people *peasants*, adding immediately that peasant self-sufficiency was never absolute. However isolated and self-reliant, peasants never cease to be members of a wider society. Peasants of colonial Latin America were obliged to pay tributes or taxes, and consequently they had to produce a surplus that could be sold in local markets. And there were always a few goods that they simply could not produce themselves. Furthermore, religious services were available normally only in the parish seat, and if a peasant landholder became involved in litigation, he had to turn to legal authority located in a distant town.

The degree to which the Latin American peasantry felt bound to the wider society was subject to extraordinary variations in time and space. The extremes were represented by isolated village communities intermittently visited by traveling merchants or perhaps itinerant priests, and by such people as the *lavradores* or copyholders of Bahia, who cultivated canefields and sold their sugar production in the market. (Boxer, 1969:150)

It would be hazardous and somewhat arbitrary to associate the peasantry with specific forms of land tenure as defined by modern law. What mattered was the *actual* control over a tract of land, whether the man was a renter, a legitimate owner, or a squatter.

The peasant worked the land himself with the help of familiars and perhaps a couple of slaves, and this circumstance determined his way of life. He was definitely tied to the land by his work. His position in the money economy was marginal at best; he had neither the leisure nor the means to take part in the culture of the distant city. He was typically nonliterate and ignorant of most events that did not immediately concern his little world. He was allowed to enjoy a great deal of economic independence as long as his interests did not conflict with those of the landholding seigneurial class. However, there have always been large areas unsuitable for livestock raising and the kind of commercial crop that would induce powerful men to invade and appropriate land held by peasants who either had no legal title to their holdings or did not know how to defend themselves against usurpation. Often, remoteness and isolation were effective defenses against encroachment, or crops of great economic potential simply had not yet appeared within the cultural horizon of a particular region. This was the case of the capitania of São Paulo prior to the introduction of coffee. Except for a few limited areas in which sugar cane could be cultivated, this region was left to a widely dispersed rather primitive peasantry, engaged in subsistence agriculture.

Yet the introduction and dissemination of profitable cash crops did not always eradicate the peasantry. An analysis of 10 local censuses carried out between 1822 and 1824 in the province of São Paulo, produced no evidence that commercial crops (sugar, coffee) had forced out the peasantry. On the contrary, in all 10 localities the recorded proportion of agriculturists who neither were slaves nor owned them was surprisingly high. In 4 localities with either sugar cane or coffee looming large in the local economy, the percentage of such cultivators varied between 41.7 and 59.1 of all householders. The only significantly lower percentage of 31.0 was found in Itú, where large cane fazendas with numerous slaves were more frequent than in any other locality. Unfortunately, the censuses do not provide information about land tenure or size of holdings; but data on cash income available for Areias and Taubaté indicate considerable economic differentiation. In fact, in coffee-producing Areias about 32.9 percent of the peasants were fairly well off, and another 32.1 percent earned a cash income at least equal to that of a skilled artisan.

Among the slave-owning agriculturalists, those who had from one to three slaves constituted the majority in all but one locality. Probably in most cases, then, the slaves merely assisted the owners in the performance of agricultural tasks, and slave ownership on such a limited basis was not incompatible with peasant status. (Willems, 1970a:34–37)

Prior to the introduction of coffee in Brazil, the liberal concession of land grants did not always lead to the formation of large rural estates. Scarcity of labor and a very limited demand for agricultural commodities, mainly corn and manioc, prevented production from rising much above the subsistence level. Few people could afford to purchase slaves, and most holdings were operated by the family and perhaps a few agregados. Most grants remained unexploited and became, as one author puts it, a "dead weight in the economic structure of the capitania" (São Paulo). (Herrmann, 1948:21) The diffusion of sugar cane cultivation near the end of the eighteenth century did little to alter the predominance of the smaller holdings. For example, in 1779 in the district of Guaratinguetá (Paraiba Valley) there were 454 proprietors of small holdings and only 19 owners of larger estates. (Herrmann, 1948:22) In 1818, when sugar cane agriculture had reached its peak, there was only one "latifundista," but there were 10 proprietors of medium-sized holdings, 359 small holders, and 136 renters. (Herrmann, 1948:70)

When coffee succeeded sugar cane in the Paraiba Valley, almost revolutionary changes occurred in the size distribution of agricultural holdings, but the peasantry did not disappear in the process. In 1890 the municipio of Vassouras, for example, had 80 proprietors owning holdings of less than 300 acres and 20 planters whose fazendas measured more than 300 acres. (Stein, 1961:269) True enough, the peasant holders controlled only 30 percent of the land; the point, however, is not that the peasants were well off but that they successfully resisted the expansionism of the seigneurial estate owners. This applies not only to the few regions mentioned here but to the entire state of São Paulo, to Minas Gerais, and to large sections of the three southernmost states of Brazil. During the eighteenth century, Portugal encouraged emigration from the Azores to southern Brazil, and several thousand families from these islands were granted small holdings along the coast of Rio Grande do Sul, Santa Catarina, Paraná and São Paulo. Up to the present day, small holdings have remained predominant in those regions.

In Colombia, the concentration of land ownership in the hands of a few, which is supposed to follow inexorably the introduction of profitable cash crops, never materialized, at least not so far as coffee is concerned. The city of Pereira, founded in 1863, was to become the major urban center of a coffee-producing area. Settlers from Antioquia were granted 12,000 hectares of land to be divided into holdings not smaller than 32 and not larger than 100 hectares. (Jaramillo Uribe, 1963b:365). In 1913 there were 3,630,000 coffee trees in the area, and almost all fincas had between 5,000 and 10,000 trees. Very few had 50,000, and only two had more than 100,000 (Jaramillo Uribe, 1963b:389) The average finca measured 4.4 hectares and was divided, in accordance with the model of the typical peasant holding, into coffee groves, pastures, and subsistence plots. (Jaramillo Uribe, 1963b:391) In 1955–1956, we should add, 99.8 percent of all Colombian coffee fincas measured between 1 and 50 hectares, covering 81.5 percent of the coffee-producing area of the country. (United Nations, 1958:27)

As in Colombia, the coffee planters of El Salvador are typically small holders: 97.9 percent own or operate fincas measuring up to 50 hectares; but in contrast to Colombia the property constitutes no more than 57.1 percent of the total area planted in coffee. (United Nations, 1958:109)

The Latin American peasant *par excellence* is the sedentary Indian of Mesoamerica and the Andes. Here agricultural traditions have been traced to pre-Columbian societies having an urban civilization, market systems, and peasants producing food to sustain royal courts, nobles, bureaucrats, priests, soldiers, and craftsmen. Numerous plant species had been domesticated in the Andes and in Mesoamerica. More than 40 species of food plants were cultivated in the Andean regions; terracing, irrigation, and the use of fertilizers secured a level of agricultural production not to be surpassed by anything the conqueror had to offer. The Spaniards added cattle, pigs, fowl, draft animals, the wooden plow, the wheeled cart, and some food plants to the indigenous technology. The beneficial effects of these additions were offset, however, by the destruction of numerous Indian communities by the Spaniards, who needed labor for their mines and industries, as well as grazing land for their cattle. Since the Spaniards were primarily a pastoral people, the burden of agricultural production continued to rest on the Indian peasant, whose capacity to adapt and to survive under adverse conditions borders on the miraculous.

Various are the origins of the Indian peasant communities that developed in colonial Spanish America. To facilitate conversion and "to assimilate Indian groups and villages to Spanish municipalities by emphasizing community institutions, in which the two countries [Mexico and Spain] seemed to share a common tradition, . . . hundreds of Indian villages were thus established or rebuilt. We can still see them today all along Mexico's roads, even though a large number have had to be restored many times over." (Chevalier 1963:191–192) Seizure of Indian lands and attempts to reduce their owners to peonage were often successfully resisted in Mexico.

> Land fights and spoliations in some regions (on which we are naturally better documented) should not conceal from us the relative tranquility of other regions, where protective measures were efficacious and native villages often remained in possession of more land than they could work. At the capital's gates, there were communities still owning good land in the mid-nineteenth century—a proof of the old system's validity. (Chevalier, 1963:219)

In Colombia, the abolition of the encomienda was followed by the establishment of *resguardos* or villages to protect the Indians. Particularly in the province of Nariño, numerous present-day peasant communities were originated by resguardos. (T. L. Smith, 1967:261)

In 1935 Poblete estimated at 3000 the number of Quechua Indian communes in Peru, the total population being 1.5 million (Poblete, 1938: 54–55, 60) Some of these communities seem to have had pre-Spanish origins, some grew out of colonial reductions, and others were formed during the nineteenth century as a measure of self-protection against encroachment on Indian lands. (Mishkin, 1946:441)

The Indian component in Latin American peasant culture

Numerous monographic studies of peasant communities in Mexico, Central America, the Andean countries, and Brazil contain detailed descriptions of cultural elements that can be traced to aboriginal societies. These elements comprise agricultural crops and techniques, tools and building materials, house forms, ways of preserving food, working habits, methods of community organization, religious beliefs and practices, crafts and arts, medicine, and mythology. Two distinct patterns are clearly noticeable in the process of joining indigenous and Iberian elements in a viable unit. In Mesoamerica and the Andean countries, where the indigenous communities were able to survive the impact of Spanish civilization without losing their basic cultural identity, selected Iberian elements were added to the autochtonous culture. In other parts of the continent, where the Indians lived in small, primitive nomadic or seminomadic bands, their lifestyle disappeared under the impact of European contact, although selected elements of the original cultures were incorporated by mestizo communities, whose way of life was basically Iberian. Much of the difference between the two areas lies in sheer numbers. If we accept the very conservative population estimates by Rosenblat, there were 4.5 million Indians in Mexico by 1492. [According to others, Indians numbered 25.2 million in Central Mexico alone. (Mörner, 1967: 31)] In what is now Colombia, Ecuador, Peru, and Bolivia there lived at least 4,150,000 Indians, but probably more. (Rosenblat, 1954:102) These native societies were not only large and dense in relation to the territories they inhabited, they were thoroughly adapted to economic exploitation by a ruling class. In contrast, approximately a million Indians inhabited Brazil by 1492, living widely dispersed in relatively small settlements untouched by exploitative economic systems. Everywhere depopulation of catastrophic proportions followed the conquest, but whereas the indigenous societies of Mexico and the Andes decreased to a fraction of their original size, except for some groups living in regions of difficult access, the tribal societies of the tropical forests and the Plata area were simply wiped out under the combined onslaught of warfare, captivity, epidemic diseases, and miscegenation. Yet much of their culture survived through miscegenation and became part of the emerging mestizo culture as it is found in the Amazon Basin, in many parts of Colombia, Paraguay, and northern Argentina, and in certain regions of Central America and southern Brazil.

Most Andean and Mesoamerican Indians lived in *corporate* communities, and the very structure of the corporate community acted as a screen or protective shield against outside influences. The relevance of the corporate community may be gauged by pointing out that if it had not had a continuing existence over three centuries, the cultural identity of the different Indian societies would have been lost. But it should also be recognized that without the corporate community, there would be no "Indian problem" *as we know it today* in Mexico, Guatemala, Ecuador, Peru, and Bolivia. The structure of the corporate community enabled the Indians successfully to insulate themselves in a world of their own. Thus defensive rejection of Creole culture later became a barrier against modernization and incorporation of Indian communities into the national society.

> The distinctive characteristic of the corporate peasant community is that it represents a bounded social system with clear-cut limits, in relation to both outsiders and insiders. It has structural identity over time. Seen from the outside, the community as a whole carries on a series of activities and upholds certain 'collective representation.' Seen from within, it defines the rights and duties of its members and prescribes large segments of their behavior. (Wolf, 1955:456)

Thus, at any time the members of such a community were prepared to reward desirable behavior and to penalize violations of the established code. The community would support the recognized rights and enforce the fulfillment of established duties of its individual members. To preserve the structure of such a tightly knit unit over three centuries, restrictions on individual behavior must have been held in constant equilibrium with the advantages accruing from membership. By refraining from mobilizing wealth within the community for capitalistic ends, the corporate community prevented its own disintegration, yet a heavy burden was imposed on its members who had to work hard and to endure poverty. On the other hand, the corporate community offered a measure of economic security that was not easily had in the outside world, where the Indian almost inevitably would fall prey to slavery or serfdom. Furthermore, within the corporate community the individual was encouraged to achieve what he had learned to be the most desirable objective of life. Most communities have always had a civil-religious hierarchy of offices that were open to the male members of the village and through which one might achieve prestige and power. The number, the designation, and the degree of functional specialization of these offices varied, but the actual government of the community was entrusted to some of the office holders, while others assumed responsibilities related to the church and the celebration of religious fiestas honoring the saints. Sponsorship of the fiestas often laid a heavy financial burden on the office holder, and only the wealthiest were chosen for the highest offices. Even these officials often assumed debts that might take several years to repay. Thus the celebration of the religious fiestas acts as a leveling mechanism, impeding permanent economic differentiation within the community. (Cancian, 1967:288–289) At the same time, the fiestas bring the people together, thus maintaining cohesion through the performance of communal ceremonies.

The civil-religious hierarchy provided, as it still does, a link between the village and the colonial or republican government. In fact, the Spanish crown fostered the corporate community mainly because its tight structure around the local hierarchy made it possible to exert its economic, social, and religious controls indirectly, and, more specifically, to exact labor services and taxes. (Wolf, 1955:457)

Linkage to the regional market center was always part of the economic structure of the corporate community, but its location on marginal land of little productive potential, as well as adherence to a traditional technology, limited the quantity of cash crops that could be produced for the market. Having little to sell, the community could not afford to buy more than a few commodities. The extraordinary stability of the corporate Indian community should not be interpreted as immutability; rather, it is the end result of lengthy reorganization that began in pre-Columbian times and was completed under Spanish rule. (Wolf, 1955:456) For example, the role of kinship in the community structure lost much of its former importance, and collective ownership of land gave way to individual ownership. The introduction of Spanish cultural elements was more often than not an addition to, rather than substitution for, indigenous elements. Religious conversion was imposed, and temples, idols, priesthoods, human sacrifices, and organized cult forms had to be given up, but numerous pre-Spanish beliefs and practices have been preserved. Adoption of Spanish costume was compulsory, but the indigenous poncho survived in one form or another. (Foster, 1960:101)

In other sectors of the culture, where change was spontaneous, Iberian traits were added by juxtaposition or amalgamation. The Spanish plow was used beside the Andean foot plow, mules and oxen were kept as well as the llama, and European food plants were added to the native ones; but Indian and Spanish arts and crafts merged to the point of constituting a "real amalgam." (Foster, 1960:101) Within the confines of the corporate community, these hybrid cultural contents acquired extraordinary stability.

Outside Mesoamerica and the Andes, the peasant community differs in origin, ethnic composition, and structure. To use Wolf's term, it is "open" rather than corporate. Its structure is open in that it interposes no barriers between the individual members and the outside world. Adherence to tradition derives from geographical isolation and lack of opportunity, rather than from self-imposed insulation and rejection of the outside world. Perhaps the most expressive symbol of self-imposed insulation is the Indian language, which the corporate community frequently succeeded in preserving. Yet no such symbolic expression of insulation exist in the open peasant community except in Paraguay, where Guaraní became the idiom of the peasantry. Portuguese or Spanish is spoken, everywhere else, indicating a greater cultural permeability.

The open peasant community is structurally unrelated to any pre-Columbian form of social life. It was founded by stragglers of the conquest, by deserters, adventurers, runaway slaves and fugitives from justice, by people trying to avoid tax collectors and military recruiters, by the many poor settlers from Portugal and Spain who tried to make a living in the vast reaches of the hinterland the Brazilians call the sertão. Rejected by the social order of colonial Latin America, the poor Iberian settlers as well as the countless mestizoes and mulattoes probably constituted the bulk of those who established open agricultural communities in tropical and subtropical rainforests, in the humid lower highlands, and in the semiarid regions of Brazil and northern Argentina. They raised cattle in the llanos of Venezuela and Colombia, in the pampas of Argentina, Uruguay, and Rio Grande do Sul, in São Francisco region and in the interior of northeastern Brazil. Left to their own devices, these settlers had to draw on whatever resources were available. In contact with many different indigenous groups experiencing hispanization, the culture of these settlers became "indianized," and the process proved highly adaptive. Along with native crops, such as maize, beans, squash, sweet potatoes, and manioc, the settlers took over the slash-and-burn agriculture of the Indians. During the dry season they cut down the jungle growth with axes, machetes, and billhooks (foice). As soon as the felled trees and underbrush were sufficiently dry, they set fire to the lot and with the help of a digging stick or hoe, proceeded to plant maize, beans, or manioc among the carbonized trunks. Such a garden plot would produce for a few years, depending on the quality of the soil. When production declined and weeding became too burdensome, the field was abandoned and the procedure of clearing and planting was repeated somewhere else. Where jungle land was plentiful, the settlers often adopted the seminomadism of the Indians. Where land was relatively scarce, the old garden plots were allowed to lie fallow for a number of years, to be utilized again when the soil had recovered its fertility. The adaptive value of such extensive agriculture appears to be related to the economic system within which it is practiced. Where markets are distant and small, transportation difficult and costly, and prices for agricultural produce low, capital investment has to be kept to a minimum. And slash-and-burn agriculture requires only the few tools used in the process and mules or carts to take the produce to the market. The rest is labor.

A paradigm of culture transfer from indigenous societies to the mestizo peasantry may be seen in the manioc complex. Not only was and is manioc one of the most widely diffused food plants in Latin America, its technological ramifications justify the term "culture complex," meaning a number of skills, techniques, utensils, tools, attitudes, and habits associated with a focal trait—namely, the manioc plant. Furthermore, there is uninterrupted continuity between the aboriginal ways in which the plant was cultivated, processed, and consumed; the transfer of these ways to the peasantry; and the present industrial complex that developed from the primitive techniques.

The manioc story

Returning from a perilous captivity among the Tupinambá Indians of Southern Brazil, Hans Staden, a mercenary soldier from Germany, published in 1557 one of the first and most reliable ethnographic accounts on South America. One passage of his book refers to the cultivation and preparation of manioc, a tropical root plant that was found to be of the utmost importance to numerous Indian tribes.

> In the places where they intend to plant, they cut down the trees and leave them to dry for one or three months and then set fire to them and burn them. Afterwards they plant the roots between the trunks, from which the roots take sustenance. This root is called mandioca and is a small tree about a fathom high, giving out three

kinds of roots. When they desire to eat the roots, they pull up the tree and break off the roots; then they take a branch from the tree and re-plant it. This in due time throws roots, and in six months it is big enough to be used for food.

They use the roots in three ways. First they rub them against a stone (board set with stone chips) and reduce them to small crumbs, after which they press out the juice with a thing made of palm branches, called Tippiti. When the crumbs are dry they pass them through a sieve and make them into thin cakes. The utensil in which they dry the meal and bake it is made of burnt clay, shaped like a large dish.

They also take the fresh roots and soak them in water until they are rotten, after which they place them over the fire and smoke them until they are dry. This dried root they call Keinrima, and they prepare it for a long time. When they want to use it they pound it in a mortar made of wood, so that it becomes white meal, and from it they make cakes called Byyw.

Again, they take the rotten mandioca before it is dried and mix it with the dry and the green roots. From this they make a dry meal which can be kept for a year or eaten at once. This meal they call Vy-Than.

The women prepare the drinks. They take the mandioca root and boil it in great pots. Afterwards they pour it into other vessels and allow it to cool a little. Then young girls sit around and chew the boiled root in their mouths, and what is chewed they set apart in a special vessel. When the boiled root is all chewed, they place it back again in the pot which they fill with water, mixing the water with the chewed root, after which they heat it again.

They have special pots, half buried in the ground, which they make use of much as we use casks for wine or beer. They pour the liquid into these and close them, and the liquor ferments of itself and becomes strong. After two days they drink it until they are drunk. It is thick, but pleasant to the taste. (Staden, 1929:137–142)

There are two kinds of plant of the genus *Manihot*—"bitter" manioc whose cultivation and preparation were described by Staden, and "sweet" manioc. The main difference lies in the content of prussic acid found in the "bitter" varieties. Hydrocyanic acid is a deadly poison that must be extracted before the manioc root is fit for human consumption. The extractive process must be considered to be a major invention of the South American natives by which they gained control over one of the most easily grown and productive food plants of the tropics. There are only speculations regarding where and when this invention occurred and how it spread. When Nordenskiöld delimited the area of diffusion in 1924, however, manioc was found from northern Argentina up to almost all parts of South America, Central America, and the West Indies, where climatic conditions permitted its cultivation. Sweet manioc was the only variety cultivated in the western part of South America. In the midwestern and eastern portions of the continent, both varieties were known. The occurrence of bitter manioc alone was limited to a few areas, mostly in the northern parts of the continent. (Nordenskiöld, 1924:36)

The wider distribution of the sweet variety, the *aipi* of the Tupí Indians, is attributed by Sauer to the resistance of some species to protracted droughts, and perhaps to lack of receptiveness which might have prevented bitter manioc from diffusing to western South America. (Sauer, 1950:508) But wherever the two varieties are found together, bitter manioc is held to be superior to aipi, mainly because the bitter varieties yield a bread, whereas aipi is only boiled or roasted, then consumed like most edible tubers.

Manioc may be planted at almost any time during the year, yet both the dryness of winter and the excessive humidity during the rainy season are believed to be disadvantageous. Most of the planting is done in late September or October. The growing cycle of manioc varies considerably with the quality of the soil and climatic conditions. The six months referred to by Staden are to be considered to be the shortest possible period. A year and more appears to be quite common in many parts of South America. However, since tubers can be left in the ground until they are needed, it is somewhat difficult to determine variations of their growing cycle. The ground most efficiently provides natural storage, but the roots may keep growing, although this seldom adds to the food value of the end product. Also, the size of plant and tubers varies enormously. Sometimes the plants reach the size of trees, the roots being equivalent to human limbs in length and thickness. But frequently a person, standing upright, can easily be seen in a manioc field, and each tuber is about the size of a large carrot.

The natives know two techniques of reducing the peeled tubers to small crumbs. There is trituration, requiring the use of stones or a mortar, or grating, which is done with a cleverly engineered contrivance, the most primitive example of which appeared to be merely a piece of bark covered with thorns and taken by the Iruma Indians from a certain palm tree. (Metraux, 1928:103) This implement probably preceded the graters such as those described by Staden that were made of a board set with stone chips, thorns, animal teeth, bones, or points of Buriti or Brejauva wood. The Manaves tribe of the upper Amazon was known to specialize in the manufacture of manioc graters that were sold to the Aiznares, the Ibanomas, and the Yurimaguas. (Metraux, 1928:103)

Grated bitter manioc is a white, starchy mush, full of hydrocyanic acid. Some Indians extract the poison simply by squeezing the mush with their hands and forming balls, which are left to dry in the sun. A more effective technique, known by hundreds of tribes all over tropical South America is associated with the so-called *tipiti*, the basket press reported by Staden and subsequently by almost every observer of Indian culture. Most Indian tribes use a plaited, basketlike cylinder, up to 10 feet long and about 6 inches wide at the opening. There is a loop at both ends of the cylinder.

> One is attached to a rafter, and the other to a stout stick, on which a woman sits, and thereby pulls upon the cylinder. The manioc is inserted through the open end before the weight is applied, and the elastic structure widens out to permit the soaked and grated roots to be packed in, till it resembles nothing so much as a well-filled Christmas stocking; but when pressure is brought to bear on the lower end the cylinder gradually elongates, and thereby contracts, crushing the roots to a pulp, from which the poisonous juice drains away. (Whiffen, 1915:98)

Ridded of its poisonous content, the manioc pulp is finally dried or slightly roasted on a hot clay plate or in a clay pot.

Manioc may be consumed in many ways. The meal is eaten together with almost every imaginable kind of liquid or solid food. The "cakes called Byyw" mentioned by Hans Staden, resemble tortillas, and some of the many kinds were recorded by observers. Writing in the middle of the nineteenth century, von Martius reported five varieties of "beiju," as the manioc cakes are currently called.(von Martius, 1867:492–493)

The poisonous juice extracted from freshly grated manioc tubers serves various purposes. Above all, it contains a sediment of starch that is dried and preserved in pots. When the sediment is heated over a moderate fire, *typyoca* or *tapioca*, a granulated starch, is obtained. Mixed with common manioc meal, tapioca yields a special cake, the *beijuteyca*.

Manipuera, the poisonous juice of bitter manioc, has a use of its own. After fermentation has taken place, the substance is boiled with pepper and salt and used as a condiment. The boiling process frees it completely of hydrocyanic acid, but the broth conserves the bitterness. Manipuera is the basic ingredient of the pepper pot used by the Indians of the Amazon and the Guianas to prepare and preserve food. "Meat and vegetables are

usually boiled together in the 'pepperpot,' which is kept constantly sim-
mering over the fire and seasoned with peppers and the expressed juice
of the bitter manioc." (Gillin, 1948:829)

Like so many food plants of tropical South America, manioc was
almost immediately accepted by the Portuguese and Spaniards. The rapid
formation of a population of mixed Indian-European ancestry apparently
facilitated the adoption of a crop that was rather at variance with European
agricultural techniques and food habits. According to early chroniclers, only
one familiar element in the native manioc complex impressed the Iberian
settlers of the sixteenth century—namely, that a "white flour," similar
to rough wheat flour, could be obtained from manioc and could be converted into "bread" or "cakes."

The "cassavie meals" (manioc) of which Knivet found large stores in
Santos toward the end of the sixteenth century, appeared to be a satisfactory substitute for European grain, which could not be adapted to
the tropics. And the native ways of utilizing manioc could hardly be
improved, except in their mechanical aspects. Thus the manioc complex
was taken over by the peasant population almost without major changes.
The slash-and-burn agriculture of the Indians was somewhat improved
by the European hoe, but the dibble has never been entirely supplanted.
The planting techniques closely followed Indian models, and the Indian
way of planting the manioc cuttings in little mounds was observed as late
as 1947 among the peasants of Buzios Island in southern Brazil. (Willems,
1952a:31) Manioc is still grated and the prussic acid extracted by means
of a basket press. Only the hand grater has been largely replaced by a mechanical device consisting of a large wheel whose broad rim is covered with
a metal grater. One person turns the crank and another presses the peeled
tubers against the rim.

An illustration in Willem Piso's *Historia naturalis Brasiliae*, published
in 1648, shows a complete manioc mill with a wheeled grater, a screw-press,
and a large oven, the *casa-de-farinha*, still found in most parts of rural
Brazil. The screw-press did not supplant the Indian *tipiti*, it only modified its shape. Instead of a tubelike contrivance, the flattening pressure
of the large wooden screw required a strong circular basket still called
a tipiti, regardless of its altered shape. But even today, hand graters are
still in use, and the screw-press is too expensive to displace all the more
primitive techniques of extracting the hydrocyanic acid. The costliest item
of the apparatus is now the large copper container in which the manioc
is dried or roasted over an open fire.

The peasants of the South American tropics make their various kinds of manioc meal, their beijus, and their cakes exactly as the Indians do. Pickles reports:

> The *farinha* entirely replaces bread in most parts of the Amazon country and is often the only food consumed by entire families for weeks on end. Boatmen and other workmen engaged in extremely hard work for long periods are quite satisfied so long as their supply of farinha is assured and the only supplies carried for long trips into the interior consist of farinha and a little dried salt beef or salt fish.
>
> As an emergency food, farinha has many advantages; it is a concentrated foodstuff, sustaining and at the same time quickly satisfying the feeling of hunger. Above all, it can be stored for long periods without being attacked by insects. (Pickles, 1942:147)

The fact that certain varieties of manioc meal and beiju could be easily preserved for many months probably contributed to the prompt adoption of the plant by the Europeans. It would indeed be difficult to explain the astonishing spatial mobility of the Portuguese in Brazil, their warlike expeditions into the unexplored hinterland, and their long-lasting wars against the French, the Dutch, and numerous Indian tribes, without the *farinha-de-guerra*—the "war meal" of the natives.

The preparation of tapioca and the many uses of the cassava juice were also taken over by the Europeans. Tapioca cake (*beiju teyca*) "when still soft, is a most delicious confection and may be eaten rolled with butter, syrup or fruit preserve." (Pickles, 1942:148) Manioc juice is widely used as a condiment in the Amazon area.

> The diluted cassava [i.e., manioc] juice from which the starch has been removed has a use of its own. The liquid is usually boiled down and skimmed repeatedly until it ceases to froth, [is] seasoned with peppers, garlic and other flavours and is used as a sauce for flavoring meat and fish. This product is known as *tucupy* and is a perfectly innocuous condiment, since all the poisonous material has been driven off or destroyed by boiling. Tucupy is sometimes concentrated by boiling gently until it attains a syrupy consistency and is then known as *cabiou*. *Tucupy de sol* is made by putting the seasoned cassava juice in a lightly corked bottle exposed in the sun for several days; during the slow evaporation which occurs, the prussic acid is eliminated. *Arube* is a powdered condiment used in the same way as mustard; it is prepared by steeping the tubers in a little water for several days, peeling them, crushing, heating with boiling water and then drying the mass after seasoning with garlic, pepper, etc. (Pickles, 1942:148)

Essentially Indian, these practices are not known in all areas of South America, where nevertheless manioc meal constitutes a major food item.

The diffusion of the manioc complex is somewhat irregular and apparently is related to the intensity of Indian influence on Iberian culture. It covers an area *at least* equal to the area covered at the time of the conquest, but the importance of manioc as a food item varies enormously. Nowhere is it greater than in the Amazon Basin, regardless of political boundaries. And outside the Amazon area it represents daily bread to millions.

In Brazil manioc has held its ground in the process of urbanization and industrialization. Manioc meal and the tubers of aipi, the sweet variety, are consumed by peasants and urbanites alike. Even in the largest metropolitan areas, inhabited by many people of recent European extraction, the consumption of manioc continues undiminished. *Farofa*, roasted manioc meal mixed with eggs and olives, is a standard addition to numerous dishes and is much appreciated by people of all social classes.

Finally, the processing of manioc has been highly industrialized, and the native implements—grater, press, and oven—have been converted into modern machinery designed for mass production. Large acreages of bitter manioc are being cultivated solely for industrial purposes, and much is exported to the United States and Europe. "The tapioca flour is used in the United States in the textile and paper industries, for making glue, laundry starch, explosives, and other miscellaneous products, in addition to being made into tapioca, which is sold on the grocery shelves for human consumption." (Stovall, 1947:155)

Among the indigenous food plants, only maize surpasses manioc in relative importance and area of diffusion. It is closely associated with the Indian peasantry from Mexico south to Chile, but it is widely cultivated in almost every part of the continent.

The extent of cultural hybridization
of the open peasant community

In many regions of Latin America the poor Iberian or mestizo peasant became a squatter on land for which there was little or no demand. He remained relatively isolated from the sources of European civilization, and his purchasing power in local markets was so low that borrowing from indigenous cultures became a matter of survival. Most of these transfers occurred during the sixteenth and early seventeenth centuries, and once crystallization had taken place, indigenous elements were perpetuated even where Indian societies had ceased to exist as culturally distinct entities.

The mestizo peasant learned from the Indian how to utilize a large variety of raw materials of his immediate natural environment for the construction of houses, shelters, storage bins, canoes, containers, hammocks, mats, pots, stools, and other implements and utensils. No attempt has ever been made to inventory all the different forms of peasant dwelling and the associated construction techniques. Often they appear to be combinations of Iberian and Indian elements, but the materials are invariably of local origin. Unhewn timber is universally used to support a thatched roof. The walls are wattled sticks that may or may not be covered with mud on both sides. Wattle-and-daub buildings are found in rural Mexico, in Central America, and in Columbia, Brazil, Paraguay, and northern Argentina. In tropical forest areas, palm leaves are often used together with wattle to build the walls. Various grasses, palm leaves, or maize straw provide thatching materials for the roof. Wooden posts and beams are bound together with twisted vine, which abounds in tropical rain forests. Wattle-and-daub techniques alternate with adobe or sundried bricks as building material, depending on the availability of suitable clay and local traditions.

Significantly, in their most primitive versions, such dwellings do not require a single piece of hardware or any item that must be purchased. After the necessary building materials have been extracted from local woods or clay pits, it takes only a few days' cooperative work of a group of neighbors to erect a house. Stove and oven are often made of mud or adobe, usually on a wooden platform. People sleep in self-made hammocks, on wooden platforms, or on straw mats. There are scarcely more than a few homemade pieces of furniture, perhaps a couple of stools, a shelf or two, and a small table roughly put together and seldom used.

A local potter traditionally provides earthenware for cooking and storage. More often than not, potters use indigenous techniques rather than the wheel to manufacture their wares. Almost everywhere basketry is well developed, and a variety of raw materials and techniques reveal a wealth of indigenous influences. Wooden containers, ladles, and spoons are common enough where suitable raw materials are available. Spinning and weaving techniques represent an amalgam of Iberian and Indian traits, but European ideas seem to be predominant in most areas.

Wherever feasible, agriculture is supplemented by hunting, trapping, gathering of forest products, and fishing. The Indian dugout is by far the most common type of boat east of the Andes. It comes in all sizes and is used both for fishing and transportation. From the Indian the mestizo peasant learned the use of vegetable poison (mostly *timbó*), to catch fish, but most fishing is done with nets, weirs, and traps. Weirs and traps are usually indigenous, whereas nets are almost invariably of Iberian origin; all types that Foster encountered in Spanish America occur in Brazil, too. (Foster, 1960:77ff.)

The large wooden mortar and pestle (*pilón, mano de pilón* in Spanish, *pilão, mão de pilão* in Portuguese) are so widely used to grind corn and other grains or coarsely grated dry manioc that they can be regarded as universal in Latin American peasant culture. Not so, however, the *monjolo*, a primitive grist mill transferred by the Portuguese from their East Asian colonies to Portugal and Brazil. (Schmidt, 1967:41ff.) The present-day monjolo is virtually undistinguishable from the one that John Mawe described in the early nineteenth century.

> Near a current of water a large wooden mortar is placed, the pestle of which is mortised into the end of a level beam twenty-five or thirty feet long, resting upon a fulcrum, at five-eighths of its length. The extremity of the shorter arm of this beam is scooped out, so as to receive a sufficient weight of water to raise the other end, to which appends the pestle, and to discharge itself when it has sunk to a given point. The alternate emptying and filling of this cavity cause the elevation and fall of the pestle, which take place about four times per minute. (Mawe, 1816:142)

The monjolo spread all over southern and portions of central Brazil, probably during the latter part of the eighteenth century, but it seems to be rare in the north, and there is no evidence that it has ever been found in Spanish America.

The only wheeled vehicle associated with the Latin American peasantry is the two-wheeled ox cart, the *carro chirrión* or *chillón* of the Spaniards and the *carro de boi* of the Portuguese. Its structural resemblance to the Roman *plaustrum* leaves little doubt about its origin. (Souza, 1958:68) Ubiquitous all over Latin America, the Iberian ox cart requires no parts or appurtenances that could not be produced by the peasant wheelwright himself. Not a single piece of metal is needed, and the wheels are solid disks, fastened to the wooden axle such that wheels and axles turn together in a wooden slot at the bottom of the cart. The friction of un-lubricated wood against wood "produces a continuous squealing which is balm to the ears of the drivers and solace—say country people—to the draft cows." (Foster, 1960:106)

In many regions the ox cart has been displaced by modern conveyances, but in 1943 there were still about 200,000 ox carts in Brazil. (Souza, 1958:138)

This is by no means a full inventory of peasant technology. Various types of primitive mills, husking devices, sieves, and sugar presses, mostly survivals of traditional Iberian transfers, can be added to the preceding listing. Moreover, it is worth repeating that none of the items described or mentioned requires skills or raw materials alien to the immediate environment of the peasant. Only insofar as the peasant depends on the outside for a few simple tools and firearms, does his technology imply linkage to a market economy. Again, such ties do not necessarily mean participation in a money economy. During the colonial period, money circulated in a notoriously limited quantity and over a relatively small range. Peasant economy was barter economy almost by implication, and barter remained the prevailing form of exchange throughout the nineteenth century.

Quite often situations arise that call for mobilization of labor beyond day-by-day availabilities. In most peasant societies of the world, mutual aid has been the response to such demands. Among the Latin American peasantry, the three ethnic components—Indians, Iberians, and Africans—apparently contributed to the implantation of reciprocal labor institutions. A man in need of help may request a number of neighbors (who may be relatives or not) to carry out a certain type of work on a particular day. Most work done by groups is agricultural, of course, but it may be the construction of a house, the cutting of timber, repair work on bridges or roads, fishing, and perhaps other jobs that exceed the capability of a single family. The host of the working party offers food and drink or/and his own help when requested by someone else to whom he owes repayment. (Erasmus, 1956) Institutionalized forms of reciprocal labor have been studied in Haiti, Mexico, Guatemala, Colombia, Ecuador, Peru, Bolivia, Chile, Paraguay, and Brazil; but they probably existed or still exist everywhere regardless of the region's prevailing ethnic composition. Words designating collective labor organization suggest different origins. *Combite* is the term used in Haiti, in Panama it is *junta*, and in parts of Colombia and Ecuador the institution is called *minga* or *cambio de mano*; among Peruvian Indians, *ayni* seems to be the word, and *mingaco* and *vuelta mano* were registered in Chile. In Brazil, the Portuguese term *adjunto, batalhão, bandeira, ajuda,* and *ajutório* are far less common than the Indian words *mutirão* or *puxirão*, which mean gathering for cooperative purposes.

There are many variations of the term according to different dialects spoken by the Indians of the Tupí–Guaraní linguistic family. Exactly as in Spanish America the *mutirão* performs not only important economic functions but is to be considered as social entertainment as well. Structural similarities with indigenous forms of reciprocal labor organization suggest close affinities, while the role of the West African *dokpwe* or collective work party, as a contributing element, seems to be less clear. (Willems, 1952b:233–235)

We shall not repeat our previous observations on the African-Indian-Iberian syncretism in Latin American folk religion, but with regard to the related field of magic it should be emphasized that similar forms of protective, preventive, and productive magic have been found in corporate Indian villages as well as in the open mestizo community. The healer (*curandero* in Spanish, *curandeiro* in Portuguese) is a ubiquitous figure; he may be a herb doctor or a kind of shaman, who is believed to control supernatural beings to perform cures but also to inflict harm (black magic) on enemies. Often enough the dividing line between herb medicine and shamanism is blurred, and the same curandero may use magic spells, incantations and prayers in administering potions believed to possess beneficial or medicinal effects.

To some extent, at least, religious brotherhoods have become part of the social network which holds the community together. In Brazil, for example, lay brotherhoods devoted to St. Benedict have been found in regions as widely differing as the Amazon and São Paulo. (Wagley, 1964: 137; Willems, 1961:86) In the Andes, the wide diffusion of the Spanish American sodality system among the Quechua Indians began in the sixteenth century (Kubler, 1946:405) and eventually became part of the religious organization of many communities. In Central American Indian communities, the brotherhood seems to occupy a similar position. (Cancian, 1967:286)

So far the description of the open peasant community has been deliberately focused on its most primitive versions, characterized by maximal reliance on subsistence activities and minimal dependence on markets; typical features have been a traditional technology, very low requirements for capital investment, reciprocal labor exchange, and an assemblage of other traits spelling self-sufficiency rather than articulation with the wider society. This somewhat oversimplified view is useful in gauging differentiating developments that derive from the very structure of the open community. In contrast to the *closed* corporate community, it "emphasizes continuous interaction with the outside world and ties its fortunes to outside demand." (Wolf, 1955:462) It does not prevent the individual peasant from using the land as he sees fit—to plant subsistence crops, cash crops, or both. The land itself may become a commodity to be bought, sold, or rented; wealth may be accumulated and even reinvested wherever market conditions invite such developments. But since developments of the latter kind depart from peasant traditions, they are dealt with in Part II.

Finally, the relationships between the peasantry and the landed estate can be divided roughly into two kinds: conflict and symbiosis. Conflictive relationships were (and still are) originated by encroachment on peasant land by large landholders. As a rule, expropriation either dislodges the peasants or converts them into dependent laborers or sharecroppers. Peasants living in symbiotic relationships with the landed estate may retain a measure of autonomy with regard to their holdings; but the small size of these holdings, combined with an archaic technology, generate the need for seasonal wage-earning jobs on nearby estates. Alternatively, peasant small holders produce cash crops, such as sugar cane, to be sold to a nearby plantation. There are other forms of symbiotic relationship, as we shall see later on, but it should be emphasized that in many regions the problem does not arise at all, since the peasants occupy marginal land or new land, located outside the sphere of interest of the landed estate.

Cultural subdivisions
in traditional Latin America

Spanish America and Brazil

The preceding chapters have indicated that the Iberian heritage imposed common cultural denominators on the societies built by the Spaniards and the Portuguese in the New World. Such common denominators were discovered in the structure of the landed estate; the patterns of miscegenation, kinship organization, and religious and political institutions; the colonial city; and the peasantry. The assumption of a common Latin American culture turned out to be tenable, but *basic* identity does not preclude *specific* differences, and some differences were found between Spanish and Portuguese America.

Apart from language and literary traditions, most of these diversities are elusive, seeming to be matters of degree rather than of kind. The scarcity of truly comparative studies further compounds the difficulties of compiling a list of clear-cut cultural differences between the two major regions of Latin America. At this point our inquiry is only concerned with *traditional* culture, not with the diversities that may have been produced by an independent existence of the Latin American states.

Let us begin a summary of our previous findings by noting the cultural implications of the conquest. Because the conquest of Brazil was predominantly private, in contrast to the officially sponsored Spanish expeditions, the Portuguese achieved a higher degree of compromise (i.e., cultural give-and-take) with Indian societies. Portuguese rule could not be imposed with the same forcefulness and display of institutional resources as Spanish rule, both because of the nature of the conquest and because Portugal's limited resources had already been overextended in Africa and Asia. The scope of Portuguese bureaucratic endeavor was more restricted, and Portuguese bureaucracy did not rise to the level of power attained by the Spanish bureaucracy.

The Portuguese were less concerned with the niceties of racial distinctions and theological orthodoxy. They developed no *formal* devices to establish *limpieza de sangre* or to legitimize children of mixed unions, and the Inquisition, never formally introduced in Brazil, was left to the initiative of local clerics and occasional *visitadores*, none of whom indulged in much witch hunting.

The relative weakness of Portuguese political institutions appears to be functionally related to the strength of the seigneurial extended family. Strongly attached to the landed estate as the customary place of residence, and acting outside the orbit of the distant seats of political auhority, the Brazilian seigneurial family seems to have reached a degree of autonomy and self-sufficiency unmatched by comparable developments in Spanish America. The rural habits of the Portuguese American seigneurial family were not unrelated to the paucity of genuine urban centers; furthermore, the Brazilian cities did not become customary places of residence for landowners, and they lacked some of the institutional apparatus of their Spanish counterparts. The Portuguese settlers were not allowed to have universities or to develop industries, and the craft guilds remained underdeveloped in contrast to those of Spanish America.

The coming of political emancipation in Brazil set in motion a succession of events that markedly differed from the course of political evolution characterizing Hispanic America. In 1806 the king of Portugal and his court, besieged by a French army, sought refuge in Brazil, and suddenly

Brazil became the center of the Portuguese colonial empire. The transfer of the monarchy was accompanied by a series of reforms that profoundly changed the colonial status of Brazil. Its ports were opened to international trade, industry was allowed to develop, banks and institutions of higher learning were established, and so was the first printing press in the New World. In 1815 the former colony was officially proclaimed "Kingdom of Brazil." Eventually the Portuguese monarch returned to Lisbon, but his son Pedro remained, invested with the powers of a prince regent. During this period of transition there were attempts at revolution, and when Portugal endeavored to restore dominance, the prince regent himself took the initiative of proclaiming independence. As noted earlier, Brazil became a constitutional monarchy under Emperor Pedro I.

Although the revolutionary potential that had accumulated during three centuries of colonialism was probably no less explosive in Brazil than in Spanish America, much of it was defused by the reforms preceding independence. In addition, the leading role of the prince regent in the process of political emancipation contributed to a relatively smooth transfer of the monarchy and its entrenchment in Brazilian society for almost seven decades. The highly centralized and integrative political structure thus established prevented Portuguese America from breaking up into a number of independent states. Revolutionary attempts to establish separate republics on Brazilian soil occurred in the north and in the south. They failed, however—perhaps less because of military repression than because of a national consensus favoring the maintenance of unity. Morse thinks that this difference between Brazil and Spanish America may be related to the following circumstances: (1) Portugal achieved national unity long before Spain did, and (2) the spirit of national unity took hold in Brazil almost spontaneously with no need for the elaborate institutional apparatus Spain had used to impose uniformity on the American territories. (Morse, 1962:166ff.) Institutional uniformity versus national unity perhaps expresses some of the cultural contrast between Portuguese and Spanish America on the eve of independence. Institutional uniformity was designed to check political divisiveness, which is traditional in Spain. It loomed in the background of Spanish regionalism, and it took the upper hand in Spanish American regionalism. There was regionalism in Brazil, of course—it could not fail to develop in a country characterized by such profound environmental diversity; but undertones of political secessionism have been the exception rather than the rule in Brazil regionalism.

The political structure of the monarchy was by no means the only unifying factor that kept Brazil from following the example of Spanish America. As pointed out before, bandeirismo had established a tradition of geographic mobility which was succeeded by periodic and massive displacements of populations. The gold rush of the early eighteenth century was one of these movements; and another series occurred in the nineteenth century; but in terms of sheer numbers, all were surpassed by the volume and scope of internal migration since 1900. The cumulative effect was to prevent regional cultures from becoming disparate and closed systems.

Augmenting and merging with the tradition of geographic mobility was a nationwide network of trade routes, particularly cattle trails that linked the people of the backlands with numerous coastal markets. (Prado Junior, 1963:237ff.) Complementing and supporting the export economy, centered around agricultural and mining products, there was

an internal movement of jerked beef and other foodstuffs, hides, and cash commodities in transshipment which has only a modest place in colonial statistics, yet which inconspicuously served to articulate those very regions which production for export appeared to isolate one from another. Here again, the point is not that internal trade was wholly lacking in Spanish America, but that in Brazil it did not center cartwheel fashion, upon a principal city, nor was it funneled through a few principal ports. (Morse, 1962:168)*

To view Spanish America and Brazil as the two major subcultural areas of Latin America may be difficult to reconcile with our emphasis on evolution. The concept of culture area seems to be based on the assumption that a given way of life, attached to a particular environmental setting, preserves its identity over a certain period of time. In other words, it carries static suggestions that may be considered incompatible with the realities of cultural dynamics. One has to admit, of course, that cultural evolution is by no means irreconcilable with cultural permanence, but in our case it may be preferable to think in terms of cultural processes occurring in particular areas and related to these areas by series of adaptive responses to environmental stimuli, both physical and social. Comparison of two areas such as Spanish America and Brazil then means looking for parallels and convergences, but also for divergences in the processes of cultural evolution. So far, our findings seem to corroborate the following statements.

* Richard M. Morse, "Some Themes of Brazilian History," *South Atlantic Quarterly*, 61, no. 2 (1962), 168. Copyright 1962 by the Duke University Press.

1. Portugal and Spain are branches of the same "tree of culture." The common cultural background led to the transfer of similar institutions, value orientations, and attitudes to the New World. These acquired continuity because the mother countries tightly controlled dependency relationships with the American colonies. A high degree of cultural conservatism or traditionalism prevented the basic institutions and value orientations of Spain and Portugal from drifting apart throughout most of the colonial period. Furthermore, during the sixteenth century a dynastic merger integrated the two countries into a single political structure that lasted 70 years (1581–1640). There would have been no cultural parallelism in America without continuing parallelism in Iberia.

2. Cultural parallelism does not necessarily impy simultaneity of evolutionary phases. True enough, some institutions (mercedes de tierra, captanias, sesmarias, the landed estate, slavery) were transplanted and disseminated almost simultaneously, but certain Brazilian developments lagged behind comparable conditions in Spanish America (e.g., the conquest and colonization of the interior, the urbanization and exploitation of mineral resources). All in all, as Portuguese America was able to catch up, initial disparity gave way to cultural convergence that probably reached its peak during the eighteenth century. The conditions under which political emancipation occurred in Brazil, as contrasted to those prevailing in Spanish America, can be considered to be the first step toward a phase of cultural divergence. This trend was again inverted with the establishment of the republic in Brazil and the introduction of a new role for the military in the political process.

3. The concept of cultural parallelism does not sit well with the role of the Catholic church in the two major cultural areas of Latin America. The institutional unity of the Church was reflected in the basic identity of tradition, dogma, and modes of action, particularly those of the religious orders, among which the Jesuits perhaps attained the highest degree of cultural homogeneity. Whatever part the Church played in producing cultural similarities in Latin America, we must attribute it to institutional unity rather than to parallel development of discrete entities.

4. Alternating trends of convergence and divergence did not affect the whole culture. It seems, for example, that the landed estate and the patripotestal extended family remained virtually unaffected. Here the previously mentioned differences and similarities between Portuguese and Spanish America did not undergo noticeable variations over a period of 300 years at least. Most aspects of peasant culture were relatively unchanged during the same era. Tenuous integration with metropolitan

political and economic institutions compelled most peasant societies to seek their own modes of adaptation geared to local resources and a primitive technology.

Subcultural regions

Homogeneous pastoral and peasant areas

Within the two major cultural regions of Latin America—Spanish America and Portuguese Brazil—the physical and social environment was sufficiently heterogeneous to push the process of adaptation in very different directions. There was, of course, nothing obliging adaptive processes to respect political boundaries, especially since neither Spain nor Portugal proved capable of remaking the emergent culture of its American territories totally in the image of its own peninsular ways of life. Indeed, adaptations occurring at the folk level were sufficiently responsive to environmental stimuli to produce a high degree of cultural uniformity regardless of political boundaries.

The gaucho subculture that sprung up in the pampas of Argentina, Uruguay, and southern Brazil provides an example of a spontaneously emerging cultural region. Escaped cattle, originally introduced by the Spaniards, had found rich natural pastures in the great plains of South America, and they rapidly multiplied to form herds of many thousands. The wealth of "wild" cattle attracted people from the present areas of Argentina, Uruguay, Paraguay, and southern Brazil, including bandeirantes from São Paulo. Although known historical sources are inexplicit, it seems that even in the early seventeenth century many people, mostly of mixed, Indian, Negro and Iberian origin, were living off the herds of wild cattle, which supplied food as well as hides and tallow for sale in the market. In time gaucho culture acquired the characteristics usually attached to the term today: a technology designed to control and exploit cattle resources, and a highly mobile life on horseback, averse to agricultural pursuits, geared to conflictive competition for "free" resources as well as to resisting recurrent attempts of colonial authorities to regulate the slaughter of wild cattle. Thus violence become an aspect of gaucho culture that later played an important role in the political upheavals of the region.

A gaucho was easily recognizable by his costume, his riding gear, his weapons (machete and lance), his food habits (meat and yerba mate), and a particular brand of folk poetry and music. Predatory exploitation of wild cattle resources depleted the herds, and gradually gaucho society shifted to cattle raising. By 1715 the *ganado cimarrón* or wild cattle had disappeared in the pampas around Buenos Aires (Coni, 1945:58), but farther north, in what is now Rio Grande do Sul, wild cattle were hunted as late as the first quarter of the nineteenth century. (Vianna, 1952:84) North of the Plate River, however, cattle were hunted not just for hides and tallow but primarily for redomestication and sale to ranchers and livestock merchants, who drove the captured herds to markets in São Paulo.

During the eighteenth century the *preadores* (captors) also began to hunt "wild" horses and mules, of which there were herds of 10,000 or more, according to Azara. (Vianna, 1952:86) Apparently the capture and taming of equines and bovines represented steps toward livestock raising that eventually changed early forms of gaucho society, which had consisted of small nomadic bands of unattached and highly independent males living in cow-hide-covered shelters and fighting each other and colonial authorities. Not surprisingly, Portuguese preadores expanding southward frequently clashed with bands of Spanish cattle hunters and ranchers moving north. Conflicts between the Spanish authorities and free-roaming bands of cattle hunters, between a "rural proletariat of vagabonds" and cattle ranchers (Coni, 1945:59), and between Spanish and Portuguese frontier bands, kept the region in continuous turmoil and consolidated the gaucho tradition of violence. The struggle between Spaniards and Portuguese had no cultural implications; there was only *one* gaucho culture, which proved pervasive enough to produce a peculiar dialect with a mixed Spanish-Portuguese vocabulary.

The gradual transition of gaucho culture from nomadic hunting of wild cattle to sedentary ranching raises the question of a possible cultural dualism similar to that of plantation areas. The granting of large estancias to individuals brings to mind the image of wealthy cattle barons controlling a mass of servile laborers and indulging in a life of luxury and leisure. However, there is no evidence of this type of cultural dualism until far into the nineteenth century. Citing Saint Hilaire, Felix de Azara, and Afredo Varela, Oliveira Vianna refers to the "democratizing action of pampa pastoralism," which reduced social distance between *estanciero* and *peón* in a way unheard of in plantation areas. Apparently, no social stigma adhered to menial work related to the capture, branding, and slaughtering or taming of cattle, horses, and mules. "The Spaniards do not mind serving as peons together with Negroes, mulattoes and Indians, even if the owner or overseer belongs to one of the latter categories." (Azara, in Vianna, 1952:290–291) In fact, owners of cattle ranchos and male members of their families worked side by side with their slaves or peons, performing all tasks involving cattle and horses.

It seems unlikely that pastoralism per se had such "democratizing" effects on gaucho society, which toward the end of the eighteenth century became a hotbed of caudillism and autocracy. A more plausible explanation lies in the economic conditions under which gaucho pastoralism evolved. If anyone was able to amass wealth, it was the cattle merchant rather than the estanciero, who probably had little choice but to work with his peons to make a living. To the extent that stratification existed, it did not generate the cultural dualism that elsewhere separated seigneurial landlords from the servile labor force. Up to the second half of the nineteenth century, gaucho culture remained sufficiently homogeneous to demarcate the pampas as a genuine subcultural area, apart from the few urban centers, of course. Later, gaucho culture gradually came to be identified with the way of life of the *peón* or cowboy. In other words, it became a class culture.

In the llanos or plains of Venezuela and Colombia, Spanish pastoralism encountered another highly congenial environment whose natural resources invited the spontaneous emergence of a folk culture similar to that of the gaucho area. In the sixteenth century the Spaniards brought a few heads of cattle to the llanos, and a century later the herds that belonged to the different *hatos* (ranchos) were reported to total 137,680. (Mendoza, 1947:64) Although the cattle were "half wild," the llaneros, mostly mestizoes, apparently never hunted wild cattle for hides and tallow, but, like gaucho society, they developed a fairly homogeneous "egalitarian" way of life. The "great house" of a hato was (and still is) a far cry from the seigneurial mansion of the plantation owners. Reliance on locally available materials as well as current construction techniques remind us instead of the most primitive peasant dwellings:

> Posts, rafters and cross-pieces are of the heart of the palm tree and other durable wood, bound together with *bejuco* (vine). The roof is palm-leaf thatch, and the floor is tamped earth. The walls are known as *bahareque*, and consist of a wattle of *cana brava* which is coated with a mixture of mud and cow dung. (Crist, 1942:16)

Like the gaucho ranchers, the llaneros had to fight numerous bands of nomadic outlaws who preyed on the herds and were believed to number about 24,000 in 1786. (Crist, 1942:75) Like the southern pampas, the llanos became the scene of political turmoil and caudillism. In fact,

Venezuelan president José Antonio Paez was a llanero who began his political career as a local caudillo.

A third pastoral subculture developed in the arid and semiarid plains that cover most of the sertão or hinterland of northeast Brazil. Pastoralism began in the seventeenth century, and most of it was originally concentrated in the valley of the São Francisco River, from which point it gradually expanded northward. The area is much poorer in natural resources than either the llanos or the pampas; periodic draughts often lasting several years had and still have devastating effects on man and beast. Adaptation to this harsh and unpredictable environment imposed an extraordinarily frugal way of life, depending almost entirely on local resources. Dried beef, and the few products of a desultory subsistence agriculture, limited to small plots, fed *vaqueiros* and ranchers alike. The daily pursuit of half-wild cattle through the thorny vegetation of the land suggested the use of tanned hides to protect the vaqueiro like a suit of armor.

> Clad in his tanned leather vest, and in skin tight leggings of the same material that come up to his crotch and which are fitted with knee pads, and with his hands and feet protected by calfskin gloves and shinguards, he presents the crude aspect of some medieval knight who has strayed into modern times. (da Cunha, 1944:92)

Such extensive use of leather led to the expression *civilização de couro*, or "leather civilization," to characterize the adaptive ingenuity of the northeastern pastoralists. It should be noted that the leather armor of the vaqueiro was somewhat paralleled by the gaucho costume worn in the Calchaqui region in northern Argentina. The *guardamonte*, the hide of a horse, was extensively used to protect the legs of the rider up to his hips. The *guardacalzón*, a slightly smaller piece of leather, served the same function. Like the Brazilian vaqueiro, the gaucho of Calchaqui wore a leather vest and a leather hat.

The cattle ranchers of the northeast are customarily depicted as an autocratic lot, ruling their huge domains with an iron hand. The *casa de telha* or tile-covered house, the residence of the owner, has been contrasted to the thatch-covered huts of the vaqueiros, suggesting a social distance similar to that of the seigneurial society of the coast. The sertão, however, completely lacks the architectural symbols of opulence that set off the lifestyle of the plantation owners from that of the impoverished cane cutters. The cattle ranches of the São Francisco region "do not exhibit any constructions of seigneurial aspect; on the contrary, they are characterized exactly by simplicity and poverty of style." (Macedo, 1952: 57) Although built of brick and covered with tiles, the buildings are suggestive of peasant dwellings rather than of seigneurial mansions. In the late nineteenth century, the cattle ranchers became town dwellers and found opportunities to branch out in business and industrial enterprise. (Vilaça and Albuquerque, 1965:45, 165) Before that time, however, it is unlikely that life on the pastoral domains could have produced the kind of cultural dualism typical of plantation areas. Isolated by immense distances from the coastal markets and dependent on the nature, which was harsh and unpredictable, the lifestyle of the rancher could not have been very different from that of his vaqueiros. Whatever social distance may have separated landowners from labor force, the subculture of the pastoral northeast was probably as homogeneous as that of the gauchos and llaneros. Like these, the northeastern pastoralists were predominantly mestizoes.

As in the pampas and the llanos, the northeastern sertão of Brazil had its society of outlaws—the nomadic jagunços, who preyed on the cattle ranches and the small isolated towns of the backlands. "Independent bands" of marauders roamed the countryside in the late eighteenth century. (Queiroz, 1968:51) For a century and a half they terrorized the population of the sertão, including the powerful cattle ranchers who adopted the self-defeating habit of recruiting bands of jagunços for private warfare and to intimidate or eliminate political rivals.

Coronelismo, the peculiar brand of Brazilian caudillism, flourished with the help of the outlaws, who found asylum from the police whenever it suited the political interests of the cattle ranchers.

Eventually, as the region entered a phase of modest economic development and urbanization, the big ranchers became town dwellers and the traditional cultural homogeneity of the area ceased to exist. Here too, the "leather civilization" of the Brazilian northeast came to resemble the way of life of the vaqueiros, the rural lower class of the pampas and the llanos.

Parallel developments in the pampas, the llanos, and the sertão— the three pastoral regions of South America—are not surprising. They reflect the interaction of similar physical environments and societies of similar cultural background. Cattle and horses were cultural transfers from Iberia, as was the marketability of cattle products—beef, dairy products, hides, and tallow. But the way of life typical of these pastoral regions was a spontaneous adaptation accomplished with the loosest possible contact with urban civilization and the institutions representing the coercive authority of the state. The three pastoral regions became areas of refuge for social rejects and deviants of colonial society: poor mulattoes and mestizoes, runaway slaves, adventurers, and fugitives from justice. All competed with the putative landowners and with one another for control of the herds; violence became a way of life, and warlike abilities had a distinct survival value. Thus the gaucho, the llanero and the jagunço became warriors on horseback, a military resource available for would-be-caudillos interested in using organized violence to conquer political office. The pastoral societies of the three areas under scrutiny, therefore, fitted the political structure of the wider society, especially as it evolved during the ninteenth century.

The Amazon Basin is perhaps the largest cultural region of Latin America. Its traditional homogeneity, preceding the rubber boom and intensive urbanization, was due to spontaneous adaptation like that which characterized the three pastoral subcultures of South America. However, relatively few Indian traits were absorbed in the pampas, in the sertão, or in the llanos. The Amazon subculture, on the other hand, assimilated indigenous elements on such a scale that in some respects at least, the way of life of the Amazon peasant was fairly close to that of the horticultural Indians. (And so it remains.) Since adaptation proceeded unincumbered by extraneous institutional impositions, political boundaries had little if any bearing on the cultural configuration of the region now shared by Brazil, Venezuela, Colombia, Ecuador, Peru, and Bolivia. The brief cultural inventory presented in the preceding chapter supports this point.

The delineation of regional subcultures was based on the criterion of cultural homogeneity. In all four areas the prevalence of a single cultural type—the gaucho, the llanero, the vaqueiro, the mestizo peasant—determined such homogeneity. It was also pointed out that as these cultural types were gradually attracted by an expanding urban civilization, homogeneity gave way to cultural differentiation and regional cultures tended to become class cultures.

Heterogenous plantation and mining areas

We are not suggesting that there were only four subcultural regions in traditional Latin America. Unfortunately, adequate data are lacking to demarcate other regions comparable in magnitude and cultural homogeneity to the ones outlined here. Nor are these regions comparable to plantation areas. A plantation area presents a combination of several contrasting subcultures held together by economic interdependence and political domination. In the coastal region of northeastern and eastern Brazil, for example, the way of life of the sugar estate owners was totally distinct from that of the slaves, and neither group could possibly be identified with that of the copyholders or lavradores mentioned by Boxer. The problem of cultural classification is compounded because the seigneurial class was highly urbanized and alternated its residence between the city and the estate. Differentiation was further accentuated by the distinct cultural traditions of the African slaves or Indian serfs who made up the labor force of the seigneurial estate.

The landed estate constituted an integrated economic and political unit, and an area homogeneously composed of such estates should be considered to be a subcultural region. But this is hardly a reason for overlooking basic differences between pampa and plantation, especially since the underlying criterion of classification is not the same as the one used to define our four subcultural regions. In this context, another difference may come to mind. The previously described pastoral cultures and, even more, the peasant culture of the Amazon Basin, were spontaneous adaptations achieved mainly with local resources. The sugar complex, however, was transplanted in its entirety from Spain and Portugal to America. Cane itself, the agricultural skills associated with its cultivation, the machinery and techniques necessary to transform cane into crude sugar and to refine it further—all these elements were completely alien to America, as was African slave labor, first introduced on a large scale in response to labor demands of the northeastern planters.

It is possible to distinguish a number of major sugar cane areas developing in succession and passing through phases of early growth, flowering, and decline—sometimes exaggeratedly referred to as a boom-and-bust cycle. During the sixteenth century, Hispaniola and Cuba, Puerto Rico and Jamaica, Martinique, Guadalupe, and most of the smaller West Indian islands developed slave-based seigneurial societies centered around the sugar complex.

In New Spain sugar cane was introduced at the same time, but large estates remained rare until the eighteenth century, when there were "twelve or fourteen great ingenios" among a total of 300 sugar fincas. (Sandoval, 1951:133) Most of these were located in different regions, Michoacan being the only state having a concentration of sugar-producing haciendas. The structure of the large Mexican estates bore a remarkable resemblance to the sugar cane plantations of the Brazilian northeast.

(Sandoval, 1951:129) In the early nineteenth century, sugar cane areas emerged in the Cauca Valley of Colombia, in the province of Tucumán (Argentina), and in the coastal plains of Peru.

Coffee was transplanted to Brazil early enough to be adapted to the pattern of the traditional agrarian society. Within the first decades of the nineteenth century, a new plantation area developed in southern Brazil, its social structure and ways of life coming to resemble those of the older sugar regions.

The cultural heterogeneity of the plantation areas was surpassed only by that of the mining regions. Not only were the distinct subcultures held together by economic symbiosis and political dominance, but mining generated its own type of urbanization, manifest in such cities as San Luis Potosí, Ouro Prêto, Taxco, and Guanajuato. "Potosí came to exhibit those common characteristics of all mining societies in such a theatrical way that it became symbolic of the process that was going on everywhere." (Hanke, 959:36) Founded in 1545, Potosí had a population of 120,000 by 1570—far more than any other city in Latin America. By the middle of the sixteenth century it had grown to 160,000, surpassing all urban centers of the New World. (Hanke, 1959:11) Like comparable cities in Mexico and Brazil, Potosí was located where the silver deposits were; mine owners and Indian laborers were integrated into a structure that came fairly close to that of an industrial city. Rapid and abundant generation of monetary wealth over approximately two centuries afforded the means to import foodstuffs and an extraordinary variety of other commodities from far and wide without much regard to cost and distance. Goods intended for conspicuous consumption came from 41 localities and countries, including Turkey, Arabia, Persia, India, and China. (Hanke, 1959:28)

Since wealth could be amassed and lost almost instantaneously, the social structure of Potosí exhibited a degree of mobility that created the sharpest possible contrast to the frozen structure of plantation society and the towns within its orbit of influence. The customary Iberian xenophobia, equating aliens with heretics and barring them from entering the colonies, apparently lost its bite, for "such was the number of foreigners that the Crown eventually became frightened of the dangers stemming from their presence." (Hanke, 1959:31) Among the aliens, the Portuguese were particularly prominent. (Hanke, n.d.:18)

If the concept of social structure means definite modes of behavior controlled by generally recognized rules, the term should not be used without considerable qualification when referring to Potosí. The social history of this city tells of a long succession of murderous feuds, bloody riots, and rebellions bordering on civil war. Creoles fought Spaniards, and mestizoes vented their grievances in a general insurrection. "Violent frays became a pastime, a recognized social activity. Even the municipal councilors went to their meetings armed with swords and pistols, and protected by breastplates and coats of mail." (Hanke, 1959:10) Hundreds of individuals lived on prostitution and gambling, and the number of "vagrants and scoundrels" was high enough to stimulate the issuance of royal orders to rid the city of their presence. To judge from yet incomplete historical reconstruction, the society of Potosí was not only infested by a disproportionately large number of deviants, but the bulk of the society engaged in modes of behavior that imperiled the very order on which continuance depended.

A system of forced labor was instituted to operate the mines. Under the so-called *mita*, a certain proportion of Indians of each territorial division had to serve in the mines for a fixed period. This meant that every year about 40,000 Indian men, women, and children were forced to migrate to Potosí. (Hanke, 1959:59) Work in the mines was so dangerous and injurious to health that the mortality rate must have been very high.

One can only speculate about the cultural impact of these forced mass migrations. The continuous presence of thousands of unassimilated Indians in Potosí implied tension and conflict, which was renewed every year with the arrival of fresh levies of Indians. Like other institutionalized forms of labor exploitation, the mita was subject to endless and acrimonious criticism. Fiscal advantages overruled humanitarian considerations, however, and the system disappeared only as the mines were exhausted. A contributing factor to the preservation of the mita was the unusual ability and competence of the administration in representing the interests of the city before the Council of the Indies. (Hanke, 1959:29)

Like the mining regions of Mexico and Brazil, Potosí became the center of ecological dominance, controlling the resources of an extraordinarily large area of Spanish America. Within a radius of 100 leagues, "nearly the total production of the neighboring regions went to Potosí, which acted like a powerful magnet." (Hanke, 1959:55) Moreover, "the extensive contraband trade through Buenos Aires had one single objective: to get to Potosí, the Mecca of all Spanish trade during that period, the Samarkand of America." (Molina, in Hanke, 1959:28)

In Mexico and Brazil, silver and gold deposits were found in areas far more extensive than the mining fields of Potosí. In Brazil the mining industry covered large sectors of what are now the states of Minas Gerais, Mato Grosso, Goiás, and Bahia. Many towns sprang up where major deposits of gold or diamonds were discovered. The intensive urbanization of the captaincy of Minas Gerais during the eighteenth century was closely associated with mining.

In Mexico the differences between the southern and northern mining areas reflected different evolutionary levels of the indigenous cultures. The southern area was part of Mesoamerica, where sedentary Indian communities provided tributary labor (*repartimientos*) and food staples to feed the mining towns. In the north tributary Indian labor was harder to come by, and the mining industry had to rely largely on free indigenous laborers, mostly migrants from the south who settled in the Indian barrios of the mining towns. "Largely because of the growth of these Indian quarters, miscegenation was more pronounced in the northern mines than in those of the south and central parts of Mexico." (West, 1949:5)

The Indians of southern and central Mexico, adapted to pre-Columbian seigneurial systems, offered little resistance to Spanish exploitation, and the mining towns developed a civil, nonmilitary political and social structure. In contrast, the nomadic Indian tribes of the northern desert were not amenable to domination and constantly harassed the mining centers, which became "virtual military garrisons with a distinctly militaristic political and social structure." (West, 1949:5) Furthermore, the lack of Indian agricultural communities forced the Spaniards to establish their own grain farms to feed the mining towns.

Silver and gold in the north led to the development of such cities as Zacatecas, San Luis Potosí, and Durango. In central and southern Mexico, the growth of Pachua, Zumpango, El Oro, Querétaro, Guanajuato, Aguascalientes, Morelia, and Taxco was closely connected with the silver mines. (Seen as an ecological and economic unit, a mining area was a territory of highly variable size, with agricultural and pastoral resources sufficient to support the mining centers.)

The cultural evolution of the nineteenth and twentieth centuries brought about changes that affected the traditional subcultural areas and created new ones of increased structural complexity. With the division of the Spanish American empire into a number of independent states, a new factor of cultural delimitation appeared. Separate and independent political existence has differentiating and integrating effects. It differentiates splinter groups from one another and from the encompassing structure that preceded them. Interactional processes are deliberately restrained between seceding units, and decisions made in one unit are not binding for any other unit. The new nations drift culturally apart, and each builds what it identifies as its own historical tradition. In Spanish America, cultural differentiation was facilitated by the absence of compelling conditions of economic interdependence. Since their markets lay in Europe, the republics could afford to cut loose from each other.

Internal integration occurred as factions, power groups, or powerful personalities asserted themselves against opposition and attained a measure of stability. External conflicts and warfare tended to reinforce national awareness and cohesion. Gradually each republic accumulated a store of tangible and intangible symbols—flags, emblems, anthems, historical shrines, stories of personal heroism, and records of political, economic, and technical achievements. Together, these provided the emotional and factual ingredients of a national identity. A steadily growing nationalism glorified the past and eventually laid claim to cultural uniqueness.

Whether or to what extent cultural evolution had sufficiently differentiating effects to generate a discrete "national character" in each of the Hispanic American republics remains an open question. Some nations exhibited greater concern for discovering and defining their national character than others, and this in itself may be regarded as a differentiating feature. But all Ibero-American nations have faced the same basic problem of extending national awareness to the many thousands of isolated peasant communities, where distinctness is often reinforced by aboriginal cultural traditions and by a defensive stance inherent in the community structure.

The claim to national uniqueness implies that each republic constitutes a cultural area in its own right. The question of whether such claims can be substantiated is taken up in Part II.

Cultural change
and persistence in
the context of an
emerging industrial civilization

Evolutionary routes
toward modern Latin America

Mechanism and conditions of cultural evolution

The history of Ibero-America encompassed many events that can be interpreted as culture changes, but it is not always easy to gauge their evolutionary significance. Defined in the broadest possible way, cultural evolution of a society refers to all the processes that produce internal diversification and increasing specialization of the diversified parts. In the social structure, evolution is virtually identical with division of labor (i.e., the dividing and subdividing of social groups and the assignment to them of specific activities). Evolution of the social structure goes hand in hand with evolutionary changes in technology and economy.

No evolutionary step can be properly gauged without taking into account the specific environmental conditions to which a society tries to respond. An effective adaptation to one environment may not work at all when transferred to another setting. The ultimate test of successful adaptation is the survival of the society; yet comparison of the adaptive capabilities of many different societies shows that the "margin of survival" is subject to considerable variations. A "narrow" margin means that the concerted efforts of the group are necessary to provide the bare essentials—to escape starvation and gradual extinction. Or it may imply a high degree of insecurity and threat of sudden extinction at the hands of superior enemies. A "wider" margin may mean more reliable and effective food-producing techniques, and perhaps a sizable surplus permitting population growth and internal specialization unrelated to the production of essentials. The viability of growing internal differentiation depends of course on *integration*—the maintenance of a common structure capable of relating the different units to one another.

In early Ibero-America the evolutionary process was enormously complicated. First of all the conquest brought massive and violent interference to many native cultures that had reached widely differing levels of evolution; from unaffiliated bands of nomadic foragers to such complex structures as the Inca and Aztec empires. Iberian interference meant of course that autochthonous evolution had come to an end, that henceforward the rhythm and direction of the evolutionary process were determined by the kind of society that emerged. As pointed out in previous chapters, the conquerors incorporated numerous elements of the indigenous cultures—not merely domesticated plants and animals, but also certain patterns of native social organization that facilitated the large-scale use of Indian labor. Where mining and urbanism could be combined, as in New Spain and Peru, a highly complex society developed as early as the sixteenth century. The almost instantaneous flowering of these regions sets into sharp relief the evolutionary process. One is inclined to view evolution as a gradual accumulation of knowledge, skills, artifacts, and organizational patterns, whereby a society "grows" or "progresses" step by step over long periods. But this picture of *primary* evolution in which autochthonous inventions and discoveries play a leading role, is often interfered with by sudden cultural transplants from other societies. Things invented or discovered elsewhere are grafted on a particular society, enabling it to develop almost at once cultural aspects that the donor society had taken perhaps a century to bring up to the present level. In other words, the cultural evolution of specific societies is not necessarily bound to rigid evolutionary "sequences" or "stages." For example, societies that are industrializing *now* do not have to go through all the phases of primary evolution that characterized the Industrial Revolution at its inception in eighteenth-century England. They can and do start with the most recent achievements in industrial technology, telescoping 200 years of primary development into a decade or two. The steelmills in Huitchipato (Chile), Volta Redonda (Brazil), or Paz de Rio (Colombia) reflect the technological level of the 1940s rather than that of earlier phases of industrial development. Richard N. Adams proposed the term *secondary evolution* or development for this kind of process, which belies the popular notion that history repeats itself. (Adams, Richard Newbold, 1967:19ff.) Secondary evolution occurs through cultural diffusion and, quite frequently, through acculturation.

Secondary evolution did not begin in the twentieth century, but it has been associated with all phases of Latin American history. The "culture of conquest," as defined by Foster, could be interpreted as a case of massive secondary development, at least as far as the Spanish and Portuguese settlers are concerned. The rapid incorporation of indigenous food plants (particularly maize, manioc, and potatoes) most certainly presented adaptive advantages to the conquerors. It seems, too, that the adoption of European domesticated animals and crops must have considerably widened the "survival margin" of the Indian communities; but the ruthless harnessing of Indian labor combined with the ravaging effects of contagious diseases introduced by the conquerors, outweighed any adaptive advances attributable to Ibero-Indian acculturation. In many areas of Latin America, particularly in the West Indies and eastern South America, contact resulted in the extinction of numerous native societies.

Thus the odds heavily favored Spanish–Portuguese rather than Indian adaptation. Only in the course of time did the Indians of Mesoamerica and the Andes find a way of adapting to "a dominant, enveloping cultural system." (Sahlins and Service, 1960:64) The corporate agricultural community, discussed in a previous chapter, was the adaptive response to Spanish domination. It secured a rather narrow margin of survival for the community, but it also stabilized relationships with the dominant sector of the society and made secondary development virtually impossible up to the present time.

The role of secondary evolution in the dominant society was complicated by several processes, which can only be outlined here. The conquest itself was tantamount to a massive transfer of Iberian culture. Secondary development requires differentiation into donor and recipient societies, and in the beginning there were neither donors nor recipients (apart from the Indians), but only Spaniards and Portuguese trying to come to grips with a strange land and its strange inhabitants. Only after the booty had been distributed through the expropriation of land and allocation of Indian labor, and only after Creole society had assumed a definite shape, differentiation into donors and recipients was sufficiently sharp to permit secondary development. By then, new ways of life had emerged that cannot by any stretch of imagination be considered to be mere cultural extensions of either Portugal or Spain. Cultural transmissions from the Iberian peninsula to the American territories was no longer a matter of legislative fiat and unquestioned acceptance; rather, it involved selection, readaptation, or rejection, all in spite of the colonial status of Ibero-America.

Secondary evolution began to take place to the extent that selected elements of Iberian culture could be fitted into the varying contexts of regional development. For example, the history of mining in Latin America recorded the successful transfer of technological inventions. (Bargalo, 1955:203ff.) The Spanish university took root in various cities, as did the Spanish craft guilds. Urban planning and urban architecture, especially Spanish and Portuguese baroque, can be cited as examples of secondary development. And of course the patterns of political and administrative organization were Iberian transfers, although many judicial and administrative attempts designed to gain or maintain institutional control over Ibero-America proved ineffectual. As indicated before, noncompliance with legal precepts became a tradition, and perhaps more than anything else, the veiled rejection ("*obedezco pero no cumplo*") of attempted legal transplants proved that cultural evolution had taken its own divergent course, which could not easily be deflected by political coercion.

Another complication arose because cultural evolution in Latin America began at widely separated levels and proceeded at vastly different rates. In the mining and plantation areas, an ingenious combination of indigenous and imported resources rapidly generated large-scale commercial, agricultural, and urban growth; a highly stratified society and considerable institutional complexity also resulted. These areas remained relatively open to secondary developments, exemplified by the introduction of coffee agriculture and the progress of mining technology.

In the more isolated regions of the hinterland, however, the situation was quite different. Here the Iberian colonist, and particularly his mestizo descendants, had to settle for subsistence agriculture having a technology more indigenous than European. Regional adaptation was achieved at the expenses of considerable cultural losses. Slash-and-burn agriculture associated with the hoe or digging stick was less apt to produce a marketable surplus than the agricultural techniques then prevailing in Iberia, where two-course or three-course land rotation was customary. In most tropical areas of Latin America neither the plow nor the toothed harrow gained entrance, and the use of organic fertilizers, common in Iberia, remained virtually unknown. (R. S. Smith, 1966:446)

Of course, in some regions the quest for a surplus was almost irrelevant, since markets were distant and scarce. Furthermore, the open peasant community was not a replica of the Iberian village community. The prevailing system of farming homesteads generated looser and less complex structures. Relationships with the outside world were likely to be intermittent and infrequent, quite in contrast to the Iberian counterparts. In other words, considerable *simplification* characterized the cultural process of the open peasant community. Many contemporary and recent critics misunderstood the functions of simplification and interpreted it in terms of "degeneration" and "reversion to savagery." However, we are dealing here with frontier adaptation to a "relatively open environment." (Sahlins and Service, 1960:52) Not only did the open peasant community survive and expand, it succeeded in preserving its basic cultural identity in spite of miscegenation and indianization.

The open peasant community did not stabilize its relationship with the dominant society. Where stabilization occurred, it resulted from isolation. The possibilities of secondary development are not a function of the limitations of the dominant society; rather, they are determined by structural changes of the wider society. In many regions these changes have been extremely slow in coming about, and seemingly "archaic" peasant traditions have survived up to the present day.

Lags and failures in secondary evolution: structural incompatibilities in the political process

With the achievement of political emancipation, the national societies of Latin America did not cease to see themselves as recipients of European culture. More precisely, the intellectual elite took on the recipient role and, acting in accord with its humanistic traditions, concentrated on the transfer of ideological rather than technological and scientific components of Western culture. By "intellectual elite" we mean the relative few who benefited from an educational monopoly and had the leisure and inclination to speculate about the situation of their society and publicly to advocate changes emulating Western models. The intellectual elite was a motley lot composed of journalists, politicians, clerics, rich dilettantes, lawyers, and even a few generals. Some wielded considerable power and assumed leading political positions; others became ideological apologists of caudillos and dictators, or protagonists of subversive movements.

And there were also those who refrained from active participation in political movements. Whether educated in Europe or America, their orientation was bound to be universalistic (or encyclopedic), with emphasis on law, philosophy, and philology. By ideological culture we mean political, philosophical, educational, esthetic, and religious thoughts and doctrines—in short, certain (but not all) products of the human mind that have been given a definite, transferable structure or shape.

Attempts to transfer selected components of Western ideological culture to Latin America generally preceded the transplant of technological and scientific components by several decades. Such lags in secondary evolution are not unusual.

> In the most advanced cultures of the present day the technological base has become an enormously complex affair, requiring sizable amounts of capital, specialized skills, organization, and great quantities of raw materials to develop it and keep it going—all of which means that it can be transmitted across cultural boundaries only with the greatest difficulty. Ideological elements, on the other hand, even those of the most advanced cultures, can be carried across cultural boundaries with relative ease. (Sahlins and Service, 1960:89)

The shift from Iberian to French and Anglo-Saxon ideological models briefly mentioned earlier was not surprising at all. Spain and Portugal were not only regarded as oppressors and exploiters, they were also felt to be backward in comparison with central and northern Europe. Rejection of Iberian cultural models ought to be interpreted as emancipation from colonialism and from Spanish "medievalism" at the same time. Spanish America produced a literature in part or totally devoted to criticism and rejection of the Iberian heritage. Brazil was less prolific in its literary expressions of rejection; criticism of the Portuguese rule took different, yet no less effective forms.

Spain and Portugal were held responsible for most of the presumably retrograde aspects of Latin America. Spaniards were said to be disdainful of work and fond of idleness "by race and birth"; they allegedly loved to acquire money without any personal effort and to spend it extravagantly. (Villarén, quoted by Zea, 1963:190) Iberian contempt for manual work and related occupations was repeatedly pointed out as a barrier to industrial development. (Zea, 1963:109) Equally damning was the criticism of Iberian education—namely, its preference for literature, rhetoric, and philosophy. Rejection of prevailing educational values of course implied criticism of the Church, which was invited to quit educating lawyers and theologians. For inculcating in the Spanish American mind the "logic of infallibility," and for "establishing political legitimacy on the ground of infallibility," the Catholic Church was accused of having implanted political absolutism (Francisco Bilbao, quoted by Zea, 1963:73)

Men like Sarmiento viewed Spain as a theocratic, medieval power, "civilizing" barbaric America; but in the sixteenth century it was allegedly a "backward and obsolete nation." (Zea, 1963:48) Catholicism was said to be incompatible with republicanism because Catholicism was authoritarian, requiring blind obedience to dogma. (Zea, 1963:50) Authoritarianism, political instability, and military interferences with the political process were equally attributed to the Spanish heritage:

> Chile ruled by an oligarchy à la Venice; Argentina trampled underfoot by the horses of the gauchos, Peru governed by the military, Venezuela involved in terrible wars over senseless constitutional reforms, Mexico with ten changes of government and three hundred military uprisings in fifty years. The dismal seeds sowed by Spain were producing their poisonous fruits. (Varona, quoted by Zea, 1963:255)

Brazilian criticism of the Portuguese cultural tradition was less articulate and more diffuse in its literary manifestations. Somewhat in contrast to Hispanic America, ridicule became a highly effective way of expressing disapproval, and the Portuguese have been a favorite target of disparaging jokes. Among the literary expressions of anti-Portuguese criticism, none is more abusive and extravagant than a book by Antonio Torres, which entered its fourth edition in 1957. (Torres, 1957) Whether joke, vituperation, or earnest attempt to formulate objective criticism, the thrust was essentially the same: Portugal and the Portuguese are "backward" and deficient in all the qualities that would have made Brazil a great country had it been colonized by the British, Dutch, or French.

As time passed, rejection of the Iberian heritage gave way to revalidation and a more balanced view of the role Iberian culture had played in the evolution of Latin America. Spain was recognized as the *madre patria* of the Hispanic American republics, but the equivalent notion and its cultural implications failed to gain currency in Brazil.

However strong the desire of the intellectual elite to cut loose from Iberian traditions and to adopt alternate models of development, some people were aware that culture changes of such magnitude cannot be enacted at will. Although politically liberated, the republics could not, as some had naïvely expected, "shake off" Spanish culture. Andrés Lama perceived the "chain" that tied Argentina to Spain in "legislation, literature, customs and habits. It binds everything, places the seal of slavery on everything and belies our complete emancipation." (Zea, 1963:237) The Cuban Enrique José Varona perceived the Spanish heritage in the "caste spirit of domination and privileges . . . the habit of exploitation that will not relinquish its old power. Everything remains the same, no freedom whatever exists. . . . The servile hand continues in servitude, in misery, and in abjection. The same instruments of oppression continue to crush freedom." (Quoted by Zea, 1963:255)

In spite of such occasional flashes of understanding, all Latin American countries proceeded to import ideological culture from various Western societies, particularly from France. In retrospect it is easy to criticize the nineteenth-century scholars, artists, writers, and politicians for their lack of originality and for their apparent inability to perceive the incongruity of numerous ideological transplants. The intellectual elite of Latin America constituted a marginal group, steeped in European political, philosophical, and esthetic traditions, yet bound to America by family ties, economic interests, and prospects of political or professional careers. They ignored, misunderstood, or scorned the indigenous and mestizo folk cultures of America. Indians and mestizoes were thought of as a liability, and quite often the indigenous societies were believed to be biologically inferior. (Zea, 1963:54–55, 200, 219) Trapped in the cultural framework of nineteenth-century Europe, the intellectual elites of Latin America could scarcely have chosen a course of action different from the one they took. To them, the redemption of Latin America lay in Europe, its institutional apparatus, its educational systems, its philosophy, and its esthetic projections. There was only dim awareness of the problems accompanying the transfer of cultural elements from one society to another. If a cultural graft did not take, the failure was attributed to the scion—the grafted item—rather than to structural incompatibilities. Such a fundamental misunderstanding generated a kind of random experimentation that probably affected political organization more than other fields of endeavor.

The United States Constitution, the French constitution of 1791, and the Spanish constitution of 1812 were widely used by Latin American legislators as models for their own charters. Components extracted from these and other sources were variously combined and sanctioned by legislative bodies or arbitrarily decreed by individual power holders. If one constitution proved unworkable or incompatible with the political designs of a caudillo or a powerful oligarchy, another combination was tried, and often enough put aside for similar reasons.

The revolutionary content of the constitutions of 1789 and 1791, particularly their democratic components, strongly appealed to the intellectual elites of Latin America. Yet the political tradition of three centuries of colonial rule did not simply come to an end with the declaration of independence. The colonial regime had been characterized by an abundant flow of royal decrees formulated with little regard for the prospects of enforcement. Unenforceable laws were superseded by new legislation, much of it equally unenforceable. This endless flow of laws was based on the implicit assumptions that *all* problems could be solved on a legal level and legislative failures could be corrected only by fresh legislation. The constitutional history of Latin America provides ample evidence that this pattern continued virtually unabated to the present time.

Writing in 1960, Raul Cereceda listed 200 constitutions and constitutional amendments enacted in 20 Latin American nations since the dates of political emancipation. (Cereceda, 1961:104–105) Because of differences in the political division of Central America and northern South America in the early nineteenth century, some constitutions were counted twice, but the total hovers around 190. These figures should not be taken as a unequivocal expression of constitutional instability, since the amendments vary in scope and significance and the period elapsed following independence—the time available for experimentation—varies as well. But comparable countries differ from one another quite significantly. Venezuela (1811–1953) had 23 constitutions and amendments, the Dominican Republic (1821–1947) had 22, Mexico (1814–1917) had 8, Argentina (1819–1957) had 10, Bolivia (1826–1947) had 13, Chile (1811–1925) had 9, and Brazil (1823–1946) had 7. Out of the 200 characters and amendments, 63 were enacted before 1850, 70 between 1850 and 1900, and 67 since 1900. Thus experimentation is not diminishing. The process has been predominantly concerned with establishing democratic rule, often tempered with measures designed to safeguard privileged positions of oligarchies, dictators, or the Catholic church. As Kingsley Davis writes:

> It is this democratic machinery which the Latin Americans, since achieving their independence, have found especially fascinating. They have constantly tinkered with it, added to it, and thought about it. They have been inveterate constitution-makers, setting forth each time the elaborate political devices which would, until the next constitution, be followed. They have tried to solve one problem after another by manipulating the apparatus.
>
> This preoccupation with the technical forms of democracy suggests that the republics are trying to accomplish something by mechanical means which requires a deeper readjustment. They resemble the neurotic patient who manages to cure one symptom after another, only to find that the underlying neurosis still remains. The trouble is that in Latin America political democracy did not grow up gradually as a result of social evolution, but came suddenly as a result of cultural diffusion. The social order was, and in many ways still is, inimical to political democracy; it, rather than the oft-cited circumstances of settlement in the new world, is the primary obstacle to such democracy. (Davis, 1942:128–129)

The social order Kingsley Davis has in mind was part of the colonial heritage that survived political emancipation and the revolutionary wars. It was the previously described autocratic, oligarchic, and feudal structure that legislative experimentation sought to change into a more egalitarian system in the following ways: by proclaiming the people to be the only source of legitimate political authority; by instituting popular elections intended to choose a president and legislative bodies with temporary mandates, and by establishing the citizen's freedom of speech and his rights to assemble and to petition for redress of grievances. Of course, privileges were abolished and all were to be equal before the law.

The task of carrying out these radical changes by legislative fiat was hopeless from the very beginning, mainly because the constitution makers belonged to the same class of people whose compliance with the new charters would have meant relinquishing their power monopoly and most of the accompanying prerogatives. If the economic interests of most intellectuals were virtually identical with those of the power holders —the rural aristocracy—we begin to wonder why such attempts to secure change were made at all. One may argue that it would have been more consistent with the realities of the existing power structure merely to legitimize the status quo by enacting conservative political charters.

To account for this apparent paradox, at least three circumstances ought to be considered. First, the intellectuals involved in the writing, discussing, or amending of charters were pursuing political or professional careers. According to a time-honored Iberian tradition one got started in politics by publicly demonstrating jurisprudential erudition—by expressing in speeches and in writing, faith in the effectiveness of the law. A candidate's ability to enforce the law was beside the point. Although critical voices were heard from time to time the political or professional status of a legislator was little affected by subsequent failure to enforce the product of his erudition.

Second, the ruling class and its intellectual exponents were extremely sensitive to European criticism of Latin American institutions. They wanted to demonstrate that the new nations were capable of keeping up with the European development, and they felt that one way of accomplishing this was to ratify charters based on European models. A constitution is a highly visible document that can be read and evaluated without reference to social realities, which often remain hidden to the legal commentator. The Latin American charters were expected to be taken at face value, and frequently they were so judged by European and American jurists and political scientists.

Third, the structure of the seigneurial class and its intellectual exponents was far from being monolithic. One cleavage that was to become almost typical in Latin America was the "generation gap" between adult members of this class, predominantly inclined to preserve their economic and political prerogatives, and the young, who had just completed their professional (mostly legal) training at a European university where they had acquired "radical" political ideas. On returning to Latin America, the young men actively involved themselves in politics and attempted to recruit followers by advocating political reforms at variance with the interests of their families and social class. They were "liberals" opposing the traditional value system of the "conservatives."

This happened, for example, in Colombia, where young intellectuals founded in 1850 a subversive association called the Republican School. This group was made up of the elites, but it wanted to dissociate from them because in the light of the liberal utopia, it had perceived the incongruities and inconsistencies of the seigneurial order. Thus it confronted the elite with the new ideologies then in vogue in the prestigious circles of Paris. The Republican School was a counterelite group with revolutionary airs and apparently committed to sponsor the transformation of the established order. (Fals-Borda, 1969:83)

The impact of this "subversive" movement was strong enough to generate a series of laws that affected the signeurial order without destroying it. Indian tributes and slavery were abolished, for example, as were ecclesiastical privileges. But soon the rebels were brought back to the traditional fold: "In the present case, a cooptation of reactionary type occurred since the rebels ceded under pressures from their elders, peers and agents of the dominant groups, through attraction by offers of sinecures and privileges; or through physical violence." (Fals-Borda, 1969:86)

The role of the Republican School of Colombia (which was not a school at all) was gradually taken over by the colleges of law, which became foci of political radicalism. Unlike their European and American peers, the law students of Latin America fought for virtually all the new political ideas invented in the Western world, and invariably these ideas were at variance with the vested interests of the ruling class. And the students were almost invariably coopted by elder politicians and converted from revolutionary firebrands into pragmatic defenders of the agrarian tradition. Usually this happened when the young revolutionary "settled down" and contracted marriage. By then the full power of the kinship group and its connubial alliances could be brought to bear on its re- calcitrant member, whose career perspectives looked dim indeed without the support of his class. The situation changed only as the social compo- sition of the student bodies of the law schools changed.

Viewed as continuous flow of ideological culture from Europe and the United States to Latin America, the process of enacting and amending political charters seems to have passed through a sequence of stages from less democratic to more democratic. Their egalitarian phraseology not- withstanding, the early constitutions placed heavy restrictions on the right to vote and to be elected to office. Again in accord with numerous European models of the time, voting rights were limited to males who were literate, exercised a "respectable" occupation, and owned valuable real estate or had a sizable income.

For example, the Chilean constitution of 1813 required literacy, a "decorous" job, and a salary of at least 300 pesos in the provinces and 500 pesos in the capital city. The electoral law of 1830 reaffirmed these requirements and explicitly disenfranchised domestic servants, industrial apprentices, and manual laborers, among others. In Venezuela the electoral decrees of 1830 and 1847 required voters to be literate and proprietors of real estate. According to the Brazilian constitution of 1824, a citizen had the right to cast his ballot in the local parochial assemblies if he had an annual income of at least 100 milreis and was not employed to perform menial services. The provincial electors, selected by the parochial assemblies, were required to have an annual income of at least 200 milreis. The electors chose the deputies and senators, but to be eligible for these offices candidates were required to have a yearly income of at least 400 or 800 milreis, respectively. The Mexican constitution of 1824 established similar property qualifications for deputies and senators. To be considered a Mexican citizen and to exercise voting rights, the constitution of 1837 required a minimum income of at least 100 pesos and literacy. Domestic servants and those who had no regular occupation or income were excluded from citizenship. To be eligible for legislative office, a person had to earn at least 500 pesos per year. The provincial constitutions of Argentina (e.g., Mendoza and Buenos Aires) established equally stringent property qualifications for voters and those running for office.

Obviously, these restrictions excluded the majority of the people from political participation. Oligarchial rule, inherited from colonial times, was effectively sanctioned by the national constitutions. The criterion of selecting voters and candidates for office was plutocratic, increasing progressively as the rank of the position to be filled.

The introduction of universal suffrage in a number of Latin American countries did little to democratize the political process. In most cases, the literacy requirement was not abolished, and this alone was enough to prevent the majority of the people from participating in elections. Yet universal suffrage in conjunction with slowly increasing literacy, particularly since the turn of the century, brought a change in the technique of harnessing political resources among the lower classes.

It has often been suggested that the literacy rate was deliberately kept down by the ruling class to keep the lower classes from voting. Regardless of whether this was the case, the seigneurial landowners soon discovered that rising literacy rates among the dependent workers, sharecroppers, and tenants could be turned to their own political advantage, as long as the existing loyalty relationships remained undisturbed. Formerly, the dependent labor force constituted a political asset only insofar as its ranks could be mobilized to demonstrate power capabilities or to fight out political rivalries or insurrections against entrenched oligarchies and caudillos. Now, universal suffrage and direct elections provided the base for a different kind of political recruitment. The more progressive landlords perceived the advantage of recruiting voters among their dependent labor force. A big landowner could enter a political contest by presenting a measurable block of "safe" voters. Such blocks could be manipulated to support political allies or to outvote competing candidates for office. On election day the voters were herded together and transported to the polling place, usually in a nearby town, where they were treated to food, drink, and fireworks. The local bosses (*gamonales, cabos eleitorais*) saw to it that the voters cast their ballots—a feudal obligation that was taken for granted by landlords and laborers alike. Traditionally, coercion was unnecessary to induce a worker to vote according to instructions. Voter registration presented no unsurmountable problem because the literacy test seldom required more than the ability to sign one's name. This system proved effective even when, as it happened in most countries, the secret ballot was introduced. The bonds of loyalty proved stronger than the chance to exercise free choice in the selection of candidates for political office. Not only were the ideological intentions of the constitution makers frustrated, but the very constitutional provisions were used to reinforce the traditional power structure.

Three major changes had to occur to undermine the traditional political process. The most important source of change lies in the rapid urbanization of Latin America and the consequent removal of political power from the rural areas into the cities. In national and provincial elections the rural voters tend to be outnumbered by the urban voters, who owe no allegiance to feudal landlords and cannot be manipulated in the traditional fashion.

Second, urbanization combined with vastly improved means of communication and transportation offered new alternatives to the rural labor force. Millions of landless laborers, sharecroppers, tenants, and small holders have chosen to migrate to urban centers, thus contributing to a gradual weakening of the traditional power structures. Formal education has played an ancillary role in this process insofar as literacy is often perceived as a prerequisite step in escaping the limitations of rural life.

Third, the rural populations, particularly the rural labor force, have become increasingly involved in "radical" political movements designed to subvert the traditional power structure. Few seigneurial landlords remain who can rely on the political loyalty of their labor force.

The cumulative effects of these three factors and possibly some minor ones have created a new set of conditions that no political charter, however well intended or innovative, could have achieved. None of these changes were originated by the lower classes, and their evolutionary significance can only be understood within the context of a changing economy.

The pattern of rebellion:
obstacle to constitutional government

In Part I the Latin American political process was presented as a dialectical interplay between autocracy and rebellion. The autocratic or authoritarian principle was embodied in Iberian absolutism and its representatives; in the status of the seigneurial landlord in relation to his serfs, slaves, tenants, sharecroppers, and the towns located within his power domain; in the Catholic clergy vis-à-vis the faithful. The pattern of rebellion, both overt and covert, was manifest in a long series of uprisings by Indians and slaves, by taxpayers and encomenderos. In addition, however, there was generalized noncompliance with laws, particularly those which established trade monopolies and sought to protect the Indians from slavery, spoiliation, and exploitation. The extensive use by powerful landlords of private armies against various foes, including rival families of seigneurial status, presaged the state of anomie that followed political emancipation in Spanish America. Far from freezing into a monolith, the ruling class split into rival factions pursuing the contest for power through organized violence. The rebellion that had been smoldering for centuries finally broke into flame and became an established procedure. During the nineteenth century "the right of revolution" became "a political article of faith and an inalienable privilege." (Royal Institute of International Affairs, 1937:144) The "right of insurrection" under certain conditions was formally sanctioned by some constitutions (e.g., those of Guatemala and El Salvador). The struggle for power was an internal affair between individuals and factions representing or allied with the upper class. As long as this was the case, no genuine revolution entailing radical structural changes was intended or attempted, although it must be admitted that once established as a pattern or customary procedure, recourse to violence furnished a recognized model or precedent for revolutionary action.

The achievement of independence can be read as the first massive success of rebellion against autocracy. Yet violent rebellion was not what it is held to be in most of the Western world—namely, an abnormal recourse justifiable only under the most unusual circumstances and fundamentally incompatible with the rule of law. In Latin America rebellion was a customary means of seizing power from someone who had taken it in the same way or was assumed to be unwilling to relinquish it except by force of arms. Once in office, whether by election or by usurpation, a leader had little choice but to assert himself by imposing autocratic rule, which in turn was used to justify attempts to overthrow him.

The interplay between autocracy and rebellion can be interpreted as a schismogenetic or regenerative cycle of cause and effect. (Bateson, 1935) The supposed intention of a power holder to stay in office (*continuismo*) becomes a stimulus for the opposition to plot the violent overthrow of the government; and subversive schemes, both alleged and real, act as stimuli for the established government to remain in power. Whenever a rebellion succeeds, the roles are inverted, but the mechanism remains the same.

It would be difficult to compile a complete list of all uprisings, revolts, mutinies, conspiracies, and coups that have occurred in Latin America since the wars of independence. During the nineteenth century Bolivia alone had 60 so-called revolutions, and a half-dozen of its presidents were assassinated. In the same period Venezuela and Colombia, respectively, had 52 and 27 revolts intended to overthrow established governments. Some of these uprisings engendered bloody civil wars; others attained their immediate objective by the mere threat of organized violence, and many aborted in the initial stages.

The keys to understanding this political process can be formulated in terms of the following questions. In the absence of respected tradition or written charters, elsewhere recognized as alternate or cumulative sources of legitimacy, what associates or dissociates people involved in the political process? In other words, what factors or forces are used to marshal support for or against a contestant? The strongest appeal lay in purely personal qualities claimed and displayed by prospective leaders. Such qualities have variously been described as charisma, machismo, personal magnetism, bravery, and ruthlessness. All seem appropriate enough, although to varying degrees. Of course, the seigneurial extended family and the landed estate, with its servile labor force and retainers, was an ideal training ground for future caudillos. It is doubtful that some of the most outstanding caudillos would have succeeded without the support of their kinship group and the resources of the family estate. Success was contingent on the contestant's ability to impose his will against opposition, and on the readiness of his prospective followers to accept the leader as long as he lived up to their expectations. The same people who had sworn allegiance to a caudillo would turn against him at the first perceived signs of weakness.

Thus Latin American government was the rule of men rather than the rule of law. Not only democracy, but any form of constitutional government, is fundamentally incompatible with personal rule and the mechanism of succession by revolt. This is not to say that political charters were useless. They could not change the political structure and the prevailing pattern of politics; but constitutional resources could be either ignored or harnessed to further the cause of personal government. Constitutions were often enacted to provide a semblance of legitimacy to the rule of a caudillo or dictator. Certain constitutional provisions, such as the "state of emergency" or "state of siege" were widely used to suppress political opposition, to postpone elections, and to perpetuate personal rule. Often victorious usurpators found it convenient to discard the existing constitution and to decree a new one, better suited to their purpose. Law was to serve man rather than the other way around. While being implanted in Latin America, the idea of constitutional government underwent a process of readaptation. The outer form was carefully preserved, but the functions were changed to fit the pattern of autocracy. To be sure there were temporary situations in which constitutional provisions, such as free elections, were allowed to function, mainly because none of the rival power contestants and their parties were strong enough to override opposition.

A century and a half of inveterate constitution making did little to alter the traditional power structure, but other forces did. Primarily, economic development was increasingly at cross purposes with the political process, especially insofar as economic advances changed the social structure in ways not anticipated by the ruling class, which made adaptive changes in the political structure inevitable.

The transition

Merchants and tastemakers: the British enclaves

The gradual expansion and diversification of international trade and the massive transfer of technology from Europe to Latin America were the first suggestions that major changes were under way. It is difficult to set a date for a cultural takeoff from a traditional baseline, but if any date at all is appropriate, it would be 1850 or thereabouts.

The secondary developments then occurring in various regions of Latin America were functionally related to the Industrial Revolution in Europe. Two aspects of the Industrial Revolution had direct bearings on the cultural process in Latin America. Increasing wealth in Europe, particularly in Britain, meant expanding markets for "colonial" commodities such as coffee, sugar, cocoa, tobacco, beef, grain, and mining products. An expanding industrial production naturally stimulated the search for new markets, and Latin America, recently liberated from the trade restrictions imposed by Spain and Portugal, was one of the chosen targets. Since Britain led Europe in industrial development, it was almost inevitable that Britain should play a key role in changing Latin American economic structure and its technological concomitants.

> Everywhere in Latin America, British merchants entrenched themselves—in Buenos Aires, Rio de Janeiro, Valparaiso, Caracas, in Veracruz, Cartagena, Lima. Great Britain, technologically and industrially advanced, became as important to the Latin American economy as to the cotton-exporting southern United States. At this point, Latin America fell back upon traditional export activities, utilizing the cheapest available factor of production, the land, and the dependent labor force. The land in Mexico, Brazil and Argentina emerged as what it had always been, a source of security, income, prestige and power. (Stein and Stein, 1970:135)

It should be added that British merchants played a similar role in Mexico, where they controlled about half the import trade after the country had won its independence. (Tischendorf, 1961:128)

No doubt, the economic response to the stimuli of the Industrial Revolution immensely reinforced the position of the landed estate. The nineteenth century, rather than colonial period, turned out to be the golden age of the latifundio, but the times also laid the foundations for the institution's structural change and its eventual decline in the general context of Latin American society. In any event, the rapidly increasing volume of Latin American exports generated the necessary monetary resources to purchase the goods manufactured in Britain, elsewhere in Europe, and in the United States. This process is usually described in purely economic terms. In the analytical context of our inquiry, however, economic stimuli and responses are viewed primarily as instrumental arrangements through which cultural diffusion occurs at a particularly high rate. The British merchants offered an increasing assortment of goods whose acceptance and dissemination implied a long series of changes. Along with the merchant came the British technician, particularly the engineer, to implant skills without which many imported artifacts would have been useless. Foodstuffs and beverages were perhaps the easiest to introduce to a society in which variety and refinement had been limited to a few wealthy cosmopolitan groups. Thus immediately after Brazil had been opened to international trade in 1808, British merchants who established themselves in the cities began to create a gradually increasing demand for such items as wheatbread, biscuits, steak (*bife, bisteca*), roast beef (*rosbife*), mutton chops, sandwiches (*sanduiche*), tea, beer, gin, whisky, rum, punch, and the type of port wine popular in England. (Freyre, 1948:56–57) Of course these products, and many others, were consumed by the members of the growing British "colonies" who performed the role of tastemakers and pacesetters for the "natives," who eagerly followed models assumed to be more "civilized." A vast and variegated array of articles of clothing (e.g., the white linen suit, pajamas, the dinner jacket, and the raincoat), household utensils, furniture and music instruments (e.g., English china, the buffet, and the piano) gained entrance in Brazil because of the commercial initiative of the British merchants and their display of cultural habits. The water-closet, toilet soap, rifles, revolvers, and pith helmets, followed suit, not all at once, and not exclusively under the impact of British industrialism and mercantile endeavor. (Freyre, 1948:56–57) Soon other European countries and the United States began to compete with the British for the Latin American market.

Gradually, the middle and upper classes of the major urban centers adopted a life style molded on Anglo-Saxon paradigms. In his study of British influence in Brazil, Freyre mentions games such as tennis, soccer, whist, and poker; the English racing horse and related institutions (jockeys, jockey clubs, derby races); five o'clock tea; suburban residence; the summer house and preference for the British "garden city" type of residential pattern; British forms of education for boys, and British parliamentary style. Most of these novelties began to enjoy increasing popularity in Argentina and Chile, too. (Cruz, 1970:169)

To gauge the scope of cultural transplants from Britain and, somewhat later, from the United States, one should be reminded of the English vocabulary that gained currency in colloquial or even in academically approved Portuguese. The following small samples were extracted from a collection of terms compiled by Gilberto Freyre (Freyre, 1948:57–58):

handicap	*sportsman*
esporte (sport)	*poquer* (poker)
match	*refe* (referee)
troli (troley)	*poni* (pony)
tender	*recorde* (record)
lore (lorry)	*craque* (crack)
beque (back)	*reporter*

coque (coke)
estoque (stock)
barca ferri (ferry boat)
esnobe (snob)
futebol (foot-ball)
gol (goal)
golquipa (goalkeeper)
breque (brake)
paquete (packet-boat)
doca (dock)
uisque (whiskey)

pudim (pudding)
iate (yacht)
truque (truck)
time (team)
cheque (check)
buledogue (bulldog)
turfe (turf)
palhabote (pilot boat)
salague (slide valve)
escuna (schooner)
bloco (block)

Many terms listed by Freyre are also current in Spanish-speaking countries.

In Brazil and Argentina, British engineers and financiers assumed a leading role in the construction of railways, gas plants, shipyards, and power plants. The Brazilian railroads measured 15 kilometers in 1851 and 28,665 kilometers in 1920. Between 1857 and 1930, the railway system of the Argentine expanded from 10 to 38,634 kilometers, and by 1913 railroads represented 36 percent of all foreign capital invested in Argentina. (Ferrer, 1967:92–93) The British also established Argentina's packing industry and contributed (as they did in Brazil) to the modernization of farming and stock raising. (Rippy, 1944:106)

> To a Brazilian it is almost impossible to hear reference to machines, motors, tools, railways, tugboats, dredges, undersea cable, telegraph, steel and iron artifacts, mechanical toys, spring chairs, china, bicycles, skates, sanitary toilets, war ships, steam boats, launches, gas or coal stove without thinking of the British. As no other people the British are related to the modernization of the material conditions of life of the Brazilians: the conditions of production, housing, transportation, recreation, communication, illumination, nutrition and relaxation among ourselves. (Freyre, 1948:90)

To this rather impressive list one could add printing, medicine, religion, teaching and even craft industries. British physicians assumed a leading role in the practice and teaching of medicine; British missionaries acted as preachers and teachers as did, to a far greater extent, American missionaries. And there were British mechanics, blacksmiths, shoemakers, tailors, and retail storekeepers who sought to improve their economic condition in Brazil. (Freyre, 1948:66)

In Mexico, Colombia, Peru, and Chile, American technicians and financiers were instrumental in the implantation of modern technology.

In these countries the general lines of technological diffusion were similar to those of the eastern parts of South America. The Mexican railway network, for example, expanded from 640.3 kilometers in 1876 to 19,280.3 kilometers in 1910. (Cosio Villegas, 1960:516, 628)

Europeans and North Americans were not only importers of whole technological complexes, such as railways, steamboats, and power plants; they also had a hand in the export trade, in banking, and in insurance. The viability of such far-reaching technological and economic changes implied certain structural adaptations of the traditional system operating in terms of kinship and feudal allegiances. A complex economic system involving large-scale production and exchange of goods over long periods, as well as customary use of currency and credit, requires standardization of procedures and relative predictability of transactional conditions. Lack of standardized procedures makes for uncertainty of outcome of planned transactions; and uncertainty increases risk and limits predictability. As long as economic transactions are defined in terms of traditional rules honored by people who are bound by kinship or feudal allegiances, an economic system of limited scope may be viable. When these structures become inadequate, however, a code of law must be established and sanctioned by the coercive authority of the state.

Most Latin American countries began to issue commercial legislation during the middle of the nineteenth century. The process was closely accompanied by the founding of corporate forms of enterprise, the *sociedad anonima* modeled after the French prototype of the *société anonyme*. In Brazil, for example, the first commercial code was enacted in 1850 when there were only 11 corporations. Yet 135 new corporations were founded between 1852 and 1859, almost all being trading, banking, transportation, and insurance companies. (Graham, 1968:25)

The following dates, referring to the adoption of the first commercial code in 15 Latin American countries, indicate a high degree of parallelism: Mexico, 1854; Venezuela, 1862; Argentina, 1859; Peru, 1853; Bolivia, 1835; Colombia, 1853; Ecuador, 1882; Chile, 1865; Uruguay, 1865; Paraguay, 1862; Nicaragua, 1877; Guatemala, 1877; Honduras, 1880; Costa Rica, 1882; El Salvador, 1882. (Faria, 1947:30–31)

Carried to the level indicated in the preceding paragraphs, secondary development shifted cultural dependence, particularly in economic matters, from Iberia to Great Britain, the United States and, to a lesser degree, to other European nations. The donor societies became dominant to the extent that they were prepared to protect through political coercion their investments and their citizens residing in Latin America. Paradoxically, political emancipation of Latin America marked the onset of what is now called "neocolonialism"; and eventually neocolonialism supplied the ideological raw material for various political movements seeking the kind of independence the revolutionary wars of the early nineteenth century had failed to achieve.

In evolutionary perspective, however, the cultural transplants of the nineteenth century are to be understood as way stations to Latin America's industrial revolution, which in the twentieth century gradually changed the relative position of the several republics in the international economic and political structure.

In the process of secondary development, the role eventually assumed by the United States far outweighed the influence Great Britain and other European countries once exercised in Latin America. In fact, cultural transplants from the United States, whether planned or spontaneous, pervaded all spheres of Latin American culture. In the present context, however, we are not concerned with enumerating North American transplants; rather, we want to reconstruct earlier developments that established the basic pattern and channels of cultural diffusion.

Early industries

The stereotype of nineteenth-century Latin America is that of an agrarian society precariously depending on the fluctuating market value of a few export crops and mining products. If admitted at all, early industrial initiatives have been depicted mostly in terms of inefficiency, poor management, and insignificant output (although accurate data about these alleged shortcomings are scarce and difficult to come by). Certainly, the output of such factories as there were did not pose a serious threat to European manufacturers. In the present context, these factories were significant because *they existed at all,* and in spite of overwhelming international competition and domestic obstacles, Latin American industry very slowly expanded throughout the nineteenth century. Our contention is that industrial enterprise did not suddenly emerge like a *deus ex machina,* but that its trajectory, irregular and inhibited as it was, reaches back into colonial traditions.

The *obrajes,* which flourished in New Spain (Mexico) and in the viceroyalty of Peru, were an ancestral form of the modern textile mill.

Overcoming the opposition of the craft guilds, which were not set up for rapid expansion, some Spaniards in Mexico showed a remarkably capitalistic orientation in organizing

> industrial establishments, *obrajes*, for the production of wool and cotton textiles. The basic equipment of these establishments was all of Spanish origin: spinning wheel, reel, cards—the wooden paddles set with iron spikes to clean wool—the horizontal loom with pedals to manipulate the sheds. Some capital was needed also to set up the water-driven machinery (*batan*) for soaking woolens in alkaline solution and for beating them until the fibers were felted together to create a uniform surface. (Wolf, 1959:185)

Prior to 1680 there were 7000 looms in the viceroyalty of Peru. The Spanish crown decreed the destruction of all obrajes to free Indian labor for mining purposes; but toward the end of the eighteenth century, there were still 150 obrajes with a total of 3000 looms in Peru. Between 1790 and 1800 textiles exported to Chile were valued at 800,000 pesos. (Romero, 1937:140)

The early textile industries were tied in with native cotton agriculture and, in the Andes, with the breeding of fur-bearing animals (alpaca, vicuña, llama). Too much insistence on agrarian pursuits has caused many to forget that processing the two major commercial crops, sugar cane and coffee, requires "factories in the field"—a veritable rural industry that followed its own lines of technological development. Signposts of this process appear, for example, in the museum that once was the residence of Bishop Colombres, who in 1821 introduced the sugar cane industry in the province of Tucumán (Argentina). Here, a primitive processing device, the old *trapiche*, is flanked by the first steam-driven machinery imported from France in 1853.

The customary emphasis on agrarian pursuits is even more astonishing because we know that the colonial economy was centered on mining rather than agriculture and that in the mining areas, such as Mexico, Peru, and large sections of Brazil, agriculture and ranching were ancillary to the extractive industries. The larger mining centers can in fact be regarded as fairly close approximations to industrial towns. In other words, the common view of Latin American cultural evolution as a transition from agrarianism to industrialism appears to be an oversimplification. Industrial pursuits were part and parcel of the traditional culture; thus we mean to sketch the path of the industrial pattern from the traditional context up to the present time.

In spite of considerable political turmoil following the struggle for independence, textile industry took hold in Mexico during 1830. In 1843, in addition to woolen and silk mills, 57 cotton mills were in operation. Rapid expansion began in the late 1890s, and most enterprises that now play a leading role in cotton and woolen manufacturing were founded around the turn of the century. (Mosk, 1954:122) In 1895 the Mexican textile mills employed 19,000 workers, a figure which in 1910 had grown to 32,000. During the same period the number of artisans engaged in craft production of textiles fell from 41,000 to 8,000, and the total production almost tripled. (Rosenzweig, 1963:444)

In Brazil the formative stage of the textile industry encompases five decades beginning in 1840. "Brazilian entrepreneurs established the cotton manufacture, employing local capital and labor along with indispensable though unpredictable government support. By 1892, basic patterns of the industry had emerged which influenced developments during the next half century or more." (Stein, 1957:185) According to the incomplete figures compiled by Stein, Brazilian textile mills increased from 8 in 1853 to 48 in 1885, and to 110 in 1905. The labor force employed by these plants went from 424 in 1853, to 3,172 in 1885, to 39,159 in 1905. (Stein, 1957:191) Before 1889 there were 626 industrial enterprises in Brazil, and between 1889 and 1914, 6946 more were established, most of them for the production of such consumer goods as shoes, hats, beer, flour, paper, glass, cigarettes, soap, and matches. There were also several foundries and ironworks producing hardware, agricultural machinery, and railway cars and wagons. (Graham, 1968:44) Although many of these early plants hardly exceeded the capacity of craft industries, Graham notes that some attained significant proportions and had moved far from that status (1968:44)

Early in the present century São Paulo had become the largest industrial center of Brazil. In 1907 it had 314 industrial plants (not including rural industries and sugar mills), employing a labor force of 24,200. By 1920 the number of industrial establishments was up to 4,145, employing a total labor force of 83,998. (Villela and Suzigan, 1973:355–356)

In Santiago (Chile) two textile mills existed before the country attained independence. In 1820 a Swiss entrepreneur established another textile plant. A brewery, a soap factory (founded by two Englishmen), and a hat factory were soon added to the embryonic industry of Chile. (Cruz, 1870:172–173)

Early industrial initiatives in Peru were probably linked to capital resources derived from the export of guano which, for several decades, represented a major source of wealth. The first textile mill, established in 1848, was followed by a crystal plant, a gas factory (1851), two lumber yards (1862 and 1870), and a foundry that produced big steam boilers for ships and for the mines. (Romero, 1949:401–403). In Colombia, early attempts at industrialization had to rely almost entirely on scarce domestic capital. Between 1830 and 1860 there was a "proliferation" of consumer goods industries in the Bogotá region.

> Handicraft and cottage enterprises were numerous, and slightly larger establishments, using newer machine methods, began to produce beer, hats, pottery, porcelain, matches, flour, glass and crystal, paper, and cloth. The paper factory lasted only some 20 years; the glass and crystal plant collapsed after a time, to be revived later. Between 1890 and 1900 a modern brewery, a bottlemaking plant, a new pottery plant, new textile plants, a tannery and a salt manufactory appeared. (Hagen, 1962:358)

The great push toward modern industrialization originated in the province of Antioquia. As in the state of São Paulo, the expansion of the international coffee trade created the capital resources and the economic climate needed for industrialization. In 1906 the first textile mill began production with 102 looms and 300 workers. Other textile plants were established in subsequent years, and by 1918 industrial employment in the Medellin area had risen to 6000. (McGreevey, 1971:199)

Obstacles and stimulants to industrialization

Although the background just presented can be interpreted as tentative first steps toward industrialization, an industrial civilization did not arise in Latin America until our day. Nor was it visible earlier in many parts of Europe or in the southern United States. Massive industrialization is a tremendously complex process, and not all its many facets are clearly understood.

Population increase is a first requirement if production of manufactured goods is to be expanded beyond the capabilities of craft industry. But as long as the vast majority of the people live as they did in most rural areas of Latin America—that is, in local subsistence economies in which exchange of goods is based on barter rather than currency, where the ties to markets are of peripheral significance—population increase can hardly be translated into a growing demand for industrial commodities. Little money circulated outside the cities, and only the multiplication and growth of urban trade centers could generate enough monetary resources to establish the necessary conditions for industrial production.

As international trade expanded, the cities did indeed grow at an accelerating rate (see Table 9, p. 232), and many new urban centers were established, particularly during the second half of the nineteenth century. Far from keeping pace with such developments, however, industrialization remained at a rather embryonic stage. Those in control of agricultural and mining resources preferred imported goods, and the state showed little if any inclination to erect the tariff barriers necessary to protect fledgling industries from international competition.

The reluctance of Latin American society to follow the example of the industrializing nations has encouraged much controversy. Political emancipation did not succeed "in creating the bases of sustained economic growth through balanced agricultural, ranching, and industrial diversification." (Stein and Stein, 1970:135) This might be interpreted as failure from the perspective of our development-oriented society, or by present-day Latin Americans, who tend to criticize "dependence" or anything suggesting "neocolonialism." However, such an interpretation makes little sense within the context of nineteenth-century Latin America. Traditionally, power, prestige, and wealth lay in landownership rather than in unpromising, uncertain, and "grubby" industrial enterprise, which was unbecoming to men respected as, or aspiring to become members of, the landholding aristocracy. The few who deviated from the norm were handicapped by lack of technical and managerial skills. The incipient European industries developed out of a rich and diversified craft tradition, and once the power of the guilds was broken, industry could draw on an abundant pool of highly skilled labor. Although there were craft industries in Latin America, they were hardly comparable to those in Europe, the Brazilian crafts being the least developed.

Lack of industrial development in Latin America is often attributed to the absence of entrepreneurship. If this term is narrowly defined as "industrial entrepreneurship," the preceding statement is tautological. If it is meant to include all forms of economic enterprise, the statement is obviously false. In many areas, particularly in Argentina, Columbia, southern Chile, coastal Peru, and southern Brazil, rapidly advancing agricultural frontiers testified to the enterprising initiative of the many who were willing to risk scarce capital in the clearing of immense areas of new land to extend the production of cotton, sugar cane, cocoa, and tobacco, or to produce new crops such as wheat (Argentina) and coffee (Brazil, Colombia, Venezuela, and Central America).

Coffee is a particularly convincing example of entrepreneurship. The clearing of large subtropical forest areas involves considerable investment of labor and capital. Furthermore, the waiting period between the planting of the young trees and the first sizable yields averages about five years, during which the young trees must be tended and the land kept free of weeds. The developing of new mining resources (e.g., guano in Peru and nitrate in Chile) further attest to the entrepreneurial initiative of Latin Americans. Thus entrepreneurship was not lacking, but it was directed primarily toward traditional economic pursuits rather than industrial development. The accelerating rate of industrialization, since the turn of the century, is largely to be attributed to immigration.

Immigration as a factor in industrialization

Secondary development, or the global transfer of cultural patterns from one society to another, seems to be more effective and perhaps faster if the patterns are transplanted together with their human bearers. During the nineteenth century, immigrants were sought after, not just to supply labor or to populate empty territory but to implant desirable skills and working habits, to stabilize political behavior, and to "raise the level of civilization." In spite of much fanciful rhetoric, elaborate justifications, and optimistic anticipations, the politicians and intellectuals who sponsored immigration in such countries as Argentina, Brazil, and Chile, failed to predict some major changes that immigrants, and particularly their descendants, were going to cause in the economic system and the social structure.

Unincumbered by traditional preconceptions about menial labor and entrepreneurial activities at any level, immigrants took advantage of economic opportunities that were shunned by the native middle and upper classes. Even if immigrants came, as the majority did, from Spain, Portugal, and Italy, whose value systems resembled that of Latin America, they found themselves in a marginal position with respect to both their original and their adoptive societies. They felt free to deviate from patterns sanctioned by either society. In fact, the adoptive society expected them to be "deviants"—up to a point, at least. It was hoped, for example, that unlike the natives they would assume positive attitudes toward menial labor and occupations implying such labor.

Empirical evidence shows that immigrants and their descendants have indeed played a leading role in business and industry.

By 1914 they owned approximately 65 percent of Argentine and 49 percent of Chilean industrial establishments. Europeans were particularly active in industries like construction, furniture, and metal products that required specialized artisan skills traditionally scarce in both republics. Since industrialization was just beginning, most of these plants were only small workshops employing a few laborers. But in both countries it was the European, not the native-born citizen, who laid the foundations for later industrial development. (Solberg, 1970:52)

In Peru, many recent immigrants entered the new and risky businesses that produced the new rich of the country. (Lipset, 1967:24) Even in a country with as little immigration as Colombia, a sample of 61 contained 25 foreign-born entrepreneurs in 1961 or 41 percent of the sample. (Lipman, 1969:38)

The entrepreneurial career of Torcuato di Tella, an Italian immigrant of middle-class origin, is one of the few cases that have been competently analysed in terms of successful adaptation of technological and managerial transfers to Latin America. Beginning in 1910, di Tella developed one of Argentina's leading industrial enterprises, which by 1939 was mass producing such items as refrigerators, hydraulic pumps, gasoline pumps, service stations, bakery machinery, electric motors, washing machines, oil pumps, and a variety of similar goods. (Cochran and Reina, 1962:212)

Technical skills unavailable among the Italian immigrants in Buenos Aires were imported from Italy, but Torcuato di Tella was not only a technical innovator and risk-taker; he also proved to be particularly skillful in organizing human relations in a way that did not violate established patterns of behavior. In fact, he turned supposed deterrents to industrialization into positive assets. Labor relations were molded on the patron-client pattern, stressing face-to-face interaction, personal dignity, and trust. Executives who were not members of the di Tella extended family enjoyed the coveted status of *hombres de confianza* (persons of trust), which in traditional Latin America was the next best thing to being a relative. (Cockran and Reina, 1962:263–265)

Perhaps it takes more than one generation of a family to attain the entrepreneurial level in the conventional sense of the term. Many immigrants started out as plain agricultural workers, as sharecroppers, tenant farmers, or small holders. Limited prospects of economic success often induced them to move to urban centers, where they attempted to establish small businesses. If successful, they frequently tried to expand into manufacturing furniture, textiles, leather artifacts, china, matches, dairy products, cigars, hats, and so forth. Often it was only the second, native-born generation that undertook the crucial move to the city. However, the many immigrants who were skilled artisans tended to go to and remain in urban centers, where they plied their trades and sometimes succeeded in developing veritable industries. The evolution from craft shop to industrial enterprise became a genuine culture pattern particularly in Brazil, Argentina, and Chile. The case of Benedicto Chuaqui, reported by Solberg, is typical.

[Chuaqui emigrated from Syria to Chile in 1908 and] eventually built a large hosiery factory in Santiago. His book, *Memorias de un Emigrante,* narrates the painful early years when he struggled to make a living as an itinerant peddler. After much sacrifice he was able to establish a small dry-goods shop, on whose single counter he slept at night." (Solberg, 1970:47)

The "itinerant peddler" of Arabic, Jewish, Italian, or Portuguese origin is a recurrent figure in all parts of Latin America. (Bastani, 1945:138ff) Many years of extreme frugality and ceaseless labor may gradually lead to economic success in form of a sedentary business, which in turn may expand and eventually become an industrial enterprise.

The close association between commerce and manufacturing occurred on all social levels. Warren Dean stresses the role immigrants of middle-class extraction played in the industrialization of São Paulo. Most of them started in the import trade and later switched or expanded into manufacturing. Their relative prosperity made it possible to secure the credit resources of their native countries, which strongly affected the rhythm of secondary development. (Dean, 1969:51ff.)

Many industries established by German, Polish, and Italian immigrants in southern Brazil, originated in craft shops. Throughout the nineteenth and twentieth centuries there have been innumerable cases of skilled weavers, carpenters, ironsmiths, tailors, machinists, watchmakers, brewers, locksmiths, harnessmakers, and brickmakers who set up shop and gradually, by using the unpaid or underpaid labor of their own families, developed their craft into a modest industrial establishment, employing a score of workers and utilizing a few machines driven by steam or water power. The market for such incipient industries was local of course, and often confined to an area settled by immigrants of the same ethnic stock.

The history of the Hering Company, one of the largest textile plants in southern Brazil, typifies the process that was repeated again and again, not just in southern Brazil but almost everywhere in Latin America where immigrants assumed the role of innovators and risk-takers. The brothers Hering, who had been in the textile business in Germany, chose Blumenau, one of the rather successful German settlements in Santa Catarina, as the seat of a small craft shop. Begun in 1879, the shop was equipped with a single circular loom. The labor force consisted exclusively of members of the Hering family.

> But when a second and third loom were acquired, additional workers had to be hired. Existing accommodations no longer sufficed. A simple wooden shack was erected in the backyard which was called "machine building" and where three circular looms, a few sewing machines, a press, some knitting machines and a cutting table were set up. (Ferraz, 1950:175)

Gradually, the factory grew, employing 1140 workers in its various branches in 1943.

A similar history characterizes the Garcia Company, another major textile enterprise, established in 1883 by a German immigrant who brought four looms and a steam boiler from his homeland. (Ferraz, 1950: 185) Virtually all the five textile plants existing in Brusque (Santa Catarina) in the early 1930s developed out of craft industries established by German and Polish immigrants.

Early leather manufacturers originated in São Leopoldo and Novo Hamburgo (Rio Grande do Sul), drawing on the raw materials of a rich pastoral area. Both towns were German settlements established in the 1820s.

> In 1844, São Leopoldo exported 7,681 saddles and 13,995 pairs of shoes. In 1920 there were, in eight municipios of Rio Grande do Sul, 540 tanneries and factories of leather artifacts managed by Germans or descendants of Germans. The center of that industry was Novo Hamburgo. In 1920 there was in Rio Grande do Sul a total of 238 factories employing more than twelve workers. Out of these 130 or 55 percent were owned by German-Brazilians. (Willems, 1946:349)

A large proportion of the remaining 45 percent was controlled by persons of Italian or Polish extraction.

Far from providing a complete picture of early industrial evolution originating in craft traditions that were transplanted by immigrants, the foregoing cases merely exemplify the process. More thoroughgoing information could be extracted from the industrial census of São Paulo state, referring to 1935. Following colonial traditions, this census included a complete record of the names of all individuals and companies engaged in any kind of industrial pursuit. The number of workers employed and of the amount of capital invested gave a fairly accurate idea of the size of the enterprise. To determine the role of immigrants and their descendants in the industrialization of São Paulo, all names that could be identified with certainty as Italian, Arabic, Armenian, German, Jewish (Ashkenazic), English, Spanish, French, and Japanese were separated, on the assumption that the bearers had either immigrated or descended from immigrants of any of those ethnic groups. The process was not totally accurate, of course, because no Portuguese names can be identified as such, and many Spanish names are undistinguishable from Luso-Brazilian names. Furthermore, in a number of cases the designation of the enterprise did not include the name of its owner. In other words, the Brazilian-born descendants of immigrants are underrepresented in the final figures, which can be taken as approximations only.

The census listed a total of 7,840 enterprises employing 213,668 workers (see Table 2). "Rural industries" were excluded from the listings, but the census took into account each owner's nationality. It seems to be significant that 246 of all plants owned by immigrants and their de-

Table 2 *Industries of São Paulo state by nationalities, 1935*

Nationalities	Number of establishments	Number of workers
Brazilian	4,402	156,218
Italian	2,029	22,721
Portuguese	406	5,528
Spanish	245	2,178
Syrian	207	6,248
German	112	1,458
Japanese	64	412
Austrian	45	605
British	27	2,018
French	20	277
American	12	841
Canadian	4	8,834
Others	267	6,330
Total	7,840	213,668

Source: Secretaria da Agricultura, Industria, e Commercio do Estado de São Paulo: *Estatistica Industrial do Estado de São Paulo, 1935*. São Paulo: Tipográfía Sequeira, 1937.

scendants employed 100 or more workers. Also, this figure is a very conservative estimate.

The vast majority of the industrial establishments listed in Table 2 consisted of small workshops employing fewer than 10 workers. They do not fit the conventional concept of industrial enterprise at all; but all could have developed into genuine industries, as some of them undoubtedly did. Here, size is not accepted as a criterion of entrepreneurship. The census data of 1935 represent entrepreneurship at different levels of development or, in other words, of an incipient phase of the industrial revolution, an assumption that has been born out by subsequent events.

The role of the immigrants and their descendants has not been restricted to the implantation and development of an industrial technology. The process outlined in the foregoing paragraphs implies a good deal of upward social mobility. Through the institutional channels of business and industry, people of the most variegated cultural origins moved to social classes higher than they had occupied when they first settled in Latin America. And by doing so they revolutionized the very class structure of which they had become integral parts. They not only changed the culture or life style of the traditional classes, social mobility itself became a highly pervasive structural element. This of course happened only in the few countries, such as Argentina, Uruguay, Brazil and, to a lesser extent, Chile and Venezuela, which attracted *large* numbers of immigrants. The impact of immigration on class structure is analyzed in another chapter.

Adaptive dimensions of industrialization

The fundamental question of whether or when the industrial model of economic production constitutes an adaptive innovation must be supplemented by more specific questions referring to the process of implantation of industry. Capital and energy must be harnessed, labor must be recruited and trained, technical and managerial skills must be available; markets have to be opened, perhaps in competition with external or internal suppliers, and political support has to be enlisted against opposing factions and vested interests. Initial success in establishing particular industries must be followed up by organizational and technical devices designed to sustain and expand production in accord with broadening markets.

To unravel some of the complexities of the adaptive process, two empirical case studies are summarized here. One was carried out in Guatemala, the other in Brazil. Both industrial enterprises were established in traditional communities, but otherwise the two cases are as far apart as possible within the universe of traditional Latin American culture. Cantel in Guatemala was a peasant community of Maya Indians; Sobrado and Mundo Novo in Minas Gerais were small towns in the economic and political orbit of coffee plantations originally based on slave labor. The establishment of a cotton textile mill in Cantel was fairly typical of the implantation process as it occurred in many different areas of Latin America. The following account summarizes the monographic study carried out by Manning Nash in 1954. (Nash, 1958)

The factory in Cantel was established in 1876, at a time when such an undertaking must have been regarded as extremely hazardous. The entrepreneurs were Spaniards rather than native Guatemalans. The spinning machines (20 all together) were imported from Britain, and so were the four engineers responsible for the technical aspects of the operation. The mill was located in Cantel because a nearby river could serve as a source of power for the machinery.

Not unexpectedly, the corporate Indian community resented and resisted the factory, which was believed to be a threat to Indian land-ownership as well as to the traditional way of life. After eight years of opposition, the Indian authorities of Cantel threatened to burn the factory down if it were not removed from the municipio. The owners had to summon military protection to prevent destruction. Local labor was unavailable, and workers had to be recruited in the surrounding area. It seems that during the first decade of operation, survival of the enterprise was related to its rather modest demand for labor. The initial labor force of about 25 workers slowly grew to approximately 100 in 1880; but in the 1890s several hundred workers were employed and since 1900 the number of personnel has fluctuated between 800 and 1000. The mill was a family enterprise (four brothers) and has remained so up to the present day.

Almost 14 years were required to overcome the initial hostility of the Indians and the rejection of factory work. A change of such magnitude raises a number of questions. Since there was no attempt to recruit labor by force, the Indians must have perceived wage earning in the factory as a rewarding alternative to farming, which unlike most ladinos (or westernized Guatemalans), they regarded as a honorable occupation. The Indians were fully aware of the importance of money and monetary income because long before the factory entered their cultural horizon, they had experienced needs that could not be satisfied without the use of currency. The problem was that a large proportion of Indian families did not own enough land to make an adequate living by their own standards. Thus an increasing number of poor Indians accepted factory work as a way out of an economic impasse. Furthermore, the mill employed women and young men who, in the traditional system, were given no opportunity to earn money at all.

In contrast to the uncertainties of farming, factory work provided a steady income. Enjoying an almost monopolistic position in the Guatemala market, and protected from international competition by high traff barriers, the mill in Cantel never had to close down. Factory work was not only stable, it was perceived to be comparatively light in comparison with farming. Aside from offering these situational advantages, factory employment entitled workers to such benefits as free housing, a school, free medical service, a clinic, the loan of small agricultural plots, and of course participation in the Guatemalan social security system.

On the other hand, factory work was so unlike anything the Indian had ever been involved in that major adjustments were inevitable. The Indian workers were not accustomed to machinery nor to the coordinated work rhythm imposed by a rather complex divison of labor. When farming his own land, one was free to set his own pace; there was nobody to tell him what to do or how to do it; and whenever he worked with others, they were relatives, rather than strangers as in the factory. Finally, he was the judge of his own performance, whereas in the mill his work was evaluated by others using criteria not always intelligible to him.

Under these conditions a high labor turnover is hardly surprising. In fact, turnover remained so high that according to Nash, eventual stabilization of the labor force would not have been predicted if the study had been made in the early 1920s. Mutual adjustments between factory and workers, occurring over a period of several decades, gradually eliminated most adaptive problems accompany the implantation process.

The use of physical punishment and abusive language in the training of apprentices was replaced by methods involving a minimum of verbal instruction and very little display of authority. In contrast to earlier times, the engineers—still Europeans—have no direct dealings with the rank-and-file labor, who are supervised by Indian foremen. The factory owners learned to make concessions to local custom. Each section of the factory is adorned with a cross or pictures of saints; workers holding office in the religious hierarchy of the village are given days off, and fiesta days are holidays for all. Gradually the mill developed the afore-mentioned services which, together with steady and rising wages, weighted the scales in favor of those who succeeded in adjusting to factory work.

In accord with the traditional Ibero-American pattern, the mill was run with a mixture of paternalism and authoritarianism. It was strictly a transaction between the entrepreneurs and the local population, but in the wake of the political revolution of 1944 a structural change of the utmost importance occurred: A labor union was organized, and most mill workers joined. The initiative came from the national level, and the local union formed part of a national federation of labor unions, which in turn was related to the international labor movement. Through the union the workers were able to gain economic and political advantages and, at the same time, to lend support to other segments of the national labor force. Integration of the Indian workers of Cantel into a national institution, encouraged and supported by the national government, altered the local power structure and partially shifted control over certain phases of the mill's operation from the paternalistic-authoritarian pattern to a more impersonal and democratic one, directly relating to the national power structure.

This is no more than a brief account of major changes occurring on the heels of industrialization, which is often believed to transform peasants and artisans into a "depressed proletariat" and generally to play havoc with traditional ways of life. Obviously, these things did not happen in Cantel. The factory was absorbed without producing any of the dire effects usually attributed to industrialization. The peasants were not forced off the land to satisfy labor demands of the mill, nor did farming fall into disrepute, thus inducing the Indian peasants to choose industrial employment instead. Cantel did not become urbanized, its class structure did not undergo major changes, and the Indian's original social system remained the chief means of prestige and social control. (Nash, 1958:148)

The case of Cantel is not without precedent. In certain areas of eastern France, western and southwestern Germany, Switzerland, Holland, and perhaps other areas of central Europe, industrialization has managed to encroach on peasant communities without destroying them. On the contrary, during the nineteenth century at least, opportunities for industrial wage earning sometimes revived peasant traditions. (Willems, 1970b)

Mundo Novo and Sobrado in the state of Minas Gerais, Brazil, had none of the peasant or corporate characteristics of Cantel. They were small towns performing political, commercial, and religious functions in a region dominated by coffee plantations. As in most parts of the country the population is composed of elements from Portuguese, African, and Indian stocks; but after centuries of miscegenation, the proportion of each component is almost impossible to ascertain. To all appearances, the Portuguese stock predominates, and the Indian component is the least conspicuous. The following description is based on a study by Brandão Lopes. (Brandão Lopes, 1967)

Industrialization proceeded much faster in Mundo Novo than in Sobrado. The first plant, a cotton mill, opened in 1905. Since 1936 three more textile plants and a paper mill have been established. All these factories are owned by a single family, of recent European extraction, which had grown rich in business. In 1950 the town had a population of 12,000 and in 1958 the industrial labor force numbered 2,200. Sobrado, with a population of 10,000 in 1950, had no more than 900 workers; all were employed by the only industrial plant, a textile mill owned by a "traditional" family of big landowners.

In both towns labor recruitment involved the kind of rural–urban migration so often depicted as an inevitable by-product of industrialization. In contrast to Cantel, where the factory moved to the very source of its labor supply, the workers of Mundo Novo and Sobrado had to move to the location of the factories. As so often in Latin America, migration was a push-and-pull movement: The demand for rural labor was declining because most landholders had switched from coffee to cattle raising, and the vast majority of the rural labor force either owned no land at all or too little of it. Thus many were being pushed out, not necessarily toward Sobrado or Novo Mundo; these towns became increasingly attractive, however, as employment opportunities there grew.

We have little information about the transitional problems relating to the change from rural to industrial labor. We are merely told that a number of workers found it impossible to adapt to the conditions of factory work. On the whole, we can assume that adaptation to a dependency relationship did not pose the same problems observed in Cantel. In Mundo Novo and Sobrado it was only necessary to transfer dependency on a patron from an agrarian structure to an urban–industrial setting. Whereas in 1900 it was somewhat difficult to recruit suitable workers, before long there was an oversupply of labor. This condition favored the entrepreneurs and encouraged the transfer of familism and feudal dependencies to the relationships between factory owners and workers, who perceived employment as a favor to be reciprocated beyond the confines of a labor contract. Workers were expected to be loyal to their employers, and loyalty meant unconditional acceptance of existing working conditions and wages. It also involved political support to the employer and to political candidates who had been approved by him. To promote or to participate in strikes, or to vote "against" the *patrão* in elections were acts of treason, punishable with dismissal. It must be added that the interpretation of industrial relations in terms of the traditional feudal system was (and still is) extremely common. Indeed, it characterizes an early phase in the incipient industrial revolution of Latin America.

Familism finds its clearest expression in the tendency to seek industrial jobs through relatives already employed in one of the plants. Far from being one-sided, this approach is approved by plant owners and managers. A job-seeker recommended by a dependable, long-time employee—a brother, cousin, or uncle—is usually given preference over competitors without such credentials.

Familism is reminiscent of a social structure in which one was either a relative or a stranger not to be trusted. It can be viewed as part of a more comprehensive pattern based on personal, primary, or "sympathetic" relationships. Through long years of employment, knowledge of family background, and standing in the community, an employee may gradually rise to a position of *homen de confiança*—a person to be entrusted with the responsibilities of a foreman, accountant, bookkeeper, or treasurer. The bonds of loyalty between a *homen de confiança* and the owners are particularly strong and cannot be defined solely in terms of contractual obligations.

On any level of employment, loyalty is (or was) perceived as a reciprocal proposition in which services rendered are to be repaid in more than one way.

> Almost all industrial enterprises in Sobrado and Mundo Novo established *vilas operarias* (housing facilities) for their employees, where they may obtain better homes and lower rents. Furthermore, some factories also provide medical assistance and hospitalization, directly or by facilitating payment. Generally, employees in financial straits are granted loans or aid in form of cash or medicine. Plant owners and managers are also constantly approached by their employees for advice and orientation to solve personal and family troubles. Political loyalty on the part of all employees is expected as something to be taken for granted. (Brandão Lopes, 1967:65)

As in Cantel, the industrial structure of Mundo Novo and Sobrado was a mixture of paternalism and authoritarianism; industrial relations were local arrangements, structured in terms of feudal loyalty, familism, and personalism.

Again as in Cantel, the changes that began to intrude on the local system originated on the national level and were distinctly political. To enlist popular support for his dictatorial regime, Brazilian president Getulio Vargas had initiated a series of major reforms designed to appeal to the lower classes, particularly urban labor. Decrees were issued encouraging the creation of labor unions and establishing, among other things, minimum wages. Increasingly effective enforcement of mandatory wage levels took one of the discretionary powers away from the local industrialists and forced them to adopt more rational techniques of management. The labor union was first interpreted by the local entrepreneurs to be incompatible with traditional loyalties, and those who joined it exposed themselves to the customary punitive sanctions. The eventual consolidation of the union and its growing influence on local labor relations would not have been possible without concomitant changes in the political structure. Population growth and increasing urbanization made it possible for populist political parties to gain a foothold in Sobrado and in Mundo Novo and to curtail the power of the traditional oligarchies. It was the beginning of the end of the paternalistic-authoritarian rule of the industrial entrepreneurs.

The two cases briefly described here characterize the implantation of industry, its adaptation to local conditions, and the changes it caused in local societies. Furthermore, both cases indicate how basic changes in the national power structure have affected hitherto localized paternalistic-authoritarian structures by imposing readaptation through the state's coercive authority.

The coming of age
of industrialism

Traditional factors and their decline

Early industrial enterprises, family-owned and family- operated, were usually small and often were craftshops rather than factories; they frequently combined production of commodities with the commercial distribution of these goods; they produced for a local or regional market whose capacity was relatively easy to predict. Typical is the case of a combined textile and business enterprise in the Brazilian state of Santa Catarina. In the early 1930s the firm was operated by a single extended family. All managerial positions in the enterprise were occupied by sons and sons-in-law of the founder, and several grandsons were being trained for leading technical positions in the company, whose shares were almost exclusively owned by the family. One son of the founder (an immigrant from Germany) was the sole distributor of company-produced goods in Curitiba, and a son-in-law held a similar position in São Paulo City. Personal relationships tied distributors to wholesale buyers, and any credit operations involved in running the various plants and businesses of the family, were transacted "among friends." In the 1930s labor relations had already developed beyond the stage of authoritarian paternalism; the workers were then capable of staging brief strikes, and the mill owners called for police "protection." But two decades earlier, the founding entrepreneur, caught in a critical situation of near-insolvency, had convened his small labor force and successfully beseeched them to continue working until he could pay their back wages.

As industrialism expanded, the traditional system began to erode. The waning of such interrelated societal traits as personalism, familism, localism, and paternalism, is of course related to sheer size. Generalized growth inevitably changes not only the structure of the individual enterprise but the total system of which it is but an integral part. A large and complex industrial enterprise is bound to exceed the managerial and technical capabilities of a single kinship group. Sooner or later functions have to be delegated to "strangers," and in the long run professional qualifications tend to override nepotism. This evolutionary trend is reflected in the advertisement sections of virtually all important Latin American newspapers, through which industrial concerns recruit executives and specialized technicians.

Expansion of productive capabilities of course indicates expansion of markets from local or regional to national and international levels, a change equally charged with structural implications. Particularly in the larger countries (Mexico, Columbia, Argentina, Brazil), coalescence of regional economic systems and their eventual integration into a national structure generated an impersonal mechanism of distribution that transcends the integrative capabilities of the customary personalistic forces. (Regarding Brazil, see Singer, 1968.)

Telescoping effects of secondary development

Industrialization in Latin America has not been a wholly spontaneous process molded on the laissez-faire capitalism that marked the Industrial Revolution of nineteenth-century Europe. *It is in the nature of secondary evolution to press what originally were successive primary changes into the mold of concomitance.* Changes in Europe that had succeeded one another at considerable intervals tended to occur almost simultaneously in Latin America. For example, when labor movements arose in Europe industrialism was already thoroughly entrenched in the society. The organization of labor unions can be understood as a collective effort to stem excessive exploitation, which had been going on since the very inception of the industrial system. In Latin America, the origins of the labor movement can be traced to the beginning of large-scale industrialization, although the movement did not reach the more isolated areas until much later. In addition, the role of the state as an intervening factor in the economic process was hesitant and ambivalent as long as industrialization was in its incipient stage. However, the rapid development of Latin American industry since the 1930s cannot be understood apart from the participation of the state. Labor movements and state intervention are dealt with in another chapter.

The ambivalent role of international trade

Growing industrialization in Latin America has been attributed to a complex of interrelated factors. Certainly it would not have been possible without the extraordinary expansion of international trade that reached a peak shortly before World War I. Economically, international trade meant large-scale export of "colonial" products such as coffee, cocoa, wheat, beef, cotton, grain, tobacco, bananas, nitrate, guano, copper, and tin. Such exports made it possible to import manufactured goods on an ever increasing scale. Translated into cultural terms, massive importation of a broad variety of commodities implied a thorough transformation of traditional consumption patterns and life styles, particularly in the middle and upper strata of Latin American society. In sociological perspective, increasing imports were contingent on accelerated urbanization and a considerable expansion of the urban middle classes.

On the one hand, the type of international trade that evolved in Latin America tends to hold back domestic industrialization. Once a market for imported goods has been established, and a solidly entrenched merchant class backed by credit institutions can use its power to perpetuate the status quo, native entrepreneurs have little chance of changing consumer preferences and successfully competing with the importers.

On the other hand, the import trade familiarized Latin American consumers with a broad assortment of new artifacts, utensils, wearing apparel, and food items. It acted as an innovator, thus unwittingly paving the way for future domestic competitors. But more important as an immediate incentive to industrialize, the traditional exports were repeatedly affected by critical price fluctuations in the world market, and soon it became increasingly difficult to maintain imports on a level necessary to satisfy domestic demands for manufactured goods. World War I drastically reduced imports from the industrialized nations and further accentuated the demand for domestic production of industrial commodities. Also, most Latin American governments erected tariff barriers to provide more effective protection from foreign competition.

No Latin American country had an active role in the events leading to the world wars and to the Great Depression of the 1930s. Nor was there any way to stave off the repercussions of wars and depression on the economy of Latin America. Whereas the world wars reduced imports, the world depression had ruinous effects on the export trade and radically reduced income from such trade. Unable to finance imports at a level that had become customary, Latin America had to industrialize further to satisfy the growing demand for manufactured goods. This became a pattern known as "import substitution."

Of course, the extent to which the cultural development of the different nations was contingent on income from international trade, varied so much that no uniform effects could be expected from the reduction of such income. Maximal effects might be expected where, up to the 1930s, exports had generated considerable wealth and relatively high levels of consumption, combined with heavy urbanization, previous industrialization, and technical skills deriving from a continuous flow of immigrants. Only Argentina, Brazil, Uruguay and, to a much smaller extent, Chile, fulfilled all these conditions. Ahead of all other nations was Argentina, where in 1914 of a total population of 7,885,237, there were 2,035,000 people in Buenos Aires, and more than half of all Argentinians were classified as urban. Between 1889 and 1914, 2,351,715 immigrants had come to stay in Argentina. Industrialization was relatively advanced at the beginning of the century, and by 1910 domestic industry was capable of satisfying one-third of all demands related to agricultural machinery. Later, by 1930, a complete petroleum refinery, almost entirely manufactured in the country, was set up. (ECLA, 1966:7)

The case of Mexico shows that the transfer of industrial skills and techniques through the import of capital goods, technical assistance, and licensing of patents rights to domestic producers may well substitute for large-scale immigration. Beginning in 1930 or thereabout, Argentina,

Brazil, Uruguay, Chile, and Mexico succeeded in increasing industrial output to a degree suggesting a radical break with past traditions, particularly with the long-established international division of labor. During the same period, although lacking the resources that a voluminous European immigration would have supplied, Colombia achieved an increase in manufacturing output quite comparable to that of Mexico or Argentina. (See Table 4, p. 217.) Between the early 1930s and 1965, similar trends are observable in Venezuela, Ecuador, and Honduras and, since 1945, in Guatemala, Panama, Nicaragua, Peru, and El Salvador. (ECLA, 1966: 22–24)

Since the increase of manufacturing outputs was determined by the difficulty of paying for imported goods with traditional exports, one would except the import coefficient to decline as the worldwide economic depression began to affect Latin America. This is exactly what happened, at least in Argentina, Chile, Colombia, Brazil, and Mexico, where imports had reached relatively high levels and the conditions for rapid industrial expansion were relatively favorable. In these countries the import coefficient fell precipitously in the early 1930s, although soon it began a series of erratically ascending and descending phases which still characterize the areas. There are several reasons for this, but a particularly important factor is the impossibility for industrialization to proceed beyond its formative phase without recurrent imports of capital goods. The technical means necessary to carry out "import substitution" can come from the outside only as long as the society has not reached the crucial point of secondary development at which it becomes increasingly able to *produce* complex machinery instead of importing it. All this suggests that if industrialization is to proceed at all, it must pass several distinct evolutionary phases. Before characterizing these, let us investigate the empirical conditions under which such changes take place. The two examples presented may seem to be excessively simple, but they uncover some of the cultural mechanisms that may be observed in the process.

The role of the immigrant in import substitution: two case studies

In a small town of southern Brazil, a German entrepreneur industrialized the production of manioc, which had been planted on a small scale within the existing system of subsistence agriculture. Recognizing the market potential for industrial starches, he encouraged the local peasants to increase the production of manioc tubers for which the new *fecularia* or starch mill would pay cash. The impoverished farmers of the region were thus induced to increase production of manioc to the point of ensuring survival of the new industry. All this happened in a brief period before World War I. All the machinery of the fecularia was imported from Germany; at that time Brazilian industry was not equipped even for such a relatively unsophisticated task. By 1934 the Brazilian-born sons of the German entrepreneur decided to build a second, much larger fecularia. This time there was no need to import anything from Germany. The machinery for the new mill was built in the nearby town of Joinville, which was then becoming a small industrial center, mainly under the influence of technicians and small entrepreneurs who had immigrated from Germany shortly after 1918.

By 1907, one of the first groups of Japanese immigrants to Brazil settled in the Ribeira Valley of São Paulo. They introduced a new crop, Chinese and Indian tea, together with the associated rural industry of processing tea in specially constructed plants.

The technoeconomic complex of growing, processing, classifying, and marketing tea was transplanted from Japan along with the necessary machinery. Japanese experts afforded technical assistance to most of the tea producers of the Ribeira Valley. In 1941 there were 23 tea-processing plants in the valley, and all but one were owned by Japanese. At that time the major producers of tea were shifting from imported processing equipment to machinery built in São Paulo by Japanese immigrants. Japan's involvement in World War II eliminated all further import possibilities, and today it would be impractical to import such items from abroad.

The cases of starch and tea processing exemplify what may be called grass-roots "import substitution." Both cases centered around the innovating role of immigrants of differing cultural origin in the process of secondary development. Usually, immigrants are perceived as permanent links with their countries of origin, but from the foregoing cases we can see that immigrants or their immediate descendants can also play a more crucial role in breaking such links, thus in furthering the industrial self-sufficiency of their adoptive society.

Industrialization resulting in import substitution is hardly contingent on the availability of immigrants. As the process become more complex and its dimensions transcend individual skills and initiatives, it depends more and more on skilled labor and technicians hired abroad for a limited time to set up a plant and train native workers in the use and maintenance of the machinery.

Stages of industrialization

In attempting to divide an evolutionary process into stages or phases, we should realize that these terms are somewhat misleading because they suggest measurable periods of time with definite beginning and ends. However, stages fade into one another; a new stage may be initiated while the preceding one is still going strong, and phenomena that characterize one stage do not necessarily vanish when a new stage takes hold. The first stage of industrialization is limited to the production of "consumer goods." These "light" or "traditional" industries process or manufacture food and beverages, often from locally available raw materials. Meat and dairy products, starch, flour, beer, wine, brandy, various soft drinks, and chocolate, are pertinent examples of early industrial endeavors in Latin America. A second complex of traditional industries involves building materials, especially lumber, brick, tiles, and cement. Simple chemicals (compounds and distillations), cigarettes and cigars, leather artifacts, soap, candles, matches, and textiles, perhaps complete the list of the more important goods produced by traditional industries. The technological complexity of the traditional industries is far from uniform. Obviously, the technical equipment and specialized skills necessary to run a brickyard or cheese factory are minimal in comparison to those required by a textile mill, cement plant, or shoe factory. Equally variable are the levels of dependency on imported capital goods; but the *essential* characteristic of the traditional phase is dependency on imported equipment and human skills. There is no country in Latin America that has not entered the first stage of industrialization. Argentina, Brazil, Chile, Mexico, and Uruguay traversed it prior to 1930. Colombia embarked on it under the impact of the worldwide depression of the early 1930s, whereas in some parts of Central America and in Venezuela there were no more than vestiges prior to World War II. (ECLA, 1966:19)

Two major effects on the traditional social structure should be pointed out. The nuclei of an industrial proletariat or working class emerged during the stage of primary industrialization. Although relatively small within the active population, they reached significant proportion in some cases. In Mexico, for example, total industrial employment, including clerical workers, exceeded half a million prior to 1930. Available figures are somewhat difficult to interpret because they do not always distinguish between artisans and industrial workers proper, or if such a distinction is made at all, it rests on debatable criteria.

In 1913 Argentina had 156,810 industrial workers, a figure that had climbed to 812, 441 in 1940. In little Uruguay, there were 65,962 industrial workers in 1936, whereas much larger Venezuela had merely 17,736 at that time. In Brazil the industrial working class increased from 150,841 in 1907 to 275,512 in 1920 and to 781,185 in 1940. (ECLA, 1966:22)

The changing pattern of international trade pushed Latin America toward industrialization, thus triggering an evolutionary mechanism with dynamics of its own. Radical choices made by a society or group of societies, particularly if they go as deep as the Industrial Revolution, inevitably limit or even exclude future options. Regardless of whether a society is able to predict all future implications of such a change, it is almost compelled to follow through and to come to grips with changes successively set into motion by the initial choice.

The internal dynamics of industrialization in Latin America led gradually to further differentiation and increasing complexity. Perhaps the most powerful impulse came from the contradictory effect of the light industries on the important trade. On the one hand they produced goods formerly imported, but on the other hand they required imported machinery, intermediate products, and sometimes raw materials. Unless export expansion keeps pace with increasing imports (which it almost never does) the situation demands relief of the import sector through further industrialization (i.e., more and more goods imported to equip and maintain traditional industries must be manufactured domestically). (ECLA, 1966:19) This means that the market for the imported products is the industrial sector itself, rather than the "final" consumer.

This type of expansion, which occurs in the second stage of the industrialization process, implies not only differentiation of the traditional market concept but also removal of a basic economic process from the direct perception and understanding of the consuming society. For example, if a Brazilian textile plant in the first stage had to purchase its mechanical looms abroad, it would no longer need to (perhaps would not be allowed to) import looms in the second stage, for now the apparatus is made in Brazil. The new industry, specialized in the manufacturing of textile machinery, may or may not have imported its own machine tools from abroad. The chances are that such equipment must be purchased abroad initially; but in time industrialization may reach the third stage, in which the technical means of industrial production—

mainly machine tools and complex equipment—are manufactured by domestic industry. Such steps of course imply heavy demands on manpower, specialized engineering skills, and capital outlay.

In such countries as Argentina, Brazil, Chile, Colombia, Mexico, Peru, and Venezuela, industrialization often proceeded at a rate that far surpassed the saving capabilities of the economy. In fact, it depended to varying extents on the availability of credit in the form of loans provided by domestic government, international credit institutions, foreign aid, or foreign investors. If advancing industrialization gradually freed a number of Latin American countries from import dependencies, it also involved new financial dependencies, tying the emerging heavy or basic industries to foreign investors or owners. Whether such investments were motivated by purely economic expectations, by attempts to marshal political support, or by a combination of both, they have to be paid off in the form of dividends, interest, and perhaps future economic and political commitments.

The amount of capital available for investment of course depends on the saving capacity of all groups and individuals directly or indirectly involved in the economic process. If domestic savings fail to satisfy capital demands, foreign savings are tapped in form of loans or direct investment by foreign industrial concerns. Although between 1950 and 1970 the proportion of foreign capital invested in Latin American industry did not exceed 10 percent of total savings, "it was instrumental in setting up key manufacturing industries by transferring know-how and organizational capabilities. This was also true in infrastructure investments and heavy industries owned by governments, which depended on foreign financing and technical aid." (Baer, 1972:98)

The crucial role of saving in the evolution of an industrial civilization elicits a few comments about the diffusion of this pattern on the individual level and in connection with the savings bank (*caja de ahorros* in Spanish, *caixa econômica* in Portuguese). Saving as a patterned form of behavior seems to stand in contrast to the prevalence of conspicuous consumption, attributed to the upper classes of traditional Latin America. And if the middle classes were as anxious to emulate upper-class behavior as they allegedly are, saving could not be expected to become a widespread habit. Although no data are available about the social composition of savings bank depositors, the relatively small size of the average deposit suggests predominance of middle-class depositors. At any rate, the number of depositors has grown faster than the traditional propensity toward conspicuous consumption seems to warrant.

Table 3 *Savings deposits in relationship to population (Colombia)*

Year	Population	Number of accounts	Accounts (in percent of population)
1956	13,792,710	1,969,890	14.3
1957	14,233,417	2,223,023	15.6
1958	14,688,206	2,435,793	16.6
1959	15,157,526	2,607,527	17.2
1960	15,641,842	2,744,134	17.5
1961	16,141,633	2,910,725	18.0
1962	16,657,394	3,118,380	18.7
1963	17,189,634	3,341,849	19.4
1964	17,738,881	3,499,611	19.7
1965	18,305,677	3,689,357	20.1

Source: Caja Colombiana de Ahorros, *Memoria del Primer Congreso Latinaméricano del Ahorro*. Bogotá: Talleres Gráficos del Banco de la República, 1968, p. 282.

Table 3 shows the recent development of saving deposits in nine banking institutions of Colombia.

Between 1956 and 1965 the total amount deposited in savings accounts rose from 365,592,000 to 1,396,915,000 pesos. (Caja Colombiána de Ahorros, 1968:282) In Venezuela, the number of savings accounts in the National Savings and Loan System increased from 4,847 in 1963 to 183,000 in 1970. (Banco Central de Venezuela, 1970:26)

Earlier data, covering only the nationwide system of federal savings banks in Brazil, report a total of 1,599,334 depositors in 1940; in 1944 the number had risen to 2,228,712. (IBGE, 1946)

Savings of this type may not represent a great deal for the total picture of an economy, or they may not even flow into the industrialization process proper. The foregoing and similar figures are significant because they express the rapid diffusion of a new form of economic behavior congruent with the exigencies of an industrial civilization. Saving is not associated with any particular stage of industrialization, but more and more of it is required as a society moves from stage one to stage two and three.

As stage three is reached and increasingly complex tools of industrial production are manufactured domestically, the industrial system as a whole proceeds toward vertical integration (i.e., it tends to produce consumer goods, intermediate goods, and capital goods). Only Brazil, Mexico, and to a smaller extent Argentina, have made considerable progress toward industrial integration. Chile, Peru, Colombia, Venezuela, and some parts of Central America are still at different points of stage two, and the rest of Latin America is still in the first stage.

Stage four of the industrialization process is characterized by growing exports of manufactured goods to foreign countries. This means that industrial commodities begin to move into a market sphere that exposes them to the kind of competition from which they are protected in the domestic market. Only the most industrialized countries have begun to make progress in that direction. It seems that Latin America itself is now the export market for industrial goods manufactured by such countries as Argentina, Brazil, and Mexico. "Thus, in 1966 Argentina dispatched 76 percent of its total exports of metal products and machinery of all types to other Latin American countries, and Brazil 73 percent." (ECLA, 1969:29)

Steel and automobiles

Particularly striking examples of the second and third phases of the industrialization process in Latin America are provided by the steel and automobile industries. Mexico and Chile first embarked on modern steel production at the beginning of the century. The steel mill in Monterrey (Mexico) augmented its productive capacity beginning in 1942, and two major steel-producing plants have been added since. In Brazil, the first modern steel mills were established in 1925 and 1937. With the opening of the state-owned Volta Redonda plant in 1946, and its rapid expansion and the addition of numerous new enterprises, Brazil became the single largest steel producer in Latin America. In 1969 Werner Baer listed 30 large and small steel firms in Brazil, but as he pointed out, about a dozen very small enterprises were not included in the list. (Baer, 1969:169ff.)

The evolutionary momentum of industrialization can be grasped by observing that by the mid-1960s the Brazilian steel industry was able to produce much equipment for its own expansion, mostly cranes, cylinders for rolling mills, compressors, hydraulic presses, parts for the construction of blast furnaces, and electric furnaces. There were about 22 enterprises employing nearly 34,000 workers, who produced equipment for the steel industry. (Baer, 1969:109) In 1964 the total direct employment effect of the iron and steel industry was estimated at 80,000 workers, but if the employment created by the principal direct consumers of steel products is included, the figure lies between 550,000 and 600,000 workers totaling nearly 30 percent of the total labor force of the country. (Baer, 1969:100)

Elsewhere in South America large integrated steel plants emerged everywhere except in the least industrialized countries. Chile's Huitchipato mill near Concepción opened in 1950. Four years later, Colombia initiated modern steel production in Paz del Rio. Peru followed suit in 1958 with the installation of a steel mill in Chimbote, and two years later Argentina opened its San Nicholas plant. Venezuela became a steel producer with the opening of its Orinoco plant in 1962. (ECLA, 1966:105) By the middle 1960s, Brazil, Chile, and Mexico were 75 to 90 percent self-sufficient with respect to steel products; Argentina was about 60 percent, and Colombia, Peru, and Venezuela somewhere between 25 and 50 percent. (ECLA, 1966:107)

Beginning in the 1930s and occurring more rapidly since World War II, the demand for motor vehicles, especially passenger automobiles, developed in strange contrast to the prevailing income distribution. The wish to acquire an automobile appears to be strong enough to override many other needs. At any rate, the import of motor vehicles climbed fast enough to have disturbing effects on the balance of payments in most countries; eventually the government intervened in the form of heavy import restrictions. These barriers in turn raised the price of motor vehicles by 300 to 400 percent above the international level. (Furtado, 1970:136) Under these conditions it became profitable, at least in major countries with considerable market potentials, to assemble motor vehicles from imported parts. Still, the acquisition of a passenger car or truck, weighed against the income level of most consumers, involved such an extraordinarily high investment that the vehicle had to be kept in serviceable condition indefinitely. (To date there are no junkyards in Latin America.) Repairing and rebuilding motor vehicles soon became a flourishing concern, and the industrial production of parts followed. In Brazil in 1944, for example, it was calculated that parts makers could supply more than 2000 different parts, including radiators, pistons, and springs. (Dean, 1969:229) Thus after the war when European and American companies began to manufacture rather than to assemble motor vehicles, part of the industrial base was already laid, at least in Brazil, Argentina, and Mexico. The trend was toward increasing self-sufficiency, and by 1967 in Argentina and Brazil, more than 90 percent of all parts were produced domestically. In Mexico the level of self-sufficiency lay between 31 and 60 percent, whereas in Colombia, Chile, Peru, and Venezuela it has not yet exceeded 30 percent. (Furtado, 1970:137)

Motor vehicle production in Brazil rose from 224,575 in 1966 to 278,936 in 1968 and to 416,304 in 1970. In 1973 it reached 600,000 units. Argentina produced 32,952 automotive vehicles in 1959, 89,289 in 1960, and 175,318 in 1967. In Mexico production and assembly of automobiles and trucks advanced from 75,199 in 1963 to 113,170 in 1966, and to 118,000 in 1967. (Furtado, 1970:137; Little, 1961:37) Although much of this extraordinary growth may have occurred at the expense of other sectors of the economy, it is difficult to believe that it could have happened without a rise of the income level of the middle class, or perhaps without a simultaneous expansion of that class. In São Paulo, for example, the automobile is now almost taken for granted by members of social segments in which it was a rare exception 15 or 20 years ago.

The growth of the Brazilian market has been attributed to an ingenious device designed to create credit for the growing mass of potential consumers who have no other access to the market. To purchase a car, a person joins a *consórcio* or group of people who agree to pay a monthly amount into a common pool. The total of all monthly payments must be equivalent to the retail price of at least one automobile. Thus every month one car is purchased and raffled off among the members of the consórcio. The monthly payments continue until every member of the group has received his car. Since most consórcios run for a period of several years, monthly payments must be readjusted to inflationary price increases. In one case, for example, payments rose from 80 cruzeiros in the first month to 220 cruzeiros in the last month.

It takes luck to "win" a car after a few payments, but even the unluckiest participant eventually gets the car he would not have been able to acquire otherwise. To the extent that the consórcio is comparable to a lottery, it fits the highly pervasive gambling complex in Latin American culture. The generalized penchant for gambling certainly helped the rapid dissemination of the *consórcios* some of which are now sponsored by automobile dealers. Unhampered by formal regulations, the proliferation of *consórcios* invited so much swindle that the institution is now closely controlled by the state.

Present levels of industrialization

There were 7.7 million industrial workers in 1950, 9.8 million in 1960, and in 1970 the total for Latin America was in the neighborhood of 12 million. These figures are significant for two reasons. First, the cumulative annual rate of growth decreased from approximately 2.4 to 2.1 percent between 1960 and 1970. (ECLA, 1969:20) This means that Latin American industry has lost some of its capacity to absorb a rapidly increasing labor force.

In the second place, the figures do not differentiate between factory workers and artisans. If these two categories are separated and the relative size of each is estimated, as in Table 4, we cannot be sure that the resulting figures are reliable indicators of the prevailing level of industrialization. Table 4 immediately reveals that our figures require some weighty qualifications; otherwise Panama would be as industrialized as Argentina and more than Brazil, and Uruguay would have attained a level superior to that of any other country.

Actually, census distinctions between factory and craft shop are based

Table 4 *Estimated structure of employment in manufacturing in Latin America, 1960*

Country	Total employment in manufacturing (in thousands)	Sector	
		Factory	Artisan
		(percentages)	
Argentina	1720	58	42
Bolivia	185	12	88
Brazil	2850	56	44
Chile	447	54	46
Colombia	748	34	66
Costa Rica	43	44	56
Cuba	400	59	41
Dominican Republic	90	50	50
Ecuador	251	20	80
El Salvador	98	44	56
Guatemala	105	36	64
Haiti	101	18	82
Honduras	44	30	70
Mexico	1556	64	36
Nicaragua	51	24	76
Panama	26	58	42
Paraguay	82	22	78
Peru	536	38	62
Uruguay	200	71	29
Venezuela	295	60	40
Total	9838	52	48

Source: ECLA, *The Process of Industrial Development in Latin America.* New York: United Nations, 1966, p. 75.

almost entirely on the number of workers employed. Thus a country with a relatively small labor force wholly employed in traditional industries and in plants barely large enough to qualify as "factories" may rank higher than countries that have already entered stage three of industrial development.

Industry is usually conceived of as competing with and eventually reducing or even destroying the artisan sector. This may be true in the long run, but sometimes crafts are deeply enough entrenched in the cultural traditions of a society to resist industrial encroachment for long periods.

Persistence of craft traditions in industrializing societies is largely a matter of socioeconomic integration. In Brazil, Colombia, and Peru, there are vast regions barely touched by industrialization; the people are no more than marginal consumers of industrial goods, and consequently they depend on local potters, weavers, blacksmiths, leather workers, and the like. Craft traditions may be expected to possess a high degree of persistence in the "Indian countries" mainly because of the corporate structure of most Indian communities and the social prestige that accompanies the manufacture of artifacts. The strength of the artisan sector in Bolivia, Ecuador, Guatemala, and Peru corroborates such an assumption, but the case of Mexico seemingly invalidates it. In Bolivia and Ecuador, survival of strong craft traditions seems to be due to a combination of at least three factors: incipient industrialization, persistence of Indian traditions, and a relatively low level of socioeconomic integration. Mexico, on the contrary, is one of the most industrialized countries of Latin America, and socioeconomic integration has advanced much farther than in any other "Indian" country.

Furthermore, the term "artisan sector" probably covers two distinct phenomena. In the economically less integrated areas (not necessarily whole countries), the artisan tends to conform to a traditional type. His outlook is static rather than dynamic—he is unlikely to assume the risk of expanding his shop to compete with other artisans for a larger share of the market; and he has no access to modern technology or capital. In other words, he is not an entrepreneur, and the sociocultural context of his life does not encourage changes. This is probably the case in such countries as Bolivia, in certain areas of Brazil and Colombia, in Ecuador, Guatemala, Haiti, Honduras, Nicaragua, and Paraguay, and in highland Peru. But in Argentina, Uruguay, southern Brazil, and Chile, in parts of Colombia and Venezuela, and in Mexico, the artisan sector is largely composed of small-scale entrepreneurs embarking on a venture that hopefully will grow. The artisan-entrepreneur has already been discussed in connection with the economic role of the immigrant, but the economic traditions of such areas as Antioquia in Colombia and São Paulo in Brazil suggest that entrepreneurship is not necessarily associated with ethnicity. At any rate the artisan-entrepreneur should not be seen as an opponent to modern forms of production. (ECLA, 1969:21)

Another way of measuring industrialization is to determine the share of the industrial product in the total gross domestic product. In trying to interpret the distances that separate the most industrialized from the less industrialized countries, bear in mind that the data of Table 5 do not differentiate between the artisan sector and the industry proper. Furthermore, where nonindustrial products (such as coffee in Brazil and Colombia) represent a very large proportion of the gross domestic product, the share of the industrial product tends to be proportionally small in spite of a high absolute level of industrialization.

Table 5 *Latin America: share of the industrial product in the total gross product in Latin America (percentages)*

Country	1950	1960	1967
Argentina	29.4	32.2	34.1
Bolivia	11.9	10.2	10.8
Brazil	15.1	21.4	21.6
Chile	21.2	23.7	25.8
Colombia	14.2	17.0	18.2
Costa Rica	9.5	11.1	14.0
Dominican Republic	11.9	14.0	14.6
Ecuador	15.7	15.6	16.8
El Salvador	12.0	13.6	17.2
Guatemala	10.1	10.5	12.9
Haiti	11.1	12.2	11.8
Honduras	8.4	12.1	14.8
Mexico	19.9	23.3	25.6
Nicaragua	9.4	11.1	12.3
Panama	8.2	12.8	16.0
Paraguay	19.4	17.3	18.2
Peru	14.1	16.7	19.3
Uruguay	17.3	21.2	21.0
Venezuela	8.0	10.6	13.4
Total (Average)	18.7	21.7	23.1

Source: ECLA, *The Process of Industrial Development in Latin America*. New York: United Nations, 1969, p. 22.

The industrialization of Latin America has not lacked for setbacks and crises. Periods of progress have alternated with years of stagnation; in some countries the process has not advanced beyond its incipient stage, in others its coming of age has all but arrived. It is more than coincidence that the largest and most populous countries (Argentina, Brazil, Mexico, and Colombia) are also the most industrialized.

Considering the magnitude and diversity of adaptive problems besetting an industrializing society, temporary reversals should not be surprising. The secondary nature of the process (i.e., the massive and rapid transfer of technology and specialized skills), calls for a rate of behavorial and institutional change that seems to be extraordinarily difficult to accomplish. Some of the stumbling blocks to industrialization are small markets, limited capital resources, and scarcity of skilled manpower. Industrial production is mass production by definition; but traditional income distribution is such that mass consumption of many commodities is no more than wishful thinking. In many parts of Latin America, industrial development runs far ahead of market expansion; thus actual outputs represent only a fraction of what industries are capable of producing. Such a trend results in "inefficient" and "high-cost" industries.

> The situation becomes especially pronounced in industries having high fixed costs. These industries require large-scale output in order to bring costs down to levels prevailing in more advanced industrial countries. Outstanding examples are the steel and automobile industries which have been established in most of the larger Latin American countries. In the case of automobiles, the situation was worsened because a large number of these countries permitted the establishment of many firms, thus completely eliminating the possibilities of economies of large-scale production. In the late sixties, the annual output of cars and trucks in eight Latin American countries was 600,000 which was produced by ninety firms (an average of 6,700 per firm). (Baer, 1972:102)

Not surprisingly, the host of problems besetting the emerging industrial order led to insistent demands for state intervention. In accord with a time-honored pattern, the state was expected to perform the role of universal provider. The state was supposed to change a totally inadequate educational system to supply skilled manpower and to provide credit for a multiplicity of purposes. The state was held responsible for the development or improvement of highways, transportation systems, power plants, irrigation systems, oil lines, port facilities, and so forth; and the state was urged to institute social security systems and minimum wages, to provide housing for the poor, and to redistribute the land. And in addition to this staggering burden, the state was assigned the role of industrial entrepreneur. Needless to say, everywhere the state was ill equipped to cope with the problems of such magnitude and diversity. Most changes required by the new role of the state were contingent on political stability or continuity, which has not been achieved yet in many countries. More about this later.

In some Latin American countries the market problem is compounded by the small size of the population. Separately, the nations of Central America would never be able to carry industrialization beyond the beginnings of the first stage. Jointly, they represent a potential market of nearly 15 million consumers of industrial products. Starting in the early 1950s, El Salvador, Costa Rica, Guatemala, Honduras, and Nicaragua entered a series of mutual agreements that culminated in economic integration "establishing mobility of goods and factors within the union and a common external tariff vis-à-vis the outside world." (Furtado, 1970: 193) Further agreements resulted in the sharing of financial, scientific, and educational resources. Economic integration immediately generated a drastic increase of intra-area exports, and the share of the industrial sector in the domestic product rose from 12 percent in 1955 to 16 percent in 1965. (Furtado, 1970:194)

Other attempts at economic integration in Latin America have failed so far to produce major changes. This is particularly true of the Latin American Free Trade Association, including all South American countries and Mexico. More promising appears to be the Andean Group, composed of Chile, Bolivia, Ecuador, Colombia, and Venezuela, which agreed on gradual liberalization of trade until a complete customs union is established among the Andean nations.

Although the political and economic obstacles to complete economic integratiion of Latin America are enormous, future decisions will be heavily influenced by evolutionary trends outside Latin America, and particularly by the development of the European Common Market.

The point of no return

Industrialization is no longer a matter of choice in Latin America. Aside from the internal dynamics of industrialization the population is expanding so rapidly that no country can afford to rule out further industrialization. An annual population increase rate of 2.9 or 3 percent for

the whole of Latin America means, for example, "that during the opening years of the 1960–70 decade there were over six million more Latin
Americans alive at the end of a year than at its beginning and that there
will be about eight million more Latin Americans on December 31, 1969
than on January 1 of the same years." (T. L. Smith, 1970:29)

These additional millions must somehow make a living, and since under
the present conditions most of them either are located in cities or tend
to migrate to urban areas, the "population explosion" results in an ever-
increasing demand for "urban jobs." Industry has demonstrated the capacity to absorb a large proportion of locally available manpower, particularly
in São Paulo, Buenos Aires, Córdoba (Argentina), Medellin (Colombia),
Mexico City, and Monterrey. Even if industrial employment fails to keep
pace with industrial expansion *and* with population growth, there are few,
if any, alternative ways of coping with the immediate problem of over-
population.

"In all probability throughout the entire history of mankind no other
large section of the earth, except the United States during the years
1790 to 1860, has ever experienced a rate of growth as high as 3 percent
a year." (T. L. Smith, 1970:29) Traditionally, all populations of Latin
America have had high birthrates *and* high death rates. A high fertility
pattern remains "functional" as long as it is counter-balanced by high
mortality rates and perhaps allows a moderate population growth. But if
death rates are suddenly reduced to a fraction of what they once were
without simultaneous changes of fertility patterns, the resulting imbalance
generates the problems that now confront most Latin American countries.

The sudden and drastic decline of the death rate was caused by a
series of cultural changes. Not the kind of changes that "just happen"—
perhaps unforeseen by-products of previous changes—but intended and
"programmed" scientific inventions that were subsequently applied to
improve the survival chances of numerous human populations. The first
major breakthrough was the eradication of yellow fever, one of the most
devastating scourges of tropical Latin America. The invention and massive
application of DDT virtually eliminated malaria, and antibiotics added
another powerful means of controlling endemic infectious diseases. Furthermore, in virtually all countries, state-sponsored initiatives designed
to provide medical assistance to the underprivileged contributed to the
reduction of death rates, particularly of infant mortality rates.

In contrast to many innovations, most new methods of control over
endemic infectious diseases encountered little if any opposition. Diffusion
proved to be relatively easy and cheap.

Even today, total health expenditures represent minor fractions of Latin America's national budgets and very small fractions of national incomes. Many insecticidal methods, in particular DDT spraying, place low demands on technical skills; these can be readily marshalled from local sources or imported from abroad. Numerous instances can be cited where a handful of professional personnel aided by a small number of moderately trained technicians have carried out successful programs involving millions of people. An important contributory circumstance has been that such programs have often required little active cooperation on the part of the public. This has been especially evident in the antimalaria campaigns, which have generally involved visits by "outside" teams and have entailed almost no subsequent disruption of daily routines. Although antibiotics and vaccines have required a greater degree of public participation, the hindrances from local inertia have generally been small. Better health and greater longevity are strongly held goals everywhere, and the means now available for achieving major improvements involve little or no conflict with other values or the general way of life. It is no accident, for example, that foreign technical assistance has been notably more successful in health than in other fields. (Stolnitz, 1958:98)*

Action programs intended to relieve human suffering—to save lives, particularly of small children—carry enough moral authority in the Western world to overrule objections and criticism. High death rates in Latin America were perceived as a solvable problem, and newly available scientific resources were mobilized without giving much thought to the socioeconomic implications of such measures. As birthrates failed to decline along with the mortality rates, Latin America was suddenly faced with a self-inflicted problem of staggering proportions. It may be regarded as an example of the not uncommon way in which planned change intended to solve one problem creates another one of even greater magnitude.

Table 6 provides a historical synopsis of population growth in all countries of Latin America. Most figures referring to the past century are extremely rough estimates even if they represent results of population censuses (as they do in the case of Brazil). Nor are many of the more recent figures to be taken literally. Only a small minority of countries took fairly adequate and mutually comparable censuses prior to 1950. (T. L. Smith, 1970:49) Table 6 was compiled on the assumption that even inaccurate

* Reprinted from George J. Stolnitz, "The Revolution in Death Control in Nonindustrial Countries," *The Annals* of The American Academy of Political and Social Science, vol. 316. Copyright 1958 by The American Academy of Political and Social Science.

Table 6 *Population growth in Latin America (census data and estimates in thousands)*

Country	Year	Population	Country	Year	Population	Country	Year	Population
Mexico, Central American, and Caribbean countries								
Mexico	1850	7,500	Cuba	1841	1,007	Honduras	1881	307
	1895	12,632		1861	1,396		1887	332
	1900	13,607		1877	1,509		1910	553
	1910	15,160		1887	1,632		1916	606
	1921	14,335		1889	1,573		1928	701
	1930	16,553		1907	2,049		1930	854
	1940	19,653		1919	2,889		1940	1,108
	1960	34,923		1931	3,962		1950	1,369
	1970	50,670		1943	4,778		1961	1,885
Costa Rica	1864	120		1963	5,829		1970	2,580
	1883	182		1970	8,553	Nicaragua	1867	257
	1892	243	Dominican Republic	1920	895		1905	505
	1927	471		1936	1,479		1920	638
	1950	801		1950	2,136		1940	836
	1963	1,336		1960	3,047		1950	1,057
	1970	1,798		1970	4,011		1963	1,535
Guatemala	1880	1,224	El Salvador	1930	1,434		1970	1,980
	1893	1,364		1950	1,856	Panama	1911	289
	1921	2,005		1961	2,511		1920	264
	1940	2,383		1970	3,530		1930	428
	1950	2,791	Haiti	1918/19	4,674		1940	566
	1964	4,284		1960	3,097		1950	757
	1970	5,160		1970	4,870		1960	1,075
							1970	1,425

South America

Country	Year	Population	Country	Year	Population	Country	Year	Population
Argentina	1869	1,737	Chile (cont.)	1895	2,695	Paraguay (cont.)	1950	1,343
	1895	3,955		1907	3,231		1962	1,854
	1914	7,885		1920	3,730		1970	2,390
	1947	15,897		1930	4,287	Peru	1836	1,374
	1960	20,010		1940	5,023		1850	2,001
	1970	23,364		1952	5,933		1862	2,461
Bolivia	1831	1,019		1960	7,374		1876	2,652
	1845	1,031		1970	8,835		1940	7,023
	1854	1,544	Colombia	1825	1,224		1950	7,969
	1882	1,098		1835	1,686		1961	9,907
	1900	1,696		1851	2,244		1970	13,590
	1960	3,019		1864	2,694	Uruguay	1852	132
	1970	4,930		1870	2,392		1860	229
Brazil	1872	10,112		1905	4,144		1908	1,043
	1890	14,333		1912	5,073		1963	2,595
	1900	17,319		1938	8,702		1970	2,890
	1920	30,636		1951	11,548	Venezuela	1873	1,784
	1940	41,236		1964	17,484		1881	2,075
	1950	51,944		1970	21,120		1891	2,323
	1960	70,119	Ecuador	1950	3,203		1920	2,412
	1970	92,237		1962	4,650		1936	3,027
Chile	1836	1,010		1970	6,090		1941	3,851
	1843	1,084	Paraguay	1887	330		1950	5,035
	1854	1,439		1889	635		1961	7,524
	1865	1,819		1914	650		1970	10,400
	1875	2,076		1924	829	Total for Latin America in	1970	274,217
	1885	2,507		1936	992			

Source: Kenneth Ruddle and Mukhtar Hamour, eds., *Statistical Abstracts of Latin America.* Los Angeles: Latin American Center of the University of California, 1971; United Nations, *Demographic Yearbook 1972.* New York: United Nations, 1973; D. M. Rivarola and G. Heisecke, *Población, Urbanización y Recursos Humanos en el Paraguay.* Asunción: Centro Paraguayo de Estudios Sociológicos, 1970.

census data and rough approximations are preferable to rejection of all counts and estimates made prior to 1940.

Determinations of natural increase rates cannot be more reliable than general population data, but even a generous allowance for errors leaves no doubt that there are considerable differences—not necessarily from country to country but between groups of countries. Mexico, the Central American countries, the Dominican Republic, Brazil, Colombia, Ecuador, Paraguay, and Venezuela, have annual increase rates exceeding 3 percent. In Chile, Bolivia, Cuba, and Haiti, the rates lie between 2 and 3 percent, whereas population growth in Argentina and Uruguay does not exceed 1.5 percent. (United Nations, 1972:65–66)

There is cautious optimism among some demographers, who believe that high fertility patterns will decline somewhat in the near future or that they have done so already in some areas. As Stycos's research in Puerto Rico has shown, a long-range decline of natural increase rates would be contingent on changes of deep-rooted behavior patterns. (Stycos, 1955) As a rule, such changes take time, especially if they meet the hostility of authoritarian governments in a position to prevent public campaigns in favor of institutionalized forms of fertility control.

Closely related to the tremendous population increase on the one hand, and widely differing levels of development on the other, appear to be the international migratory movements within Latin America. Although largely unnoticed, they have been voluminous enough to reduce the increase of population in the donor countries and to add to that of the recipient countries. Not surprisingly, Argentina's relatively high standard of living, combined with job opportunities superior to those of its neighbors, has attracted numerous migrants from Bolivia, Paraguay, Chile, Uruguay, and Brazil. In Argentina in 1954 there were 369,395 immigrants, coming from Paraguay (133,104), Chile (74,890), Uruguay (53,961), Brazil (52,266), Bolivia (48,567), and Peru (6,607). (Argentina, 1956:37) Many more migrants have come to Argentina since 1954, particularly from Bolivia and Paraguay. Although no reliable figures are available, there has been also a steady flow of migrants from Paraguay to Brazil, particularly to the state of Mato Grosso. (T. L. Smith, 1970:50)

In January 1971, when Venezuelan authorities forcibly returned a number of Colombian families to their native country, allegedly because of illegal entry in Venezuela, the ensuing reaction in the Colombian press called attention to a very substantial migratory movement from Colombia to Venezuela. Particularly since 1960, the flow of Colombian migrants has seemingly increased, and in 1971 the number of Colombians in the state of Zulia alone was estimated at 300,000, of whom 200,000 were living in Maracaibo. (*El Tiempo*, Bogotá, January 20, 1971)

In Central America, Honduras has been the recipient of a continuous flow of immigrants from densely populated El Salvador, and the tropical regions of Costa Rica have attracted numerous settlers from Nicaragua. (T. L. Smith, 1970:49) Finally the Caribbean area has been the scene of substantial migratory movement from Haiti into the Dominican Republic.

Too little is known about international migrations within Latin America to assess their demographic or social implications. They may relieve pressures here and fill gaps there. In some areas they may change the ethnic composition of the working class, as they certainly do in Argentina; but at least in two countries—the Dominican Republic and Honduras— they have caused or contributed to bloody conflicts.

The changing city

Rates and patterns of growth

To place urban growth within the context of the Industrial Revolution easily suggests a close correlation between the two phenomena. Many Latin American cities began to grow considerably and to acquire at least some symbols of modernity long before industry was playing a noticeable role in the socioeconomic system. The export trade rather than industry paid the way of early modernization of such cities as Rio de Janeiro, São Paulo, Buenos Aires, Montevideo, Santiago, Lima and Mexico City. And in the past century many new cities were founded that took roots and developed without any industry at all. La Plata in Argentina and Belo Horizonte in Brazil are conspicuous examples of modern cities that remained without industry for decades. Dozens of cities emerged and developed during the nineteenth and twentieth centuries in the coffee-producing areas of Brazil and Colombia without the benefit of industrialization. In fact, recent urbanization without industrialization has been the rule rather than the exception in Latin America. On the other hand, at various times since the early 1900s many of the old cities began to feel the impact of industrialization. Their physical and social structure changed sometimes beyond recognition. The most extreme case is probably São Paulo, whose colonial past is now almost completely obliterated. Yet there is no doubt that urbanization is running ahead of industrialization; in other words, whatever the growth rate of industry, it has not been able to keep up with the expansion of the cities.

Considerable confusion has been created by the habit of calling any city "preindustrial" if it has remained, for whatever reasons, without any industry at all. There are no preindustrial cities in Latin America now because they all depend on the technological and institutional achievements of an industrial civilization. None could survive in its present form without such sources of energy as electricity, steam, and fossil fuel. None could do without mass-produced goods, imported from distant industrial centers by rail, ship, truck or airplane. And the extensive trade system that keeps the city supplied with essentials would bog down without the services of modern communication and transportation systems. There are many nonindustrial cities in Latin America, but none is preindustrial, not even those that have preserved the picturesque quaintness of their colonial past.

Of course, the foregoing assertions may lose validity if a city is merely defined as a residential aggregate with a population of 2000 or more, because many of the smaller localities have few, if any, of the cultural characteristics of a city. Thus the percentages of Table 7 stipulating populations of 2000 or 5000 as the lower limit for urban centers, ought to be taken as rough approximations only. Furthermore, the percentages of Table 7 do not reflect the distribution of either urban or rural populations. If, for example, 50 percent of the inhabitants of a given country are classified as urban, are they concentrated mostly in one single metropolitan area, or are there several major urban centers? The cultural implications of either possibility are obvious. If a country's urban population is distributed over a number of cities, located in different regions and performing diverse functions, the chances are that different styles of urban life will develop, styles discernible in the physical and social structure of each city. In a highly decentralized system, cities may become as different from one another as Medellin and Cartagena, Quito and Guayaquil, or

Table 7 *Percentage distribution of urban and rural population in Latin America*

Country	1950 Rural	1950 Urban	1960 Rural	1960 Urban	1970 Rural	1970 Urban
Argentina	35.8	64.2	32.4	67.6	—	—
Bolivia	74.2	25.8	70.1	29.9	—	—
Brazil	69.2	30.8	60.6	39.4	45.1	54.9
Chile	42.2	57.8	37.1	62.9	31.8	68.2
Colombia	63.6	36.4	53.9	46.1	38.0	62.0 (1972)[a]
Costa Rica	71.0	29.0	62.2	37.8	—	—
Cuba	50.7	49.3	45.4	54.6	38.8	61.2 (1971)[a]
Dominican Republic	76.2	23.8	69.5	30.5	60.3	39.7
Ecuador	72.3	27.7	65.3	34.7	60.9	39.1 (1972)[a]
El Salvador	72.3	27.7	67.4	32.6	60.6	39.4 (1971)
Guatemala	76.0	24.0	69.0	31.0	—	—
Haiti	89.9	10.1	87.4	12.6	—	—
Honduras	82.7	17.3	77.5	22.5	76.8	23.2
Mexico	54.2	45.8	46.4	53.6	49.3	50.7
Nicaragua	71.9	28.1	66.1	33.9	51.4	48.6 (1972)[a]
Panama	64.0	36.0	59.0	41.0	52.4	47.6
Paraguay	72.2	27.8	66.2	33.8	64.3	35.7 (1970)[a]
Peru	72.0	28.0	64.2	35.8	52.6	47.4
Uruguay	33.3	66.7	29.2	70.8	—	—
Venezuela	51.1	48.9	38.3	61.7	24.3	75.7 (1970)[a]
Latin America	61.0	39.0	53.9	46.1	—	—

[a] Estimate.
Source: United Nations, Economic Commission for Latin America, *The Economic Development of Latin America in the Post-War Period*, II. E/CN. 12/659/Add. 1, April 7, 1963; United Nations, *Demographic Yearbook 1972*. New York: United Nations, 1973.

Bahia and Pôrto Alegre. On the other hand, in a highly centralized urban system, the possibilities of cultural differentiation are as limited as they are in such countries as Chile and Uruguay.

In most countries of Spanish America the dominance of the capital city is uncontested. Dominance is reflected in relative size, institutional centralization, and industrial concentration. The proportion of the total population residing in the capital city conveys a measure of the degree of dominance which, according to Tables 8 and 9, exhibits a broad range of variation. However, in each country dominance of the capital is limited by the number of "principal cities," which absorb some of the total pop-

Table 8   *Estimated percentages of population living in capitals and principal cities of Spanish America and Haiti (about 1970)*

Country	Number of principal cities	Percentage of total population in principal cities	Percentage of total population in capitals
Mexico	22	16.4	17.3
Costa Rica	5	7.6	11.3
El Salvador	4	9.9	9.8
Guatemala	4	2,2	14.1
Honduras	4	6.5	8.9
Nicaragua	4	7.6	14.6
Panama	4	7.6	29.2
Cuba	5	8.9	11.7
Dominican Republic	5	5.1	16.3
Haiti	3	1.5	8.1
Argentina	13	15.4	35.0
Bolivia	5	5.3	11.3
Chile	5	9.8	30.3
Colombia	19	24.0	10.3
Ecuador	1	12.2	8.0
Paraguay	3	2.4	18.4
Uruguay	4	8.1	49.0
Venezuela	7	15.6	10.5

Source: Adapted from Kenneth Ruddle and Mukhtar Hamour, eds., *Statistical Abstracts of Latin America*. Los Angeles: Latin American Center of the University of California, 1971, p. 63; and D. M. Rivarola and G. Heisecke, *Población, Urbanización y Recursos Humanos en el Paraguay*, 2nd ed. Asunción: Centro Paraguayo de Estudios Sociológicos, 1970, p. 62.

ulation. The more "principal cities" there are, and the higher the proportion of the population living in such cities, the more decentralized the urban system concerned. The "principal city" concept is not only relative but somewhat arbitrary. Principal cities in Argentina, Mexico, and Colombia are urban centers with populations of 100,000 or more. If the same size category were applied to Uruguay, Costa Rica, or Haiti, however, there would be no principal cities at all. A city of 50,000 may be functionally important within the urban network of Paraguay or Honduras, but it would hardly have the same status in Mexico or Argentina. In other words, the category of "principal city" was adapted to the size and corresponding urban differentiation of the countries under scrutiny.

The most urbanized country in Latin America appears to be Uruguay. (See Tables 8 and 9.) With almost 50 percent of its population living in

Table 9 *Population of capital cities in Latin America (in thousands)*

City	Year	Population	Percentage of total population
Mexico City	1950	3050	8.7
	1960	4871	8.1
	1970	8360[a]	17.3
San Jose	1950	87	10.9
	1960	101	7.6
	1969	203	11.3
El Salvador	1950	162	8.7
	1960	256	10.2
	1969	349	9.8
Guatemala City	1950	294	10.5
	1960	573	13.4
	1970	731[a]	14.1
Tegucigalpa	1950	100	7.3
	1960	165	8.8
	1970	232	8.9
Managua	1950	109	10.4
	1960	235	15.3
	1965	262	—
Panama City	1950	128	15.9
	1960	273	25.4
	1972	418	29.2
Havana	1953	785	13.7
	1966	990[a]	11.7
Port-au-Prince	1950	134	4.3
	1960	240[a]	6.0
	1969	340[a]	8.1
Santo Domingo	1950	182	8.5
	1960	370	12.1
	1969	655	16.3

Montevideo, the country also presents the highest degree of urban centralism—indeed, no more than 8.1 percent of all Uruguayans reside in the four next largest towns (see Table 7). Argentina and Chile are usually mentioned together with Uruguay as highly urbanized countries dominated by a single metropolitan area. Chile appears to be particularly close to the model of highly centralized urban system. More than 30 percent of all Chileans live in Santiago, but only 9.8 percent in five principal cities. Argentina, however, presents a different picture. Although

Table 9 *(Continued)*

City	Year	Population	Percentage of total population
Buenos Aires	1950	6062	18.8
	1960	6763	14.8
	1970	8191*a*	35.0
La Paz	1950	321	10.6
	1960	360	9.7
	1969	525	11.3
Brasília	1960	142	—
	1970	272	0.3
Santiago	1952	1350	22.8
	1960	1907	25.9
	1970[a]	2781	30.3
Bogotá	1951	639	5.5
	1964	1662	9.5
	1969	2294	10.3
Ecuador	1950	210	6.6
	1962	355	7.9
	1969	496	8.0
Asunción	1950	207	15.6
	1962	305	16.8
	1970	437*a*	18.4
Lima	1961	1436	14.5
	1970	2815*a*	20.7
Montevideo	1963	1204	46.4
	1970	1415*a*	49.0
Caracas	1950	495	9.8
	1969	787	10.5

a Estimate

Source: Adapted from Kenneth Ruddle and Mukhtar Hamour, eds., *Statistical Abstracts of Latin America*. Los Angeles: Latin American Center of the University of California, 1971, p. 63; and D. M. Rivarola and G. Heisecke, *Población, Urbanización y Recursos Humanos en el Paraguay*, 2nd ed. Asunción: Centro Paraguayo de Estudios Sociológicos, 1970, p. 62.

35 percent of the population is concentrated in Greater Buenos Aires, there are 13 cities with more than 100,000 inhabitants, and Córdoba was reported to have a population of 800,000 in 1970. Although Paraguay is much less urbanized than any of the aforementioned countries, the dominance of Asunción is not in doubt. A high degree of urban centralism, combined with heavy urbanization, characterizes Panama, whereas the Dominican Republic, Guatemala, and Nicaragua are somewhat less ur-

Table 10   *Urbanization of five major regions of Brazil, 1970*

Region	Total population	Urban and suburban population	Percentage	Percentage of urban population living in capital cities
North	3,650,750	1,649,430	45.2	72.8
Northeast	28,673,770	11,980,937	41.7	36.3
Southeast	40,331,969	29,347,170	72.5	40.1
South	16,683,551	7,434,196	49.3	21.9
Center–West	5,167,203	2,493,011	48.2	47.2

banized, and the dominance of their capital cities appears to be less pronounced.

A somewhat different pattern prevails in Costa Rica, Honduras, Cuba,
and Bolivia. Although their urbanization differs in many respects, the
relative position of their capital cities seems weak in comparison to their
principal cities.

A clearly decentralized urban system prevails in Colombia, Ecuador,
El Salvador, and Venezuela, where the combined population of the principal cities outweighs that of the capital. Decentralization is most strongly
accentuated in Colombia, where the combined population of 19 principal
cities is more than double the number of Colombians residing in Bogotá.
Ecuador's position seems to be unique insofar as Guayaquil, the only
"principal city," has been growing much faster than Quito, the capital.

Mexico combines a high urbanization rate with a high percentage of
the total population concentrated in the metropolitan area of Mexico
City. However, that percentage is not significantly higher than the proportion of all Mexicans living in 22 major cities. Notwithstanding the
unequivocal dominance of Mexico City, the urban system of the country
is relatively decentralized, particularly in view of the fact that, as in
Colombia and Venezuela, the medium-sized cities have a higher growth
rate than the capital.

If one wishes to include Brazil in Table 8, its position would be unique
indeed. Of course, Brasília, the new capital, should not be regarded as a
genuine expression of prevailing urbanization trends. Rio de Janeiro, the
old capital, is the second largest urban concentration of Brazil, but its
share of the total population did not exceed 4.5 percent in 1970, suggesting
the highest degree of urban decentralization in Latin America. How-

Table 10 (Continued)

Number of capital cities	Number of principal cities	Percentage of total population living in capital cities	Estimated percentage of total population living in principal cities
6	2	33.0	4.7
9	12	15.2	4.7
5	26	29.4	12.6
3	11	9.8	8.9
3	3	14.5	5.4

Source: Fundação IBGE, Anuário Estatístico do Brasil, 1971. Rio de Janeiro: Instituto Brasileiro de Estatística, 1971.

ever, the continental size of Brazil and its extraordinary diversity of ecological and sociocultural conditions place this country into a category by itself. Here, internal differentiation, reflected by strikingly diverse levels of evolution, makes statistical averages almost meaningless.

However, if Brazil is divided into five ecological and sociocultural regions, each one can be regarded as comparable to a major Spanish American country. The north, covering three states and three territories, comprises the largest area and the smallest population, one third of it being concentrated in the six capital cities (Table 10). The only two major urban centers of the entire Amazon area are Belém and Manaus. In sharp contrast to the north stands the northeast, where about 30 percent of all Brazilians are located. Each capital of the nine component states is a major city, and two metropolitan areas, Recife and Bahia, have more than a million inhabitants (Table 11). Although twelve cities were classified as principal, they absorb no more than 4.7 percent of the total population.

The most highly urbanized area by far is the Southeast. The two largest metropolitan areas of Brazil—São Paulo and Rio de Janeiro— are located in the southeast. Together with Belo Horizonte they account for more than 25 percent of the total population of the southeast, but 26 principal cities with populations of 100,000 or more absorb about 12.6 percent of the area's inhabitants, indicating a significant degree of urban decentralization. The highest degree of urban decentralization, however, is found in the south, where agglomeration in the three capital cities is not only the lowest in Brazil, but among the lowest in Latin America. And it is not much higher than the proportion of people living

Table 11 *Population of capital cities of Brazil*

Region	1872	1890	1900
North			
Porto Velho			
Rio Branco			
Manaus	29,334	38,720	50,300
Boa Vista			
Belém	61,997	50,064	96,560
Macapá			
Northeast			
São Luis	31,604	29,308	36,798
Teresina	21,692	31,523	45,316
Fortaleza	42,458	40,902	48,369
Natal	20,392	13,725	16,056
João Pessòa	24,714	18,645	28,793
Recife	116,671	111,556	113,106
Maceió	27,703	31,498	36,427
Aracajú	9,559	16,336	21,132
Salvador	129,109	174,412	205,813
Southeast			
Belo Horizonte			13,472
Vitória	16,157	16,887	11,850
Niterói	47,548	34,296	53,433
Rio de Janeiro	274,972	522,651	811,443
São Paulo	31,385	64,934	239,820
South			
Curitiba	12,651	24,553	49,755
Florianópolis	25,709	30,687	32,229
Pôrto Alegre	43,998	52,421	73,674
Center–West			
Cuiabá	35,987	17,815	34,393
Goiânia			
Brasília			

in 11 principal cities. The Center–West, an immense area with a sparse population, has few urban centers of any significance apart from the two state capitals and Brasília.

Within the southeast, the state of São Paulo (Table 12) presents such an extraordinary picture of urban development that some special attention is required. In 1970, 17,958,693 or 19.1 percent of all Brazilians resided in São Paulo, and 80.3 percent of the state's population was classified as urban. If only cities having more than 20,000 inhabitants are included,

Table 11 (Continued)

1920	1940	1950	1960	1970
		27,244	51,049	48,272
19,930	16,038	28,246	47,882	84,334
75,704	106,399	139,620	175,343	312,160
		17,247	26,168	36,491
236,402	206,331	254,949	402,170	633,749
		20,594	46,905	86,307
52,929	85,583	119,785	159,628	265,595
57,500	67,641	90,723	114,799	220,520
78,536	180,185	270,169	514,818	859,135
30,696	54,836	103,215	162,537	264,567
52,990	94,333	119,326	155,117	221,484
238,843	348,424	524,682	797,234	1,060,752
74,166	90,253	120,980	170,134	263,583
37,440	59,031	78,364	115,713	183,908
283,422	290,443	417,235	655,735	1,007,744
55,563	211,377	352,724	693,328	1,235,001
21,866	45,212	50,922	85,242	133,117
86,238	142,407	186,309	245,467	324,367
1,157,873	1,764,141	2,377,451	3,307,163	4,252,009
579,033	1,326,261	2,198,096	3,825,351	5,921,796
78,986	140,656	180,575	361,309	608,417
41,338	46,771	67,630	98,520	138,556
179,263	272,232	394,151	641,173	885,564
33,678	54,394	56,204	57,860	100,865
	48,166	53,389	153,505	381,056
			141,742	272,002

Source: Fundação IBGE, *Anuário Estatístico do Brasil*, 1971. Rio de Janeiro: Instituto Brasileiro de Estatística, 1971.

we find that the number of such cities rose from 16 in 1940 to 28 in 1950. In 1960 there were 47 urban centers of that size, and in 1970 the number had risen to 88. The percentages of the state's population residing in cities with populations in excess of 20,000 were as follows: 26.7 in 1940, 35.5 in 1950, 45.6 in 1960, and 62.7 in 1970. (IBGE, 1962:2–3; 1971:165ff.)

Table 12 *Growth of urban population in São Paulo*

Year	Cities with population of 20,000–50,000	Cities with population of 50,001–100,000	Cities with population of 100,001 or more
1950	20	7	2
1960	26	15	7
1970	55	17	20

Source: IBGE, *Estado de São Paulo. Sinopse Preliminar do Censo Demográfico.*
Rio de Janeiro: Serviço Nacional de Recenseamento, 1962; Fundação IBGE, *Anuário Estatístico do Brasil,* 1972. Rio de Janeiro: Instituto Brasileiro de Estatistica, 1972.

The degree of centralization of the urban system of São Paulo is indicated in Table 12, which divides all cities into three size categories. That cities of more than 100,000 should have tripled every 10 years since 1950 might have been expected, but the somewhat surprising substantial increase of cities with populations between 20,000 and 50,000 suggests that the development of very large metropolitan areas such as São Paulo City, absorbing one-third of the state's population, is not incompatible with a fairly high measure of urban decentralization, particularly at the level of small provincial cities.

The disintegration of the traditional city

The phenomenal pace of urban growth was bound to explode the physical structure of the traditional Latin American city. Urban expansion is usually related to massive in-migration, and rightly so, but one should not forget that the flow of inmigrants merely added to the relatively high natural increase rates of most urban populations. Since it was impossible to accommodate the swelling urban masses within the tight physical structure of the colonial town, residential aggregates began to spring up outside the old city perimeter.

These structural changes affected all social classes, even the old upper class, which is always depicted as being closely attached to the area around the central plaza. If members of this class chose to relocate in new residential areas, the traditional center must have ceased to be synonymous with social preeminence. In contrast to other social strata, relocation of the upper class was clearly a matter of choice reflecting changes of the traditional life style. The process occurred gradually of course, and in many cities die-hard families hold on to their old town houses to the present day. On the whole, the exodus from the central city into "suburban" residential areas began much earlier than was formerly assumed. In Guatemala City, for example, the suburbanization process was well under way by 1900. It was an innovation imported by newly rich merchants of alien extraction and accepted by wealthy native landowners and entrepreneurs, most of whom did not belong to the old upper class. At any rate, by 1948 some of the old families had already moved out of the center. (Sander, 1969:142) A similar pattern characterized the Panamanian capital. An early trend to establish new residential barrios outside the prestigious center began to change the structure of Panama City prior to World War I. (Sander, 1969:25)

In spite of its isolation, Bogotá was one of the first colonial cities in which the traditional upper class began to desert the center. Of 418 "old or historic" families that had been living in five barrios of the old center, only 7.5 percent resided in the same area after 1938–1940. Apparently the exodus occurred gradually over a period of 40 years. (Amato, 1968:77)

The dislocation of the traditional upper class has been a universal phenomenon in urban Latin America. It began at different times and proceeded at widely varying rates, but there is hardly any city with a population of 500,000 or more in which the process has not been completed. Of course, the relocation of the upper class ought to be viewed in the perspective of a general population exodus from the urban core into new residential areas. Eventually the urban center came to be increasingly specialized in nonresidential functions.

Contrary to what some observers seem to believe, the traditional upper class was not nearly large enough to populate the immense residential barrios which have sprung up in the last half century or so. Even if we attribute a prodigious fertility rate to the 410 historical families of Bogotá, they could not have populated more than a tiny fraction of the residential barrios that have developed north of the old city. And if their numbers are multiplied to include the "new upper class" of bankers, high-ranking bureaucrats, wealthy businessmen, and professional people who bear none of the illustrious names of the past, the total would represent hardly more than one-third of the people living in the northern sections of Bogotá.

As a matter of fact, the bulk of the people who populate the new barrios are members of a highly differentiated middle class; but it is not always possible to establish a clear spatial separation between middle-class and upper-class districts. Sometimes, as in San Salvador, for example, the upper-class barrios have moved away from the urban center, and areas of formerly high standing have been taken over by the middle class. (Sandner, 1969:112) In Managua, on the other hand, residential ranking of new barrios has been more stable, and apparently middle-class areas are geographically distinct from upper-class districts. (Sander, 1969:83) The patterns observable in San Salvador and Managua have been repeated in many cities; but clearly segregated upper-class barrios are probably less common than the mixed residential areas, where streets flanked by rather unassuming row houses alternate with clusters of isolated "villas" symbolizing recent economic success or the more conservative taste of old established families. Often the ethnic origin of the owner is reflected in the architecture of his residence. Immigrants from Arabic countries, especially, have tended to invest their newly acquired wealth in elaborate mansions of Moorish design.

The physical structure of most Latin American cities expanded without totally obliterating the original core area. The old part of the city frequently has been partially or totally preserved. This is the case, for example, in many Mexican cities, in the Central American capitals, in Bogotá, Cartagena, Quito, Lima, Córdoba, La Paz, Bahia, and Recife. The extent to which the old center was preserved is not unrelated to its original size and the prevailing types of construction. Except for a few architectural monuments, for example, there was little incentive to preserve colonial Rio de Janeiro, whose old center was largely rebuilt during the nineteenth century. On the other hand, colonial Lima, Quito, and Bahia were so abundantly endowed with magnificent edifices, religious and secular, that reconstruction would have been considered to be unnecessary at best and vandalism at worst.

In a few cases, however, physical expansion assumed such extraordinary proportions and proceeded at such a high rate of speed that the old urban center was virtually erased, and the past is now barely recognized in a few isolated structures. Buenos Aires and São Paulo are the most impressive examples of this. Both cities were swamped with European immigrants, particularly Italians, who were more inclined to build a city in their own cultural image than to respect local history. Both cities financed their vertiginous growth from the proceeds of an extremely profitable export trade, and both cities took the course of early industrialization. But Buenos Aires had a considerable start over São Paulo. Between 1855 and 1860 its population rose from 90,076 to 181,838, and in 1872 it reached 204,634, whereas in the same year São Paulo had no more than 31,000 inhabitants. When São Paulo was still essentially a colonial town, Buenos Aires was rapidly becoming a metropolis. Its population rose to 663,854 in 1895, to 950,891 in 1904, and to 1,231,698 in 1909. Long before the turn of the century, "the aristocratic element shifted to the city's northern edge along the streets of Córdoba and Santa Fé and left the blocks adjoining the Plaza de Mayo (old center) to commercial and business houses." (Scobie, 1971:164) As elsewhere, the preference for new residential areas was largely determined by British and German residents who "started to move northward to homes in Belgrano, San Isidoro and San Fernando, and some Porteños followed the trend initiated by European tastemakers." (Scobie, 1971:164) Of course the exodus from the old center was almost irrelevant, given the rapid development of huge new barrios whose inhabitants had never lived anywhere near the old city. By 1910 Buenos Aires had assumed the morphological features that made it the "Paris of South America." The sumptuous architecture of the business district and the palatial homes of the upper-class residential areas, all emulating the most elaborate Parisian models of the 1890s, were designed to last and to survive the architectural changes of recent decades. Although high-rise buildings are multiplying now, they are far from dominating the city.

Early industrialization led to the development of working-class barrios, mainly in the following satellite cities: Avellaneda, Cuatro de Junio, Lomas de Zamora, Quilmes, General Martín, and Vincente Lopes. In 1954, 72,713 industrial establishments employing a total of 829,463 workers were located in Greater Buenos Aires, that is, the federal capital proper, plus 17 cities (partidos) surrounding the federal district. (Czajka, 1959: 193)

São Paulo's first great leap forward came between 1890 and 1900, when the population climbed from 64,934 to 239,934, partly under the impact of Italian immigration. In 1910 the population was estimated at 375,000, and by 1919 it had risen to 526,000. The old center rapidly lost its residential functions, and a number of new barrios emerged all around the "hill," where the original town was located. In Higienópolis, which in the early 1900s was a kind of suburb in relation to the center, the traditional upper class built "palatial homes, unsurpassed in splendor and luxury by the great mansions of Europe." (Wright, 1907:212) The burgeoning middle class built its own barrios south and west of the core area, and the lower class followed the path of industrialization in the northern barrios of Braz, Mooca, Lapa, and Penha. In 1950 in the area of greater São Paulo there were, 24,519 industrial establishments employing a total of 484,844 workers. By the time of World War I, a British company had initiated the construction of a number of garden cities, such as Jardim

America, Jardim Europa, and Pacaembú, which soon attracted increasing numbers of middle- and upper-class residents. As in Buenos Aires, the "garden city" represented a radical break with architecture and life styles of the past. It was no longer the patio house, flush with the street and neighboring houses, turned inward for privacy, but rather the isolated villa surrounded by lawns and shrubbery, facing the street and affording ample opportunity for ostentation.

With a few exceptions, the edifices that replaced the colonial buildings of traditional São Paulo were a far cry from the elegant structures that filled the financial and business district of Buenos Aires. In the mid-1930s the inadequacy of most buildings erected between approximately 1880 and 1920 caused another radical break with past traditions: Vertical lines rather than horizontal began to dominate the urban profile. São Paulo of 1970 has been called a "jungle of skyscrapers" conforming to the stereotype of a "North American" city, whereas Buenos Aires still carries the connotations of a "European" city. In 1970 greater Buenos Aires and greater São Paulo had 8,191,000 and 8,137,401 inhabitants, respectively.

Buenos Aires and São Paulo are the most impressive but by no means the only cities in which traditional urban past was almost completely superseded by massive and extremely rapid modernization, and the usual population movement from the colonial center to peripheral residential areas had little relevance. Montevideo, Santiago, and, more recently, Caracas experienced equally hectic phases of modernization, reducing previous urban nuclei to a few isolated architectural monuments.

The development of new residential areas has been accentuated in recent decades by the proliferation of so-called shantytowns or squatter settlements. Given the extraordinary rate of growth and size of these settlements, as well as the problems they have caused, Chapter 13 is entirely devoted to the phenomenon.

All in all, the disintegration of the traditional city represents an inversion of the centripetal (i.e., centralized) structure of the colonial town; a centrifugal (i.e., decentralizing) process now has carried the various social classes into different directions away from the old town. People formerly lived in fairly close proximity, permitting a kind of face-to-face symbiosis, which gave way to spatial segregation and impersonal interdependence unrelated to one's place of residence. The new barrios are worlds apart, each having its particular set of institutions, its life style, and its value orientations.

Four patterns of urban expansion

If and when a city begins to expand, the areas next to the old city perimeter seem to be the most desirable ones to extend into the surrounding space in the existing street design—the checkerboard pattern in Latin America. This is what happened everywhere, as long as sea, river, swamp, or steep hills did not make *circumferential extension* impossible or impractical. Often the land was owned by city people who welcomed the opportunity to sell their holdings (*chacaras* and *quintas*) to the highest bidder, but often enough circumferential expansion involved dislocation of lower-class populations inhabiting the fringe barrios of the city.

Yet at spots in the irregularly extending circumferential areas, expansion resulted into bulges following railways or, more recently, key highways leading to ports or important cities of the interior. Within the general context of growing zonal specialization, these *sectorial extensions* harbor industry and working-class neighborhoods, or they may become residential barrios of various kinds.

Of the four patterns, however, *dispersive nucleation* has caused the most drastic changes in the traditional urban structure. As land became a marketable commodity and urban expansion a matter of private entrepreneurship, residential projects more or less distant from the advancing city perimeter began to attract people in search of housing. Called *loteo, lotificación,* or *urbanización* in Spanish and *loteamento* in Portuguese, the process of dispersive nucleation consists of dividing a rural property into small lots, which are offered for sale to urban residents. Often land is speculatively bought and left unused for years until its market value has risen high enough to yield expected profits. But apparently many owners sold or sell whenever opportunity arises. Although empirical studies of *urbanizaciones* are too scanty to allow generalizations, in many cities it was possible for a person with a small income to purchase land in suburban areas. In Bogotá, for example, the availability of relatively inexpensive land is believed to have staved off for a while the emergence of shantytowns. (Pineda Giraldo, 1969:59) Prior to 1945, an abundance of relatively cheap land in many suburban areas of São Paulo made it possible for numerous working-class families to acquire a lot on which to build a modest house. As a rule, these nuclei had no city water, no sewer system and no electricity. The streets were unpaved and unlighted, and in most cases people had to walk a long way to public transportation.

It was part of the speculative scheme of the landowners to use the first group of settlers as a political lever in demanding those urban services from the city administration. Once the improvements had been granted at the expense of the taxpayers, the demand for the land would increase, thus, too, its market value. Of course, such speculative designs were not always successful, and many such lower-class settlements differ from shantytowns only insofar as the inhabitants are legal owners of the land.

On the other hand, dispersive nucleation produced numerous middle- and upper-class settlements on land that had already been improved or "urbanized" before being put on the market. Major projects of this kind were sometimes fashioned after European models and often initiated by such European enterprises as the City Company of São Paulo, which then implanted new architectural styles and new modes of urban living.

Dispersive nucleation generates a large number of more or less isolated residential aggregates, each having its individual layout separated from similar settlements by stretches of unused land. The integration of all these aggregates into a network of urban services (e.g., streets, transportation, water, sewerage, electricity, telephone service, police protection, and public schools) presents almost unsurmountable problems, especially in the rapidly growing metropolitan areas of the capital cities. Of the four patterns under scrutiny, dispersive nucleation is doubtless the one that justifies the title of this chapter. In recent years the disintegration process has assumed a more controlled form as most cities tried to subordinate further urban development to a master plan; but controlled or not, dispersion goes on in the form of public housing projects as distant from the city and as mutually discontinuous as any loteamentos.

Many of the formerly isolated nuclei have grown together in the meanwhile, presenting huge compact urban areas (e.g., the northern part of Bogotá or the suburbs of Rio de Janeiro following the Central Railway). Another radical break with the traditional pattern of urban centralism becomes obvious in many of these new areas: They cease to be merely residential or industrial, developing instead their own commercial, banking, and entertainment centers, often surprisingly similar to parallel developments in the United States.

The last of the four patterns of urban expansion refers to conurbation or integration of formerly distinct communities into the urban complex. As a rule, such localities were predominantly rural before they were affected by the expanding city. And more than a few trace their origin to colonial times. Yet almost everywhere a gradual sectorial expansion along arterial roads eventually reached these communities and transformed them into residential and/or industrial suburbs. The process has been quite common in Latin America, but its frequency and dimension depend on traditional settlement patterns prevailing in the area in which the city is located. Thus, for example, San José, the capital of Costa Rica, was surrounded by a ring of such autonomous communities, which were eventually absorbed by the expanding city: Escazu, Desamparados, Guadalupe, San Juan, San Vicente, San Pedro, and Curridabat, originally peasant settlements and later centers of small rural districts, are now residential barrios of San José. Contrary to the idea that in Latin America suburbs are lower-class barrios, most of these integrated areas are socially differentiated into lower-class, middle-class, and sometimes upper-class neighborhoods. (Sandner, 1969:68–69)

Social composition of urban populations

Migration as a source of diversity

Urban society in Latin America has always been heterogeneous. Iberians, Indians, and Africans represented different racial stocks and strikingly different cultures that often failed to coalesce in the social environment of the colonial town. Nor were these cultural divisions completely synonymous with the cleavages of the system of stratification. Although Indians and blacks were usually relegated to the lowest ranks, there were poor urban whites and many people of mixed ancestry whose status aspirations were chronically at variance with their positions as determined by social and economic contingencies beyond their control. In the first part of our inquiry it was made abundantly clear that the lower urban strata, particularly mestizoes and mulattoes, did not resign themselves to the lowly ranks assigned them by the ruling class. The medieval notion of a God-given station in life, which provided rigidity and ideological support to European society, failed to take hold in Latin America except perhaps in the self-anointed aristocracy.

Accelerated growth, combined or not with industrialization, substantially augmented the sociocultural complexity of the city. Aside from expectable changes in occupational structure, migration, both internal and international, is the factor that has been adding to the cultural heterogeneity of the Latin American city.

Most internal migrations proceed from rural areas to urban centers, often to smaller cities first and to metropolitan centers later. The more distinct the original culture of the migrant, the more pronounced its likely effect on the cultural diversity of the city. In Mexico, Guatemala, Ecuador, Peru, and Bolivia, where the rural population is overwhelmingly composed of culturally distinct indigenous communities and migrants are mostly Indians, the impact on the city appears to be quite different from the changes caused by rural–urban migration in the cities of Chile, Costa Rica, or Cuba, where the rural population is considerably more westernized.

From the percentage of urban inhabitants who were not born in the city in which they live at the date of a population census, we can gain a fairly accurate idea of the volume of internal migration. Not all of it is rural–urban, of course, but birthplace data justify the assumption that a large majority of such migrants do indeed originate in small communities and rural areas.

Comparison of the three federal districts including the national capitals of Brazil, Mexico, and Venezuela, shows closely parallel migratory trends. In 1950 the percentage of inhabitants who were not natives of their respective capitals amounted to 43.5 in Rio de Janeiro, 46.4 in Mexico City, and 48.6 in Caracas. (T. L. Smith, 1970:105) Particularly high percentages of in-migrants were found in major Colombian cities, according to the census of 1951. In Bogotá, 56.7 percent of the population had moved to the city from other regions; in Barranquilla that percentage amounted to 48.8, and in Medellin 55.5 percent of the total population had migrated in. (T. L. Smith, 1970:108) In Colombia internal migration has affected all major cities to roughly the same degree, but such movement has gravitated very heavily toward Lima in Peru. Of the 2,815,000 inhabitants Lima had in 1970, about 60 percent are believed to have come from other regions of the country. (Valdivia Ponce, 1970:15)

The role of Santiago as a recipient of in-migrants resembles that of Lima, but the majority of the Chilean migrants proceeded from urban rather than rural centers. In 1957 36 percent of the 1,118,000 inhabitants of greater Santiago were natives of other regions of Chile, but 63 percent of all migrants had been born in urban areas. (Universidad de Chile, 1959:97–98)

Regarding Brazilian cities, a sample of 4228 adults living in six urban centers of widely differing size and located in three states, revealed that 25.8 percent were born in the city in which they were living, 14.4 percent were natives of other large cities, 36.2 percent had come from small towns, 13.4 percent from fazendas or hamlets, and 9.8 percent were aliens. (B. Hutchinson, 1963:43)

Although the number of foreign immigrants has been rather negligible in the demographic picture of most Spanish American cities, it has

Table 13 *Population of greater Buenos Aires
according to place of origin*

	1869	1895	1914	1936	1947	1957
Total population (in thousands)	230	783	2035	3430	4724	6370
Population according to origin (percentage)						
Natives of Buenos Aires	50	42	40	52	55	42
Natives of other Argentine provinces	3	8	11	12	29	36
Aliens	47	50	49	36	26	22

Source: Gino Germani, "The Process of Urbanization in Argentina," United Nations Economic and Social Council General, E/CN 12/URB/LA/4. New York: United Nations, September 1958.

loomed very large in Buenos Aires. As shown in Table 13, estimates based on four national censuses indicate that the percentages of foreign immigrants in the population of greater Buenos Aires rapidly decreased while the proportion of migrants from other provinces of Argentina rose from 3 percent in 1869 to 36 percent in 1957.

According to another source, the proportion of internal migrants in the population of greater Buenos Aires amounted to 27.08 percent in 1960. (Lattes and Lattes, 1969:49)

Córdoba, the second largest and second most highly industrialized city of Argentina owes its population gains—from 386,828 in 1947 to 702,465 in 1967—largely to in-migration. In these 20 years in-migration represented 48.3 percent of the total population increase. (Sanchez and Schulthess, 1967:8)

Of all the major Brazilian cities—except Brasília of course—São Paulo probably is the only one that has grown over a period of 60 years (1900–1960) more by in-migration than by procreation: Between 1900 and 1920, internal migrants there and in Buenos Aires represented only a minority in the total migratory flow, most of which originated in Europe. But since 1920 internal migration rose sharply, and from 1930 on foreign immigrants represented no more than a tiny proportion of the total migratory volume. Between 1900 and 1920, 64.4 percent of São Paulo's population increase was due to in-migration. In the following two decades the total migratory flow rose to 66.5 percent; between 1941 and 1950 it went up to 70.5 percent, and during the subsequent decade it fell to 58.4 percent. (Camargo, 1968:110–111)

The assumption that foreign immigration necessarily generates cultural heterogeneity ought to be qualified. In Argentina, Uruguay, and Brazil, Italians composed the largest single immigrant group. Between 1857 and 1950 Argentina had a net immigration of Italians amounting to 1,774,178. The next largest contingent were the Spaniards, of whom 1,251,336 settled permanently in Argentina. All other groups were small in comparison to Italians and Spaniards, and their total, distributed over 16 nationalities, amounted to 852,018 between 1857 and 1940. (Hechen, 1955:150–152)

Between 1819 and 1962 Brazil reported 5,638,730 immigrants. Among the national groups composing this total, the Italians numbered 1,623,155 or 28.5 percent, the Portuguese followed closely with 1,453,852 (25.7 percent), and the Spaniards totaled 708,271 (12.5 percent); the 252,339 German immigrants accounted for 4.4 percent, and the 224,504 Japanese represented 3.9 percent of all immigrants reported by Brazilian sources. We can estimate that approximately half these immigrants settled permanently in Brazil, except for the Japanese, whose "fixation quotient" has been close to 90 percent.

Without minimizing the cultural differences between Italians, Spaniards, and Portuguese on the one hand and Latin Americans on the other, there can be no doubt that the cultural affinities more than offset the differences. Perhaps the most convincing evidence is that immigrants from the Iberian peninusla and Italy have assimilated to their adoptive societies at a rate that has been unmatched by any other immigrant group. In any event, these groups were not a source of cultural diversification in Latin American cities. On the contrary, they probably contributed to the continuity and unity of basic cultural patterns, among which family and kinship organization and religious beliefs and attitudes are the most obvious examples. The role of these immigrant groups has not been confined to Argentina, Uruguay, and Brazil. Particularly pervasive and ubiquitous has been Spanish immigration, which left no Latin American country untouched. Especially Uruguay, Venezuela, Central America, and Mexico have attracted Spaniards by the thousands ever since the 1850s, when intercontinental migration began to reach sizable proportions.

Social mobility

The centrifugal expansion of the Latin American city, reflects three processes: unprecedented population growth, changes in the system of stratification, and changes in the life style of the different classes. By changes in the system of stratification are meant increasing social mobility, particularly upward mobility, a restructuring of the three major classes, and greater differentiation and general expansion of the middle class. "Social stratfication" designates a system of ranking people according to such criteria as descent, somatic characteristics, wealth, political power, occupation, education, and religious affiliation, and perhaps others. Ranking criteria and the relative weights assigned to them are a function of culture: At any given time a society may classify its members in a way that differs from ranking patterns of the past, and different societies have been found to adhere to diverse ranking systems.

One important variable, the criterion of descent, may carry enough weight to overrule or control all other measures. To descend from parents who belong, by birth, to a particular group, often carries a number of privileges defined by law or custom. Descent may allocate political power, including the prerogatives to exploit human and natural resources, to monopolize certain professions defined as honorable, to have access to the universe of literature and fine arts, and so forth. In the other direction, descent may prevent one from obtaining political power and bar him from the sources of economic wealth; it may condemn one to dishonorable, vile, or unclean occupations and automatic exclusion from the cultural resources that only formal education can make available. Since these different life styles are rigidly determined by descent, they are beyond the control of the individual. One is born and dies in such a stratum, called a *caste*. There are only two castes in some societies, but often there are several, constituting a genuine hierarchy. The caste concept is relevant here because Latin American systems of stratification have been described as caste systems developing into class societies. In Part I we indicated that neither Spanish nor Portuguese America ever presented a social structure that could be regarded as a caste society, although local communities often bore certain characteristics of caste systems. But the strictures of local caste systems did not necessarily carry over into other communities, particularly not into cities in which a person's ancestry was unknown or could be concealed.

The concept of caste has been widely applied to the structural arrangements of communities composed of Indians and mestizoes (Andes) or Indians and ladinos (Mesoamerica). A case in point is the Peruvian town of Muquiyauyo, whose population used to be divided into two castes —the Indians and the mestizoes. The difference was cultural rather than biological: Indians lived on communal land, spoke Quechua, wore the traditional dress, and had no formal education. Mestizoes were individual landowners, spoke Spanish, controlled business and local government, and had access to formal education. Intermarriage between the castes was "theoretically prohibited." Anybody descending from Indian parents was automatically registered as Indian and anybody of mestizo parentage was considered a mestizo. (Adams, 1959:82–83) But apparently biological descent was an ambiguous thing, for the mestizoes too had Indian ancestors, and there was no reliable way of telling a mestizo from an Indian by somatic appearance alone. In other words, if an Indian left Muquiyauyo and went to a larger town where he was unknown and where he succeeded in living like a mestizo, he would have overcome the caste barrier. We do not know whether or to what extent this happened in the nineteenth century, but we do know that caste was local rather than national. By 1943 the Indian way of life had changed so thoroughly in Muquiyauyo that all Indians were then registered as mestizoes and the caste order had become a class system.

In a class system, descent is *not* the overruling criterion of rank. It may or may not coexist as a sort of booster with a number of other criteria or variables relied on by sociologists to determine class "membership"—mainly wealth, occupation, and education. These variables surely are aspects of what has been called *class culture*, but class culture cannot adequately be described in terms of a few selected elements. Like any other culture or subculture, it is a way of life reflecting a person's upbringing; the house and neighborhood he lives in; the way he dresses, speaks, eats, and drinks; his occupation and income; his habits of spending money or saving it; his religious affiliation; his leisure pursuits; his political interests and participation in political activities, and perhaps other modes of behavior that symbolize class status in a particular society. Since descent does not exclusively determine who does or does not belong, class is open to those who wish to belong and who have demonstrated the capability of internalizing the modes of behavior and acquiring control of the symbols by which members of a class identify one another. In other words, it is social mobility that characterizes a class system in contrast to a caste order. Ancestry (*abolengo*) is not an unsurmountable obstacle to social ascent, nor does it protect a person or family from sliding down the social scale. Upward mobility is regulated insofar as there are recognized channels through which one can move from a lower to a higher level. In Latin America, for example, the Catholic Church has been such a channel, mainly because the scarcity of priests has compelled the hierarchy to recruit candidates to the priesthood whereever they can be found.

The existence of channels of social ascent does not carry any implications relating to the extent to which such channels are used. It has never been claimed that upward mobility was easy or frequent in traditional Latin America, but it certainly occurred on a moderate scale, and its frequency increased substantially during the nineteenth century. This becomes immediately clear if the proliferation of new employment opportunities is taken into account. The expansion of export and import trade in many cities: The emergence of a network of banking and insurance institutions (formerly quite insignificant), and the creation of a modern infrastructure composed of railways, domestic steamship companies, gas companies, waterworks, and electrical power companies, meant thousands of clerical, technical, and managerial positions of middle-class rank. In other words, the appearance of new opportunities rather than the elimination of barriers opened avenues of social ascent to people who formerly would have found it impossible to lead a middle-class existence in an urban environment. This kind of social mobility has been termed "structural," in contrast to "exchange mobility," involving "exchange of positions in a relatively fluid social system." (B. Hutchinson, 1962:10) The latter type depends on individual ambition and drive, but it would be misleading to interpret the two categories as mutually exclusive.

Usually these structural changes, if admitted at all, are thought of in connection with the modernization of existing cities and the "loosening" of traditional systems of stratification. Little attention has been paid to the *urban frontier* and the extent to which it affected social mobility. Hundreds of new cities have been founded during the last century, mostly in regions that formerly had been undeveloped or only sparsely populated. Often enough such cities grew beyond the 50,000 or 100,000 mark within a few decades and offered a broad range of positions in their economic and administrative structures.

The case of Pereira in the department of Caldas, Colombia, exemplifies the process of structural mobility within the cultural context of the urban frontier. Pereira was founded in 1863 by migrants from Antioquia who played an exceptionally energetic role in establishing rural and urban settlements in Colombia. There were neither Indians nor Africans to work for the settlers, and consequently there was no way of reenacting the kind of ethnic stratification that characterized other areas of Colombia. In 1871 the government distributed 12,000 hectares of public land to be divided into holdings not inferior to 32 and not exceeding 100 hectares. (Jaramillo Uribe, 1963b:365) In fact, the small family-owned and family-operated farm has remained the prevailing form of land tenure around Pereira. At first founded on cocoa, rubber, and gold, the economy shifted to coffee, sugar, and cattle and eventually branched out into industry. In 1905 Pereira had 19,036 inhabitants, by 1918 their number had risen to 24,735, and 10 years later the figure stood at 50,699. In 1938 Pereira had a population of 60,492, which during the following 25 years rose to 203,437. In 1963 the city had 10 industrial plants employing a labor force of 10,000. (Jaramillo Uribe, 1963b:382–386) In 1971 the population of Pereira was in the neighborhood of 230,000.

There is enough evidence to convince us that the original settlers did not belong to the privileged strata of Colombian society—settlers who accept small holdings of land and cultivate them without slaves or serfs, never do. Differentiation into social classes followed rather than preceded the development of Pereira. "Of twenty-three local members of the *Asociación Nacional de Industriales*, at least ten, now managers and owners of industries, came from the sector of small merchants, white collar employees and industrial workers, and their fortunes have been made during the last fifteen years." (Jaramillo Uribe, 1963b:413)

The case of Pereira is not unusual at all. There were or are similar urban frontiers in many areas of South America, particularly in Venezuela, Colombia, Brazil, and Argentina. Perhaps the largest number of entirely new cities, all founded in the present century, covers the western region of São Paulo and the north and west of the neighboring state of Paraná (Brazil).

Among the few empirical studies of social mobility in Latin American cities, Bertram Hutchinson's comparative essay on Buenos Aires, Montevideo, and São Paulo is particularly relevant to this chapter. This intergenerational study assigns one of six hierarchically ordered status categories to the fathers of the informants. Tables 14 and 15 leave out one of the two alternative classifications of the Uruguayan sample, opting for the one that assigned the lowest status to small farmers in the parental generation.

The "status" category in Table 14 should not be confused with class. Informants who perceived their own status to be higher or lower than their father's had not necessarily moved into a different social class, although this may have happened in some cases. The similarities among the three cities are rather striking, particularly insofar as upward mobility is concerned.

Table 15 indicates that exchange mobility, in Hutchinson's terminology, is more frequent than structural mobility. São Paulo may differ from the two other cities because its structural transformation is more recent and

Table 14 *Status category of male informants
related to that of their fathers by city (percentages)*

Informant's status relative to father	Buenos Aires	Montevideo	São Paulo
Higher	43.4	39.0	40.5
Same	33.1	35.0	42.5
Lower	23.5	26.0	17.0
Number of informants	1632	1718	1099

Source: Bertram Hutchinson, "Social Mobility Rates in Buenos Aires, Montevideo, and São Paulo: A Preliminary Comparison," *América Latina*, 6, no. 2 (1962), 15–16.

consequently offers more opportunities than either Montevideo or Buenos Aires.

The results presented in Tables 14 and 15 are preliminary and tentative. They certainly should not be considered to be typical of all large urban centers of Latin America, although it would not be unreasonable to expect similar results if comparable studies were carried out in such cities as Mexico City, Monterrey, or Medellin.

Small, nonindustrialized cities located in less developed countries are seldom expected to generate a great deal of upward mobility. A study of Sucre, Bolivia, indicates the need for extreme caution with generalizations about urban stratification. The population of Sucre was reported to lie between 30,000 and 40,000 by 1940. Twelve groups of interrelated families representing less than 1 percent of the population derived their income from businesses, professions, civil service, investments, and agricultural

Table 15 *Variations in social and directional mobility with change*

Percentages of social mobility due to exchange of position and structural change			
	Buenos Aires	Montevideo	São Paulo
Exchange mobility	68.6	69.1	53.3
Structural mobility	31.4	30.9	46.7

Percentages of directional mobility due to structural change			
Upward mobility	47.2	42.4	62.3
Downward mobility	2.3	13.6	8.8

Source: Bertram Hutchinson, "Social Mobility Rates in Buenos Aires, Montevideo, and São Paulo: A Preliminary Comparison," *América Latina*, 6, no. 2 (1962), 15–16.

estates. They were regarded as upper class. From 20 to 30 percent of the people of Sucre constituted the middle class—not exactly a trifling figure for a town of this kind.

Sucre's lower class is composed of *cholos*—people of Indian or mixed ancestry—who are reputed to be highly aggressive and ambitious. "The ideology of the upper and middle classes recognizes a *cholo* hostility which has a long history of sporadic open expression." (Hawthorn, 1948:25) The cholo men are mostly skilled traders and holders of many small offices of the city's business and government, the women are shopkeepers and domestic servants. Social mobility in Sucre was found to be "high" and "about half of the families in the upper class had middle or lower class status not more than two generations back." (Hawthorn, 1948:26)

The restructuring of the three major classes

Urban growth greatly expanded and diversified the occupational structure, and in so doing it affected all social classes. To the extent that industry entered the urban scene, a rapidly growing mass of industrial workers was added to the lower rungs of the social structure. The demand for technical skills and the chronic scarcity of such skills has had differentiating effects on the working class and has opened prospects of socio-economic ascent.

The changes urbanization has generated among the middle class should not be mentioned without reference to a rather peculiar controversy involving the concept of the Latin American middle class. In the past, Latin American society was often depicted as a "two-class structure"; and implicitly or explicitly, the existence of a middle class was denied. If admitted to exist at all, this class was supposed to be very small, economically unstable, without a value system of its own, and committed to emulating the values and lifeways of the upper class. Some authors have found class consciousness weak or totally lacking, not only in the middle class but in the lower class as well. In other words, "the presence of a middle class patterned on the model of those which exist in western Europe and the United States has been doubted or denied by many analysts of Latin American society." (Wagley, 1968:195) It ought to be added that most of these "analysts" were North Americans who took the ethnocentric attitude that if the Latin American middle class did not conform to their own model, it was not fit to be called a middle class. Such terms as "middle group," "middle mass," "middle sector," and "middle stratum" were proposed to substitute for class, and the term "middle sector" has found many takers indeed.

Admittedly, other Latin American social and cultural phenomena, too, may not live up to models built by North American and European scholars, and in such cases consistency would require a new terminology. We may find that Latin American labor unions, rural cooperatives, city councils, country clubs, and perhaps a host of other institutions, are quite different from their North American and European counterparts and therefore ought to be called something else. However, we propose to view social class like any other phenomenon to be scrutinized—that is, *within the context of Latin American culture and in the terms of that culture*. As far as the middle class is concerned, neither an ideology "of its own" nor economic stability nor ethnic homogeneity is an acceptable cross-cultural prerequisite. If social classes are *open* strata, as has been assumed here, we can expect the members of the lower and middle classes to strive toward a class status superior to their own. Emulation of values and life styles attributed to higher classes should be interpreted as a reflection of social aspirations that characterize rather than adulterate social behavior in a class society.

But aspirations should not be confused with the way middle-class people *actually* live. Identification with upper-class values means little if occupation, income, family background, education, and other circumstances confine a person to a way of life far removed from that of the upper class.

Most attempts to order the urban populations of Latin America along class lines are based on occupational census data. So, for example, is Iturriaga's assertion that between 1895 and 1940 the urban middle class in Mexico increased from 776,439 (6.12 percent) to 2,382,464 (12.12 percent) of the total population. At the same time, the urban *clases populares* increased from 14.17 to 22.40 percent and the urban upper class from 0.39 to 0.57 percent of the total population. (Iturriaga, 1951:28)

Or let us take Uruguay as a contrasting example. We are informed that in the provincial cities of this small country with a large middle class, the upper class represents 3 percent, the middle class 24 percent, and the lower class 73 percent of the total urban population, whereas in Montevideo, only 1 percent of the population belongs to the upper class, 40 percent to the middle class, and 59 percent to the lower class. (Rama, 1960:110) The class structure of Argentina in 1947 was similar: 44.2 percent of the gainfully employed urban population were included among the lower classes, and 30.6 percent were middle and upper class. (Germani, 1955:149)

Available information about income distribution in São Paulo City in 1967 provide some clues concerning the class structure. The figures refer to "domiciles," apparently covering all gainfully employed members of each residential unit or family. We find that 63.1 percent of such units fell into the low-income group (up to 500 cruzeiros or approximately $125), 33.4 percent earned between 500 and 1500 cruzeiros, and 3.5 percent made 1500 cruzeiros or more per month. (Prefeitura, 1968:160) The low-income group of this inquiry seems to coincide with lower-class status, whereas upper class implies an income considerably above the 1500-cruzeiro level. A cautious estimate would probably place about 30 percent of all residential units in the middle class.

In some Latin American countries the urban middle class seems to be smaller and the lower class larger than in Buenos Aires, Montevideo, or São Paulo; but whatever the figures may be, they represent way stations along an evolutionary curve that reflects varying degrees of social mobility.

The extraordinary differentiation of the urban middle class suggests the types of subdivision that have been proposed in Europe and in the United States. Upper and lower middle class or *burguesia* and *pequena burguesia* (i.e., *bourgeoisie* and *petite bourgeosie*) are among the terms most frequently used in accounting for obvious diversity. Apparently urban class systems, particularly the middle ranges, are too fluid to make any such subdivisions meaningful. In the largest cities, upward mobility has produced frequent associations of considerable wealth with undesirable ethnic background, lack of formal education, and social skills, making assignment of class status hazardous. Perhaps an even greater source of uncertainty lies in the many new and little-known occupations being generated by an increasingly complex technology and economic organization. If there is little doubt about the status of physicians and lawyers, such professionals as market analysts, industrial chemists, computer programmers, economists, laboratory technicians, and the many specialists performing administrative and managerial functions in large industrial enterprises, are comparatively unknown quantities in terms of status allocation in a fluid class structure.

Almost as indefinite as the recent accretions to the middle class appears to be the so-called new upper class. Rich merchants, bankers, industrialists, high-ranking civil servants, military officers, and successful politicians of middle-class origin (sometimes handicapped by Syrian, Lebanese, Japanese, Indian, or Negro ancestry) are often believed to be "social climbers" desirous of being admitted to the exclusive ranks of the traditional upper class or "aristocracy." On the other hand, the old aristocracy supposedly shows little inclination to "recognize" the *arrivistas*, and when they request membership in certain exclusive clubs symbolizing upperclass status, they are blackballed. There are of course such "boundary-maintaining" mechanisms designed to keep "undesirable" elements out of the country club, the Rural Society, or the *Social Register*; but in the long run, political and economic power, not membership in the country club, decides who belongs or does not belong to the upper class. And there is little doubt that almost everywhere the traditional seigneurial upper class has been losing out to a new upper class composed of generals, bureaucrats, wealthy industrialists, merchants, and bankers.

The city of Córdoba: a case study of structural change

The events that transformed Córdoba from a traditional to a modern industrialized city are paradigmatic within the Latin American context: Rapid growth superimposed on an old Spanish town, numerous immigrants from Italy and Spain, and industrial developments attracting thousands of people from the surrounding provinces. The population of Córdoba jumped from 54,763 in 1895 to 134,935 in 1914 and has not stopped growing. In 1970 it had reached 800,000. Our knowledge of these changes, which have been studied in detail—a rarity in Latin America —seems to justify the insertion of a summary of what happened to the class structure as it existed up to 1920, approximately.

There was of course a seigneurial upper class, but in contrast to other similar structures, it had no agrarian roots. It was a thoroughly urbanized, self-styled "doctoral aristocracy" composed of men who held degrees from the local university. These men were lawyers, doctors, engineers, notaries (*escribanos*), and clergymen who monopolized the leading positions in government, church, bureaucracy, the university, and the judiciary, or who practiced one of the recognized "liberal" professions, such as law and medicine. Since their privileged status was contingent on a college degree, they were vitally interested in preserving the boundary-maintaining function of the university. Apparently there was a general consensus that the doctoral aristocracy was superior to the "common people."

Although some members of the privileged class of Córdoba owned real estate, the majority had only income from the professions or civil service. Few families could afford the kind of ostentation and conspicuous consumption that are thought to accompany upper-class status. To make up for such shortcomings, the doctoral aristocracy developed a style of life characterized by pomposity and formalism in dress, speech, and manners. Erudition and refinement were greatly respected, as was the command of stylized language in conversation and oratory. (Agulla, 1968:26ff.)

On a slightly lower level, but tied to the doctoral aristocracy, stood the estancieros or big landowners. Control of the people living on the hacienda or within its orbit assured them of a leading position in politics. When older, they retired to Córdoba to seek advantageous marriages for their daughters and college degrees and high-level employment for their sons. Often these wealthy landowners indulged in luxury and ostentatiousness to compensate for "the dark hue of their skin." (Agulla, 1968:30)

The commerce of Córdoba was controlled by the *pelucones*, mostly people of Spanish, Italian, and French extraction who had grown wealthy by dint of hard work and frugality.

> Success in business made it possible for them to rise to the doctoral aristocracy through their sons, who used to comply with the rite of passage of a college education. The sons of the *pelucones* were brought up in an atmosphere of strict family morality and with a great appreciation of formal education, particularly of a university career. They thus accepted the laws of the game imposed by the doctoral aristocracy to the point of always being available to rise to its level through marriage. (Agulla, 1968:32)

There was of course a rather well-differentiated lower class of people who worked with their hands, of small merchants and employees who apparently had little chance to rise in the social structure.

The gradual decline of the doctoral aristocracy was not unrelated to rapid population growth. Agulla observed that an aristocracy numbering approximately 100 families could not perform its governmental functions in a city of 135,000 inhabitants. (Agulla, 1968:35) What was difficult in 1914 became even more problematic with the population growth of subsequent decades.

The functional decline of the old upper class of Córdoba becomes clearly visible if one scrutinizes its role in three institutional sectors that had been its traditional power domains. Controlling positions in politics, the judiciary, and the university increased from 62 in 1924 to 132 in 1960. At the same time, the extent to which the doctoral elite held controlling posts in politics decreased from 67.3 percent in 1924 to 7.0 percent in 1960. Its hold on such positions in the judiciary fell from 100 percent in 1924 to 48.8 percent in 1960. The university sector was under complete control of the doctoral elite until 1937, but in 1951 its members held no more than 22.3 percent of leading positions in the university, mainly because of massive government intervention and summary dismissal of professors. By 1960 participation of the doctoral aristocracy in the university sector was up 61.1 percent, but control had shifted to the newly founded Catholic University. (Agulla, 1968:41, 44–45)

The changes that transformed Córdoba into the main center of Argentina's automotive industry came from the outside in the form of capital, technology, and skilled manpower. Between 1947 and 1966 immigration amounted to 48.3 percent of the total population increase. (Sanchez and Schulthess, 1967:8) A new lower class of skilled and unskilled factory workers, a new middle class of technical and managerial specialists, and a new upper class of industrialists, top managers, and financiers were added to the existing structure. Labor unions and entrepreneurial bodies constituted influential pressure groups taking a strong hand in the decision-making process. National political developments beyond local control (such as peronismo) tended to undermine or openly subvert the existing class order. Steeped in humanistic traditions, the doctoral aristocracy had little chance to preserve its power monopoly in a technocracy; but the 1960s was a period of transition characterized by two conflicting sets of values—one "residual" and the other "emergent" representing side by side, tradition and modernity. (Miller, Greco, and Agulla, 1966:41)

In 1970 the physical structure of Córdoba clearly reflected the socioeconomic changes that had been taking place. A new diagonal street pattern was playing havoc with the colonial grid geometry, circumferential expansion had removed the urban perimeter several miles from the old colonial center, and high-rise buildings had begun to dominate the city's skyline. A very large proportion of middle- and upper-class families had moved to a completely new residential barrio, Cerro de las Rosas, which was already developing its own commercial establishments.

Among the Latin American cities with similar histories of modernization, Córdoba appears to be unique for its persistence in Spanish colonial scholasticism until the early twentieth century, when this tradition had long ceased to dominate the ideological culture of other cities. Unique was also its intellectual upper class, which might have been able to salvage more of its power, had it been able or inclined to establish a firmer hold on the economy.

The shantytowns
and the cities

Shantytowns and slums

The proliferation of squatter settlements or shantytowns in virtually all major urban centers of Latin America constitutes one of the most problematic aspects of urban growth. The term "squatter settlement" emphasizes illegal, de facto occupation of a site, whereas "shantytown" stresses the improvised and flimsy nature of the buildings composing such settlements. Occupation of unused land in the vicinity of an urban center is typically a concerted action carried out by a group of families who erect the first shanties and are usually followed by other groups. Within a few weeks several hundred families may have established residence on land owned by a public entity or by individual proprietors. Such a settlement is called *barrio de invasión, tugurio, callampa, rancho, barriada,* or *villa miseria* in Spanish and *favela, mucambo,* or *vila de malocas* in Portuguese. Shantytowns are often referred to as slums, but it may be preferable to confine the term "slum" to deteriorating urban districts, where older resi- dences are partitioned into the largest possible number of tenements and rented to people unable to afford or find lodgings in more desirable neigh- borhoods. Slums are not created by the people who inhabit them, and if they are remodeled or replaced by new buildings, the slumdweller certainly has no part in the process.

In contrast to the slum, the squatter settlement is an *addition* to an existing urban aggregate, and it is built by its own inhabitants on unused land (or water). A slumdweller can never hope to own the building he lives in, but the squatter expects or hopes eventually to obtain legal title to the land on which his house is built. Shantytowns are forms of urban growth, slums are not.

The origin of the squatter

Shantytowns have been more often criticized than studied. They are frequently described as "pathological" aspects of urbanization, as "can- cerous" growths on the organism of the city. Critics focus on the unsuit- ability of the terrain, the flimsiness of the dwellings, the small size of the structures, and lack of plumbing. The entire settlement is condemned be- cause of the absence of piped water, sewers, electricity, transportation, hos- pitals, schools, police protection, and other institutional facilities that go with "normally" developed residential areas. The settlers are found to lack experience in urban living, formal education, and the skills necessary to find employment. At worst, the population of the shantytowns is viewed as a mixture of poor people, drifters, vagrants, criminals, and prostitutes. Perhaps more than any other terms, the words "marginal" or "marginaliza- tion" have been used to describe a process that is believed to exclude shan- tytown populations from full participation in the culture of the city, par- ticularly in the sharing of its institutional facilities.

We do not know enough about the shantytowns to generalize about the social origin of the settlers. The notion that most of them are migrants coming directly from peasant villages has received little support, but since research has been concerned with large metropolitan areas rather than with provincial cities, some qualifications seem to be in order. As a matter of fact, much rural–urban migration proceeds in steps, and smaller and medium-sized cities appear to be way stations between the hamlet or village and the capital city. It was found, for example, that Indian peasants from the Mixteca Alta (Mexico) area formerly went to such cities as Oaxaca, Veracruz, or Puebla, and to Mexico City later. (Butterworth, 1970:101) But since the shantytown is a permanent fixture of virtually all provincial cities, one can only conclude that many migrants remain there and that the contingent of greenhorn peasants in such cities must be considerably higher than in the capitals. According to our own observations in intermediate cities including São Luis do Maranhão, Natal (Brazil), Tucumán, Salta (Argentina), and Temuco (Chile), the squatter settlements do indeed have a rural character.

Most inquiries are vague or omissive regarding the rural or urban nature of the locality indicated by the squatter as his place of origin. In a study of two shantytowns in Bogotá, 95.8 and 79.6 percent of all informants in the respective areas had come from a *cabecera* or county seat, whereas only 4.2 percent and 20.4 percent, respectively, indicated a *vereda* (countryside) as their place of origin. There is no doubt about the peasant character of the vereda, but a cabecera may be a provincial town or just a slightly urbanized village. (Cardona Gutierrez, 1968:69) The chances are that the class culture to which most migrants belong is more rural than urban, regardless of whether the cabecera is an overgrown village or a town of several thousand inhabitants.

Step migration from the original community to a metropolitan squatter settlement ought to be considered as a sequence of adaptive phases during which the migrant finds the opportunity to acquire useful knowledge and to familiarize himself with urban ways of life. Before settling down in a shantytown, a substantial proportion of migrants spend some time in slums. Attempts to move out into a squatter barrio may not succeed, or the living conditions in such settlements may not live up to expectations, thus determining further moves.

Table 16, referring to the aforementioned squatter settlements in Bogotá, indicates that relatively few migrants had come directly to the barrio in which they were living at the time of the inquiry. Table 17 shows that in most cases considerable time had elapsed between the migrant's arrival in Bogotá and his move to either one of the two barrios.

Many adults living in shantytowns are not migrants, however. A study of four settlements in Santiago, for example, revealed that 42 percent of all heads of families were natives of Santiago; 12 percent had been living there for 30 or more years, and in 30 percent of all cases between 10 and 29 years had elapsed since the informant had moved to Santiago. (Portes, 1969:20) In three shantytowns near Barranquilla (Colombia), 30.4 per-

Table 16 *Barrios in which informant lived prior to moving into Policarpa Salavarrieta and John XXIII*

| | John XXIII | | Policarpa Salvarrieta | |
Number of Barrios	Number	Percentage	Number	Percentage
0	29	32.6	58	9.9
1	33	37.1	244	41.6
2	15	16.9	141	24.0
More than 2	12	13.4	144	24.5
Total	89	100.0	587	100.0

Source: Ramiro Cardona Gutierez, "Migracíon, Urbanización, y Marginalidad," in Ramiro Cardona Gutierez, ed., *Urbanización y Marginalidad*. Bogotá: Publicación de la Asociación Colombiana, de Faculdades de Medicina, 1968, p. 70.

cent of all informants were natives of the city, 45 percent had been living in the barrio for less than 10 years, and 24.6 percent had been there for more than 10 years.

Studies made in Lima, Mexico City, Santo Domingo, Guatemala City, Panama City, Caracas, Montevideo, Buenos Aires, and Rio de Janeiro confirm that many squatters either were natives of the city or had been living there for a number of years. The proportion of people who had moved from a rural area *directly* to the shantytown was found to be small. (Mangin, 1967:68–69)

Invasion as concerted action

If it would be a distortion of facts to depict the shantytown as a displaced peasant community, it would be equally mistaken to deny the sur-

Table 17 *Time elapsed between arrival in Bogotá and settlement in Policarpa Salavarrieta or John XXIII*

| | John XXIII | | Policarpa Salvarrieta | |
Years	Number	Percentage	Number	Percentage
0	19	25.0	51	9.2
1–4	24	31.6	212	38.4
4–15	21	27.6	228	41.2
More than 15	12	15.8	62	11.2
Total	76	100.0	553	100.0

Source: Ramiro Cardona Gutierez, "Migración, Urbanización, y Marginalidad," in Ramiro Cardona Gutierez, ed., *Urbanización y Marginalidad*. Bogotá: Publicación de la Asociación Colombiana, de Faculdades de Medicina, 1968, p. 70.

vival of significant rural elements among urban squatters. Little is known
about the actual process of selecting and seizing a piece of land, obtaining
building materials, and erecting the first clusters of shanties. There is no
doubt that in many cases a number of families act collectively and with
astonishing speed. The more people are involved and the larger the number
of buildings erected in the shortest possible time, the more difficult the
removal of the squatters. If, as it sometimes happens, a few hundred people
occupy a site during a single night, building 50 or 100 improvised huts within a couple of days, the local authorities face a situation that may prove
politically embarrassing. Forcible eviction of a few may pass unnoticed,
but ejection of hundreds of people, including women and children, will
likely be branded as inhuman and cruel.

Much depends on careful planning and determination.

> In Lima, after months of planning, thousands of people moved
> during one night to a site that had been secretly surveyed and laid
> out. They arrived with the materials to build a straw house, all their
> belongings, and a Peruvian flag. They were determined and, in several
> cases, returned to the sites two or three times after police burned
> their belongings and beat and killed their fellows. (Mangin, 1967:69)

Reconnoitering of prospective sites and a realistic appraisal of the like-
lihood of mounting a successful invasion require knowledge of the local
topography, ownership conditions, and chances of marshaling political support. Public land is preferable to individually owned land, but sometimes
unexpected help comes from politicians who try to capitalize on imminent
invasions. In Barranquilla, for example, "invasions of public and private
land were encouraged by demagogues who later entered negotiations to sell
the (private) land to the municipio. Eventually, it acquired the sites that
had been invaded, a measure which, in a sense, legitimatized the occupation and encouraged further settlements." (Usandizaga and Havens, 1966:
29–30)

Careful harnessing of political resources by invasion leaders has been
reported from Venezuela. "The outstanding credential of the leader (or
leaders) is that he usually has the backing, either tacit or explicit, of one
of the political parties that shares governing power in the city. . . . This
link is essential because it protects the leader against official reprisal." (Ray,
1969:33–34) Reprisal means forceful removal of the settlers by the police.
Thus since force is rarely employed in Venezuela, success of invasion strategy is indicated.

Referring to the favelas of Rio de Janeiro, Anthony Leeds emphasizes

the "shrewd awareness" of political chances and the tendency of the squatter to shift behavior to get the most out of politicians in return for votes.
(Leeds, 1969:79)

Adaptive value of cultural survivals

Supported or not by politicians or idealistic advisers, planned invasions
can hardly be credited to peasants freshly arrived from the countryside.
Knowledge acquired during years of urban residence must be involved;
but adaptation to urban ways does not imply complete loss of rural cultural elements. In fact, survival of these elements has a distinct adaptive
value in many shantytowns, mainly in those located in provincial cities.
São Francisco, for example, a squatter setttlement in the immediate vicinity
of São Luis do Maranhão, in a city of 380,000, has preserved a somewhat
rural character. Each dwelling has its own garden in which papayas, banana
trees, sugar cane, and other food plants are raised. In the broad alleys, fowl,
pigs, and goats feed on grass, weeds, and scraps. The houses are wattle-
and-daub constructions covered with thatch or tiles. We had the opportunity to verify the existence of similar settlements in a number of Latin
American cities including Tucumán and Temuco.

The most valuable skills the migrants transfer to the city are construction techniques. Here a detailed knowledge of building materials appears
to be crucial. The settler has an eye for trees, vines, grasses, weeds, palm
leaves, bamboos, clay, and the like; but of course his experiences vary with
the resources of his native environment. Clay occurs in most regions and
can be utilized in several ways. In Spanish-American countries it is mostly
used in the form of adobe or sun-dried brick; but *bahareque* or wattle-and-
daub is quite frequently seen, particularly in Colombia and Venezuela,
and in Brazil it is probably the most common construction technique.
Palm leaves, straw, wild grasses (*Anetherum bicorne* and *Andropogon bicorne*, called *sapé* in Brazil), or locally produced tiles are used as roofing.
Exceptionally useful are several species of bamboos (*guadua* in Colombia
and *taquara* or *taboca* in Brazil), which produce a durable and versatile
building material. In Colombia, *guadua* is skillfully used to erect rather complex houses, often several stories high and strong enough to withstand
earthquakes. (Castro, 1964)

Most of the traditional materials and techniques are quite common, not
only in peasant hamlets but in smaller towns, and they are generally familiar to lower-class people who have grown up in such localities. Using lo-

cally available and usually "free" materials, the poor are quite capable of erecting serviceable dwellings within a few days. In an urban environment scraps of wood or metal may substitute for the traditional materials. What matters is the transfer of skills whose adaptive value can hardly be questioned.

Also, the kinship organization of the migrant is often adaptive in urban squatter settlements. In Peru, "there is a strong tendency for relatives from the provinces to join the barriada families, particularly aged parents who abandon land in the provinces and can act as caretakers of grandchildren and property while both husband and wife work." (Mangin, 1970:26)

In the shantytowns of Mexico City, kinship seems to play a similar role. "The majority of the migrants from Tilantongo [an Indian municipio in the state of Oaxaca] arrive, usually without notice, at the doorsteps of a relative or compadre already established in the mushroom slum of the city. If employment is found they usually stay in Mexico City." (Butterworth, 1970:102) Among the many thousands of Mexicans who have migrated to Monterrey, particularly since 1940, kinship has played a vital role in providing continuity to the migratory flow and in assisting newcomers to get established. It was learned that 84 percent of all migrants arriving between 1961 and 1965 had relatives of friends living in Monterrey, and two-thirds of these received some kind of help, mostly in the form of food and shelter. (Browning and Feindt, 1971:60)

Next to the kinship group, it is probably the regional association of migrants from the same town or municipio that mediates adaptation to life in the shantytown. Related or not, families from Tilantongo stick together in Mexico City, as do the migrants who settle in the barriadas of Lima. Mangin identified more than a thousand such regional associations or clubs, noting that they "sponsor activities which permit social continuity not only during the stressful initial period of adjustment to life in the metropolis but for a lifetime." (Mangin, 1970:32) In both cities selected patterns of regional cultures tend to become permanent fixtures, probably as long as the flow of migrants from the same localities is not disrupted.

Shantytown populations

Censuses of shantytown populations should be considered with extreme caution. The Brazilian Census Bureau classifies as a *favela* any settlement composed of at least 50 dwellings built without permit on land that is neither owned by the inhabitants nor equipped with sewers, piped water, electricity, gas, or telephone service. There is no officially sanctioned street plan, nor do the inhabitants pay property taxes or fees. Even if this or a similar definition were agreed on, application would be difficult because almost all settlements are affected by constant changes which, as we shall see, prevent the simultaneous use of the foregoing criteria except in very recent settlements. Table 18 is an abbreviated version of data compiled by Ramiro Cardona. (Cardona Gutierrez, 1968:207–210)

The concept of *barrio popular* covers a wide range of lower-class settlements, and some of them cannot be regarded as shantytowns at all in the previously defined sense. None of the figures included in Table 18 stands for a homogeneous and unchanging category of settlement. Nor do these figures approach the reliability of census data—they are merely extremely crude estimates that at least in some cases, seem to be either far too high or far too low. The State Department of Statistics in São Paulo, for example, carried out a census of all favelas in that city in 1968. A total

Table 18 *Population in different types of barrio popular*

City	Year	Shantytown population (in thousands)	Percentage of city population
Greater Buenos Aires	1965	800	10
Rio de Janeiro	1961	900	27
São Paulo	1960	70	2
Recife	1961	375	50
Pôrto Alegre	1960	86	13
Bogotá	1967	100	5
Medellin	1964	53	5
Cali	1964	75	5
Greater Santiago	1966	266	10
Guayaquil	1957	105	24
San Salvador	1961	5	2
Tegucigalpa	1967	35	18
Mexico City	1966	1500	33
Panama City	1965	35	11
Lima	1966	500	24
Arequipa	1961	63	39
Santo Domingo	1967	150	25
Caracas	1962	263	23
Maracaibo	1960	175	35

Source: Ramiro Cardona Gutierez, "Migración, Urbanización, y Marginalidad," in Ramiro Cardona Gutierez, ed., *Urbanización y Marginalidad*. Bogotá: Publicación de la Asociación Colombiana de Faculdades de Medicina, 1968, pp. 207–210.

of 37 shantytowns were identified, and their total population amounted to 26,737. This figure bears no resemblance to the estimate of 1960. (Departamento de Estatística, 1968) To account for the constantly changing conditions of the barrios populares in Lima, for example, the term *barriada* has been replaced by *pueblo joven* (young settlement), of which there were 270 in 1970, with a total population of 727,000.

Shantytown dynamics

To place the situation of the squatters in a realistic perspective, we must emphasize first that to the settlers, the housing and economic conditions of the shantytowns are superior to those of the rural areas, towns, or the urban slums whence they came. Consequently, remigration figures are low. (Mangin, 1967:89) For example, of 6019 families living in 37 different squatter settlements of São Paulo City (in 1968), only 181 (2 percent) were willing to return to their places of origin. (Departamento de Estatística, 1968)

Moreover, faced with a choice, most settlers refuse to give up their shanties for better houses located in newly built residential districts. Recent resettlement of shanty dwellers in Rio de Janeiro had to be carried out by the police. Immediately following the population transfer, all buildings were burnt down to prevent the people from returning to the settlement. A similar tendency to refuse resettlement has been noted in the villas miserias of Buenos Aires, even in those that were periodically flooded. (Romano de Tobar, 1968:30) Such attitudes are to be interpreted in terms of "uniquely satisfactory opportunities" offered by the squatter settlements to the poor.

[The shantytowns] are characterized by "progressive development," by which families build their housing and their community in stages as their resources permit, the more important elements first. The procedures followed by these self-selecting occupant-builder communities, free to act in accordance with their own needs, enable them to synchronize investment in buildings and community facilities with the rhythm of social and economic change. (Turner, 1970:1)

Occasional references notwithstanding, there seems to be little awareness of how widespread this pattern actually is. In 1959, carrying out inquiries in Los Nogales, a *callampa* or shantytown of Santiago with a population of about 20,000, we noticed the changes taking place. Many settlers had begun to erect brick walls around their original hovels. In some cases the new walls were only a yard high, other constructions had already reached the roof level, and some had been completed. Once the roof was put on such a structure, the innards of the old dwelling were removed and the family had a fairly adequate, permanent house. In 1959 Los Nogales had electricity, and there were buses providing transportation to the center of Santiago. In 1970 the reconstruction of Los Nogales had been completed. The original shanties had given way to solid row houses, all streets were paved, and the total impression was that of a modest working-class neighborhood.

Alagados, a large squatter settlement near the central part of Salvador (Bahia), presents different phases of development side by side. At first glance the swampy shallows of Tainheiros Bay seem to make for an extremely poor site. The choice proved strategically sound, however, at least from the standpoint of the squatters. All coastal lands in Brazil, are owned by the federal government, which is not known for prompt and decisive action. To build a settlement on water was to protect it from immediate intervention by municipal and state authorities, which had no jurisdiction in the case. Besides, fishing in the bay was profitable enough to supply additional food.

The first squatters built wooden shacks on piles connected with each other and with the shore by boardwalks. Small entrepreneurs soon built several shanties which were offered for sale or rent. At the same time the most active settlers organized to defend the interests of the new settlement. Predictably enough, electoral campaigns afforded opportunities to exploit political rivalries to the advantage of the settlement. Apparently these efforts succeeded because the population of Alagados was not removed but was allowed to grow from 8,875 in 1960 to 73,370 in 1968. At the same time, the number of buildings rose from 2,524 to 14,674, and in 1968 the people of Alagados represented 8.2 percent of the total population of Salvador. (Rios, 1969:16ff.)

Very soon the squatters discovered that the shallows could easily be filled in by dumping refuse and dirt in the bay, and at the request of the people, Alagados became the garbage dump of the city. Local entrepreneurs extracted paper, bottles, and metal scrap for resale and unloaded unusable waste in areas to be filled in. The fresh dumping grounds produce a terrible stench, but hundreds of vultures are constantly busy in devouring organic matter.

In 1970 a large section of the bay had been filled in, and numerous streets flanked by new houses had replaced the old boardwalks and wooden shacks. Three types of building were clearly recognizable. The earlier wooden type, erected on piles, had an average living space of 43.8 square meters, divided into three rooms. Where the bay had been filled in, the wooden shanties tended to be replaced by a more solid construction of *taipa* (pounded clay), slightly larger and divided into six rooms without plumbing. Finally, more recently built dwellings had brick walls and an average living space of 65.1 square meters. In 1969, 11 percent of all buildings had been connected to the city water system and 49 percent had indoor plumbing. (Rios, 1969:38) Further changes in the type of construction were foretold by the first brick-and-concrete building of more than one floor, which was being erected in 1970.

Although a substantial proportion of the inhabitants of Alagados held no legal title to the site they occupied, thousands had succeeded, probably through political patronage, in legalizing their situation. In fact, these families were paying a (token) fee to the federal government, and a third category had obtained a temporary permit from the federal Port Authority. (Rios, 1969:73–74) In the meanwhile, sites are staked out in the bay, piles are driven in, and new shacks erected to accommodate the steady flow of new inhabitants. In 1969 Alagados had 754 commercial establishments and 30 industries, employing a total of 2231 workers. (Rios, 1969: 62–64)

In Guayaquil, Cartagena, São Luis do Maranhão, and Recife, some squatter settlements are located in shallow coastal waters or mangrove swamps. The inventiveness of the settlers is particularly impressive in the case of the *mocambos* of Recife, which were reported as early as the seventeenth century. In the delta region of the Capiberibe and Beberibe rivers, covered by extensive mangrove swamps, thousands of squatters built dwelling sites out of accumulated mud and set up their mocambos or shacks on these platforms.

Adaptive advantages of squatter settlements

The economic advantages of squatter settlements are rather obvious. Initial investment, mostly in the form of labor, is insignificant. If there is no immediate threat to the survival of a new barrio, the settlers begin to improve their primitive dwellings or perhaps to replace them with more solid constructions. This process, which usually takes a few years, depends mainly on whether the squatter is able to earn a living. His chances are uncertain and subject to fluctuations; but since he does not owe rent, taxes, fees, or any other regular payments related to land and home, the construction process can be adapted to the ups and downs of the income. The higher the investment level, the more determined the collective effort of the settlers to stay and to stabilize the situation of the barrio.

Sometimes threats of eviction affect the willingness of the squatters to invest labor and meager savings in buildings that may be evacuated and razed by local authorities. As a rule, however, the settlers prefer to improve their dwellings in spite of legal uncertainties. The fact that they do not own the land does not prevent them from buying, selling, or leasing their houses. For the lack of titles they keep all documents (such as paid water and electricity bills) that could possibly be used to prove ownership of the house in the case of sale or disputes with local authorities. In a number of cities the squatters realize the possibility of claiming monetary compensations for their houses in case of removal and resettlement. In the late 1950s when thousands of rancho dwellers in Caracas were resettled in newly erected superbloques (high-rise apartment blocks), they received compensation according to the estimated value of the old dwelling. (Matos Mar, 1968:290)

The ceaseless endeavor to assure survival and amelioration of the settlement is not solely due to the squatters' desire to stabilize their situation; they also want to preserve their chances of earning a livelihood in the nearby city. Contrary to the rather widespread belief that shantytowns are areas of refuge for the unemployed and the unemployable, for drifters and vagrants, the population of such barrios is deeply involved in the economic system of the city. Rather than areas of refuge, the shantytowns are strategically advantageous areas of economic and political initiative, designed to secure for their residents a role in the structural transformation of the city.

Data on unemployment in the shantytowns are difficult to evaluate because many squatters have found ways of earning a living that cannot easily be fitted into conventional categories colored by middle-class conceptions. In the three previously mentioned shantytowns of Barranquilla, the average unemployment was 8.8 percent. (Usandizaga and Havens, 1966:39) A 1956 survey of the barriadas in Lima revealed that 71 percent of all "economically active" inhabitants were permanently employed and 27 percent had temporary jobs. Estimates or inquiries made in other cities (e.g., Santiago and Rio de Janeiro) yielded percentages varying between 12 and 27 percent. (Mangin, 1967:737)

Many shantytown dwellers are versatile enough to fit several occupational categories. Personal services, trade, and employment in industry or business—the three broad categories covering most economically active persons in any given barrio—are not mutually exclusive. Not only do many people shift from one category to another, they often engage in several activities, that place them in more than one division. The first category includes domestic servants, washerwomen, charwomen, bootblacks, gardeners, messengers, and others who commute to their working place. The traders have either a stand or small shop of their own, or they are street vendors. Shops are usually located in the settlements, but stands are found anywhere in the city, particularly in the open markets. The location of at least six *barriadas* in Lima appears to be a function of the nearby wholesale and retail markets, where most squatters have found opportunities to earn some cash. (Matos Mar, 1968:35)

Most traders sell their wares in the streets of the city. In fact, a substantial proportion of the retail trade of many cities is plied in public places by men, women, and children, many of whom live in squatter settlements. Shining shoes and peddling newspapers on foot are mostly in the hands of children, whereas newspaper and magazine stands are often family businesses. Lottery tickets, however, may be sold by anybody. In certain areas of Bogotá, Quito, and Lima, the sidewalk trade is extensive enough to convey the impression of a crowded marketplace, particularly on the eve of a popular holiday. An inventory of merchandise sold on the sidewalks of several city blocks adjacent to the central market of Lima in December 1970 included the following items: chinaware, leather goods, cutlery, straw hats, combs, brushes, mirrors, costume jewelry, shoestrings, toys, ladies' underwear, cosmetics, basketry, socks, shirts, skirts, blouses, dresses, sweaters, shoes, monkeys, parrots, canaries, parakeets, and other birds. Municipal authorities disclosed that during the preceding month of November, 500 peddlers had been arrested for having no documents to prove how and where they had purchased the goods they were selling. In many cities a large proportion of the goods sold by sidewalk merchants is contraband. The merchants are not likely to be directly involved in smuggling operations; they merely retail wares that have changed hands several times.

A motley group are the laborers. The dividing line between skilled and unskilled, specialized and unspecialized workers is uncertain. Men employed as unskilled laborers in the city may work as bricklayers, carpenters, electricians, painters, or plumbers in the settlement, often on their own houses, or they may help neighbors, compadres, or relatives to improve or enlarge their houses. Distinctions between working hours and leisure time are generally meaningless. Many shantytown dwellers welcome opportunities to work on weekends, as in São Paulo, for example, where many construction workers receive special pay for late hours and weekends.

Almost as common as the constant search for supplementary sources of income is the frequent changing of jobs. The temporary nature of many jobs, combined with low wages, induces many to try out various ways of making a living. One may change from unskilled laborer to sidewalk merchant, from selling lottery tickets to hawking American cigarettes, only to return to a wage-earning job. In Brazil, *biscateiro* is the equivalent of our idea of jack-of-all-trades, master of none. In a shantytown of Fortaleza, a nonindustrial city of northeastern Brazil, the occupational picture some 10 years ago was as follows: (F. Ribeiro, n.d.:13)

Heads of families gainfully employed	3263
Washerwomen being the sole breadwinners of their families	1337
Biscateiros	1026
Unemployed heads of families	2396

In many families it is the wife rather than the husband who holds a steady job (as maid, cook, or washerwoman)—a condition that is reflected in the matrifocal structure of numerous families.

Intensive participation in the economic process of the city would hardly be conceivable if illiteracy rates were as high as they are sometimes said to be. Table 19 provides some random data on illiteracy in shantytowns, but the percentages refer mostly to older people. With the exception of very recent settlements, schooling is available, and the proportion of children who do not attend at least grammar school seems to be relatively small in most barrios.

As a rule, the settlers are strongly interested in formal education, and

Table 19 *Illiteracy in shantytowns*

City	Year	Percentage	Source
Santiago	1960	12.7	Willems, 1967b
Santiago	1968	8.0	Desal-Celap, 1968
Santiago	1969	10.0	Portes, 1969
Guatemala	1965	20.0	Cuevas, 1965
Lima	1961	10.0	Matos Mar, 1961
Rio de Janeiro	1965	34.0	Bemdoc, 1965
Montevideo	1963	16.0	Bon Espandin, 1963

cases have been reported of people erecting a school building and hiring teachers at their own expenses when their request for a public school had been rejected. (Mangin, 1967:78)

The significance of knowledge acquired in school is reflected in the diffusion of reading habits, which actually contradicts the notion that shanty-town dwellers are completely isolated from their urban environment. In the three squatter settlements of Barranquilla, for example, the number of families in which newspapers were read, turned out to be almost twice as high as the number of nonreading families. (Usandizaga and Havens, 1966: 74) In the callampas of Santiago the readers of newspapers and magazines are even more numerous.

Low and irregular income of most squatters would seem to render unlikely acquisition of such relatively expensive items as radios and television sets, yet both are quite common in most settlements. Transistor radios are taken for granted, but in cities like Caracas, Bogotá, Lima, Buenos Aires, Santiago, and Rio de Janeiro, numerous families possess large sets. Mangin counted more than 50 television sets in 10 blocks of the barriada Pampa de Comas (Lima), and Abrams discovered that 30 percent of all ranchos in Venezuela had television sets, 32 to 35 percent had refrigerators, and some 15 percent owned automobiles. (Abrams, 1964:18) In the favelas of Rio de Janeiro (and probably elsewhere, too), owners of television sets often charge admission fees to neighbors who wish to watch particular programs. Although data are unavailable, one is inclined to think that expensive items such as television sets could not be had if the people owed rent or mortgage payments on their dwellings. Since they are not obliged to meet with such expenses, occasional savings may be invested in items that may seem incongruous with prevailing income levels. Besides, radio and television keep the shantytowns in touch with the city and the nation.

There is a widespread tendency to view the inhabitants of squatter settlements as a homogeneous class or part of such a class. This position is probably justified for newly established barrios, but a settlement that survives attempts at eradication soon enters a phase of socioeconomic differentiation. Several analysts emphasize the high degree of economic initiative in the barriadas of Lima and the favelas of Rio de Janeiro.

There is a tremendous proliferation of small enterprise. When a squatter settlement has become more or less established and accepted by the government, banks appear (mobile banks in panel trucks appear long before this point), movie houses are built, chain stores open, horse race lottery shops open, etc. Even from the outset, however, the local people begin buying and selling to and from each other at a great rate. In a Lima barriada of approximately 1500 houses, we counted more than 100 houses where something was sold. (Mangin, 1967:76)

Mangin also reports that similar observations have been made in Rio de Janeiro. (Mangin, 1967:77)

Of course some people are more successful than others, and before long economic differences can be discerned by inspecting the material possessions of the squatters. Also, the flow of incoming settlers tends to become more heterogeneous once people perceive that the chances are favorable to convert illegal occupation of the land into legitimate ownership. Public servants and white-collar employees, small merchants, teachers, lawyers, and physicians may move into a barrio, mainly in the hope of becoming house owners with a minimal investment of capital. In the barriada Pampa de Comas (Lima), the membership list of a club contained a medical doctor, a branch manager of a bank, a police lieutenant, two college students, a lawyer, and several owners of urban businesses. (Mangin, 1967:75)

Not a few squatter settlements have become lower-middle-class barrios over time.

Are shantytown dwellers marginal?

Although systematic research on squatter settlements has been spotty and limited to a few metropolitan areas, we may ask whether the previously reported data are compatible with the popular notion that the shantytowns are "marginal" settlements, or that the lifeways of their inhabitants can best be characterized in terms of "marginality."

Attempts to define the uncertain and extremely flexible concept of marginality could be summarized as follows: The shantytown dwellers are structurally and culturally segregated from the nearby urban society. They are impotent and embittered spectators of urban life, which they can neitheir understand nor participate in. They vegetate in apathetic despair and hopeless misery, without internal cohesion, incapable of concerted action, therefore permanently disorganized. A combination of poverty, political impotence, and general ignorance seems to reduce their chances of cultural participation to a minimum. The situation of the squatters could be normalized by "integrating" or "incorporating" the shantytowns into urban society. This means eradication of all traces of alleged marginality. Better housing, schools, hospitals, health insurance plans, and recreational facilities, but above all full employment, should be provided for all.

In the foregoing and similar proposals one can read all shades of demagoguery, political radicalism, reformist doctrine, and benevolent paternalism; but the common denominator seems to be the assumption that moral responsibility and initiative should rest with the state. Self-help is often emphasized, but it should always be accompanied by public assistance. The settlers should be encouraged, for example, to build their own houses, but the materials should be donated by public agencies. *The kind of self-help that thousands of squatters have actually demonstrated, has been barely noticed.* Inquiries about particular settlements always uncover items which can easily be interpreted as symptoms of marginality. Undoubtedly, there is a great deal of poverty and malnutrition, and many buildings are indeed too small and primitive. Often there is no piped water, sewerage, or electricity. The streets are either mudholes or dustbowls; many children seem to be neglected, and many couples live in "free" marital unions.

We can object to many such inquiries because they imply that poor conditions are immutable: They describe situations rather than processes, and little if any attention is paid to the inner dynamics of the settlement under scrutiny. The material just presented clearly indicate that incessant efforts are made by the settlers to improve the quality of life in their barrios and to intensify their involvement in the economic and political processes that link them to the urban structure. *These conditions are clearly irreconcilable with the concept of marginality.*

Marginal perhaps are recent squatter settlements established by migrants totally unfamiliar with the culture of the city of their choice. Or the amelioration of a shantytown may be delayed by an economic depression and high rates of unemployment. A case in point is Tucumán (Argentina), whose sugar industry has been in critical conditions for a number of years. The villas miserias of Tucumán, largely inhabited by migrants from Bolivia, show little change in comparison with similar settlements in Rosario or Salta, for example. But in spite of occasional failures, the idea of immutability does not appear to be supported by facts.

Equally inconsistent with the foregoing data, it seems, is Oscar Lewis's much debated "culture of poverty" concept. Doubtless poverty is an effective equalizer, and the lifeways of the shantytown dwellers bear a high degree of similarity regardless of nationality and ethnicity. The culture traits Lewis encountered in Mexico and Puerto Rico are probably ubiquitous in most squatter settlements, but the crucial mark of the culture of poverty is as incongruous with shantytown dynamics as the marginality concept:

Once [the culture of poverty] comes into existence it tends to perpetuate itself. . . . By the time slum children are age six or seven they have usually absorbed the basic values and attitudes of their subculture and are not psychologically geared to take full advantage of changing conditions or increased opportunities which may occur in their lifetime. (Lewis, 1966:xlv)*

The ways of life of known squatter settlements do not correspond to the picture of immutability suggested by Lewis. On the contrary, one of the most salient characteristics is an unusual adaptability to unstable environmental conditions, particularly the capacity for taking advantage of such varying conditions.

The eradication of the shantytowns

There seem to be four ways of "dealing" with shantytowns: (1) Emerging settlements are destroyed without regard to the fate of the invaders. (2) No action is taken, and the development of a barrio is left to the resourcefulness of its inhabitants. (3) Local institutions provide assistance in developing existing shantytowns and "integrating" them into urban society. (4) Populations of shantytowns are transferred to newly constructed housing developments.

Needless to say, these "policies" are not mutually exclusive, and almost everywhere in Latin America, action or inertia has been determined or directed by power groups of various kinds. To trace these complicated, often confused and contradictory developments would be outside the scope of the present inquiry.

Virtually all Latin American societies have shown growing concern with various urban problems, including squatter settlements. In particular, Mexico, Venezuela, Colombia, Peru, and Chile have carried out massive construction programs for low-income housing since the 1950s. Brazil followed in the 1960s with the establishment of the Banco Nacional de Habitação (National Housing Bank), which between 1965 and October 1971 had financed 753,000 housing units, and most of these were turned over to low-income families in all major cities of Brazil. (Conjunctura Econômica, 1971)

* Oscar Lewis, "The Culture of Poverty," in *La Vida*. New York: Random House, 1966. © Copyright, 1965, 1966, by Oscar Lewis.

Many attempts to transfer shantytown population into housing developments have met stiff opposition. Although rents or payments in case of purchase have been kept relatively low, the people were forced to budget the additional money they owed the financing institution. This approach may be feasible as long as there is a regular income, and as long as this income is not affected by inflation, layoffs, or unemployment. However, this is exactly where housing developments are inferior to squatter settlements. Almost everywhere except in Cuba, compulsory or voluntary transfer of populations from shantytowns to public or private housing developments is an attempt to "integrate" those populations into a formal urban housing market which economic conditions had compelled them to avoid. (Leeds, 1969:60) The obvious advantage of adopting the betterment of housing conditions to a fluctuating and unpredictable income has been definitely lost. In Brazil the so-called *monetary correction*, an automatic adjustment of mortgage payments to a high rate of inflation, means a periodic increase of financial liabilities without a simultaneous raise of real wages. Small wonder that in the state of Guanabara alone, 137,385 housing units stood unoccupied and 24,867 were "closed" in 1971. (Cavalcanti, 1971:129)

In some cities an unexpected "solution" to this problem has been attempted by forceful occupation of newly erected housing. During the revolution of January 1958, thousands of rancho dwellers in Caracas occupied a number of high-rise buildings that had been constructed for shantytown dwellers. In 1968 Matos Mar found that 96 percent of all these apartment buildings were illegally "occupied" or "rented" and that the inhabitants of 4580 housing units had not paid any rent since 1958. (Matos Mar, 1968: 285) Similar forms of invasion and occupation have taken place in Santiago over a period of several years. Although the forced occupation of low-income housing seems unlikely to gain many practitioners, collective refusal to pay rent or interests may. The *superbloques* or large housing units, concentrating thousands of people within a very small area, facilitate and perhaps encourage concerted action.

Many low-income housing developments have been located at great distances from the city, and this has raised much opposition. The problem of distance is often compounded by thoroughly inadequate and costly transportation systems. The transfer of populations from shantytowns into faraway suburbs almost always destroys a symbiotic network of relationships to favorably located urban labor markets. In other words, resettlement leads to economic disintegration rather than integration—an unintentional outcome of inadequate planning whose cost is borne, of course, by the settlers.

A study of two resettlement projects in Rio de Janeiro revealed that distance from labor market, combined with poor, time-consuming, and relatively expensive transportation, relatively high monthly payments, and isolation from urban life, had been generating a great deal of dissatisfaction. In one of the new housing developments (Vila Kennedy), 36 percent of all informants would have preferred to return to the old favelas. No such possibility existed, but in recent years many families in Vila Kennedy had sold their houses to lower-middle-class families and moved to favelas in Rio. (Salmon, 1969)

In the other housing development studied by Salmon the situation was more favorable insofar as existing economic relationships to the city were not disrupted. Consequently only one-fifth of all informants, given the opportunity, would have returned to their former place of residence. There existed in both suburbs a clear correlation between preference for squatter settlements and income: the lower the income, the more frequent the desire to return to the former settlement.

The most serious general shortcoming of resettlement projects is their failure to solve the problem of the poorest stratum of squatters. Since most new housing developments are conceived of as self-paying or self-supporting propositions, the tenant, to be eligible, must show proof of a regular income. Such eligibility requirements automatically exclude the unemployed, the underemployed, and, all those who have no steady job. For the last several years Rio de Janeiro has been gradually eliminating the favelas and resettling the people in new low-income residential areas. While this is happening, more favelas are being established outside the city limits, on land that is not under the jurisdiction of Guanabara State (synonymous with the city of Rio de Janeiro.)

It would seem that wherever the eradication of shantytowns is attempted in the terms described in this chapter, it is likely to solve the housing problem of a rather privileged stratum among the urban squatters, while the rest are merely dislocated and deprived of whatever adaptive arrangements they had been able to make in the original settlement.

The changing
political system

Political significance of structural change

The political implications of urbanization and the emerging industrial
order are fairly obvious. As a rapidly increasing proportion of a national
population tends to concentrate in cities, power potentials shift from rural
to urban areas. This means that power contenders have to seek support
among the urban masses. Nowadays neither elections nor revolutions can
be won without support of the major cities. Not only did the geography
of power change, the techniques of marshaling the political support of
urban populations are quite different from those which characterized the
political organization of the rural areas.

The previously outlined changes in the urban structure produced new power contenders and increasing diversity of interests to be pursued through political means. In the literature, the social classes themselves are often presented as political actors. Taken literally, the idea of a social class being capable of concerted action is a serious distortion of reality. Most of the time, however, the term "class" seems to be no more than a shorthand expression designating a specific group organized to defend or expand the interests of certain segments of a society. Political parties, labor unions, associations of manufacturers, peasant leagues or cooperatives, federations of planters, (coffee, cocoa, cotton, sugar cane, etc.), student associations, military circles, and professional societies have been known to serve the interests of particular social classes. Not to mention short-lived action groups mobilized to demonstrate power capabilities or to intimidate or remove powerful individuals from office.

The extraordinary growth of urban population by itself appears to impose changes, if only by opening up in the politico-administrative structure new positions that are too numerous and often too specialized to be filled by members of the traditional elites.

Not surprisingly, most of these new aggregates embodying interests of diverse social classes, are opposed to power monopolies held by individuals or exclusive oligarchies. To ensure access to and participation in government, they strive for what may broadly be called "democratization" of the political process. This does not mean commitment to any specific form or type of democracy, even if the current constitution suggests such a commitment. Rather, democratization involves the mobilization of political support to remove personal and institutional obstacles to the access of a particular faction, party, or other aggregate to participation in, or control of government. Success is often achieved at the expenses of competing groups, which then strive for further "democratization."

By undermining or destroying traditional forms of political control, urbanization and industrialization have generated social conditions leading to the involvement in the political process of an increasing proportion of the national populations. In addition to participation in elections, involvement means support of, or opposition to, subversive movements designed to seize power by violence. Rather predictably, the foreground is now occupied by the growing middle class and the urban working class, which in the past had played a small role (or no role) in the political process, and more recently they have been joined by the peasantry. Whereas in the past the struggle for power was typically confined to rival factions belonging to the same seigneurial class, *all* classes are now involved in the power struggle insofar as their diverse interests are represented by political parties, labor unions, associations of manufacturers, student associations, peasant leagues, guerrilla groups, factions within the armed forces, cliques of various kinds, and uncounted informal or impromptu bodies acting on a local level.

Political evolution then seems to proceed in the direction of growing politicization of the masses and diversification of political interests and the social aggregates representing such interests. At the same time, representative democracy, at least in the form of constitutional charters and political ideology, becomes one of several alternative approaches to securing access to or control of government.

Persistence of traditional trends

The changes attributable to massive urbanization and industrialization, significant as they are, have not produced a complete break with the past. In a previous chapter the traditional political process was presented as a kind of seesaw movement between autocracy and rebellion which reached its fullest expression in the nineteenth and early twentieth centuries. Both autocracy and rebellion showed an unexpected capacity for adapting to virtually all changes that have affected the structure of Latin American societies. The caudillo developed into the modern dictator, who recognized the vital importance of mass support and technical expertise in government. Eventually, military dictatorship began to rid itself of its personalistic and charismatic traits to become "an exponent of the thoughts and attitudes of the armed forces" (Sepúlveda, 1970:176). Military regimes, such as those of Argentina and Brazil, have recently demonstrated that they can regulate succession to the presidency without violent confrontation, which would hardly be possible with a chief of state who conformed to the model of autocratic personalism of the past. But authoritarian rule has found its way also into the various democratic structures that at one time or other have been erected with varying degrees of staying power.

Representative democracy in Latin America has always been characterized by the extraordinary amount of authority vested in the president. Nowhere is presidentialism more pronounced than in Mexico.

A prime characteristic of the system of executive supremacy is that it is virtually self-perpetuating. Although no reelection is one of the most sacrosanct principles of the Mexican Revolution, succession to the presidency has inevitably been determined by the incumbent chief executive and his immediate advisers. Also characteristic is the political impotence of the Mexican Congress, which is little more than a ratifying agency for executive decisions. (Glade and Anderson, 1968:130)

Although there have been sporadic attempts to restrict the constitutional authority of the president in some Latin American countries (e.g., in Costa Rica), the predominant pattern is close to the one spelled out by Carlos Astiz for Argentina: "The theoretical recognition of the preference for a strong chief executive has been reinforced by political custom. The result has been the widespread belief that in Argentine politics, things get done by the executive branch, if they get done at all." (Astiz, 1970:12)

"Political custom" has probably been more effective in determining behavior than constitutional provisions, but some of these, created to meet such emergencies as martial law, and state of siege, can be and have been widely used to suspend constitutional articles designed to limit presidential authority. An ambitious president with autocratic leanings who dissolves parliament often meets only token resistence, or if the existing constitution does not permit him to be reelected, he may rewrite the law to legitimize his intention to stay in power—a pattern known as *continuismo*. As in Cuba under President Machado, parliament may lend its rubber-stamp approval to constitutional amendments allowing reelection of the chief of state. (Fitzgibbon, 1965:147)

Needless to say, the entire politico-administrative structure is typically imbued with authoritarianism. Within their subdivisions, governors, superintendents, and mayors have powers comparable to those of the president, particularly if they are appointed by higher authority and are not responsible to a provincial or local electorate. Even members of parliament, once elected, tend to act with little regard for their constituencies. Likewise, effective decision-making power is centralized at the top level of the bureaucratic hierarchy, and little if any authority is delegated downward. But on all levels of the bureaucratic hierarchy one may encounter informal power structures linked to politically influential personalities who are capable of affecting policies concerning appointments, promotions, transfers, and dismissals. Often some sectional chief becomes a little cacique, surrounded by a retinue of sycophants who expect their allegiance to be rewarded with favors or privileges, concession of which usually violates regulations.

The old power contest between the central government and recalcitrant local caciques, coronels, or gamonales, representing kinship groups and landed interests, has lead to the restriction of political authority vested in municipal government, which was usually manipulated by local autocrats. Even when municipal officials are elected, their powers are so limited that the body can hardly be considered to be a self-governing structure. Whether political centralization occurs in dictatorships or in representative democracies, it ought to be seen as a concession to the authoritarian principle. Even in countries such as Chile and Costa Rica, often praised for their adherence to democratic rule, very little authority is delegated to local governments.

Considering the extraordinary pervasiveness of the autocratic or authoritarian principle, it would be surprising indeed if the political parties had been able to stay clear of such influence. Contrary to certain stereotypes, Latin American parties are not inherently devoted to any version of representative democracy. Political parties have often been extensions of the personal power of dictators, mere organizational devices to organize support and to manipulate the masses. But whether a party strives for representative democracy, socialist revolution, nationalist revival, or dictatorship, its structure is likely to be "elitist." Power is concentrated at the top level, and relevant decisions are made by a single leader or a small party oligarchy.

To the extent that political parties are engaged in recruiting leaders for the nation at large, they contribute toward the perpetuation of the autocratic pattern. They are not alone in the performance of this function, however. The military are for obvious reasons the most powerful competitors; but as we shall see, the university has no minor role in perpetuating the pattern of authoritarianism. As indicated in a previous chapter, autocracy may be interpreted as an aspect of patrimonialism, particularly insofar as it is based on charisma and personal allegiance. The mass of loyal followers expect and often demand the exercise of discretionary power. The capacity for making the right kind of decision is assumed to be inherent in the personality of the leader. No legislative body, no board of ministerial advisers, no party directorate, could possibly improve on the wisdom of the leader's discretionary decision making, or so the people believe. What Tannenbaum once wrote about the patrimonialistic role of the Mexican president is applicable, to some extent at least, to most Latin American countries.

In a subtle sense, the mass of rural population, Indian or mestizo, illiterate or schooled, expects the president of the country to play the part of the great father. There is an implicit submissiveness, a bending of the head, which unconsciously forces upon the president the exercise of arbitrary power. Only the president can make a final decision. No other power is final, no other authority is absolute. He who would govern must also rule, or he will not be able to govern. Like every father, he must rule personally, in detail, and cannot delegate his authority. If he does, he will risk losing it. (Tannenbaum, 1953:130)

Patrimonialistic residues may be seen in the use of the armed forces for the furtherance of private ambitions, often made possible through personal allegiance of troops to their commanding officers. Again, Mexico of past decades could be considered as a model for numbers of countries.

It used to be customary for the general to move with his own troops. He had raised them, and trained them, and they were his people. It took three unsuccessful revolutions after 1920 and the purging of hundreds of army officers before the principle could be established that the troops did not belong to him, and that he could be moved without them. (Tannenbaum, 1953:132)

The assumption that the troops "belong" to the commanding general relies on the time-honored confusion of private and public domain, certainly one of the major characteristics of patrimonialism. A similar obfuscation may be found in a variety of situations and in otherwise different countries. The use of an elective or appointive office for personal gain is probably the most typical manifestation of patrimonialism. Since colonial times, low and irregularly paid salaries have contributed to the preservation of a tradition according to which the civil servant in direct contact with the public expects to receive bonuses for services pertaining to his regular duties, and the public in turn does not expect to be served well unless some *propina* or *gratificação* is offered to the functionary in charge. Moreover, a government employee who has any authority at all to make decisions, is not perceived as a servant of the people, but rather as a dispenser of favors, a role that fully agrees with his self-image.

Elective offices, particularly these pertaining to various legislative bodies, are widely used for a broad range of transactions in which the legislator exerts his power to dispense favors in return for personal gains.

Attempts to eradicate patrimonialistic practices in bureaucracies and legislatures have met with more success in some countries than in others. However, the state has been compelled to take on a great many new functions involving concession of credits, subsidies of various kinds, tax rebates, and direct investment in new industries, highways, port facilities, and the like; therefore, the patrimonialistic system of the past has been revivified in unexpected ways.

If autocracy has preserved its historical role, so has rebellion, although it has found new modes of expression. The traditional coup d'etat, which changed little except the personnel in control of government, has not disappeared by any means. Nowadays, however a coup cannot succeed without the support of military groups. Gone are the days when power contenders could seize political control with the help of improvised private armies.

Representative democracy and populismo

Analysts of Latin American society once believed that feudal residues, caudillism, and dictatorship—the "archaic" forces, in Lambert's terminology—were gradually being overcome and that political evolution was moving in the direction of representative democracy. In the light of actual events, such a view is unrealistic. In a previous chapter it was suggested that democracy was added to the many cultural imports from Western Europe and the United States, but it was quite incompatible with the prevailing social structure in which power was concentrated at the top level. To make democracy acceptable at all, its principles had to be adapted to the existing power structure, and the most effective way of accomplishing this was to disenfranchise the illiterates and all those who did not fit the property and income requirements set up by the constitutions. Income and occupational criteria were gradually dropped, but in most countries illiteracy has been recognized as a "legitimate" barrier to political participation up to the present day. The main effect of such constitutional barriers was to restrict the electorate to a small minority of the total adult population—a minority that could be relied on not to upset the applecart; a minority that could be coopted or otherwise manipulated.

Electoral fraud was another device employed to adapt democracy to the established power structure. Although as one might imagine, reliable data are hard to come by, fraudulent practices were and still are widely used to keep a ruling elite or an autocratic ruler in power. Prior to Perón, few elections in Argentina were honest, and during the 1930s electoral fraud was one of the "pillars" of the establishment. (Imaz, 1970:16) The results of most Brazilian elections prior to 1930 were distorted to some extent by fraud. Ballot boxes were stuffed or stolen; voters were intimidated, coerced, or simply kept from casting their ballot; "friends" of the power holders were allowed to vote several times, often under the names of children or persons deceased. Electoral fraud was so widespread that in several countries institutional safeguards, such as Brazil's *justiça eleitoral*, were created to stem abuse.

Systematic adaptation of representative democracy to the traditional power structure was a distinctive phase of the political process which extended throughout the nineteenth and far into the twentieth century. At some time, however, this process reversed itself—that is, there appeared a tendency to adapt the power structure to democratic rule. This reversal did not come about simultaneously in the different countries, nor did it immediately halt the opposing process. This second phase in the history of representative democracy is obviously related to urbanization, industrialization, and all the structural implications of these processes. It should also be noted that neither phase had much continuity: Many governments were overthrown, legislative bodies were forcibly dissolved, constitutions were discarded or rewritten, and dictatorships were established and disestablished. In other words, both phases were often disrupted by events that temporarily abolished democratic rule.

Nevertheless, a number of changes indicated that the second phase was under way. New political parties sponsoring the causes of the middle class, the workers, and the peasants transformed the traditional power play between conservatives and liberals into a more complex form of political competition. Whereas the older parties were vertical structures cutting across lines and keeping their lower-class segments in a tight dependency relationship, many of the new parties, particularly the socialist, groups tended to be horizontal structures recruiting the bulk of their members among the same social strata. Yet the traditional pattern of rebellion or inconformity continues *within* most political parties; factions typically precipitate around dissident leaders and ideological heresies. Thus Uruguay's two parties are split many ways, and so is Colombia's two-party system. Attempts to integrate Marxist groups into disciplined, monolithic communist parties have consistently failed, and everywhere the radical left is composed of a number of factions.

Proliferation of new political parties has been accompanied by ideological polarization, and polarization means, above all else, the emergence of parties or factions advocating causes that are totally or partly, irreconcilable with the established order.

At any rate, new parties must recruit followers, and followers are almost useless unless they are allowed to participate in elections. Thus all new parties were vitally interested in voter registration, in fighting electoral frauds that benefited entrenched power holders, even in making the vote a legal obligation of all qualified citizens. An increasing proportion of the population participated in elections. Chile, for example, has come a long way since 1937 when all registered voters represented no more than 10.4 per-

Table 20 Voting population in presidential elections of fifteen
Latin American countries (percentages of registered voters)

Year	Argentina	Bolivia	Brazil	Chile	Colombia	Costa Rica	Ecuador
1944	—	—	—	—	—	—	—
1945	—	—	83.1	—	—	—	—
1946	85.3	—	—	76.2	—	—	—
1947	—	—	—	—	—	—	—
1948	—	—	—	—	—	—	62.0
1949	—	—	—	—	—	—	—
1950	—	—	72.1	—	—	—	—
1951	86.5	—	—	—	—	—	—
1952	—	—	—	86.1	—	—	65.0
1953	—	—	—	—	—	67.2	—
1954	81.0	—	—	—	—	—	—
1955	—	—	59.7	—	—	—	—
1956	—	86.0	—	—	—	—	71.0
1957	—	—	—	—	—	—	—
1958	90.3	—	—	83.5	58.0	64.7	—
1959	—	—	—	—	—	—	—
1960	—	—	81.0	—	—	—	—
1961	—	—	—	—	—	—	—
1962	—	—	—	—	49.3	80.9	—
1963	80.1	—	66.2	—	—	—	—
1964	—	—	—	56.2	—	—	—
1965	—	—	—	—	—	—	—
1966	—	—	—	—	—	81.4	—
1967	—	—	—	—	—	—	—
1968	—	—	—	—	—	—	—
1969	—	—	—	—	—	—	—
1970	—	—	—	83.2	52.6	—	—
1971	—	—	—	—	—	—	—

cent of the total population and only 9.16 percent of these voted in the presidential election of that year. (Petras, 1969:110)

The oligarchical structure of the first Brazilian republic (1891–1930) is unquestioned. Indeed, in "no election prior to 1926 did the winning presidential candidate receive as many as 600,000 popular votes. As late as 1919, when the republic's population already was over 26,000,000, Epitácio da Silva Pessô won the presidency with *less than 290,000 popular votes.*" (Johnson, 1958:155)

Developments since World War II are summarized in Tables 20 and 21. Although the reliability of some data is doubtful, voter registration sug-

Table 20 *(Continued)*

Guatemala	Honduras	Mexico	Nicaragua	Panama	Paraguay	Peru	Uruguay
97.6	—	—	—	—	—	—	—
—	—	—	—	—	—	—	—
—	—	—	—	—	—	—	—
—	—	—	—	—	—	—	—
—	—	—	—	—	—	—	—
—	—	—	—	—	—	—	—
71.4	—	—	—	—	—	—	77.6
—	—	—	—	—	—	—	—
—	—	74.1	—	—	—	—	—
—	—	—	—	—	—	—	—
70.5	—	—	—	—	—	—	67.9
—	—	—	—	—	—	—	—
—	—	—	—	80.1	—	83.8	—
—	—	—	—	—	—	—	—
—	—	71.7	—	—	—	—	71.3
—	—	—	—	—	—	—	—
—	—	—	—	—	—	—	—
—	—	—	—	—	—	—	—
—	—	—	—	—	—	76.1	77.1
—	—	—	79.1	—	65.3	94.4	—
67.6	—	69.3	—	67.1	—	—	—
—	—	—	—	—	—	—	—
—	—	—	—	—	—	—	—
—	—	—	—	—	65.2	—	—
—	—	—	—	—	—	—	—
—	—	65.1	—	—	—	—	—
—	68.2	—	—	—	—	—	—

Source: Kenneth Ruddle and Philip Gillette, eds., *Latin American Political Statistics*. Los Angeles: Latin American Center of the University of California, 1972, pp. 105–114.

gests, on the whole growing involvement in the political process, at least in Argentina, Bolivia, Brazil, Chile, Costa Rica, Ecuador, El Salvador, Mexico, Paraguay, and Uruguay. There seems to be a tendency to reduce the gap that initially sets apart participation in elections in a number of countries, but voting in presidential elections has been subject to great fluctuations. However, since many voters must travel long distances by uncomfortable, expensive means of transportation to reach the balloting place, most percentages can be considered to be rather high.

Table 21 *Registered voters in fifteen Latin American countries*
(percentages of total population)

Year	Argentina	Bolivia	Brazil	Chile	Colombia	Costa Rica	Ecuador
1944	—	—	—	—	—	—	—
1945	—	—	16.1	—	—	—	—
1946	21.6	—	—	11.5	—	—	—
1947	—	—	—	—	26.6	—	—
1948	24.1	—	—	—	—	20.6	14.2
1949	—	—	—	10.4	—	—	—
1950	—	—	22.0	—	—	—	—
1951	51.1	8.1	—	—	44.6	—	—
1952	—	—	—	18.4	—	—	16.5
1953	—	—	—	18.2	—	32.7	—
1954	51.5	—	26.4	—	—	—	—
1955	—	—	26.1	—	—	—	—
1956	—	29.2	—	—	—	—	22.8
1957	51.0	—	—	19.1	42.6	—	—
1958	—	13.3	22.0	21.4	37.1	32.2	24.9
1959	—	—	—	—	—	—	—
1960	50.5	14.1	21.9	—	28.5	—	—
1961	—	—	—	25.1	—	—	—
1962	54.5	32.6	24.6	—	32.5	37.1	—
1963	53.1	—	23.9	—	—	—	—
1964	—	35.5	—	53.6	35.1	—	—
1965	52.0	—	—	34.0	—	—	—
1966	—	33.7	—	—	—	38.0	—
1967	—	—	—	—	—	—	—
1968	—	—	—	—	—	—	—
1969	—	—	—	34.0	—	—	—
1970	—	—	31.4	36.2	36.2	—	—

Increased electoral participation does not necessarily imply striving for representative democracy. Juan Perón was elected president of Argentina in 1946, and in spite of his assumption of more and more dictatorial powers, the elections of 1951 and 1953 confirmed his regime. After eight years of dictatorial rule, and after having been forcibly removed from the presidency in 1945, Getulio Vargas was elected president of Brazil again in 1950. General Rojas Pinilla, who had imposed dictatorship on Colombia between 1953 and 1957, lost the 1969 presidential election by a slim margin.

Such electoral behavior does not suggest genuine commitment to representative democracy, but it seems to express a desire for democratization of the political process in the previously defined sense. It is certainly part and parcel of what is often loosely referred to as *populismo*. The term ap-

Table 21 (Continued)

El Salvador	Guatemala	Mexico	Nicaragua	Panama	Paraguay	Peru	Uruguay
—	12.9	—	—	—	—	—	—
—	—	—	—	—	—	—	—
—	—	—	—	—	—	—	32.6
—	—	—	—	—	—	—	—
—	—	—	—	—	—	—	—
—	20.5	—	—	—	—	—	53.3
—	—	—	—	—	—	—	—
—	—	18.2	—	—	—	—	—
—	—	—	—	—	—	—	—
—	21.5	—	—	—	—	—	55.6
—	—	—	—	—	—	—	—
—	—	—	—	40.5	—	17.7	—
—	—	—	—	—	—	—	—
—	20.5	30.9	—	—	—	—	57.2
—	—	—	—	—	—	—	—
31.5	—	—	—	—	—	20.9	58.2
—	—	—	—	—	37.2	18.9	—
—	—	—	37.1	—	—	—	—
36.1	19.5	32.9	—	40.4	—	—	—
—	—	—	—	—	—	—	—
39.3	—	—	—	—	—	—	—
—	—	—	—	—	—	—	—
41.0	—	—	—	—	40.1	—	—
—	—	—	—	—	—	—	—
42.3	—	42.6	—	—	—	—	—

Source: Kenneth Ruddle and Philip Gillette, eds., *Latin American Political Statistics.* Los Angeles: Latin American Center of the University of California, 1972, pp. 105–114.

parently means different things to different people, but populismo is essentially an urban phenomenon, related to extremely rapid city growth and frantic attempts to marshal political support among the urban masses through nontraditional approaches. Populismo thus refers to political attitudes and expectations of the urban masses, but also to the techniques of creating and manipulating such attitudes and expectations for the benefit of politicians, political parties, or political movements.

The belief that government should be directly if not immediately responsive to the popular will may be defined as "populist legitimation." Such a belief would tend to undermine the system of representative democracy, which provides a political infrastructure standing between public sentiment or demand and governmental response." (Walker, 1967:416)

Some analysts define populism as "the rule of the masses, different from that of political parties." (Ianni, 1970:5) Others see it as active participation in decision making by the poor, the disinherited minorities (e.g., Indians), and the effectively disenfranchised in society at large. (Petras, 1969: 203) It has also been said that "populist politicians exacerbated the political climate by clamoring for drastic reform of the existing social and economic order and blaming the 'Oligarchy' and its congressional delegation for the nation's lack of progress." (Roett, 1972:15)

To be sure, populism is all this and more. Due to its experimental nature and the impossibility of organizing the support of the urban masses by traditional means, it takes diverse forms presumably adapted to the atomized structure of the modern city. It often degenerates into demagoguery, bypassing political parties and legislatures; it resorts to revolutionary rhetoric or violence; it may seek stable support from new parties and labor unions, or it may be no more than an individual's personal flair for getting votes in democratic elections.

Whatever its form, populism addresses itself to the masses, disenfranchised or not, poor, or hovering above the poverty level. Populist politicians tend to use political parties in a highly personal way, if at all. They certainly do not fit parties with a strong discipline, and they oppose the "cult of personality." Leftist they may be, but they are hardly submissive members of the traditional communist parties, for example. To the extent that populist politicians possess charisma, they make the most of it. Whether they are of the right or the left, they draw their ideological sustenance from nationalism. Plinio Salgado, national chieftain of the Movimento Integralista, the Brazilian version of fascism, tried in the 1930s to implant "a mística da pátria" (the mystique of the fatherland) and to turn the national conscience against the exploitation of Brazilian resources by foreigners, particularly Americans. A representative of the extreme right, he found many followers among populists who later opted for a combination of nationalism and Marxism.

To sum up, populism implies politicization or even political mobilization of the "urban masses," especially the underprivileged and frustrated segments of these masses. In some cases it has reached the peasantry as well. This trend runs hand in hand with attitudes, programs, and possible actions directed against traditional power holders. Furthermore, populism is highly pragmatic and eclectic in its choice of ideological underpinnings and in its strategies of gaining mass support and carrying out socioeconomic change.

Vargas tried to merge a corporatist state with a labor movement. His fascist ideas failed to take hold in Brazil, but he was extremely effective in mobilizing urban labor and in building a powerful labor party. Juan Perón did for Argentine labor what Vargas had done for the Brazilian working class; unlike Brazilian labor, however, the peronistas withstood the pressures of a military regime without signs of weakening. In Brazil, populist approaches have been attempted in all democratic elections since Vargas's death by suicide, from the presidential down to the municipal level. In São Paulo, Ademar de Barros and Janio Quadros successfully posed as populists, and Lionel Brizola, governor of Rio Grande do Sul, was "the most dynamic left-wing populist." (Skidmore, 1967:281) In Peru it was Victor Raul Haya de la Torre, founder of the Alianza Popular Revolucionaria Americana (APRA), whom Cotler called a "typical case of Latin American populism" (Cotler, 1967:5). Populist trends are clearly visible in the Christian Democratic Party of Chile, in the Accion Democrática of Venezuela and in the Movimiento Nacional Revolucinario of Boliva. Far from advocating revolutionary causes, Alianza Nacional Popular in Colombia nevertheless assumed a rather pronounced populist stance through its most vocal leader, Maria Eugenia Rojas de Moreno, daughter of dictator Rojas Pinilla and senator of the republic, who possesses a popular appeal resembling that of Eva Perón. (McDonald, 1971:188)

Needless to say, there has been a populist component in the revolutions that, changed to varying degrees, the societies of Mexico, Bolivia, Cuba, and temporarily at least, Guatemala.

There can be no genuine representative democracy without a strong legislature, and strong legislatures have been rare in Latin America. By "strong" legislature, we mean a body of elected representatives that performs a relevant role in political decision making and is capable of checking the power of the chief executive. As suggested before, a strong legislature is hardly compatible with the authoritarian role assigned by most constitutions to the chief of state. The customary corrective of what is felt to be abuse of presidential power is subversion rather than reliance on legislatures.

It is unrealistic to expect the politicized urban masses to believe in the effectiveness of legislative bodies for the solution of major social problems. With exceedingly few exceptions, legislatures are either controlled by conservative forces resisting radical changes, or they are divided into irreconcilably opposed factions. Conflicts over vital issues are not easily accom-modated. In fact, the inability to resolve conflicts seems to be a major stumbling block to concerted action by Latin American legislatures. For example, the incapacity of the Peruvian congress to agree on one of the three presidential candidates, none of whom had gained the necessary one-third of the votes, led to the establishment of a military government in 1962. "If Peru was to avoid a military takeover, it was clear that the lead-ing parties would have to cooperate to select a president and guaranty him their support. Once again, however, the reformers were unable to reconcile their differences, even temporarily." (McCoy, 1971:344)

In the Venezuelan senate, allegiance to political parties is said to control senatorial behavior to the point of destroying the ability of this legislative body for autonomous conflict resolutions. (Kelley, 1971:491) Most legis-latures must obey precedural rules that facilitate procrastination of vital decisions almost indefinitely. For the last decade, the Colombian legisla-ture has avoided a floor discussion of several drafts of a law proposing "ur-ban reforms" that would contravene powerful real estate interests.

Only Chile, Costa Rica, and Uruguay have or had "strong" legislatures capable of autonomous decision making. Costa Rica is an extreme case of a country that has imposed constitutional limitations of presidential pow-ers, but those who praise Costa Rican democracy ought to be reminded that the present regime was born in the bloody "revolution" of 1948 and that the representative democracy then established has not affected the hegemony of the traditional elite. "The system has permitted this class to permit formal political participation to everyone in the country and yet to preserve its position as decision maker for the society as a whole." (Denton, 1971:106) And the role of the Uruguayan and Chilean legislatures sud-denly ended with the establishment of military regimes in 1973.

Revolutions

In preceding chapters no attempt was made to spell out the intended meaning of the term "revolution." In the past, many authors, including Latin Americans, have overused the word. Almost any kind of rebellion, revolt, or insurrection designed to overthrow established government has been labeled a revolution. Such indiscriminate use of the term has failed to indicate that most rebellions were not meant to change anything but the person or persons in control of government, whereas a few profoundly

affected the social structure and the institutional apparatus of a given country. Only the latter type seems to fit the concept of revolution as a radical
interference in the structure of a society. Revolution in this more specific
sense has become indeed one of the most significant accretions to the Latin
American cultural tradition of defying, subverting, or overthrowing established authority by violence or threat of violence. More than ever before,
the "right of revolution" has become "a political article of faith and an
inalienable privilege." (Royal Institute of International Affairs, 1937:144)

Revolutions are often assumed to be radical, swift, and political, although
it is not supposed that the transformations brought about by revolutions are
merely changes in existing political regimes. But what about such concepts
as the "Industrial Revolution" or the "Agricultural Revolution"? These
events were neither swift nor limited to the polity. They were not political
revolutions at all, although they affected the political structure of all
societies concerned.

Here the view is taken that whether sudden or gradual, revolution implies "*radical* transformation of a system, the substitution of one principle,
or basis, of organization for another." (White, 1959:181) Both the Cuban
Revolution and the Industrial Revolution generated *radical* transformation
of existing systems. The first was sudden and extremely limited in time and
space; the second has been gradual, of long duration and far-reaching effect.
However, it should be added that revolutions typically seek continuity in
time by institutionalizing systemic change.

If taken in White's sense, revolution seems to alternate with evolution,
or sequences of change *within* a given system. Thus "evolution and revolution are correlative and complementary concepts, not mutually exclusive
or opposite." (White, 1959:281) One can also view evolution as sequential
change, apparently punctuated by revolutionary phases implying systemic
changes. This conceptualization of revolution seems to be particularly appropriate for Latin America because it fits the idea that revolution is part
and parcel of the cultural process, rather than an "abnormal" or "pathological" phenomenon.

The first Latin American revolution that could be said to have brought
about a radical systemic transformation occurred in Mexico. The Mexican
Revolution was not, however, a clearly defined movement with a distinct
ideology and a leadership committed to a comprehensive program of national scope. The initial uprisings were intended to recover village land that
had been despoiled by large landowners. The revolution "moved by fits
and starts, and in numerous directions at once; it carried with it the bas-

tions of power and the straw-covered huts of the peasantry alike. When it was finished, it had profoundly altered the characteristics of Mexican society." (Wolf, 1969:26)

In its first phase the Mexican Revolution was almost entirely concerned with eradicating the landed estates, abolishing debt-servitude, and ameliorating the conditions of the working class. The constitution of 1917 decreed land reform and liquidation of the large estates, including the huge holdings of the Church. It subordinated land ownership to the national interest and issued labor legislation seeking to protect the workers against exploitation. The mostly radical steps, however, were not taken until 1934, when General Lazaro Cardenas began to carry out agrarian reform and labor organization on a large scale.

> Cardenas did what no Mexican leader had attempted before him: he dismantled the political power of the hacienda owners and distributed hacienda lands among the peasantry. Before Cardenas about 17 million acres of land had been redistributed; during the six years of his tenure in office this total was raised to 41 million acres. Most of this land was granted to village communities under communal forms of tenure (*ejidos*). (Wolf, 1969:45)

The political mobilization of rural and urban labor provided the revolutionary government with the mass support it needed to consolidate its power and to confront internal and external opposition, particularly the United States.

Not only did the revolutionary state capture these as yet untapped power potentials, it also succeeded in centralizing the politicoeconomic structure by establishing "a relationship of direct dependence on the machinery of government among the major interest groups in national life." (Glade and Anderson, 1968:27) Potential or actual power contenders, such as the military and regional caudillos, labor leaders, and foreign concerns, were thus effectively neutralized. Some revolutionary changes may perhaps be labeled as "socialist," but nationalism rather than socialism was the ideological mainspring of the Mexican Revolution. Like all nationalisms, it created a strong collective consciousness and a united front against foreign encroachment on the economic resources of the land and its institutions. In the name of nationalization, foreign land holdings, oil fields, and railroads were expropriated and the revolutionary state assumed an unprecedented role in promoting economic development and sociocultural change. By accepting development banking as a legitimate exercise of political authority and by using credit as a political sanction, the state channeled capital resources into the economic system and embarked on rapid industrialization. (Glade and Anderson, 1968:109–111) At the same time, the educational system was completely restructured, and massive attempts were made to incorporate the Indians into the nation.

In structural terms, the Mexican Revolution did away with the semi-feudal seigneurial class of big landowners and broke their political stranglehold on the nation. It enfranchised the peasantry and carried out a land reform that, in spite of numerous shortcomings introduced significant changes to the village communities. And, as indicated in a previous chapter, it created the prerequisites for structural mobility that expanded and transformed the Mexican middle class into an achievement-oriented segment of the society.

The example of Mexican nationalism and state-sponsored socioeconomic development, which has not been lost on Latin America, is certainly related to similar changes that have occurred in every republic south of the Rio Grande. It is also true that many accomplishments of the Mexican Revolution, which cost an estimated 2 million lives, were achieved elsewhere without violent upheavals.

If revolution brought political stability to Mexico, it failed to do so in Bolivia, where the Movimiento Nacional Revolucionario seized power in 1952. A reliable history of the Bolivian Revolution has yet to be written, but there is no doubt that it brought radical systemic transformation to the nation. As in Mexico, agrarian reform, abolition of Indian servitude, and political enfranchisement of the Indians (now called peasants) were the immediate concerns of the revolutionary leaders. As in Mexico, the natural resources of the country came to be controlled by the state, the mines were nationalized, and peasants and workers were organized in *sindicatos*. Since the Indians constitute a clear majority in Bolivia, the right to vote and to bear arms, unheard of under the old regime, implied a major shift in the distribution of power. At the same time, the power monopoly of the landholding seigneurial class was destroyed as land reform, preceded or accompanied by Indian uprisings in some regions, spread throughout the country. A total of 7,906,283 hectares (out of 109,858,100 hectares) was affected by the agrarian reform, and in 1967, 191,459 families had received titles to their holdings. (Heath, Erasmus, and Buechler, 1969:373–374)

Unlike their Mexican counterparts, the leaders of the Bolivian Revolution were unable to obtain enough support to secure political continuity for the regime established in 1952. Several military coups have taken place since then, but they have not reversed the structural changes brought about by the revolution.

The most radical revolution by far occurred in Cuba. Beginning with the collapse of the regime of Fulgencio Batista and the seizure of Havana by Fidel Castro's rebel forces, the revolutionary transformations of Cuban society proceeded faster than comparable changes in Russia or China. A radical land reform was carried out within six months. Before the second year was over, all United States industrial and agricultural holdings in Cuba were expropriated, as well as most Cuban enterprises. (Wolf and Hansen, 1972:328) The defeat of the American-supported attempt to invade Cuba intensified nationalistic feelings and brought international prestige to the revolutionary leadership. The Cuban Communist party had done nothing to assist the rebels in their struggle against the Batista government, yet three years after the victorious entry in Havana Fidel Castro proclaimed himself and the revolution to be "Marxist-Leninist."

Deprived of the American-controlled sugar market, Cuba sought and found an economic relationship with Russia which has greatly benefited both countries. The price Russia pays for Cuban sugar can be twice the world market price and still be only one-third of what it would cost Russia to produce domestic sugar. "By using Cuban imports to meet the rise in domestic sugar consumption, the Soviet Union can reduce the domestic price of sugar while at the same time providing Cuba with a stable market for its exports over the medium term." (Furtado, 1970:244)

The first priority of the revolutionary regime was agrarian reform, but the process went much farther in Cuba than in either Mexico or Bolivia. As in Mexico, the revolution succeeded in generating enough popular support to confront the United States and to neutralize internal dissent; but unlike Mexico, Cuba witnessed a massive exodus of its middle and upper classes, which certainly helped eliminate political opposition. As in Mexico and Bolivia, nationalism became the ideological basis of the revolution— nationalism directed against foreign, particularly American, domination of the Cuban economy. Ex post facto conversion to Marxism should probably be interpreted as ideological reinforcement, clearly ancillary to nationalism.

At the time, Castro's position, clearly defined in his Moncada address, was more populist than Marxist; it reflected more the influence of José Martí, the "Apostle" of Cuban independence, than any Marxist current of thought. . . . Confronting a fragmented, subnational political order, Castro adopted a political stance and strategy that were importantly geared to erasing the former cleavages within the Cuban society and to building a nationally integrated state. (Manitzas, 1971:3)

Equally concerned with ethnic cleavages, nationalism, and land reform was the abortive revolution in Guatemala. Following the overthrow of Jorge Ubico's dictatorship in 1944, there came a decade of revolutionary changes under the administrations of Juan José Arvalo and Jacobo Arbenz. Under Arbenz, the relatively small group of local Communists gained increasing influence on the government, and the threatened expropriation of large holdings owned by United States citizens brought about the American-supported overthrow of the Arbenz government by Castillo Armas in 1954. What the United States had failed to do in Mexico and Cuba was easily accomplished in a small country, divided by political dissent and surrounded by unsympathetic neighbors. (Adams, 1961:268–269; 1870: 184ff.)

A great many hypotheses have been advanced to "explain" the three major revolutions of Latin America and to isolate the (causative) variables. Analysts have pointed to ruthless exploitation of labor, political oppression, extreme cleavages in the class structure, corruption and graft in government, foreign domination, and similar conditions that presumably lead to violent eruptions, providing enough "social tensions" have accumulated and a "catalytic agent" is there to spark the explosion. (Draper, 1965:116)

Such causes of discontent and social tensions, however, are neither new nor limited to the few countries that have experienced revolutionary change. Latin American history is full of violent eruptions due to a broad spectrum of "catalytic agents"; but exceedingly few of these eruptions developed into full-fledged revolutions. Perhaps the most impressive incident, known as La Violencia, occurred in Colombia. It began in 1948, cost an estimated quarter-million lives, and extended well into the 1960s.

La Violencia was a phase in a long chain of similar, but less bloody outbreaks having roots in the nineteenth century. The situation of the Colombian peasantry and working class was hardly less desperate than that of their Mexican counterparts, but exploitation and oppression did not produce a genuine revolutionary climate. Large areas of the country, deeply affected by continuous fighting, approached a state of anarchy, but no Carranza or Zapata emerged to provide a sense of direction or orientation. Surely, many local groups of peasants took over haciendas and in some cases proclaimed independent "republics." Eventually, a few guerrilla bands declared a commitment to revolutionary ideologies, but they were no match for the well-equipped and adequately trained regular forces.

La Violencia was hardly more than a phase in the old power struggle between the conservatives and the liberals. In a sense, it confirmed the hypothesis that Latin American social structure is basically unreceptive to political pluralism: that political parties "sometimes forcibly try to eliminate other parties." (McDonald, 1971:3) In the case of Colombia, both parties lost control over their rural members and eventually fighting sank to the folk level of blood feuds and predatory warfare.

Although the Colombian civil war was largely a matter of meaningless bloodshed in which political issues played hardly more than a marginal role, rural guerrilla warfare erupted in Venezuela, Peru, and Bolivia. Most of these movements, committed to a Marxist or Marxist-derived ideology, apparently had been initiated on the assumption that the peasantry would join them in a generalized class struggle that would eventually spread to the cities and bring about the proletarian revolution. These radical expectations were based on faith in the universal validity of a political ideology. All these attempts fell short of producing the expected results and were eventually suppressed by regular forces. For a few years the guerrilla syndrome shifted to the cities, where it gained notoriety through acts of terror, but political support failed to materialize. Fidel Castro and his small band of guerillas in the Sierra Maestra seem to have served as model on which revolutionary strategies and political expectations were based. It was assumed that Castro's campaign could be reenacted and its success duplicated under conditions bearing no more than a remote resemblance to the Cuban Revolution.

In view of numerous failures to revolutionize Latin American society by violence, one has to admit that only under uncommon structural conditions does violent revolution have a chance to succeed. As long as an established government can count on substantional political support, as long as it controls a loyal and well-equipped army, the chances of revolutionary groups to seize power are nil.

Although some aspects of the Cuban Revolution are still controversial, it is clear that the government of dictatoɪ Fulgencio Batista proved incapable of achieving the political support indispensable to an effective confrontation with the small revolutionary forces. On the contrary, whatever precarious support may once have existed among a poorly integrated society was eroded by the misuse of coercion and by the growing renown of the rebels. On the other hand, the exceptional quality of the rebel leaders enabled the guerrilla bands to accomplish the rare feat of gaining the confidence and active support of the mountain peasantry. Apparently this was done primarily by carrying out radical changes in the areas controlled by the revolutionary groups.

By the summer of 1958 the Rebel Army administered an area of
5000 square miles; it had carried out an agrarian reform which included the distribution of 6000 head of cattle, and had established 25
schools. By the end of the war, significant sections of the Sierra Maestra
peasantry had been radically politicized. (Wolf and Hansen, 1972:324)

While the Batista regime was rapidly losing ground, the rebels gained
enough support from different segments of the society to win a military
victory over the demoralized army. It could be argued of course that the
outcome might have been quite different if Castro and his followers
had presented themselves at the very beginning as protagonists of a Communist revolution.

The telescoped chain of events characterizing the Cuban Revolution
stands in strong contrast to the protracted and somewhat diluted processes that culminated in revolution in Mexico. Along with many other,
rather striking differences between the two revolutions, at least two similarities are obvious: The regime of Porfirio Diaz collapsed suddenly after
a disastrous military confrontation with the rebel forces. Like Batista, the
Mexican dictator lacked political support, and the Mexican army could not
suppress the rapidly spreading uprisings. Carranza, one of the first and most
successful rebel leaders, did not have to face Castro's problem of establishing his credibility among the peasantry of northern Mexico. Carranza
was a peasant, and so were his followers. As in Cuba, mass support and
consolidation of revolutionary gains on a regional basis could not fail to
exercise a decisive influence on the development of the revolution.

In Bolivia the revolutionary process was different insofar as it seems to
have occurred almost simultaneously at two levels. The determining factor
was the power struggle between the Movimiento Nacional Revolucionario
and the armed forces representing the *Rosca*, "the combination of mining
and landed interests that had traditionally ruled the country." (Blasier,
1967:44) Supported by the urban middle class and perhaps the miners,
the MNR won an easy victory over the traditional power holders. But "the
old regime no longer existed as a group with faith in itself and power to
enforce its beliefs; it was a shattered conglomerate of special interests without the force or talent to impose the principles which supported their privilege." (Patch, 1961:127)

While the MNR wrested political power from the *Rosca*, the Indian
peasantry through its sindicatos, prepared to fight for a redistribution of the
land. There was an obvious connection between the enactment of a land
reform law by the revolutionary government in 1953 and the peasant rebel-

lion. Nor was the rapid spread of the movement unrelated to attempts by radical leftist groups to help organize it (Malloy, 1970: 202ff.). However, certain factions within the MNR were apparently opposed to national agrarian reform. Although the general confusion makes reliable reconstruction of the facts extremely difficult, it appears that peasant sindicatos did indeed seize land and livestock and that bloody clashes with groups of opponents occurred. (Heath, Erasmus, and Buechler, 1969:44ff.; Malloy, 1970:203). It is unlikely that the government would have decreed a general land reform in 1953, if it had not been under pressure from the Indian peasantry. "To sign the decree, President Paz journeyed to Ucurena, by now the symbolic center of *el movimiento campesino*. There, on an open air platform surrounded by thousands of armed Indian peasants, the land reform became law." (Malloy, 1970:206–207)

There is no question that the idea of a radical subversion of the established social order has a tremendous appeal to the segments of Latin American society that have little to lose and much to gain from revolutions such as those in Mexico, Bolivia, and Cuba. To gain any credibility at all, coups d'etat must now be presented to the masses as genuine revolutions, and no power holder can hope to stay in office long unless his revolutionary rhetoric is accompanied by more or less drastic changes.

In the political panorama of Latin America, Chile appears to be unique, a revolutionary power contender having become president there by popular vote. However, as in Bolivia, revolutionary change was precipitated by politicized peasants who took agrarian reform into their own hands, forcibly occupying numerous haciendas. As in Bolivia, too, such actions seem to have contributed to a growing scarcity of agricultural products in the urban market and to a rise in food prices. Attempting to carry out socialist reforms within the constitutional framework of representative democracy, president Salvador Allende was constantly hampered by strong opposition and mounting economic problems. The military, who had been under severe pressure to intervene, eventually overturned the government in a bloody coup that culminated in the alleged suicide of Allende. A military dictatorship was established that had, at least initially, the support of a substantial proportion of Chilean society.

Militarism and military government

According to Claudio Veliz, there were 81 successful military coups in Latin America between 1930 and 1966. Except in Mexico and Uruguay, power was seized by military groups as often as nine times in Bolivia and Ecuador; seven times in Argentina and Paraguay; six times in Brazil and Haiti; four times in Cuba, the Dominican Republic, Peru, and Venezuela; two or three times in Chile, Columbia. Honduras, and Panama; and once in Costa Rica and Nicaragua. (Veliz, 1967:278)

In the nineteenth century, military power holders were virtually indistinguishable from caudillos, although some caudillos were civilians. Prior to 1920 several hundred successful and unsuccessful insurgencies occurred in which the military played a leading role. The frequency with which military chieftains became contenders for power in the political process has induced quite a few authors to discuss this phenomenon in terms of *militarism*. From a comparative, cross-cultural standpoint, however, the concept of militarism hardly seems to be applicable to Latin America.

No Latin American nation exhibits the characteristics of a type of society in which warfare and preparation for war are raised to a dominant position in the value system. At a primitive level, such as represented by Indian tribes of the Great Plains, a man could gain social distinction only as a warrior. His feats in combat were carefully recorded, and they served as points of reference in the incessant competition for status. Military chiefs and military societies were part and parcel of the political organization of the tribe. At a highly complex level, such as represented by Japan prior to 1945 and Germany prior to 1918, war is glorified, perhaps more often in word than in deed; preparation for war is a national priority, and the highest social rewards are associated with a military career. In imperial Germany, military bearing and military discipline pervaded all walks of life. The second best thing to being an officer of the army was to be an officer of the military reserves, a considerable distinction in civilian life. The military establishment was of course, a privileged institution, the officer corps being the highest ranking stratum of the society. There was a clear separation between military and civilian authority at the lower levels of the social structure, but not at the top. The ruling dynasty and the nobility identified themselves with the military establishment. The emperor was, above everything else, the highest-ranking officer of the armed forces, and commanding positions in the elite regiments were open only to members of the nobility. A military coup would have been redundant because the army had all the political power it could desire. Such is the cultural orientation of a militarist society. Needless to say, no Latin American republic bears or bore any resemblance to the true militaristic model. Military government, even military regime, yes; militarism, no. Most current definitions of militarism seem not to recognize that militarism as we understand it is a genuine culture pattern, and as such it implies far-reaching, if not complete, cognitive and emotional consensus of the society at large.

Since the very inception of an independent Latin America, relationships between civilian and military authorities have been shot through with antagonisms, rivalries, and inconsistencies. Up to the present time countless attempts have been made to protect civilian government from military interference. On the other hand, time and again civilian power contenders have tried either to involve the armed forces in the political process or openly to enlist support for political objectives. Contempt, hatred, and fear of the military establishment have alternated with enthusiastic praise and hero worship of distinguished soldiers. The not uncommon appraisal of the "man on horseback" as the villain who has thwarted the establishment of representative democracy is not only a gross oversimplification of rather complex processes, it also represents an ethnocentric assumption that the military should be under complete control of an elected government and that they should never be involved in politics. In the present context the military are accepted "as an integral component of Latin American society *interacting* with other elements rather then *acting* against them." (McAlister, 1966:28) Whether deplorable or not in the perspective of some political ideologies, the political role of the Latin American military is read here as a cultural pattern, a "normal" rather than a "deviant" circumstance.

Perhaps the armed forces have played a pivotal role in politics because the military establishment, more than any other institution, encompasses the two opposing principles characterizing the political process in Latin America: authoritarianism and rebellion. The military chieftain embodies the autocratic or authoritarian principle. Carried to its ultimate consequence, autocracy appears to be unwilling to respect constitutional limitations when it perceives structural hazards menacing the society it is supposed to protect. The overthrow of what is believed to be a weak, inept, or corrupt government is felt to be a functional extension of the autocratic role of military power contenders.

However, the Latin America armies have often been unable to stave off rebellion in their own ranks. Local uprisings by garrison commanders or groups of officers trying to oust a provincial government and then "march on the capital" have been rather common in many countries. Such attempts are breaches of military discipline, of course; and since they force the loyal troops to take action, the fabric of the army is torn asunder by warfare between military factions. Also, plots and conspiracies of subaltern officers against their superiors are not unusual. Fulgencio Batista staged the so-called Sergeant's Revolt in Cuba (1933); corporals and sergeants in the air force and marines revolted in Brasília in 1963, and in 1964 noncommissioned officers involved themselves in a naval mutiny in Rio de Janeiro.

It would be naïve to expect the military to remain exempt from the structural inconsistencies affecting the society at large. Factionalism is the price the military establishment has to pay for assuming an active role in the political process.

Assumption of an active political role by an army does not necessarily mean that overthrow of an established government will occur. Certain informal and rather subtle ways of intervening in politics are perceived to be at variance with the interests of the nation as a whole or of the army as the chief custodian of such interests. Interventions of this type usually take the form of pressure brought to bear on the chief executive, his ministers, and perhaps leading members of the legislature. In other words, the army assumes the role of an overseer of the political process or, as some prefer, "a constitutional caretaker."

Although the election of military officers to the presidency of a republic, to the governship of a state or province, or to membership in a legislative body cannot be interpreted as direct intervention, it certainly opens channels through which the military establishment may seek to exercise its influence.

Military intervention by open rebellion and takeover of governmental function appears to belong either to the "arbitrator" type or to the "ruler" type. (Perlmutter, 1969:382–404)

> [The former] imposes a time limit on army rule and returns the government to civilian hands while it resumes its role as a guardian of the constitution. The ruler-type army challenges the very legitimacy of the political system it overthrows: it seeks to remain involved in politics to bring about a transformation of the political system. (Roett, 1972:4–5)

If taken literally, transformation of the political system would mean revolution in the previously defined sense.

It would be difficult to understand the power potential of the Latin American military establishments without taking into account the processes of professionalization and modernization undergone by the armed forces since the late nineteenth century. Following the established pattern of cultural transfer from Europe and the United States, "military commissions," mainly from France and Germany, were contracted to provide training cadres for certain Latin American armies. To the extent that this implied procurement of sophisticated weaponry, and training in its use, modernization ran parallel to professionalization. In accordance with the general trend of development, military technology became increasingly important and complex, requiring acquisition of highly specialized skills. Particularly since World War II, thousands of Latin American officers have been sent to the United States for long periods of training.

Professionalization and modernization not only multiplied the power potential located in the armed forces, they created a much broader base for military intervention and participation in technological development. In some countries (e.g., Argentina and Brazil), the military have provided technical expertise necessary for industrial development.

The political role of the military has frequently been related to the class structure. By restricting recruitment into the officer corps to members of the ruling upper class, the armed forces became to varying degrees structural extensions of that class, therefore instruments of class hegemony. The Chilean army seems to have been in such a position between 1830 and 1879. (North, 1966:12) Far more common, however, was the manipulation of the armed forces by caudillos. As indicated before, some caudillos came from the upper class, some did not. Those who made it to the top used the army to keep themselves and their loyal followers in government rather than to further class interests. In fact, not infrequently they sought to curtail the power of the landed elite when it interfered with their personal political designs.

In spite of some complexities, it is less difficult to perceive an alliance between military and the seigneurial upper class than to find unequivocal evidence for structural relationships between middle class and the military establishment. To be sure, sooner or later *all* armies of Latin America began to recruit officers from the middle class, and the middle-class element has been clearly dominant for some decades now. Exactly what this means in terms of political orientation of the armed forces is unclear. Empirical evidence shows that everywhere the armed forces have actively opposed the violent and radical revolution sought by various leftists. Therefore, we could borrow Marxist parlance to state that the military identify themselves with the interests of the "bourgeoisie." Even if the "corporate self-interest of the military" turns out to influence political orientation of the military more decisively than conceivable "identification with the middle class," Marxist interpreters would probably not hesitate to brand such an attitude as "bourgeois."

To associate the military with specific and presumably overriding interests of the middle class is a far more difficult task than imputing a vague "bourgeois" orientation to the armed forces. Studies carried out in Venezuela and Ecuador are rather inconclusive. (Springer, 1965; Needler, 1964) The proposed middle-class orientation in military political behavior seems to imply that middle-class interests are homogeneous, an assumption that would be difficult to maintain. In the increasingly complex structure of most Latin American republics, neither middle- nor upper-class interests could be considered to be homogeneous.

The recurrent controversy over the role of the military in the modernization process has entered a new phase, since "a new type of military began to invade politics. In Argentina, Brazil, Bolivia and Peru they seized power and declared that they will stay for a long time until the 'modernization' process of the society will be completed." (Sepúlveda, 1970:176) Not only have the military establishments taken the initiative in economic and technological development, they have preempted the concept of revolution for the goals they have been trying to accomplish. It may be argued that with the possible exception of Peru, the proclaimed revolution hardly went beyond political rhetoric. The Peruvian military government has actually been carrying out a vast land reform that is clearly at variance with the interests of the traditional seigneurial class. And without venturing into the hazards of a structural revolution, the Brazilian military regime has been able to introduce some rather spectacular changes, including tax reform, large-scale economic planning, and a nationwide urban housing program for low-income groups.

Generally speaking, the armies of Latin America constitute the only cohesive forces in an area recurrently characterized by erosion of power, lack of basic consensus, and the threat of violent confrontation among diametrically opposed political groups. Whereas in most Western nations political dissent and competition for power do not affect the basic consensus embodied in the constitution, such consensus is rare in Latin America. It appears that Latin Americans refuse political commitments that rule out alternatives.

Traditional lack of basic political consensus has been exacerbated by rapid socioeconomic differentiation and a steadily growing number of interest groups, reflected by the multiplication of intransigent political parties and movements. Not surprisingly, intervention by the military is frequently perceived to be the last resort. If the military do not assume the role of national savior willingly, it is forced on them by civilians who feel they have reached the end of their rope.

The rural world
in transformation

The quest for agricultural surplus:
the expansion of food production

Urban growth of the kind and magnitude that characterizes *all* Latin
American countries could not have occurred without concomitant changes
in the food-producing segments of the society. The production of basic
foodstuffs—grain, potatos, yams, manioc, beans, fruits, green vebetables,
fish, and meat—supposedly depends on techniques so primitive that it is
hard to imagine how so many large urban populations could be supplied
with enough staples to prevent starvation. Many analysts of primitive agriculture believe, for example, that the productivity of slash-and-burn agri-

culture is too limited to support urban civilizations. But this view appears to be at variance with history: Until a few decades ago, all agricultural staples (corn, beans, rice, and manioc) that fed the urban populations of, for example, Brazil, were produced by swidden cultivators.

Few countries in Latin America do not import at least certain foodstuffs to avoid critical shortages, yet everywhere the bulk is produced domestically. Whatever the technological level of agriculture and animal husbandry, production has risen substantially by extensions of the cultivated area. In Brazil, for example, the total area in farms rose from 197.6 million hectares in 1940 to 265.1 million in 1960. In Mexico, the total cropland with annual harvests grew from 8.3 million hectares in 1949–1951 to 14.5 million in 1964–1966, an increase of 75 percent. (Venezian and Gamble, 1969: 72) In Venezuela, the total arable area expanded from 22,127 million hectares in 1950 to 26,215 million in 1961. (Heaton, 1969:98) In Peru, "it appears that output increases have occurred through increased land area or livestock numbers as contrasted with yield increases per unit of land area or livestock unit." (Coutu and King, 1969:50) No such increases are feasible in Chile, Uruguay, and the Caribbean republics where cultivable land resources are insignificant or nonexistent.

The extension of cultivated areas not necessarily accompanied by modernization of agricultural techniques. On the whole it proceeds along traditional lines, particularly when virgin lands are opened to agricultural and pastoral pursuits. Although, the occupation of new land has been going on since the conquest, its rhythm accelerated in the nineteenth century and even more so over the last 50 years.

Colonization of virgin land, often referred to as agricultural frontier, appears to be far more significant than the available studies suggest. The term "colonization" is used here merely to designate the establishment of new human settlements in areas that had not been permanently inhabited before, or where previous occupation has been based on less intensive use of the land. In contrast to more specific meanings often associated with the term (T. L. Smith, 1969:94ff.), colonization in the present context may be completely *private* insofar as it is carried out by individuals who either purchase or rent a piece of land in the open market or simply occupy land as squatters. Such colonization may be organized or unorganized. It is organized if the land is surveyed and parceled and if the owners have invested in roads, railways, perhaps irrigation systems, and other facilities, to assure a viable community life and access to markets. It is unorganized if all these tasks depend on the settlers' own initiative. Organized colonization implies legality of purchase or rental contracts, whereas unorganized colonization connotes either squatter settlements or merely legal acquisition of surveyed but unimproved land without benefit of infrastructure.

Public colonization, on the other hand, means that land is made available by the state to persons who meet certain qualifications. The land may already belong to the state, or it may be purchased or expropriated by the state for the purpose of establishing rural settlements.

Public colonization has a long history in Latin America. In Brazil, for example, it goes back to the early nineteenth century, when the imperial government began to sponsor European immigration. The costs of recruitment and transportation were born by the state; land and agricultural implements were provided free, and small cash subsidies were often paid to help the settlers get established. It would take many pages to describe the legislative efforts made since independence by different countries to promote colonization of one kind or another, but on the whole the results were modest compared with the prevailing legislative exuberance.

In recent decades public colonization has been almost synonymous with agrarian reform (i.e., redistribution of land). Whereas private colonization implies no size, large or small, of new holdings, public colonization has been concerned with relatively small agricultural holdings. Frequently public colonization has also involved attempts to modernize agricultural technology.

Whether private or public, the colonization of virgin lands plays a role that has not yet been fully recognized. One may even venture to suggest that extensive agricultural frontiers have sprung up about which no reliable information exists at all. In the cetnral region of Maranhão, Brazil, for example, approximately 600,000 persons are said to be involved in rural settlement and colonization. (Chardon, 1966:170–171) Agricultural and pastoral frontiers have been opened in the Amazon Basin. In the Colombian Amazon, frontiers have been developed by the Institute for Agrarian Reform (Incora), but along with officially sponsored settlement, much spontaneous, nonorganized colonization has been going on. In the Caquetá territory alone, Incora data cite 3,500 individual farms established by 1972, and the total population of Caquetá had risen to 300,000—triple that of seven years ago, according to *Colombia Today* (vol. 7, no. 10, 1972). From a study comparing directed and spontaneous settlers, we learn

that the governmental assistance program for the directed colonists in Caquetá has not been effective. No significant differences were found between the two groups in terms of their level of education, level of living, adoption of new practices, attitudes, labor efficiency, and material possessions. The directed settlers had more access to credit, the extension service, and to new agricultural techniques. However, the same colonists had less livestock, sold less on the market, were less satisfied in Caquetá, and tended to have less wealth and to be living on a lower level of income than the spontaneous settlers. The spontaneous settlers' experience in agriculture was their most important advantage. (Tinnermeier, 1964:234–235)

Agricultural frontiers exist in the Bolivian, Peruvian, Ecuadorian, and Venezuelan sections of the Amazon Basin. Brazil has attempted to develop the agricultural and mining resources of the area by establishing federally administered territories (Amapá, Roraima, Rondônia) and by building major highways crossing the subcontinent and linking the southern and eastern regions of the country to the north (Belém) and to the west (Rio Branco). The trans-Amazonian highway, now under construction, will further tighten the integration of northern Brazil. Insofar as highways generate large-scale, spontaneous colonization along their axes, they can be considered to be frontier areas of a rather unusual kind. In contrast to many remote pioneer settlements, they lie within the immediate reach of major urban markets. (See, e.g., Valverde and Dias, 1967.)

Agricultural frontiers located in distant jungles and savannas of the Amazon Basin are far less effective surplus producers than those that have sprung up in more accessible though undeveloped areas of Latin America. To some it may be surprising that colonization of new lands has played a highly significant role at distances of no more than a few hundred miles from major metropolitan areas. For example, agricultural frontiers have been moving south from Antioquia, Colombia, into Caldas and Tolima. At the same time, an "unparalleled land rush" moved toward the Gulf of Uraba. In the municipios of Turbo and Arboletes, the population grew from 15,000 in 1951 to about 100,000 by 1966. Bananas, African oil palms, coconuts, rice, and corn are the principal crops. (Parsons, 1968:93)

In Colombia as well as in southern Brazil, settlement of virgin lands has been a continuous process that is traceable to the middle of the nineteenth century and even earlier. Beginning in the first or second decade of the present century, colonization reached the western regions of the states of Rio Grande do Sul, Santa Catarina, Paraná, São Paulo, and the so-called *Triângulo Mineiro*, in the state of Minas Gerais. The newly occupied lands were by no means planted exclusively in coffee. Low winter temperatures rule out coffee agriculture in Rio Grande do Sul and in the highlands of Santa Catarina and Paraná. Almost everywhere rice became an important commercial crop; corn was raised primarily to fatten hogs, and increasingly large areas were planted in pastures to raise beef cattle. In the southernmost states, wheat has been a growing concern, particularly since World War II.

Privately organized colonization of new lands was a fairly common occurrence, even in the nineteenth century. For example, the Jewish Colonization Association, formed in 1891 in London, established its first Argentine colonies in 1891 and 1892. (Taylor, 1948:338) The German immigration into Rio Grande do Sul induced many owners of extensive sesmarias to parcel undeveloped lands and sell them to immigrants. References to such colonization projects go back to the middle of the nineteenth century. (Willems, 1946:108ff.)

Contrary to the widespread beliefs that land resources are monopolized by the big estate owners to prevent rural labor from "seeking economic independence" (Wolf and Mintz, 1957:389), or merely to "have enough to distribute among their numerous heirs" (T. L. Smith, 1963:353), an open market for land developed and became increasingly important in the process of allocating land resources.

An outstanding instance of organized settlement of virgin land by a private company occurred in the Brazilian state of Paraná. In 1920 the northern and western regions of this state were almost totally uninhabited. Shortly after World War I, the state government began to sell the land to private developers with the understanding that it would be parceled and resold to agricultural settlers. Eleven major land concessions were made, the largest by far being the Companhia de Terras Norte do Paraná. Founded with British capital, this company purchased almost 4700 square miles of virgin land, constructed a rather elaborate infrastructure of roads linked to a trunk railway, and began to sell the land in 1930. The company's stated policy was to encourage small and medium-sized holdings by extending credit to purchasers who could afford no more than the required down payment. (Willems, 1972:330–331) Favorable market conditions, associated with the exceptional quality of the soil and relatively advanced agricultural techniques, prevented the smallest holdings from developing the social problem associated with the minifundio.

Private colonization did not stop at the boundaries of the company land but spread beyond in a westerly direction until reaching the Paraná River. In 1960, this frontier area covered 64 (new) municipios and encompassed a total of 125,262 holdings on 4,195,244 hectares. (Willems, 1972:336)

Between 1940 and 1965 the population of northern Paraná leaped from 340,000 to 2.7 million people within an area of 18,569 square miles (Nicholls, 1969:49) During the same period the population of western Paraná went from 145,000 to 1.6 million. (Nicholls, 1969:53)

Contrasting private colonization of virgin areas with public reclamation and colonization of land that had previously been used in a rather desultory fashion, the Yaqui and Mayo River projects in northwest Mexico are probably the most spectacular examples of change brought about in the production of basic foodstuffs.

In 1958, 568,000 acres of land were under irrigation on the Yaqui River and 198,000 on the Mayo. The amount of land under irrigation in 1958 was about twenty times as great as in 1910 and about three times as great as in 1948. . . . By 1958 government investment in social overhead capital projects such as dams, roads, and major canal networks quadrupled the total value of agricultural production in the area. (Erasmus, 1967b:13)

With the addition of the Fuerte River area to these two reclamation projects, directed technological change succeeded in transforming northwest Mexico into a major surplus-producing area of commercial crops including wheat, rice, cotton, and sugar cane. (Dozier, 1969:12)

Cultural change among the peasantry

Almost without exception, recent changes affecting the traditional way of life of the Latin American peasantry are exogenous. They originate in the context of urban civilization, and they are introduced into peasant communities by people who either are city-bred or have been thoroughly exposed to the stimuli of an urban-centered technology and market economy.

Of course certain changes in the rural world of Latin America are clearly detrimental to the peasantry. Transition from a primitive subsistence agriculture to commercial farming is usually thought to benefit the peasant. In northern Panama along the Panamerican Highway, however, swidden cultivators were induced to plant their land in sugar cane to be bought by a local mill, and changes threaten rather than improve the narrow survival margin of the peasants. As they ceased to produce subsistence crops, the peasants became almost totally dependent on store-bought food. Because of unpredictable price fluctuations on the sugar market, their cash earnings sank to a level no longer sufficient to cover their living expenses. They were economically worse off than before, although it could be argued that the change was not irreversible.

If we confine ourselves to the analysis of changes definable in terms of "modernization," we do not imply that such changes are necessarily desirable or advantageous to the people who are affected by them. Modernization of the rural world is seen here merely as an integral part of the evolutionary process—more specifically, as an inevitable corollary to urbanization and industrialization. As a city grows, it extends its tentacles into the surrounding rural areas in search of food supplies. In all major cities of Latin America, the wholesale trade in food staples is so lucrative that numerous specialists will traverse the countryside in trucks to buy up large quantities of grain, potatoes, fruits, fresh produce, eggs, fowl, hogs, and perhaps fish. Depending on road conditions and distances, at least three alternatives are available: (1) The wholesaler drives directly to the farms to buy up seasonal food staples; (2) the producer meets the wholesaler halfway in "distribution markets" (e.g., the *feira de distribuição* of the Brazilian northeast, described by Forman and Riegelhaupt 1970:200); or (3) the producer himself takes his staples to the urban market. In some urban centers, the wholesale trade of food staples appears to be an ethnic speciality of such groups as Arabs (Syrian, Lebanese), Italians, or Japanese. In some regions, as in southern Brazil, the halfway distributor frequently owns a general store, buying from the local peasants and selling to urban wholesalers. We still do not know exactly how these patterns are distributed and combined, to what extent they vary, and how they change.

Scope and depth of the changes covered by the catchall concept of modernization must be viewed in terms of the *total distance* traversed by the peasantry of the 1970s since the days when urban markets were remote, small, and undifferentiated, and the production of food crops afforded only the most tenuous relationship to urban markets. To the extent that peasant producers entered the orbit of urban markets, they became increasingly involved in the money economy. This meant, among other things, westernization of traditional peasant cultures. Domestic production of textiles, mats, hammocks, baskets, pottery, canoes, nets, and gourd and wooden containers was often discontinued, and the craft items were replaced by manufactured articles bought in the market. Many such artifacts and techniques were clearly of Indian origin, others were either Iberian or hybrid composites. Pieces of factory-made furniture began to appear in peasant households. Ingenious manufacturers launched cheap products adapted to the needs and budgets of rural dwellers. In southern Brazil of the 1930s an inexpensive collapsible bed, mass-produced in São Paulo, rapidly spread even to the most inaccessible rural regions. Nowadays in Argentina, Uruguay, southern Brazil, and Chile, tools and artifacts associated with domestic crafts are likely to be found only in museums, except in localities where the tourist trade has brought a revival of certain folk traditions. In Mexico, modernization of Indian peasant cultures appears to be correlated with the expansion of the highway system.

The closer to the national network of roads, the more receptive to changes the Indian communities tend to be. They are more inclined to produce for distant markets, including those demanding new crops, and indigenous crafts decline in the process. Along with technological change, Spanish is increasingly substituted for the indigenous language. But villages not yet within reach of the highway system stick to autochthonous idioms, crafts, and crops, and local markets reflect, even today, a high degree of economic self-sufficiency.*

A similar situation prevails in the Andean countries, but often enough there is no immediate substitution of the new for the old, and modern elements coexist with traditional ones. For example, the people of Contadero, a Colombian community located in the high plains, practice crop rotation (corn–potatoes–cereals–corn) in their lots. "Commercial fertilizers are applied in limited quantities to potatoes, but only rarely applied directly to cereals, corn or pastures. Limestone is occasionally applied, and potatoes are regularly sprayed with insecticides. . . . [and] practically all the women and older girls spend their spare time spinning and weaving wool." (Adams and Havens, n.d.:22, 24)

Similar association of modern and traditional techniques can be observed in numerous highland communities of Peru, Ecuador, and Bolivia, but one would have to search far and wide to find Brazilian peasant women spinning and weaving textiles for domestic consumption.

To describe the range of agricultural practices of San Pedro, a small town in the Cauca Valley of Colombia, Miles Richardson selected three local peasant households. In one, Anibal Pinzón tills his small holding with a hoe and plants maize with an iron-tipped digging stick to feed his family. This he does at the time of the waning moon. To shell the maize, he puts the ears in a burlap sack and beats it with a stick. Simon Gutierrez, another agriculturalist of San Pedro appears to be a farmer rather than a peasant. Unlike Pinzón, who was taught agricultural skills by his father, Gutierrez received his training from a school. He gets hybrid seeds from an experiment station in a nearby city and rents a tractor to do the heavy work, paying no attention to the moon. The maize is shelled with a hand-

* The author is indebted to Dr. Ronald Spores for information concerning the Mexican peasantry.

driven mechanical sheller and fed to a breed of chicken developed by Gutierrez himself. The sale of chickens and eggs furnishes the main source of
his income.

The Lozano brothers of San Pedro are equally progressive. Their holding is mostly pastures, where they keep 50 dairy cows. They plant maize
from selected seeds and use a rented tractor to till a field of about 11 acres.
The maize is shelled by someone from a nearby town who comes over to
San Pedro with his motor-driven mechanical sheller. The crop is sold to
the highest bidder. (Richardson, 1970:38–40)

Coexistence of traditional and modern elements in the same peasant
community ought to be distinguished from the blending of such elements
into a single complex. Coexistence is an inevitable by-product of cultural
transition, whereas blending means mutual validation of the discrepant
elements. This process has been described, for example, in a monograph on
Zinacantan, a municipio of Chiapas, Mexico. The local cargo system, described in a previous chapter, requires steep cash investments in prestige
positions in the religious hierarchy. Savings were rarely sufficient to defray
the expenses involved in the proper execution of a yearly round of ceremonies and the incumbent usually had to borrow heavily to meet the expenses. The new alternative was to increase cash income by expanding the
production of maize on rented land.

> The really successful operators have in recent years been able to
> borrow money from Mexican government banks, to hire laborers
> (mainly Chamulas) and to plant up to 15 hectares of land in maize.
> In good years the surpluses are such that they can not only supply
> family food with ease, but hold the surpluses for the best possible
> profits in the market in late summer. The surplus cash controlled
> by these large operators is impressive by Zinacanteco standards, and
> it can be converted into much more rapid movement through the
> cargo system and the achievement of power and prestige that reaches
> well beyond the potential for men without land or entrepreneurial
> skills. (Vogt, 1970:60)

In other words, the power associated with high office in the traditional
religious hierarchy is sufficiently attractive to validate market-oriented entrepreneurship, and increased cash income in turn opens new avenues to
potential holders of high office, which may cost in the neighborhood of
14,000 pesos. In a sense, the innovation has a revitalizing effect on traditional components of the community structure.

How do innovations spread to peasant producers within the range of
urban markets? The process has a number of facets, but most are known

only in a very general way. In the vicinity of the largest metropolitan areas, truck farming is extremely important, and truck farming is almost by implication highly intensive. In view of high land values and extremely favorable marketing conditions, one might assume that this type of agricultural endeavor is controlled by urban entrepreneurs. In the proximity of such cities as São Paulo, Curitiba, and Pôrto Alegre, however, truck farmers are predominantly small holders and members of certain ethnic groups (Italians, Portuguese, Japanese, and Germans) who work their vegetable gardens and dairy farms almost in the same way as their European or Asian counterparts. (For São Paulo, see Viotti Costa, 1958:113ff.) In the province of Buenos Aires, people of Spanish and Italian stock prevail among the owners and renters of chacaras, quintas, huertas, and dairy-farms. (Taylor, 1948:218) In the Chancay Valley, 60 kilometers north of Lima, Japanese immigrants own the *granjas avicolas* (chicken farms) supplying the market of the Peruvian capital. (Matos Mar, 1969:8)

It is likely that the agricultural skills of these ethnic groups stem from their original societies and, perhaps, from ethnic associations centered in the city. This is doubtless the case among Japanese settlers in Brazil. Whether intentionally or not, the immigrant is often the innovator in areas of mixed settlement. In fact, communities located in the Brazilian northeast have attempted to attract Japanese farmers, hopefully to further the dissemination of modern agricultural skills among the local peasantry.

Rural migrants returning to their native communities after a prolonged exposure to modern agricultural technology may act as innovators. More than any other country, Mexico has benefited from the experiences of many thousands of *braceros* participating in seasonal migration to the United States. We know so little about the modernization process of peasant agriculture that any attempt to weigh the various innovating forces according to their relative importance would be extremely hazardous. One high-ranking factor, however, appears to be the city-based agricultural entrepreneur. More often than not, he invests in medium-sized holdings, often on land that has been under cultivation for many years, but expansion of urban markets and improved transportation networks make agricultural ventures of a new type profitable. It is the agricultural entrepreneur, individually or corporately, who introduces the results of modern agrobiology: new strains of food plants, new crops, chemical fertilizers, fungicides, and insecticides, along with modern machinery. Seldom are successful innovations lost on the local peasants.

The Paraiba Valley between Rio de Janeiro and São Paulo exemplifies the process under scrutiny. Cultivated since the seventeenth century, it witnessed the gradual disappearance of coffee agriculture, eventually becoming a food-producing area specializing in rice, potatoes, and beef cattle. Since these staples are easily absorbed by the two metropolitan markets and a number of smaller urban markets throughout the valley, most producers can afford to invest in machinery, irrigation, and fertilizers. More than the peasant, of course, the city-based entrepreneur has the background, the connections, and the capital to take full advantage of the advances of modern agronomy. Since the 1920s government-sponsored research institutes, experimental stations, and agricultural colleges have become centers of diffusion of agricultural technology, so to speak. Quite frequently, the innovating functions of these institutions have been initiated by skilled specialists and capital resources imported from abroad.

Most of the technical assistance programs, however, were preceded by systematic efforts by American Protestant churches to implant modern agricultural technology in many regions of Latin America. The introduction of technological innovation was felt to be an extension of religious proselytism, but the impact of proposed technological change went far beyond the boundaries of the newly established Protestant communities. This has been the case, for example, in Chile. In 1919 the Methodist Foreign Mission Board purchased El Vergel, a 3800-acre hacienda near Angol in Malleco province.

> At a time when Chilean agriculture and husbandry were almost entirely dependent upon the initiative of the individual hacienda owner, El Vergel became a major focus for the diffusion of new farming and breeding techniques. All the major crops of the country, except grapes, underwent improvements in quality and quantity. . . . In recent years, large-scale experiments in reforestation and the introduction of new grasses for pastures have been combined with new techniques designed to combat soil erosion. (Willems, 1967b: 191–192)

An agricultural college is attached to El Vergel, and in 1959, there were 80 students receiving professional education there. Since 1928, moreover, 42 Mapuche Indians have been graduated from El Vergel. (Willems, 1967:192)

> The Brazilian counterpart of El Vergel is the College of Agriculture in Lavras, Minas Gerais. Founded in 1908 by the Board of World Missions of the Presbyterian Church in the United States, it has played a pioneer role in the modernization of Brazilian agriculture and animal husbandry. Like El Vergel, it was many years ahead

of similar initiatives by state and federal government. . . . (Willems, 167b:193)

Three major achievements have been attributed to the Lavras school. By adopting the organization of the American land-grant college, it combined practical instruction with the academic standards of a university; by associating praxis with theoretical learning, it successfully fought the widespread prejudice against manual labor, and scientific agriculture was given the status of a professional career. Finally the college provided agricultural extension services, thus became a center of diffusion of modern skills among farmers of the area. (Maddox, 1956:98)

In 1956 Maddox listed a total of 41 agricultural projects controlled by United States religious agencies and located in 13 Latin American countries (Argentina, Bolivia, Brazil, Chile, Colombia, Costa Rica, Ecuador, Guatemala, Honduras, Mexico, Nicaraugua, Peru, and Venezuela). Most of the projects are farms designed to produce food for the missionaries and their students.

Even though the product of the farms move principally to the mission kitchen, the missionaries frequently introduce new crops or try out new practices that appear to have promise for the community in general. Moreover, many of the farms lend pure-bred studs—bulls, rams and boars—to neighboring farmers. On the demonstration plots of mission farms, there is often some experimental work with crop varieties and fertilizing practices. (Maddox, 1956:39)

Of the numerous organized attempts made by government agencies and institutions to disseminate new agricultural skills, two must suffice here to illustrate scope and nature of the process.

In 1943 a cooperative program involving the Mexican Ministry of Agriculture and the Rockefeller Foundation was established; its objective was to raise the productivity of corn and wheat agriculture. Yields had changed little between 1925 and 1945, but they began to rise significantly after 1945. The overall figures for Mexico show that corn yield moved from 626 kilograms per hectare in 1940–1944 to 1204 kilograms in 1965–1967. The impact of the improvement project on wheat production has been even more striking. Average yields rose from 762 kilograms per hectare in 1940–1944 to 2600 kilograms in 1965–1967. (Myren, 1969:439) As a consequence, Mexico can now satisfy domestic demands for wheat and export surpluses.

The differentials between corn and wheat yields teach a basic lesson in cultural diffusion and innovation. The wheat farmer tends to be a commercial entrepreneur who grows wheat on irrigated holdings measuring an average of 17 hectares. He is totally market oriented, therefore receptive to any innovation that may increase his profits. The corn producer is more likely to be a peasant, and he is more subsistence oriented. As a rule, he sells only what his family cannot consume. Since his cash income tends to be much smaller, his receptivity to innovations implying capital investments is less pronounced. The size of the average corn land plot per farmer has been estimated at 3 hectares—a size category hardly amenable to mechanization. Besides, corn predominates 748,318, or 54.8 percent of all farm units, whereas wheat predominates on 28,388, or 2.1 percent.

> It is probable that corn is grown on at least two thirds of the farms by some two million farm families, while wheat is grown by less than 50,000. If so, there are 40 times more corn farmers than wheat farmers, and consequently 40 times as many decision-makers to be reached with information about new production practices. (Myren, 1969:444)

The Mexican project revolutionized the agricultural technology of a whole country. The second case of organized change, however, was concerned solely with a community of 1850 Quechua-speaking Indians constituting the resident labor force of Vicos, a single seigneurial estate in the highland of Peru. The project was initiated in 1952 by Cornell University in cooperation with the Peruvian government. It was intended to improve the standard of living of the Vicos population, and "to study the independent variables involved in increasing agricultural and human productivity." (Holmberg and Dobyns, 1969:407) Underlying the innovation program was the idea that after five years the Indians would take over the estate and become landowners rather than agricultural serfs, as in the past. Since the innovators were in complete control of the estate, it would be possible to mount a coordinated program of carefully supervised guided change, greatly surpassing mere technological change. While new seeds, fertilizers, insecticides, and fungicides were being introduced to improve the quality and quantity of the potato crop, the organization of the community itself underwent transformations designed to develop self-reliance and the capacity for autonomous concerted action. Formal schooling was improved and expanded, and a clinic was installed at which modern medical practices are used in the treatment of diseases affecting the local population. (Holmberg, 1961:45ff.) The economic outcome of the Vicos experiment is an independent peasantry, producing a large surplus of potatoes that can be sold for cash in the national market.

Stratification in rural society

What is the place of the peasantry in the class structure of Latin American society? From the preceding pages at least two safe conclusions can be drawn: Regardless of regional differences, the peasantry is neither homogeneous nor static as far as social class is concerned. In other words, there is considerable socioeconomic inequality within the peasantry, but often the peasantry's relative position within a given structure is subject to change; vertical mobility, up or down the social ladder, seems to be the rule rather than the exception. Furthermore, there appears to be a linkage between the expansion of urban markets, modernization of transportation networks, dissemination of technological innovations, and upward mobility. In many regions the peasant is being transformed or replaced by the agricultural entrepreneur.

To place the peasant in the class structure, a relationship between size of holding and status has often been postulated. The pitfalls of such an assumption are rather obvious: The socioeconomic implications of size depend on soil quality, level of technological development, proximity and size of urban markets, community structure, and perhaps other variables. In São Paulo, Japanese farmers often prosper on five or so hectares, while a neighbor of different ethnic background ekes out a precarious living on a holding of equal size and quality. On investigation one is likely to find that the Japanese farmer has acquired skills that his neighbor lacks, and that he and the members of his family work seven days a week, from dawn to dusk. The neighbor's working habits are relaxed, however, and probably he gets little or no help from his family. He religiously observes Sundays, as well as another 20 or 30 saint's days a year. The Japanese can rely on his cooperative for credit and marketing facilities, but the neighbor is completely ignorant of cooperatives. After a few years the Japanese has saved enough to invest in a sewing machine for his wife and perhaps a small truck for taking his produce to the market. It is highly unlikely that his neighbor will ever reach the point of making similar investments. The Japanese spares no sacrifice to send his children to secondary schools and possibly to one of the new colleges. If the neighbor's children go to school at all, they seldom advance beyond second or third grade in primary school. In other words, the differences are significant enough to place the two families on different class levels, although they control holdings of identical size within the same ecological universe. The preceding situation is instructive, but relatively frequent only when peasants of radically different background inhabit the same area.

In unimproved regions of northern Mexico, northern Chile, northwestern Argentine, and northeastern Brazil, family holdings of 100 hectares or more may not suffice to make a living, whereas in northern Paraná, the quality of the soil and marketing conditions are so exceptional that a family will not find it difficult to live on 10 hectares or less, even if no modern agricultural techniques are used.

The social differentiation of the peasantry has been obfuscated by depictions of the rural world of Latin America exclusively in terms of latifundio and minifundio. Although the "minifundio" has been defined repeatedly as a holding too small to provide an income that by local standards is considered to be necessary to satisfy the basic needs of a single family, there is a strong tendency to regard *all* small holdings as minifundios. For reasons difficult to fathom, "magic significance" has often been attributed to five hectares as the " 'break-even' point on subsistence." (Schaedel, 1965:91) In view of numerous and drastic regional (rather than national) variations, such generalizations carry no validity whatever.

On the other hand, the latifundio is supposed to be an extremely large estate that is only in part exploited, but most of the time data about size and land use are disregarded, and any holding measuring more than 200 or 300 hectares is classified as a latifundio.

Such oversimplifications obviously reduce the structure of rural society to a "dismal dichotomy"—the "landed few" and the "landless many. . . the upper elite (proud, educated, inheritors of the national patrimony, carriers of the world tradition) and the lower masses (illiterate and disinherited and hopeless)." (Nelson, cited in Schaedel, 1965:93) To anyone who has had extensive firsthand contact with rural Latin America, the assumption of a two-class structure appears to be out of touch with reality.

There is a rather remarkable attempt to classify farms and farming areas not by size but according to the number of persons employed (see Table 22). If all "subfamily" farms employing fewer than two persons are discarded as "substandard" or minifundios (which in many cases they are not), and if all "multifamily" establishments employing more than 12 persons are arbitrarily assigned to the "upper elite," we find a surprisingly large residue, seemingly irreconcilable with Nelson's "dismal dichotomy." There are "family farms" employing 3 to 3.9 persons—presumably all members of a single family—and medium-sized "multifamily" holdings employing from 4 to 12 persons. Together these two categories represent a varying but always substantial segment of the rural population. Yet by no stretch of imagination could these individuals be assigned either to the "upper elite" or to the "illiterate, disinherited, and hopeless lower masses."

As Table 23 indicates, the percentage of family and medium-sized multi-

Table 22 *Number and area of farms in eight Latin American countries*

Country and item	Percentage of total farms in each country by size class				
	Subfamily[a]	Family[b]	Multifamily, medium[c]	Multifamily, large[d]	Total
Argentina					
Farms	43.2	48.7	7.3	0.8	100
Area in farms	3.4	44.7	15.0	36.9	100
Brazil					
Farms	22.5	39.1	33.7	4.7	100
Area in farms	0.5	6.0	34.0	59.5	100
Chile					
Farms	36.9	40.0	16.2	6.9	100
Area in farms	0.2	7.1	11.4	81.3	100
Colombia					
Farms	64.0	30.2	4.5	1.3	100
Area in farms	4.9	22.3	23.3	49.5	100
Ecuador					
Farms	89.9	8.0	1.7	0.4	100
Area in farms	16.6	19.0	19.3	45.1	100
Guatemala					
Farms	88.4	9.5	2.0	0.1	100
Area in farms	14.3	13.4	31.5	40.8	100
Peru					
Farms	88.0	8.5	2.4	1.1	100
Area in farms	7.4	4.5	5.7	82.4	100
Venezuela					
Farms	67.7	22.2	7.9	2.2	100
Area in farms	2.9	5.0	13.2	78.9	100

[a] Farms employing fewer than 2 persons.
[b] Farms employing 2 to 3.9 persons.
[c] Farms employing from 4 to 12 persons.
[d] Farms employing more than 12 persons.
Source: Data for all countries except Venezuela from Solon L. Barraclough and Arthur L. Domike, "Agrarian Structure in Seven Latin American Countries," *Land Economics*, 42, no. 4 (November 1966), 395; and an article on tenancy studies made by the Inter-American Committee for Agricultural Development, quoted by Barraclough and Domike. Venezuelan data added by approximation from 1961 agricultural census data.

family farm units varies between 56.2 in Chile and 9.7 in Ecuador, and the percentage of the total farm area covered by family holdings and medium multifamily units goes from a 10.2 in Peru to 59.7 in Argentina. In Chile, Peru, and Venezuela, however, so much land has been redistributed in connection with agrarian reform projects that the figures of Tables 22 and 23 should be considered with caution.

Table 23 *Family farms and medium multifamily farms in eight Latin American countries*

Country	Percentage	Country	Percentage
Argentina		Ecuador	
Farms	56.0	Farms	9.7
Area in farms	59.7	Area in farms	38.3
Brazil		Guatemala	
Farms	72.8	Farms	11.5
Area in farms	40.0	Area in farms	44.9
Chile		Peru	
Farms	56.2	Farms	10.9
Area in farms	18.5	Area in farms	10.2
Colombia		Venezuela	
Farms	34.7	Farms	30.1
Area in farms	45.6	Area in farms	18.2

Source: Data for all countries except Venezuela from Solon L. Barraclough and Arthur L. Domike, "Agrarian Structure in Seven Latin American Countries," *Land Economics*, 42, no. 4 (November 1966), 397; and an article on tenancy studies made by the Inter-American Committee for Agricultural Development, quoted by Barraclough and Domike. Venezuelan data added by approximation from 1961 agricultural census data.

Only detailed knowledge about tenure, land use, land value, and marketing conditions of carefully circumscribed regions may justify the association of size categories of land holdings with social class. Let two regions serve as examples. First, the agricultural area around São Paulo City, including 36 municipios and 11,624 agricultural holdings on 562,825 hectares, supplies much of the food crops, beef, and fowl consumed by a metropolitan population of about 8 million. In this area farms measuring between 20 and 100 hectares can be classified as medium-sized. In 1960 these holdings represented 25.8 percent of all agricultural establishments and 25.4 percent of the total acreage in farms of the area. The other region encompasses 32,193 holdings and 863,584 hectares of northern Paraná and 125,262 holdings and 4,195,244 hectares of western Paraná. Of all units in 16 municipios of the northern section, 27.7 percent of the farms were between 20 and 100 hectares, amounting to 38.2 percent of the total area in farms. In 69 municipios of the western section the corresponding figures were 36.1 and 29.6 percent, according to the agricultural census of 1960. (Willems, 1972:339)

More than farm size is implied by the concept of rural social class, but whatever socioeconomic attributes are associated with particular size categories, the medium-sized holdings, in the previously indicated sense, strongly suggest the existence of a rural middle class about which very little is known. Our data also suggest that a relatively large and perhaps "lower" segment of this middle class is still rooted in peasant tradition, while members of another, more progressive stratum begin to resemble the agricultural entrepreneur who is a farmer rather than a peasant.

Functions of agrarian reforms

From previous references to agrarian reforms, one can conclude that radical changes in the allocation of land resources rank very high among the priorities of certain political parties, social movements, and, above all, established governments committed to revolutionizing the traditional agrarian structure. Whatever versions of land reform may have been proposed or carried out, the ultimate objective appears to be a "more equitable income distribution" among the rural populations of Latin America. Not unexpectedly, the issue has generated an avalanche of polemic literature, much proposed and actual legislation, and relatively few empirical studies on the effects of agrarian reform projects. In the present context only the latter are relevant.

Of course, the socioeconomic functions of large-scale redistribution of land would not be restricted to the peasantry. In fact, most reformers are concerned with the landless labor force rather than with small holders, who would be expected to benefit only to the extent that their holdings are of the "subfamily" or minifundio type. To provide for the landless labor force, at least four alternatives are open: (1) The large estates could be parceled out and turned over to individual families; (2) the resident labor force could take over the state collectively and run it as a cooperative enterprise; (3) the labor force could be resettled on new land (as has been done, (e.g., in Venezuela, Colombia, and to a small extent in Bolivia); and (4) the state could claim ownership of all or at least all larger holdings, instituting a system molded on the Russian or Chinese model of collective farm organization. In Cuba, where all estates of more than 67 hectares are owned and operated by the state, the fourth alternative has been chosen.

Thus three of the four available options call for the large estate to bear the brunt of agrarian reform. On the other hand, the cases of Cuba and Chile suggest that medium-sized properties may equally be affected by reallocation policies.

Since farms of *all sizes* are surplus producers for a rapidly increasing

urban population, we must ask whether a radical and thorough redistribution of land would affect food supplies and price levels of food staples
in the urban market. Furthermore, to the extent that domestic economies
depend on export crops, agrarian reforms may pose a serious threat to the
entire economic system if reallocation of land is accompanied by a general
decline of agricultural productivity.

To assess the changes among the peasantry due to agrarian reforms, one
may want to distinguish political from economic changes. The two types,
do not necessarily coincide, although it could be argued that economic
gains would not have been possible without prior liberation of the rural
labor force from the bonds of servitude. In Mexico and Venezuela political
enfranchisement occurred long before full-scale agrarian reform programs
were carried out. This is not to deny that the abolition of coercive labor
exploitation has economic consequences: It most certainly eliminates or
curtails that part of the landowner's income which flowed from the fees
and services of the serfs.

In Mexico, agrarian reform created the *ejido* system, a "land-holding
village type of settlement pattern," which reflects certain traits of pre-
conquest community organization. Under the ejido system, the community
rather than the individual peasant owns the land. In the relatively few collective ejidos, all the land is cultivated cooperatively and the profits are
distributed among the workers; under the individual ejido regime, "a
farmer would be given the use of the land for lifetime, and could pass it
on to an heir, but he could not sell it nor could he rent it, but had to
work it himself. If the land lay idle for two years in succession, it could
be taken away and returned to the community for assignment to someone
else." (Whetten, 1963:4) These restrictions were intended to prevent ejido
land from falling back into the hands of large landowners.

In Mexico, environmental conditions and cultural traditions vary so
greatly that it would be naïve to expect uniform effects of land allocation
to ejidos. The level of living of the *ejidatarios* rose "where climate and soil
make agriculture profitable, as in parts of the south and in the northeast.
But elsewhere it has hardly changed at all, and in comparison to other segments of Mexican society, it may have declined." (Villegas, 1964:132)
The Mexican experience shows that as long as enfranchisement and reallocation of land are not accompanied by the implantation of modern agricultural techniques and credit facilities, land reform will not generate major
economic changes. Furthermore, in Mexico, many holdings of individual
ejidatarios apparently are too small to be economically viable. In fact,
439,000 peasants hold less than one hectare of land apiece. Although the

revolution destroyed the traditional seigneurial class, it did not prevent the rise of a new class of large landowners who now, according to Chevalier's estimate, control about 3.5 million hectares of crop land. (Schaedel, 1965:96)

In Venezuela only 4 to 5 percent of all cultivated land had been redistributed by 1964, but the National Agrarian Institute was "deliberately trying to keep land redistribution secondary to a broad program of rural development including the colonization of new lands, road building, construction of irrigation systems, mechanization, electrification, and supervised credit." (Erasmus, 1967a:369) Apparently such efforts have been successful, at least in the lowlands of Venezuela.

> Radios are common everywhere, and bicycles are numerous in settlements near paved highways leading to cities or large towns. Near urban areas rural families possess many consumer goods. At one agrarian reform settlement near Maracay all families had radios, over half had refrigerators and sewing machines, a third had television sets, a fifth had gas stoves and a sixth had washing machines. The greater affluence of most Venezuelan rural families compared with those of Bolivia and even Mexico is very apparent. They have acquired a strong taste for consumer goods and are well on the way to becoming an internal market for Venezuelan manufacturers. (Erasmus, 1967a:370)

Between 1959 and 1965, a total of 118,737 farm families were directly benefited by land reform activities of Venezuela's Agrarian Institute. In spite of serious shortcomings of the program, the total value of crop and livestock production on these farms increased from 115 million bolivares in 1961 to 449 million bolivares in 1965, corresponding to 13 percent of the total agricultural production of Venezuela. (Heaton, 1969:193)

In Bolivia the agrarian reform affected 84 percent of the cultivated land, but only a small portion of it actually changed hands. For the most part, there were transfers of property rights to the peasants who previously had been cultivating the land for the owners. Carried out at once and under political pressure, the Bolivian land reform had little effect on the archaic agricultural technology of the Quechua and Aimara Indian communities. Not unexpectedly, the newly enfranchised campesinos began to consume a much larger portion of their food crops, causing acute food shortages in the cities due to inflated prices. But in the mid-1960s the urban markets appeared to be well supplied with food. (Erasmus, 1967a:361)

Two conflicting tendencies were noted by Charles J. Erasmus in 1963. In some communities the increased surplus was invested in the traditional religious ceremonies, whereas in others the peasants preferred to improve their housing or to invest in bicycles, radios, and metal beds. (Erasmus, 1967a:361–362) In the province of Nor Yungas (Department of La Paz), the economic rise of the Indian peasant was followed by a worsening of the economic conditions of the townsmen. "Hacienda owners lost most of the traditional income from their estates; mestizo overseers lost their relatively lucrative salaried positions and were thrown back on the scanty resources of the town; town mestizos lost their virtual monopoly in the purchase of campesino products." (Léons, 1970:276)

Like the ladino in Mesoamerica, the mestizo in Bolivia and Peru has become, more than ever before, the model of westernization. The agrarian reform has provided the means of purchasing shoes, transistor radios, and mestizo-style town houses. The formation and growth of "campesino towns" is to be considered the most consequential aspect of Indian acculturation. The peasants build houses in town "not only to take advantage of town services and social life, but also to enhance personal prestige. Most of the town houses are permanently occupied, though some are used only on Sundays and holidays, while the family continues to live in the country house close to the fields." (Léons, 1970:268) The population of Arapata, a town in Nor Yungas, had grown from 24 in 1950 to 751 in 1964. As the Indians become urbanized, they acquire political and commercial skills, along with formal education and the command of Spanish. (Léons, 1970:268–269)

In some parts of Bolivia, particularly in the Department of Cochabamba, the Indian peasantry were active in the pursuit of land reform. In the more isolated hacienda communities of Chuquisaca, however, the new order had to be imposed on the reluctant peasants, and the effects of the reform law failed to change the most crucial aspects of land tenure. Under the traditional system, large tracts of land has been leased by the owners to *arrenderos* (renters), who had to be men of substantial resources to fulfill contractual obligations. The arrenderos in turn assigned smaller tracts of land to *arrimantes*. In fact, the arrendero assumed the role of a petty patron to his arrimantes, who depended for additional labor on the *vivientes* who joined the household of the arrendero as dependent field hands. (Heyduk, 1971:70ff.) The land reform law canceled all rental obligations of the arrenderos to the landowners, but it brought no benefits to either arrimantes or vivientes, whose dependence on the arrenderos continued unchanged. (Heyduk, 1971:89)

In contrast to Bolivia, the agrarian reform initiated by the Peruvian military regime in 1969 avoided the fragmentation of the large agricultural estates of the coast and certain areas of the interior. The stated purpose of the Peruvian land reform is to prevent "concentration" as well as "pulverization" of holdings. Where it is deemed desirable, for economic reasons, to maintain the technical and structural unity of existing estates, these are turned over to peasant cooperatives composed of the resident labor force. (Garcia, 1970:5ff.) Apparently, the Peruvian government has been trying to avoid mistakes made in other parts of Latin America, and current agrarian policies are adapted to regional particularities. No dependable data are available to use in assessing the impact of the Peruvian land reform, which has been proceeding rapidly.

In Chile, the Marxist government installed in 1970, as other governments before, was under heavy pressure to extend and accelerate the agrarian reform that had been initiated in the 1960s. Land reform policies in Colombia and Ecuador have failed to generate major changes in the structure of the traditional rural society.

Cooperatives and syndicates

Two organizational devices are closely associated with culture change in rural Latin America, particularly with agrarian reform: cooperatives and sindicatos. Both are exogenous to the peasantry, and consequently dependent on the usual mechanisms of diffusion and adaptation. In fact, ability of cooperatives and sindicatos to integrate the peasantry into domestic markets and national political structures depends on the possibilities of implanting such structures into the peasant community in the first place.

The rural cooperative was invented in Western Europe in the middle of the nineteenth century under specific socioeconomic conditions. Since it enabled the peasants collectively to do what they could not have done as individuals—namely, to hold their own in a highly competitive market—the cooperative spread rapidly and became an increasingly complex means of dealing with market mechanisms, including the capital market. The success of a cooperative is contingent on large agricultural surpluses, competitive urban markets, literacy, and neutralization of all structural obstacles that might thwart the formation of effective voluntary associations in traditional communities.

Not surprisingly, cooperatives have been most successful in areas of recent immigration from Europe and Japan (e.g., Argentina, Uruguay, southern Brazil), where the structural pattern of voluntary association for entrepreneurial purposes was part of the cultural heritage of the immigrants. In most other regions the transplantation of the cooperative pattern has been only partly successful, but detailed knowledge of actual conditions is scarce. Apart from the collective ejido in Mexico, the cooperative as a landholding *and* entrepreneurial entity, succeeding the individually or corporately owned large estate, is a new experience of uncertain future.

Syndicates of hacienda workers and peasants are labor unions transplanted from an urban to a rural setting. To achieve formal recognition and to enjoy the advantages of arbitration, the syndicate must conform to structural patterns instituted by a legislative act of the state. It would seem that sindicatos can succeed only to the extent that the peasantry and the rural labor force have been politically mobilized, and political mobilization in turn depends mainly on the initiative of political forces alien to the rural world. Revolutionary governments either organize peasant unions or they recognize existing unions and integrate them into a nationwide structure (Mexico, Cuba, Bolivia). In Venezuela the *Acción Democrática*, not the government, sought to recruit peasant support for radical social reform after 1941. The number of Venezuelan peasant unions increased from 130 in 1958 to 3476 in 1965. One reason for the growth is said to be the distribution of the benefits of agrarian reform to the syndicates rather than to individual peasants. The syndicates are related to the political system through their leaders, who are militant members of political parties. (Mathiason and Powell, 1972:314)

Syndicate-type peasant organizations are political two-way streets: They are channels of distribution of benefits to individual peasants, but they also perform the function of harnessing political support for political parties or revolutionary or populist governments, which in turn exercise control through the application of sanctions (withholding of benefits).

> Because Venezuela's peasant federation has two highly competitive subdivisions, each linked to one of the two major political parties (Democratic Action and Christian Democrats), the party in power must pay more attention to syndicate demands than in Bolivia and Mexico, where for the most part the peasant syndicates have been captives of a one-party system. (Erasmus, 1967a:370)

The examples of Peru, Colombia, Chile, and Brazil indicate that a wide variety of political forces, all urban centered, may attempt to induce the peasants and hacienda laborers to join syndicates. Often rural migrants returning from politically active urban centers become foci of unionization. Particularly in Peru, such initiatives have capitalized on chronic dissatisfaction and a long history of uprisings, usually related to land despoliation by the owners of large estates. The Indian comuneros are primarily interested in the recuperation of land, whereas the rural proletariat, particularly on the large coastal estates, look at the sindicato as a means of attaining higher wages and more favorable working conditions. The preferred weapon of salaried workers has been the strike, whereas the Indians often seek to take possession of land belonging to haciendas. (Cotler, 1968:20)

In Peru, rural unionization began shortly after World War I, and its agitated history has been punctuated by violence. Based on newspaper reports, Carlos Malpica compiled a list of 46 violent confrontations, involving 211 killings, between 1956 and 1964. Fifteen attempts to occupy hacienda land caused the death of 59 persons. Twenty-three individuals were killed in connection with strikes intended to achieve higher wages or better working conditions, and 55 killings were related to refusals to fulfill traditional feudal obligations. (Espinoza and Malpica, 1970:230–231) The history of the Peruvian rural syndicates reinforces previously presented evidence that Indian peasant behavior does not match the stereotype of conformity and apathy.

The complexity of the Peruvian agrarian problem is reflected by occasional instances of several groups of peasants laying claim to the same land. In Yanamaroa Valley, south of Jauja, the militant peasantry swept away the traditional hacienda system. The resident labor force claimed the hacienda land on the grounds that they had lived there and had cultivated it. However, the nearby Indian community based their claim to the same land on the assertion that the territory had been stolen from the Indians by the *hacendado*. By 1967 the conflict relationship between the two contestants had broken into open violence. (Alberti, 1970:79–80)

In most Latin American countries rural unionization has been of little practical consequence, and in a few cases peasant syndicates have achieved a notoriety that appears to be incommensurate with their role as political power contenders. Probably no organization has received more international attention than the peasant leagues of the Brazilian northeast under the leadership of Francisco Julião. Anthony Leeds correctly described the various Brazilian peasant aggregates as "groupings of mutually antagonistic organizations whose formation is, in large part, being encouraged in a paternalistic manner by representatives of the controlling and more powerful mediatorial elites of the country." (Leeds, 1964:192) Julião, the organizer of the peasant leagues, belonged to the landholding upper class of Pernambuco; he was a lawyer and member of the state legislature. Like many other populist politicians, he sought support for his own political career among the rural population, preaching the gospel of radical agrarian reform. The peasant leagues, however, saw little development outside the state of Pernambuco. (Leeds, 1964:192–193) Like most comparable phenomena elsewhere in Brazil, they failed to survive the "revolutionary" purges of 1964.

The evolution of the large estate

One of the most perceptive analyses of the large agricultural estate in Latin America discerns two types of social systems in agriculture—the *hacienda* and the *plantation*. (Wolf and Mintz, 1957:381) The study refers only to Middle America and the Antilles, but its conceptual framework can easily be applied to South America. Since we are concerned with the large rural holding rather than with the agricultural estate in the narrow sense of the term, the cattle ranch should be added to the proposed typology.

It is probably true that the largest rural properties are specialized in livestock raising and that except for the pampa region of Argentina, Uruguay, and southernmost Brazil, as well as parts of northern Colombia, the land occupied by the big cattle ranches is so inferior in quality that it could not be used for cultivation unless huge sums were invested in basic improvements. Or if the soil is not poor, the livestock-producing areas are distant from markets and hard to get to. Thus ranchos measuring 10,000 hectares are found all over central Brazil and in arid interior of the Brazilian northeast, in the llanos of Venezuela, and Colombia, and in northern Mexico.

The only major change that has affected the traditional ranch is the introduction of new breeds of cattle that produce more beef and are better adapted to the tropics. To the limited extent that pastures are man-made rather than natural, the dissemination of highly productive and draught-resistant grasses has contributed to the development of the pastoral economy.

Of course ranching keeps population density down to a minimum, and where pastoralism succeeds agriculture, as it does in some regions, human settlements tend to shrink and sometimes disappear completely. Whereas an agricultural estate may require a large labor force, a cattle ranch is run by a very small group of cowhands. *Gado cria o deserto* (cattle creates the desert), say the Brazilians; and in the mind of the people, pastoralism is irreconcilable with development. Yet ranching is highly attractive in areas where poor or exhausted land can be bought cheaply and labor and capital are scarce. Thus relatively high returns may be secured with small investments in land, labor, and capital, since the growing urban markets are virtually insatiable in their demand for beef.

Of the two types of agricultural estates, the hacienda represents tradition and the plantation stands for modernity. What was described as the landed estate in a previous chapter is roughly identical to the hacienda. At least up to the middle of the nineteenth century, virtually all landed estates seemed to be haciendas in the sense proposed by Wolf and Mintz. Although modernization has cut a wide swath in contemporary rural society, the hacienda type as a mode of life and a way of combining capital, land, labor, technology, and social and political sanctions is still very much alive. (Wolf and Mintz 1957:382) Furthermore, transition from the family-owned, labor-intensive, paternalistic, and technologically archaic hacienda to the corporation-owned, capital-intensive, and technologically modern plantation is almost never achieved in a single step.

Santa Amelia, an agricultural estate in the Central Valley of Chile, combines characteristics representing both the hacienda and the plantation. In 1960, a thousand hectares of arable land belonging to the estate were irrigated and under cultivation. Potatoes, wheat, rice, and grapes were produced exclusively for the market. Milk from 80 Holstein cows went into a small cheese factory located on the estate. There was also a thoroughly modern chicken farm under the supervision of a professional veterinarian. The *mayordomo chefe*, or general manager, was assisted by eight technicians, each specialized in a different field (dairy industry, chicken farming, viticulture, fruit culture, horticulture, etc.). Four of the specialists were graduates of agricultural schools. A few skilled workers, such as mechanics, carpenters, and masons, were employed on a full-time basis.

Undoubtedly Santa Amelia had reached a technological and managerial level of development characteristic of the plantation, but labor relations were still imbued with traditional elements. Although all services rendered by the 160 resident laborers (*inquilinos*) were remunerated, only a small fraction of the compensation was paid in the form of money wages (200 pesos or 20 cents per day). Each worker received a hot meal at noon and one pound of wheat per work day. Free housing, a small subsistence plot, and the rights to cut firewood and to keep three large animals on pasture land constituted the main perquisites in lieu of monetary remuneration. In addition, each worker could cultivate one hectare of marginal land, which was redistributed every year.

Although no worker was expected to render services that had not been formally stipulated, it would be impossible to define the worker—owner relationship in contractual terms alone. The owner, a member of the traditional seigneurial class of Chile, was still expected to perform the role of the "symbolic father," to whom his workers would turn in situations of distress. *He* was asked for advice in cases of marital trouble; *his* assistance was requested when sickness or death struck a family; *he* was approached for loans; *he* was asked to arbitrate disputes among neighbors. Many of the independent small holders of nearby villages even consulted the owner of Santa Amelia for the same reasons his own inquilinos did.

Santa Amelia had been in the owner's family for several generations. In his grandmother's time the hacienda had been five times as large, including among its resident labor force the population of several villages that were no longer part of any estate in 1960. In spite of successive partitions, the present owner had inherited the paternalistic role of his predecessors. Although a full-time social worker had been hired to serve the inquilinos, these still preferred to approach the owner for assistance.

The "great house" of Santa Amelia had been designed to symbolize the family's claim to seigneurial status. Although of relatively modest proportions, its architectural style and furnishings were modeled after the French chateaux; it was surrounded by a small park of European trees and shrubbery, dotted with "classic" statuary along the paths. Although the hacienda type of operation allocates resources to this and similar forms of conspicuous consumption intended to support status claims of the owner's family, the accounting system of the plantation, geared to maximizing returns on invested capital, preclude such use of profits. Whatever social aspirations the individual shareholder of a plantation may wish to express by conspicuous ostentation, they tend to be divorced from the operation of the corporate estate.

Santa Amelia reflects an extremely common way of combining hacienda tradition with the technical and managerial progress of the plantation. Modernization cannot be measured exclusively in terms of investments in tractors, irrigation systems, fertilizers, hybrid seeds, or degree of internal specialization. The process has many facets, and some of these are unrelated to technological and organization complexity.

Of course Santa Amelia is a relatively small operation in contrast to the sugar cane plantation of Cartavio in Peru, for example. In 1964 Cartavio measured 5200 hectares and cultivated another 1000 hectares of rented land. It employed 1600 agricultural workers, 1000 laborers in its sugar mill, 200 day laborers, and 110 white-collar workers.

Cartavio is a real city with the factory, the administrative buildings, two churches, the hospital, the grade schools, the church-affiliated secondary school, the commissary, movie theatre and the residential districts for the labor force built around it. Here live 16,500 inhabitants. . . . The technical revolution, labor unions and perhaps the fact that a large proportion of the capital came from the United States have resulted in improvements for the labor force. (Collin-Delavaud, 1967:8)

In Cartavio, mass employment combined with union influence on salaries and working conditions, as well as a number of highly institutionalized fringe benefits, would render impracticable the personal paternalism characterizing the labor relations of smaller estates.

Almost entirely unnoticed so far has been the residential dissociation of rural labor force and plantation in the state of São Paulo. Although no quantitative data are available, it appears that in the more densely populated, more highly urbanized areas of the state, the plantation workers have been moving away from the estate to establish residence in nearby towns, from which they commute to their place of work. They are *diaristas* rather than *colonos*. The viability of this trend seems to be contingent on the kind of infrastructure—a dense highway network and transportation facilities—that has been emerging in many parts of the state. It seems to indicate the end of the effectiveness of traditional perquisites that were assumed to tie the labor force to the estate and that renumeration has become entirely monetary; labor relations, moreover, are now totally contractual and consistent with the socioeconomic structure of the plantation.

The diffusion of tractors may be regarded as one of the most significant indices of technical modernization. In Argentina, the number of tractors used in agriculture rose from 1,800 in 1922 to 120,000 in 1962. (Fienup, Brannon, and Fender, 1969:168) According to the Brazilian agricultural census of 1950, 5,937 farms used a total of 8,372 tractors, and 4,497 of these farms using a total of 6,385 tractors were located in southern Brazil. (Schuh, 1970:155) In 1970 Brazilian industry produced 15,000 tractors, and the number of tractors in agriculture exceeded 100,000. (Cavalcanti, 1971:87) In Venezuela the total of tractors in use on farms rose from 14,667 in 1961 to an estimated 16,773 in 1965. (Heaton, 1969:198) Mexican total investment in agricultural machinery including tractors increased at an annual rate of 5.4 percent from 2,564 million pesos in 1950 to 4,317 million in 1960. There is no reason to assume that this growth rate has diminished. (Venezian and Gamble, 1969:109)

For decades the landed estate has been involved in passionate controversy in which fact it is difficult to distinguish from fiction. To many critics it epitomizes all that keeps Latin America from developing a more equitable socioeconomic system. However, even when changes in the political power structure remove the barriers to radical agrarian reform, the large estate does not disappear. The old landholding aristocracy may lose its controlling position, but a new class of big landowners is allowed to emerge, as in Mexico. In Cuba the large sugar plantations were taken over by the state, and Peru is anxious to preserve the large coastal plantations by transforming them into cooperative holdings. Whatever the ideological justification of such policies, it seems to be realized that indiscriminate fragmentation of the most intensively cultivated and modernized plantations would spell economic disaster for societies dependent on export crops and on the production of large economic surpluses to feed growing urban populations.

Elsewhere in the world, modernization of agriculture appears to be accompanied by widespread rural exodus: The proportion of the total population engaged in agricultural pursuits tends to shrink to a fraction of what it is now in most regions of Latin America. In the United States, for example, it has shrunk to 3.5 percent of the economically active population (1970), whereas in The United Kingdom in 1972 the percentage had reached an all-time low of 2.5 percent. (United Nations, 1973:305, 310) Where this occurs, the economic structure of the urban areas is prepared to absorb the rural excess population. However, if countries such as Mexico, Colombia, Peru, Chile, and Brazil were capable and determined fully to modernize their agricultural systems following models set by the United States, Canada, or Western Europe, the ensuing rural–urban migration would probably create socioeconomic problems of staggering proportions, particularly since most cities of Latin America are already besieged with extremely serious population problems.

Kinship, education,
and religion

The dynamics of kinship and family

The forms of kinship

Our previous findings, particularly those related to industrialization and urbanization, left little doubt about the high degree of adaptability of the traditional kinship complex to a changing social structure. However, it seems reasonable to assume that the structural changes accompanying urban growth and the emergence of major industrial complexes would leave their mark on kinship behavior and family structure. Unfortunately, research on kinship and family remains one of the most neglected fields of study, particularly in Spanish America. Much of what can be said

337

about the "changing family" is based on limited evidence that may or may not be validated by further testing.

A glance at published results of research undertaken since approximately 1940 suggests the persistence rather than the disruption of the traditional kinship complex. However, most studies were carried out by social anthropologists and rural sociologists, who have a penchant for tradition-oriented peasant communities and hacienda-like structures. It is therefore possible that findings related to kinship and family are unintentionally weighted toward persistence rather than change.

At this point a sharpening of our conceptual tools is appropriate. So far we have distinguished the nuclear family, the extended family, and the kinship group. It was suggested that the extended family comprises several nuclear families bound together by frequent interaction, sometimes by sharing a common residence or a cluster of neighboring dwellings. The kinship group was conceived of as a larger unit encompassing various extended families united for political action or corporate enterprise. This tripartite division was thought to be roughly equivalent to Wagley's suggested division: the nuclear family consisting of husband, wife, children, the kindred, and the ancestor-oriented kin group. (Wagley, 1963:184–204) Kindred differs from extended family in that the kindred is perceived *not* in terms of a network of established obligation-relationships identical for all participants, but rather in the perspective of a particular individual, as the total of all those relatives (consanguine, affinal, and ritual) with whom he continuously or periodically interacts. One may assume, as Kottak suggests, that "each individual has his own personal kindred, the limits and specific personnel of which are unique." (Kottak, 1967:429) Nevertheless, there is likely to be some overlapping, at least as far as the members of a nuclear family are concerned.

According to one authority, the ancestor-oriented kin group claims descent through male and/or female links from "a certain 'apical' ancestor" (Kottak, 1967:429), for example, the famous sixteenth-century Indian chief Tibiriçá, who is believed to be the ancestor of the paulistas who, now bear the name Tibiriçá.

The three categories proposed by Wagley are not only useful in contrasting the kinship system of upper and lower classes, as Kottak suggested, but also in measuring changes.

The nuclear family

Two major changes have affected the conjugal or nuclear family: It has acquired a higher degree of autonomy in its relationships to more inclusive kinship groups, and its internal structure has changed. The relative "emancipation" of the nuclear family should be viewed as a process of decentralization by which the tutelage of the more inclusive kin group slips and eventually loses its hold on its component conjugal units. In other words, the nuclear family gradually expands its functional autonomy, often in opposition to traditional patripotestal authority. Long vanished are the times when a person of legitimate Spanish descent was not allowed to marry without paternal consent, and arranged marriage as a transaction between kinship groups is hardly more than a dim memory. Often enough the kin group is no longer capable of preventing the dissolution of marriages. Among the Chilean upper class, for example, young couples sometimes defy the sanctions of their orthodox Catholic kindred and separate, even contracting new unions disapproved of by the church. (Willems, 1967b:49)

Although intergenerational clashes occur, the process is primarily one of gradual erosion, rather than a cataclysmic change. Hutchinson noted the cohesiveness of the upper-class kinship groups in Vila Reconcavo, Bahia. The individual still moved in the orbit of the kindred that had not yet lost its capability of placing young people in business or a profession, and of caring for and protecting members who require such attention. (H. W. Hutchinson, 1957:130–133) The kindred acted as a center of sociability, cousin marriages were still frequent, and the patriarch was still accorded deference and respect; but he had no strong control over the nuclear units, which had reached the point of making their own decisions.

The growing autonomy of the nuclear family appears to be related to changes in its own structure. Perhaps no single factor has altered the conjugal family more than female education and the widening of occupational prospects for women. Up to the end of the nineteenth century formal education went rarely beyond the three R's, but in the middle and upper classes at least, "girls go to secondary schools and often to college to take advanced degrees as do their brothers." (H. W. Hutchinson, 1957:131) This trend delays marriage until the early twenties and instills a sense of independence that may or may not be translated into a professional career. In all of Latin America the teaching profession, at least at the elementary school level, is almost entirely in the hands of women, and many do not give up teaching when they get married. But high schools, liberal arts colleges, nursing, and social work offer rapidly increasing professional chances for women. On the lower levels of the middle class, there is of course a broad choice of occupational opportunities in business, banking, and insurance, and lower still, factory work has long been acceptable for females.

These changes are significant because employment of whatever kind removes the female from the strictures of traditional family control. Furthermore, the working woman is a breadwinner, a role that had previously been monopolized by father or husband. By contributing to the family budget, a woman is implicitly demonstrating potential independence. Although marriage continues to be the first choice of most girls, a professional career or employment is becoming an increasingly viable alternative; at worst, work is a last resort to fall back on if a marriage breaks up or terminates with the husband's premature death. In relatively conservative Bahia in the early 1950s, marraige had already assumed "an aspect of companionship." (H. W. Hutchinson, 1957:131) On the whole, the marrying woman of the 1970s is considerably older, far better educated, and more capable of sharing authority with her husband than was her mother or grandmother.

Possible changes of middle- and upper-class sex patterns are most difficult to assess. Outwardly at least, relationships between young men and women appear to be quite removed from parental control and the traditional strictures of chaperonage. In virtually all large cities of Latin America, the associations between unmarried men and women are virtually undistinguishable from those of North American or European cities. But in our attempts to gather information about current sexual mores, we were often advised that beneath the surface of informality, the traditional attitudes are lingering on, that an unmarried woman still must protect her reputation, and that suspected loss of virginity may still ruin a girl's chances of marriage. Apparently, surgical restoration of the hymen is even more frequent now than it used to be 20 or 30 years ago. This would mean of course that a certain proportion of unmarried women engage in sexual relations that do not lead to marriage. Most of our informants agreed that as a rule, male adolescents now refuse to get their sexual initiation from prostitutes. Apparently, unmarried girls are now available for this function.

In a previous chapter it was suggested that on the lower-class levels the nuclear family was less rigidly structured and sexual behavior of the female was not circumscribed by the implacable sanctions that controlled middle- and upper-class women. Scarcity of reliable studies makes it almost impossible to tell whether the lower-class family has changed and if so, exactly what the changes are. Occasional statements referring to the "disorganization" of the urban family ought to be received with considerable caution. In fact, so-called indicators of "disorganization," such as the consensual union and illegitimacy, often represent the perceptions of middle-class culture. The consensual union ought to be read as a viable alternative to civil or religious marriage rather than as a deviation from middle- or upper-class patterns. There is no overall evidence that consensual unions are less stable than conventional marriages. The frequency of consensual unions varies considerably within the lower classes of different regions, but virtually nothing is known about the determinants of such variations. In a recent study of a shantytown in Bogotá, it was discovered that 27.27 percent of all marital unions were consensual. (Neglia and Hernandes, 1970:155) In San Lorenzo (Ecuador), 80 percent of 207 couples who had been living together for five years or more reported "strictly consensual unions," but Whitten learned that at least 15 were incorrectly referring to their "stable consensual unions" as civil marriages, and a few other young people lied because they wished to make a favorable impression on the anthropologist. (Whitten, 1965: 119)

Consensual unions do not imply polygynous arrangements, but where these exist, they have to be consensual. Whitten found 18 men of San Lorenzo living in polygyny. Nine of these subjects had one or more wives in addition to a legal spouse, and all others had exclusively contracted consensual unions. Whitten also observed economic advantages in polygynous arrangements.

> A man with a farm, a shop, and a cantina can keep all three operations running profitably if he has one wife living on the farm and another in the cantina, while he himself runs the shop. Polygynous marriages that combine economic diversification and an explicit preference for one wife over another are as stable as monogamous marriages in San Lorenzo, but whatever marital form is manifest at a given time, the norms of serial polygyny govern it. (Whitten, 1965: 127–129)

The consensual union is not a male-imposed pattern, at least in the contemporary urban environment of Latin America. Often enough, women find it less difficult than men to earn a living, and the possibility of having to provide for an unemployed and perhaps malingering husband holds little appeal to most women. A consensual union may thus seem to be preferable, and it can be terminated without legal complications. It has often been said that the poor cannot afford the fees and ceremonial outlay of marriage as sanctioned by state or church. The extent to which poverty has contributed to the preservation of the consensual pattern is impossible to say. Marriage is expensive, but so is divorce—where, indeed, it is legally available. In most countries there is no legal divorce, but where consensual unions are not felt to deviate from "normal" behavior, the indissolubility of marriage, decreed by church and state, may be ignored by those who have little to lose by not complying with legal precepts.

Of course consensual unions produce illegitimate offspring, and it may well be that both patterns are becoming increasingly nonadaptive now that benefits derived from social legislation are contingent on legitimacy of marriage and offspring.

The kindred

The growing autonomy of the nuclear family does not imply the disintegration and gradual disappearance of the kinship group as an interactional unit. On the contrary, available evidence suggests that the more independent role assumed by the nuclear family may be functionally related to the support it receives from the kindred. No demonstration of autonomy could be more convincing than the decision to break away from the native community and its component kinship structures, and to migrate to faraway urban centers. However, studies carried out in Mexico, Colombia, and Peru show the crucial role of kinsfolk already located in the city, in assisting newly arriving migrants to find housing and jobs. In San Lorenzo, a township of coastal Ecuador, "personal kindreds are partially localized within a household, neighborhood, and town, and partially dispersed between towns and between a given town and the rural hinterland." (Whitten, 1965:139) Since most people are involved in shifting subsistence agriculture, spatial mobility is essential, and spatial mobility would be costly and difficult if a person could not rely on his dispersed kindred for housing and food as long as he wishes to stay. An individual is expected to reciprocate when called on, however. Thus a single household may be composed of one or several nuclear families, but because people travel often in pursuit of a livelihood, membership tends to fluctuate within relatively short periods of time.

From the study of San Lorenzo, one of the few inquiries dealing with kinship patterns of the lower class, we find that the Negroes of San Lorenzo rank several notches above the laborers attached to, or dependent on, haciendas or plantations. In San Lorenzo, a person's kindred is an asset rather than a liability, and ambitious individuals are able to manipulate the kin group to their advantage and to move up to middle-class level. (Witten, 1965:148ff.)

In view of the reciprocity of all kinship obligations, however, it can be argued that the personal kindred cannot be exploited indefinitely. Indeed, we can assume that people at lower-class levels have little to offer one another; thus if they are frequently approached for economic assistance, kinship is likely to act as a leveling mechanism, redistributing among the poorer members of the kindred the savings a nuclear family has been able to accumulate.

The study of Arembepe, a fishing village of Bahia (Brazil), reports indeed the leveling effect of the personal kindreds. There is no lack of entrepreneurship in Arembepe, but even the most resourceful individuals are eventually defeated by the obligation to help destitute relatives. (Kottak, 1967:428)

Kottak thinks that his observations in Arembepe apply to most of northeastern and north central regions of Brazil. However, both Kottak and Whitten are referring to a lower class in which people have retained some control, however limited, of economic resources. The point is crucial, because without such control the adaptive role of the kindred tends to shrink and eventually to disappear.

We assume that the desire for economic success, stimulated by the "revolution of rising expectations," interferes with traditional kinship obligations. A person confronted with the choice of helping destitute relatives and rising to a higher socioeconomic level, may well choose the latter. Evidence that this happens is extremely scarce, however. In San Lorenzo, one upward-mobile family decided to sever ties with relatives in rural areas and with all those who could not reciprocate on an equal basis. This was done when the family had reached a level of prosperity which would have rendered aid to needy relatives most effective. (Whitten, 1965:155)

The leveling effect of strong kinship ties may at times act as a barrier to technological and economic development. In a case reported by Foster from the northern coast of Peru, efforts were being made to modernize fishing techniques. When such aid was offered to a young fisherman, he declined it on the grounds that if he earned more money he would have to take care of more relatives, thus forfeiting the chances of bettering his own situation. (Foster, 1962:92) The fisherman's attitude reflects dissatisfaction with the leveling effect of the kindred, but apparently he did not feel strongly enough to defy the system.

Both Whitten and Kottak found that in the lower classes the kindred had a rather limited range. In contrast to the ancestor-oriented kin group of the upper class, people do not go beyond the first ascending generation in reckoning descent. The kindred usually consists of the parents and grandparents of a man and of his wife, his and her parents' siblings, and his and her siblings and first and second cousins. In San Lorenzo, third cousins are equated to first and second cousins if, for pragmatic reasons, it is deemed desirable to recognize them as kinsmen at all. (Whitten, 1965:146–147; Kottak, 1967:433)

In the upper class, possession of control over vast economic and political resources makes it practical to reckon kinship on a far more inclusive basis. The chances are that kinship can be used to increase rather than to redistribute wealth. There is an obvious advantage in having the largest possible number of kinsmen distributed in joint agricultural and industrial enterprises, in the higher echelons of the civil service, in the military and in various legislative bodies, in the universities, and per-haps among the high dignitaries of the Church. Instead of the personal kindred, it tends to be the ancestor-oriented kin group that protects wealth and status of its members and limits "access to strategic resources." (Kot-tak, 1967:437) This appears to be the case of the Eleadoro Gomez kin group reported by Strickon. (Strickon, 1965:337) For generations the Gomez have acted as a corporate power in Argentine agriculture, industry, politics, and administration. Studies of descent groups made in Spanish America duplicate almost exactly our knowledge of Brazilian kinship structures. In Argentina, as in Brazil, one marries into one's own class, and often the choice falls on a cousin. Cousin marriages have also been reported from Costa Rica. In fact, there is nothing in the portrait of Costa Rican family and kinship organization that could not be applied to Brazil, too. (Biesanz and Biesanz, 1944:48–104)

However, it is far from certain whether the ancestor-oriented descent group has preserved its capability of concerted action. Initially, kin groups of this type were interactional units, but in the course of time so many lines branched off from the common trunk, meeting such diverse fates, that interactional coherence was preserved only among the lines that had the means to live up to the seigneurial tradition. In 1959 we found that Chilean upper-class families supported poorer relations and prevented them from sliding into middle-class oblivion. (Willems, 1967a:50) But for how long can upper-class status depend on charity, however discreetly provided? Some of the most illustrious family names of São Paulo are in fact now found among the middle class. The bearers are aware of their distinguished descent, but long ago they lost all personal contact with the sector of the descent group that maintains its position of wealth and power.

Most students of kinship in Latin America have been surprised by the number of consanguine and affinal relations whom a single individual, in rural as well as urban settings, is often able to recall. Remarkable as such genealogical memories may be, the question that comes to mind refers to the functional implications of such mnemonic records. Do all these hundred or more relatives, presumably priding themselves on their common descent from a famous ancestor, really constitute an interactional unit? Or do they meet only at birthday parties and funerals? Do they meet *at all* for any sort of corporate endeavor?

The chances are that any member of an ancestor-oriented kin group interacts only with a fraction of all those relatives, and not all interactions imply mutual responsibilities of great economic or political consequence. Furthermore, on questioning different members of the same descent group, the observer will probably be given a somewhat different set of relatives by each member interviewed. If this happens, it would follow that the ancestor-oriented kin group is in the process of becoming a personal kindred.

The evolutionary implications of the hypothesized changes are clear. Taken in its totality, the ancestor-oriented kin group is too unwieldy to preserve its adaptive value. Too many of its branches have sunk to lower social levels and cannot profitably be mobilized for corporate enterprise. Besides, in the highly dispersive life of the big city it is difficult to engage in social intercourse with several hundred relatives, many of whom have little to offer except occasional favors of little consequence. The personal kindred, on the other hand, may meet more precisely the needs and capabilities of the individual. Lauterbach found the kindred group rather then the descent group to be important in the enterprises of various Latin American countries.

> In some cases a family-owned enterprise employs hired high-level executives from outside the family, but more frequently family influence extends not only to ownership but to management. In other words, the managerial group in a given firm is likely to come entirely or in large part from the famliy, though some of the relatives concerned—especially the young ones—may also have received executive training. (Lauterbach, 1966:7)

Over the last 10 years, the role of the kindred in major enterprises has shrunk, particularly in Brazil, where numerous investment opportunities are no longer restricted to shareholding members of kindreds.

Although joint ownership and management of economic enterprises by kinship groups imply continuous cooperation over long periods, other forms of interaction are clearly limited to situations of distress. One of the exceedingly rare studies on kinship behavior in a large metropolitan area was carried out in São Paulo in 1967. Based on a random sample of 461 nuclear families, the author proceeded to uncover Ego's possible relationship with 16 kinds of consanguine and affinal relatives. The results indicate that the nuclear family is indeed part of an interactional network that includes a varying number of relatives.

One of the three basic questions referred to "verbal interaction" or exchange of information with different members of Ego's personal kindred. It was found that "the higher the socioeconomic status of the nuclear family, the greater the number of different types of relatives with whom the nuclear family interacts." (Berlinck, 1969:97) The second question did not refer to *actual* cooperation but rather to hypothetical situations of emotional crisis in which Ego might approach relatives for help. The investigator learned "that the higher the socioeconomic status of the nuclear family, the smaller the number of different types of relatives the family would ask for help." (Berlinck, 1969:98) The third question was designed to ascertain the types and number of relatives the nuclear family would expect to receive help from in situations of financial distress. The findings indicated that no relationship exists between the socioeconomic status of the family and the number of types of relatives from whom the family would expect help in a financial crisis. It was also found that the more relatives were living in the city, the larger the number of different relatives who would be expected to offer help. (Berlinck, 1969: 139)

The author concluded that in cities such as São Paulo, among the upper and middle-upper classes "extended kinship structure is a viable adaptive mechanism, and consequently it is maintained in the system." (Berlinck, 1969:141) Since we are dealing with hypothetical rather than actual forms of aid, the findings suggest that the kindred has been maintained, not because of its *actual* adaptive role but because it is still *believed* to be able to perform that role.

Presumably, there is very little in the size, functional relevance, and composition of the kindred that is not subject to variations in time and space. Among the skilled and unskilled laborers of Argentine cattle ranches, the kindred elaborated the concuñado relationship in preference to other structural aspects of the kinship system. A *concuñado* is a man's wife's sister's husband. This relationship is recognized anywhere in Latin America, and the Spanish term has a Portuguese equivalent. However, among the Creole laborers of Buenos Aires province, "the brothers-in-law of a concuñado become Ego's concuñado as well, and this usage is extended indefinitely." In recommending persons for jobs on the estancia, a senior employee may bypass a close relative in favor of a concuñado for strategic reasons or because the former is unreliable. (Strickon, 1965: 330–331)

Whatever variations of the kinship pattern are encountered, the overall picture indicates that in spite of substantial changes in the relative position of the nuclear family, the kindred has been able to preserve many of its traditional functions. And Wagley may be correct in suggesting that kinship will continue to play an important role in ordering social relations. (Wagley, 1968:193)

Formal education

The dual position of education

Institutionalized education holds a unique position in any cultural system: It is an integral aspect of the culture it is designed to transmit from generation to generation. In other words, the instrumentalities and organizational devices—charters and techniques of instruction, bodies of instructors, technical equipment, and material structures—that are involved in the transmission are subject to the same cultural laws that pattern, for example, kinship, economy, polity, and religion. This dualism is of little consequence as long as a society is untouched by revolutionary transformations, but it suddenly assumes critical proportions if major changes affect a culture and, with it, existing educational traditions.

For a long time, the "content" of education—the ideas, beliefs, values, attitudes, and skills to be transmitted—may go for granted. But technological and economic changes and the emergence of new scientific knowledge or new political or religious ideologies, may necessitate a radical revision and thorough substitution of educational contents. Such manifest needs for change may be advocated by certain groups and opposed by others. Professional educators may participate on either side, but the chances are that the majority will defend the status quo of formal education. Conflict may also arise about the identity of the recipients of formal education. The social class or group that controls the educational institutions may have political or economic reasons for wanting to prevent certain segments of the society from gaining access to these institutions. Or, educational privileges may be opposed on the same grounds on which political and economic privileges are opposed.

All these things have occurred in Latin America, and for the last half-century approximately, the educational systems have been in a state of almost continuous turmoil, particularly on the higher levels, where those who have completed professional initiation requirements are rewarded with access to scarce economic and political resources. The situation has been complicated because formal education is particularly sensitive to the shortcomings of secondary development. As indicated before, the intellectual elites who determine the content and form of education have been under the sway of European and North American models whose adaptability to Latin American conditions has been a source of discord for the last 30 or 40 years.

The traditional educational system of all Latin American countries rather accurately reflected the social structure. It almost completely ignored the lower classes; it was androcentric, top-heavy, and authoritarian. The state was very reluctant to assume an active role in the establishment and diffusion of a school system designed to benefit the masses. Any form of education that went beyond the teaching of the three R's remained, until the first two or three decades of the twentieth century, a privilege of middle- and upper-class men. Women were not expected to acquire more than the rudimentary skills necessary to read the prayer books. Indeed, female illiteracy among the upper classes was fairly common, up to the second half of the nineteenth century.

The "elitist" nature of the educational system was illustrated by the overriding interest of Latin American societies in higher education. Whereas the beginnings of elementary education have elicited little or no interest, several republics have been vying for the glory of having the first university in the New World.

We shall not repeat our comments about the dominant role of the Catholic Church in the educational system, the authoritarian character of education, and its humanistic content. The Church lost most of its hold in the nineteenth century, and education went through a process of secularization; but it did not lose its authoritarian structure, nor did it cease to be a class-bound institution. The development of international trade and the incipient industrial revolution caught the educational system almost completely unprepared. It ought to be added that in Latin America, formal education had always been designed to promote *understanding* rather than *change* of man's place in the world. (Rivera, 1971:69) It was not primarily intended to transmit skills and knowledge that could be readily used to transform the physical and social environments. In other words, it lacked the pragmatic orientation that seemed to be demanded by the rapidly spreading emphasis on science and technology.

The demand for change: primary and secondary education

The quest for change in modes of traditional education boiled down to two major issues: the implantation of knowledge and skills more suited to the emerging industrial order, and the opening of the educational system to larger segments of the population.

As might be expected, the quest for change became a vindication of political parties representing the interests of the middle and lower classes. Urbanization and simultaneous modifications in the occupational structure provided a pragmatic basis for the eradication of illiteracy. Middle- and upper-class employers had little use for illiterates, and migrants in search of urban employment had slight chance of success without some command of the three R's.

Where foreign immigrants constituted a substantial proportion of the population, particularly in Argentina, Uruguay, and southern Brazil, the demand for a primary school system was most insistent. In fact, where the state failed to provide schooling, the immigrants and their native-born descendants often established their own educational system, which tended to perpetuate languages other than Spanish or Portuguese, and, with the languages, cultural traditions that were perceived to be at variance with the process of assimilation.

Often enough, illiteracy was (and still is) perceived and discussed out of cultural context. Believers in the redeeming effects of formal education per se demanded schools, not only in the cities but in the remotest and most isolated rural areas, where reading and writing skills were unrelated to the local culture, and the acquisition of such skills could not have generated change except when accompanied by technological and economic innovations. To the limited extent that educational opportunities appeared in such areas, schools not only failed to "improve" matters, they did not even succeed in implanting literacy, mainly because the children who could be induced to attend classes, tended to forget whatever skills they had absorbed there. Nothing in the local culture required or stimulated reading or writing.

Except for Argentina, Uruguay, and Chile, the dissemination of the three R's proceeded at a very slow pace. In Brazil, for example, 66.4 percent of the people were illiterate in 1872. By 1920 that percentage was still as high as 60.1 percent. (Azevedo, 1943:346) Obviously, the eradication of illiteracy was an uphill struggle among a population whose natural increase rate went up to about 2.8 percent per year. At any rate, by 1970 the illiteracy rate had been reduced to about 25 percent of the population of 6 years of age and older, at a cost of 111,416,760 cruzeiros, or more than twice the amount spent on primary education in 1969. (Cavalcanti, 1971:111–113) Like most national averages, the illiteracy rate of Brazil hides regional cleavages as pronounced as, say, the difference between Uruguay and Bolivia, or between Mexico and Guatemala.

Table 24 shows widely varying rates of illiteracy; however, most, if not all these figures have been significantly reduced in the years since the data were collected. Brazil's spectacular success should not be con-

Table 24   *Illiteracy among population of 15 years of age and older, by sex (percentages)*

Country	Year	Male	Female
Argentina	1960	7.98	10.25
Uruguay	1963	9.01	8.51
Chile	1960	15.17	17.50
Costa Rica	1963	15.25	16.04
Paraguay	1962	19.16	31.47
Panama	1960	23.12	23.41
Cuba	1963	24.15	19.97
Colombia	1964	25.17	28.87
Peru	1961	25.61	31.47
Mexico	1960	29.82	39.26
Ecuador	1962	31.62	36.91
Venezuela	1961	31.98	41.58
Dominican Republic	1960	33.33	37.57
Brazil	1950	45.20	55.94
El Salvador	1961	46.10	55.50
Nicaragua	1963	49.46	49.01
Honduras	1961	51.28	58.53
Guatemala	1964	55.80	68.22
Bolivia	1950	57.64	77.22
Haiti	1950	87.25	91.55

Source: Adapted from Kenneth Ruddle and Mukhtar Hamour, *Statistical Abstracts of Latin America 1970*. Los Angeles: Latin American Center of the University of California, 1971.

sidered to be an isolated case. One could easily argue, however, that in all countries *functional* illiteracy is probably higher than the figures of Table 24 suggest.

More than elementary education, the secondary school system opens channels of social ascent to middle-class and, indirectly, to upper-class levels. All secondary school systems in Latin America have been criticized because they constituted effective boundary-maintaining structures tending to preserve the educational monopoly of the middle and upper classes. There were relatively few secondary institutions, and these were, with few exceptions, in private hands, therefore dependent on tuitions and fees high enough to exclude low-income segments of the population.

Like most educational institutions, the secondary school was a transplant from Europe, and with it had come the belief that secondary education should merely serve to replenish the ranks of the elites, furnishing a channel toward the institutions of higher learning. The principle of limited facilities and controlled access was taken for granted in Europe, and the first timid changes following World War I conjured visions of an "academic proletariat," unemployable, frustrated, and the potential focus of social revolution.

Educational ideologies changed as the North American model began to displace European elitist ideologies. The change is reflected, for example, in the *Manifesto dos Pioneiros da Educação Nova* (Manifesto of the Pioneers of the New Education), published in 1932 by a group of 26 Brazilian intellectuals. In this almost revolutionary document, education at any level is defined as "a social function and essentially a public service which the state is required to provide in cooperation with all social institutions." (*Manifesto*, 1932:113) The pioneers demanded that there be only one system for everybody—coeducational, laic, compulsory, and without charge on all levels up to the age of 18. Secondary school, they insisted, should be

for the people, not limited to the preservation and transmission of the classics, but designed, by its democratic structure, to be accessible and to afford equal opportunities for all. On the base of a common general culture it should comprise specialized sections serving the humanities and sciences, as well as manual and mechanical crafts. (*Manifesto*, 1932:114)

Although it was not proposed to do away with private schools, the state was expected to provide parallel facilities countervailing the economic advantages of a privileged minority.

The *Manifesto* was evidently far ahead of political and economic developments that eventually led to the implementation of some of its demands. An educational system does not change because a group of progressive intellectuals demand reforms, but primarily because particular segments of the society are powerful enough to carry through such demands against the opposition of the traditional power holders. At any rate, the structural changes, particularly in Argentina, Costa Rica, Chile, Panama, and Uruguay, were such that major reforms of secondary education could be initiated. In 1955 enrollment in Argentine secondary schools had reached 27 percent of the total school-age population. In 1960 it had risen to 31 percent, the highest proportion of all Latin American countries except Uruguay, where it had gone from 24 to 32 percent. During the same period, secondary school enrollment grew from 23 to 30 percent in Panama, from 16 to 28 percent in Costa Rica, and from 19 to 23 percent in Chile. All other countries were lagging behind, but growth rates between 1957 and 1962 indicate significant changes in the rank order of development. In Venezuela the proportion of the school-age population enrolled in secondary institutions increased by 153 percent; in Cuba it rose by 137 percent, and in Nicaragua by 116 percent. (Solari, 1967:459)

Two aspects of Venezuela's spectacular development are particularly significant. The total number of secondary institutions including technical and normal schools grew from 357 in 1960–1961 to 659 in 1969–1970. Half these schools (329) were classified as technical institutions, suggesting erosion of the traditional dominance of the academic type of *liceu*. Furthermore, the enrollment in public (free enrollment) schools rose from 78,621 in 1960–1961 to 218,304 in 1969–1970. At the same time enrollment in private institutions increased from 26,380 to 69,648. (Dirección General de Estadística 1972:502, 505) Since enrollment in public schools was three times higher than that in private schools, we can conclude that the system had ceased to be the barrier to social ascent it once was.

A similar trend has been noticeable in most countries, especially in the highly industrialized and urbanized areas. In Brazil, total enrollment in middle schools jumped from 1,076,201 in 1959 to 3,205,689 in 1968. In 1959 only 373,187 students were enrolled in public secondary schools, but in 1968 their number had risen to 1,744,513. For the first time in Brazilian history, the number of students attending public secondary schools was significantly higher than the total enrolled in private schools. (Fundação IBGE, 1970:249)

In 1931 there was no industrial or agricultural secondary school in Brazil at all. Between 1959 and 1968 the enrollment in industrial schools went up from 22,312 to 121,192, and that in agricultural establishments rose from 5,679 to 18,222. (Fundação IBGE, 1970:250)

As secondary school systems expand and an increasing proportion of such schools are public and free, more members of the lower classes will surely gain access, and they can then use the system as a channel of upward mobility. A study by Havighurst and Gouveia revealed that in five Brazilian states enrollment of students from the working class was close to 30 percent in the first cycle and 22.1 percent in the second or more advanced cycle of the system. (Havighurst and Gouveia, 1969: 58–59) It was also found that working-class students prefer commercial, industrial, and agricultural schools to academic ones, and that far more working-class students were enrolled in academic schools than in private schools. (Havighurst and Gouveia, 1969:68, 75)

Relatively high enrollment figures of working-class students in private secondary schools seems to be related to the number of such schools that are organized as profit-oriented private enterprises. Educational entrepreneurship is found in all parts of urban Latin America, but probably more in Brazil than in Spanish America. The establishments are stratified insofar as they charge widely differing fees, and the least expensive institutions are night schools attracting students who work in the day and often come from working-class families.

Does the secondary school system serve as channel of upward social mobility? Havighurst and Gouveia found that more than 60 percent of all students in their sample had attained a higher level of education than their fathers. (Havighurst and Gouveia, 1969:79). In one of our own studies, a sample of 399 students of all secondary schools of five municipios of São Paulo State was analyzed to determine intergenerational differences in educational achievement. Table 25 shows that 83.2 percent of all fathers and 87.2 percent of all mothers had less education than their children currently enrolled in a middle school. Having children in secondary school does not itself raise either the family or the children to middle-class status, but a middle-school education ought to be regarded as one of several alternative steps to social ascent. In Brazil, no more than 40 percent of the students enrolled in secondary institutions complete a full seven-year course. (Havighurst and Gouveia, 1969:27) But we can assume that even a few years in secondary school, attended anywhere in Latin America, will probably cause a student to seek white-collar employment; and particularly in the larger cities, there is a wide range of jobs in private business and civil service for which this kind of education is adequate. The traditional prejudice against manual labor is dying hard,

Table 25 *Formal schooling of parents of 399 students of secondary schools in five municipios of São Paulo, 1968*

Schooling	Father		Mother	
	Number	Percentage	Number	Percentage
None	45	11.28	83	20.80
Grade school incomplete	183	45.86	161	40.35
Grade school complete	104	26.07	104	26.07
Secondary school incomplete	33	8.27	22	5.52
Secondary school complete	7	1.75	28	7.00
College (complete and incomplete)	27	6.77	—	—
No answer			1	.26
Total	399	100.00	399	100.00

and even low-paying white-collar jobs are felt to be socially superior to better-paying manual work.

The changes affecting the structure of secondary education are rapidly closing the gap between male and female enrollment. In fact, by 1968 the proportion of girls in all secondary schools of Argentina, Chile, Cuba, the Dominican Republic, and Panama was higher than the percentage of boys. In Brazil female enrollment had jumped from only 18 percent in 1932 to 49 percent in 1967. In Venezuela it was up to 49 percent in 1969 as against 32 percent in 1938. Perhaps the most rapid development occurred in Paraguay, where in 1938 females represented only 8 percent of all secondary students. In 1969 female enrollment was close to that of males which was 53.4 percent. In Colombia in 1968 the sex difference was neglible, and female enrollment in Ecuador had reached 41 percent in 1961. The proportion of females enrolled in secondary schools in Bolivia, Guatemala, Honduras, and Mexico was close to 40 percent in 1968–1969, and in El Salvador it had reached 47 percent. (Ruddle and Hamour, 1971:153; UNESCO, 1961)

Does the secondary school actually transmit the knowledge and skills it proposes to pass on? The question seems to be unanswerable at present. One clue to the effectiveness of secondary schools may be seen in the degree of professionalization of the teaching staff. In Mexico, 50 percent of all teachers had no credentials in 1968. In Bolivia the percentage was 46.7 in 1969, and in Ecuador it was reported to be 90 percent in 1965–1966. On the other hand, in Argentina only 2.7 percent had no credentials, and in a number of countries the percentage lies between 10 and 30 percent. (Ruddle and Hamour, 1971:152) Of course credentials are often of dubious value, since they are issued by institutions of "higher" learning whose academic status compares unfavorably with national standards of most Western countries. There certainly are wide gaps from country to country, and these are even broader among different regions of the same country. Usually, intellectual competence in all branches of learning is heavily concentrated in capital cities.

The Latin American university

The extraordinary amount of controversy and conflict surrounding Latin American institutions of higher learning is primarily concerned with the same two issues that have been raised in connection with the secondary systems: the demand to adapt the university to a rapidly changing culture and the demand to open it to larger segments of the society. However, the university is set apart from the middle school by several factors. First, the role assigned to the institution of higher learning in Western civilization involves not only the autonomous selection of cultural contents or subject matter to be transmitted, but also the creation of such subject matter through organized research, much of which affects the cultural evolution. Second, social accessibility is far more crucial insofar as the university controls admission to the professional ranks of the society, therefore to the middle and upper strata of the class order. Third, unlike those enrolled in the lower levels of the educational system, the university students are adults, capable of playing an active role in decision-making processes affecting the organization and functions of the university.

The foregoing aspects of the university assume particular significance in Latin America because the transfer of European forms of university organization was not achieved without adaptive distortions. The European model had been sacrificed to structural vicissitudes and cultural norms, and the resulting institution was almost diametrically opposed to a true transplant. The intellectual elites of Latin America had been conditioned to copy rather than to challenge European models of higher learning. Furthermore, allegiance to exogenous paradigms often prevented the Latins from gearing the selection of subject matter to the realities of their own societies. The European institution of the *catedra*—the "chair" that the European professor, once invested, occupies for life—was highly compatible with Latin American patterns of behavior. Its monopolistic and fossilizing effects were magnified by native authoritarianism.

In addition to the distortions of the European model just mentioned, there was an obvious lack of resources or, in some countries perhaps, refusal by the state to appropriate sufficient funds to free the teaching staff from the need to practice law, medicine, or a technical or managerial profession. In fact, remuneration was (and still is) so low that most professors subordinate their teaching duties to their professional activities. The Latin American professor is not only a part-time teacher, he is also an absentee functionary who often leaves the teaching to an assistant whose loyalty is assured because his employment depends on his personal relationship with the *catedrático*, the tenured occupant of the chair.

The European idea of university autonomy, intended to protect academic freedom and the independence of research, was readily accepted in Latin America; where the principle could be preserved against political pressure, however, it often transformed the university into a bastion of scholastic traditionalism and organized resistance to modernization.

Authoritarianism found perhaps its most uncompromising expression in the structure of the traditional university. It could be expected, therefore, that the university would become a focus of rebellion, according to the familiar pattern of political behavior. That the first organized rebellion should occur in the Argentine University of Córdoba is not surprising at all. In 1918 Argentina was undergoing rapid economic development. Thousands of European immigrants and their native-born descendants were pressing for access to the higher levels of a rigidly stratified society, and in Córdoba they were confronted with one of the most antiquated institutions of higher learning on the continent. Since its very inception it had been a power domain of the upper class, and through it, the upper class had controlled access to all important political, judicial, administrative, and ecclesiastical positions of the regional society. The student rebellion of 1918 should thus be interpreted as integral to the structural change analyzed in a previous chapter. The demands of the students, formulated by the First National Student Congress, meeting in July of 1918 in Tucumán, are highly significant for two reasons: They had a strong impact on the students of most Latin American universities for years to come, and they epitomized the changes that have been advocated and fought for up to the present time by many student bodies, under widely varying conditions. Of the 10 major proposals of the Congress of Tucumán, the most incisive was the demand for student participation in the governance of the universities. Several other resolutions were intended to break down the aristocratic isolation of the university and to relate it to social realities, particularly to the problems of the region where it was located. (Valdes, 1965:179) The action of the students of

Córdoba constitutes a major change in itself and the beginning of what has been labeled the "politicization" of students and universities.

In the present context it is not possible to follow the long and complex string of student rebellions since the Congress of Tucumán. They spread to all countries, and they reflect alliances with or subservience to a number of political parties or movements. Street and campus demonstrations, strikes, violence (particularly when police or troops attempted to suppress public outbursts), occupation or destruction of university buildings, intimidation of faculty, and conversion of the campus into a center of revolutionary activities, are some of the major instruments chosen by student groups to express dissatisfaction with existing policies. Since almost all major universities are state institutions, student rebellions imply or are meant to be confrontations with constituted government.

There are several possible classifications for student rebellions. If objectives are the criterion, three major categories can be distinguished. Some revolts are concerned with immediate issues of limited scope. The students protest or strike against professional incompetence or absenteeism; they revolt against university authorities, whom they accuse of making high-handed decisions incompatible with student interests; they protest against inadequate food services and the lack of scientific equipment, library facilities, and dormitory space. One of the most bitterly resented shortcomings, attributed to numerous universities, has been the failure to establish facilities to admit all students who have passed entrance examinations.

The second category of student revolts transcends such limited objectives, and the young people battle for a more thorough or radical reform, which would enable the university to play a leading role in national development.

Finally, some student groups strive for a revolutionary transformation of the entire social structure. They do not believe that the university could change the society; but it is felt that a revolutionized society would bring (as it presumably did in Cuba) the desired changes to the university. Where student groups of this kind were able to gain temporary control (e.g., in Caracas and in Quito), the university ceases to perform its educational functions and becomes a focus of revolutionary politics, allied and coordinated with outside political groups. (See Peterson, 1970.)

The Latin American public university is extremely unstable. Temporary gains of student protests and rebellions are frequently offset by repressive action of authoritarian governments (e.g., those in Argentina and Brazil).

Most of the time, disruptions caused by the actions of revolutionary student groups are not approved by the majority of the students, especially those enrolled in medical and engineering schools. Apparently, however, no effective organizational device exists to resolve conflicts within student bodies.

Of course, the students are not the only ones to demand changes in the traditional university structure. Much pressure has come from the segments of the society that were vitally interested in technological, economic, and organizational development. For example, the inadequacies of the technical schools is reflected by the observation that in Brazil "most of the major steel firms have special training programs for their engineers, both within the company and at universities. Volta Redonda (the state-operated steel plant) even established its own engineering school." (Baer, 1969:105–106) Every year thousands of Latin Americans are sent to the United States, Europe, or Japan to acquire specialized technical or scientific skills unavailable at home. And whenever new industries are established, it is usually the imported specialist who sets up the plant and trains nationals to take over operations when they become capable of doing so.

The proliferation throughout the continent of private institutions of higher learning suggests attempts to overcome the lag between the felt need for specialized education and the existing institutional facilities. Only 5 private universities were founded in Latin America during the nineteenth century, but 13 were established between 1900 and 1945, and 10 between 1946 and 1962. (Steger, 1965:55–56) In 1969 there were 119 private universities. The total number of component schools (*faculdades*), plus isolated establishments not integrated in a university, amounted to 633 in Spanish America by 1969. Brazil had 26 private universities by 1969, but there are no reliable figures on the total number of private faculdades. (Ruddle and Hamour, 1971:161) Most private institutions of higher learnings are owned and controlled by Catholic religious orders or by a bishopric. Some are lay institutions, however, and a few have acquired a reputation for being geared to the needs of a modernizing society: One of these, the University of Concepción in Chile, was probably the first Latin American institution to undergo (in 1960) radical structural change.

Apparently there were 115 public universities in Latin America by 1962. (Steger, 1965:56) Seven years later this figure had reached 140. Of these, 34 were located in Mexico, 14 in Argentina, 22 in Brazil, 17 in Colombia, and 21 in Peru. Of all 254 universities existing by 1968–1969, Mexico had 51, Argentina 38, Brazil 48, Colombia 40, and Peru 28. (Ruddle and

Table 26   *Latin American students enrolled in institutions of higher learning*

Country	Number of students		Increase (percentage)
	1962	1968–1969	
Argentina	166,000	271,496	63.5
Bolivia	7,900	22,910	190.0
Brazil	93,200	282,653	203.9
Colombia	29,000	62,844	116.7
Costa Rica	3,800	11,436	201.0
Cuba	26,000	35,490	44.2
Chile	31,000	52,937	70.8
Ecuador	9,000	19,600	117.7
El Salvador	2,400	4,536	89.0
Guatemala	4,000	11,890	197.0
Haiti	900	1,527[a]	69.6
Honduras	1,500	3,459	130.0
Mexico	142,000	188,011	32.4
Nicaragua	1,300	5,993	361.0
Panama	3,900	10,083	158.5
Paraguay	3,300	6,940	110.3
Peru	26,000	83,509[b]	214.0
Dominican Republic	5,000	9,893	97.8
Uruguay	16,000	17,561	9.8
Venezuela	24,900	72,649	19.1

[a] 1966–1967.
[b] 1967.

Source: Adapted from Hanns-Albert Steger, "Einige für das Verständnis des latein-amerikanschen Hochschulwesens wichtige historische und ökonomische Aspekte," in Hanns-Albert Steger, ed., *Gründzuge des lateinamerikanischen Hochschulwesens.* Baden-Baden: Nomos Verlagsgesellschaft, 1965; Kenneth Ruddle and Mukhtar Hamour, *Statistical Abstracts of Latin America 1970.* Los Angeles: Latin American Center of the University of California, 1971.

Hamour, 1971:161) Argentina, Brazil, and Mexico, the three most indus-trialized nations, contained 54 percent of all institutions.

The figures of Table 26 are approximations. They do not include normal schools whose status within the different educational systems is too variable to allow generalizations. In all countries a large majority of the students are enrolled in public institutions. The only exception seems to be Colombia, where enrollment in public schools did not exceed 53 per-cent of the total in 1968. With 41.7 percent, Costa Rica had the highest female enrollment, but Argentina was a close second with 41.6 percent in 1968–1969. In general female enrollment was close to or somewhat higher than one-third of the total. Only in Guatemala and Haiti was it under 20 percent. (Ruddle and Hamour, 1971:166)

The most significant changes do not lie in mere enrollment but in the emergence of new schools, or divisions within schools, specializing in the teaching of the natural sciences, mathematics, and the social sciences. Many of these schools now attract a substantial proportion of all students. In Mexico, for example, 26.1 percent of all students were enrolled in schools of economics and business administration in 1967. In Argentina it was 25.3 percent in 1969; and in most countries, the amount varied between 10 and 20 percent. The traditional bias against the study of the natural sciences and mathematics, *outside* the medical and engineering schools, seems still strong enough to hold enrollment to less than 10 percent. On the other hand, the traditional pull of law and the humanities continues to be strong. About 25 percent of all students are enrolled in law schools in Uruguay, Paraguay, and Guatemala. In Argentina and Brazil, law students constitute 16.7 and 19 percent, respectively, of all students. The humanities still have a powerful appeal in Costa Rica and in Brazil, where 28.1 percent of all students are enrolled in such courses. In Brazil, this trend is probably due to the proliferation of *faculdades de filosofia e letras* sponsored by states, municipalities, and religious orders, and frequently located in provincial towns. They attracted 44,802 students out of a total of 278,295 in 1969. (Cavalcanti, 1971: 117) What is happening in Brazil appears to be part of a generalized process that is bringing college education to numerous provincial cities where no comparable opportunities had been available. Supported by local politicians and populist governments, the rapid diffusion of such institutions certainly exceeds available economic, technological, and human resources, even in the most developed countries. There is little doubt that the majority of these institutions are colleges in name only.

We have very few reliable data on the Latin American university as channel of upward mobility. Analysts who engaged in (limited) research are in virtual agreement that relatively few students come from the working class. (Silvert, 1964; Scheman, 1963; Ganon, 1965) Hutchinson's analysis of a sample of 500 students of nine schools of the University of São Paulo in 1955 shows that 9.2 percent were of working-class origin and 16.1 percent came from the lower ranks of the middle class. (B. Hutchinson, 1960:151) However, such studies do not reflect the total extent to which the university serves as a channel of socioeconomic ascent. It usually takes more than one generation to cover the social distance between working class and university. It is safe to assume, for example, that most of the numerous bearers of Italian names among the university students of Buenos Aires, Montevideo, and São Paulo came from immigrant families that once occupied the lowest ranks of the social order; but it is likely that most of these families have belonged to the middle class for two generations or more.

To study the function of the university with regard to some of the ethnic groups located in São Paulo, we examined lists of students who had been accepted by various schools of the university. We singled out the individuals who could be identified without a shadow of doubt as members of certain ethnic groups by name alone. Most of these names were Slavic, Japanese, Jewish, German, Chinese, and Arabic. No attempt was made to include Italian names, and of course individuals of recent Portuguese and Spanish extraction could not be identified by name.

Among 420 students who had been admitted to the school of engineering, 37.6 percent bore "ethnic" names, and of these, 47.5 percent were of Japanese extraction. In a sample of 807 students who had been admitted to 20 medical schools in the state of São Paulo, 33.8 percent were bearers of "ethnic" names in the previously defined sense. Both lists were published in one of the newspapers of São Paulo City. (*Estado de São Paulo*, February 3 and 19, 1967)

These results may be read as a very definite trend toward a substitution of the traditional elites. They exceed by far the proportion of the total population that is constituted by any of the component ethnic groups.

Differentiation of the religious structure

Challenges from within and from without

The cumulative effects of culture change, described in previous chapters, could not fail to generate major adaptations in the religious structure. The Catholic Church was in no position to avert developments that it perceived to be at variance with its functions of creating social solidarity, of uniting men horizontally, and establishing "the vertical liaison of souls with God." (Bastide, 1951:344) Because of its union with the state, the Church had always held a salvation on monopoly; it had, at least nominally, controlled access to the supernatural to the exclusion of all other religious bodies. But the assumption that the Church was capable of carrying out this monopoly has been a major source of misinterpretations. At least two major changes reflect the contrast between the nominal position of the Church and its actual power capabilities. Beginning in the second half of the nineteenth century, the salvation monopoly of the Church was successfully challenged by a wide range of competing religious groups whose eventual consolidation resulted in a *pluralistic* religious structure. It is our contention that religious pluralism developed in a "power vacuum"—a kind of no man's land of "nominal" or "cultural" Catholics who could not effectively be reached by the Church.

The other major area of change lies in various attempts of the Church to come to grips with its internal problems, to stem institutional decay, and to mobilize its human resources. Of course, these two processes of change are not unrelated. For the first time since the conquest, the Catholic Church was forced to face competition with proselytizing emissaries who enjoyed the powerful backing of North American and European institutions. From the point of view of some Protestants, it was a kind of delayed Reformation that eventually reached Latin America.

Structural changes in the Catholic Church: reform or revolution?

The most serious obstacle preventing the Catholic Church from performing its self-assigned role was the scarcity of priests. It has been estimated that in 1750 there were 779 inhabitants per priest on the continent. In 1960 the average number of parishioners per priest was 15,332. (Houtart and Pin, 1965:23, 150) In the late nineteenth century, the clergy were ill-prepared to indoctrinate the faithful and to enforce the moral order the Church stands for.

Wherever the political relationship between government and the Vatican made it possible, the Church mounted a far-flung reform movement that eventually reached all regions of Latin America. Thousands of priests were imported from Europe and, much later, from the United States, to take over vacant parishes, dioceses, seminaries, monasteries, schools, and missionary centers.

In some countries, particularly in Brazil, the massive influx of European clergy began with the separation of church and state in 1891; in others it started much later, depending mainly on political relationships with the Vatican. Most foreign priests were members of religious orders, others belonged to the secular clergy. And in the wake of this clerical migration there came European nuns to take charge of schools, hospitals, and orphanages. The friars and monks who went to Latin America by the turn of the century viewed themselves as true missionaries entrusted with reconverting the people who had strayed from orthodox Catholicism. One of the basic objectives of the reform was the recruitment and training of native-born persons for the priesthood; but the creation of a native clergy turned out to be a formidable task indeed. In fact, up to the present time, the Church has not been able to recruit enough native-born priests to take the place of the foreign clergy. In 1960, out of a total of 37,636 Catholic priests, an estimated 50 percent were citizens of Spain, Italy, Germany, the United States, the Netherlands, France, Switzerland, Canada, and Austria. (Houtart and Pin, 1965:156-157)

The massive transfer of priests and nuns from Europe and North America was an aspect of secondary development that was accompanied by predictable adaptive problems. The priests came from extremely hetero-geneous national cultures, and in each, the development of the Catholic Church had proceeded along somewhat differing lines. The Spanish, Portuguese, and Italian clergy were known for their conservative attitudes regarding the role of the Church in society; the Dutch, German, and North American priests were more inclined to favor reform and experi-mental approaches to the problems of reconversion. On the whole, the foreign clergy who came to Latin America prior to World War I had been trained to purify the faith and to reestablish the moral authority of the Church, but they were hardly prepared to preach or carry out major social reforms to accomplish their purpose.

Compounding the problems of adaptation, more than half of all foreign priests belonged to a bewildering variety of religious orders. With reference to Brazil, for example, it was found that even in the 1960s, when the proportion of demographically Brazilian clergy was beginning to increase, 55 percent of members of men's religious orders (7515 in 1963) were foreigners, as opposed to 16.5 percent of the secular clergy; more than 65 percent of all priests (12,141 in 1963) were members of religious or-ders. (Ireland, 1972:350)

In addition to being very different from one another, religious orders are more rigidly structured than the Church as a whole; their members are bound by vows of obedience to their superiors, who have tended to issue directives not always adaptable to Latin American conditions. Ireland reports that in Brazil, 165 European-controlled orders set up their own school systems and initiated their favorite movements, always depending on directives from superiors abroad and employing models designed with European needs in mind. In addition to the problem of viability of foreign models, there has been an almost total lack of integration of these orientations and action programs into a horizontal structure. Small wonder then that ecumenism has been "easier between the Catholic Church and other churches, than between rival movements within the

Church." (Ireland, 1972:351) Needless to say, the situation in most parts of Spanish America is hardly different from that of Brazil. (See, e.g., Adams, 1970:278ff.)

It gradually dawned on the more innovative members of the clergy and laity that moral exhortation and the prospect of otherwordly rewards and punishments alone would not suffice to stem the growing alienation of the masses. Emile Pin's diagnosis of popular attitudes toward the Church and its priests in Valdivia (Chile) would fit almost any urban environment in Latin America:

> The priest is believed to be a member of a class other than that of the workers, for he does not live with them and does not maintain any contact with them. To them the Church is something totally alien. It is not a position of hostility, but of practically ignoring its existence. The Church is something for the rich and the women. (Pin, 1963:65)

Ideological alienation was intensified by the inability of the Church to recruit enough priests to serve the rapidly growing urban populations. By 1960 urban parishes had reached almost totally unmanageable sizes. In 1960 the estimated average population of urban parishes varied between 15,000 for Bogotá and 60,000 for Havana; but in most major cities the average parish encompassed from 20,000 to 30,000 people. (Houtart and Pin, 1965:151) Considering the extraordinary growth rate of all cities and the very limited success the Church has had in recruiting priests, one can only assume that parish populations have further grown since 1960.

It became increasingly clear to the innovators that the Church would have to embark on two major courses of action—namely, advocating structural changes that could deal effectively with major "social evils," and mobilizing lay members to help carry out the reforms deemed necessary.

Both courses were fraught with peril. First of all, striving for radical reform or revolutionary change would almost certainly generate factional conflict within the Church, involving laity and clergy alike. Furthermore, lay participation in crucial phases of what was visualized as "directed" social change might challenge the tradition of ecclesiastic authoritarianism.

Moreover, the responsibility for the execution of radical or revolutionary changes of the social order had been preempted by a number of socialist parties and factions. Any intrusion on the premises of what was understood to be "leftist" ideology might cause the intruder to be tagged as "communist."

Whatever the chosen course of action, the Church's dilemma was virtually inescapable, since any decision would be a political decision or, at least, would have political implications. The power of the Church, to use Adams' suggestive terminology, is *derivative* rather than independent. (Adams, 1967:40) It derives from a long-standing though sometimes precarious alliance with the ruling class, which was and still is vitally interested in maintaining the political status quo. By venturing into the high-voltage field of structural change, the Church would risk alienating the power holders, thus foregoing their protection. By refraining from radical reform, the Church would further lose its already feeble hold on the masses.

There had been factional conflict indeed between conservative and radical wings within the laity and the clergy, with some lay organizations defying Church authority by cutting themselves off from hierarchical control. (Ireland, 1972:348) In the 1960s "Christian radicalism" became rampant among lay youth organizations and a small sector of the clergy, but one would hardly expect the Church to move everywhere at the same pace and in the same direction. In Chile, for example, the Church played a pioneer role by developing a social ideology, based on such key concepts as the "Christian revolution" (Vallier, 1967:220) Translated into action during the 1950s, this "revolutionary" ideology brought distribution of Church land and technical training to underprivileged peasants, and cooperatives to shantytown dwellers.

In Argentina and Colombia, on the other hand, the Church has shown great reluctance to underwrite radical change. In fact, certain areas of highland Colombia may be the only remaining regions of Latin America in which the Church perpetuates an independent power domain, exercising almost absolute control over the rural populations.

Through its lay organizations, often under the leadership of "radical" priests, the Church has attempted to reach the people by organizing cooperatives, labor unions (*sindicatos*), and a variety of schools intended to bring literacy and technical skills to the lower classes. In Brazil, particularly in the northeast, educational campaigns were thought to be more meaningful if they included systematic efforts to make people aware of their own environment, "both as it *is* and as it *could* be." (de Kadt, 1970:103) This process, called *conscientização* by its advocates, came close to promoting subversion of the power structure.

Not surprisingly, Catholic reform movements met with repression in countries where they were perceived as threats to the established social order. The Brazilian military regime dissolved most activist organizations and exiled or jailed lay leaders and clergy alike. However, allowing leeway to a few radicals, the Church can appear to be satisfying demands for social change without compromising its middle-of-the-road trajectory. It seems to be acceptable to have one priest who is referred to as "the Communist," providing he is not successful. In Guatemala, however, one of the very few radical priests "was proving to be so threatening to the government that the Church sent him out of the country." (Adams, 1970:304) A few years later three American priests were expelled from Guatemala because of their announced intention to support revolution. (Adams, 1970:309)

The image of the revolutionary priest was embodied by Camilo Torres Restrepo, an able sociologist and Catholic chaplain at the National University of Colombia in Bogotá. After years of conflict with the hierarchy, Father Torres requested release from his clerical duties to join a "just revolution," which was being fought by a number of guerrilla bands. This he did "in order to be able to give food to the hungry, drink to the thirsty, dress the naked, and bring about the well-being of the majority of our people. I believe that the revolutionary struggle is a Christian and priestly struggle." (Fals-Borda, 1969:164) Father Torres was killed in combat with Colombian police forces.

The emergence of religious pluralism:
Protestantism, Spiritualism, and African religions

To understand religious differentiation in Latin America, it must be recognized that the Catholic Church had lost control of large segments of the society. National censuses inform us that around 97 percent or some similar proportions of the population of any given country is Catholic, but nothing could be more misleading than these figures. If Catholicism is measured in terms of religious practice as required by the Church, those proportions shrink to less than 20 percent, often to less than 10 percent, of the total population of a particular area. People may declare themselves to be Catholic in a somewhat hazy sense, but seldom is a definite commitment implied. Such "cultural" or essentially uncommitted Catholics are found in all social classes, but as one moves down in the social order, their proportion appears to be not only larger but correlated to the size of the local parish and the availability of priests. In other words, there has been, since the early nineteenth century, a steadily growing no-man's land in which people felt free to develop new and perhaps experimental approaches to the supernatural world *as they perceived it*. And by the middle of the nineteenth century this no-man's land had become a mission field for a variety of Protestant churches.

The diffusion of Protestantism proceeded from two different sources, however, and as two parallel and almost entirely separate processes. Early Protestant nuclei were established by European immigrants who merely wished to maintain their religious practices, usually without any proselytic intent. British subjects living in most major port cities and capitals were somewhat grudgingly allowed to build their chapels and pursue their customs. The significance of the British Protestants does not lie in numbers, but rather in their success at establishing small enclaves, backed by their mother country, thus challenging the salvation monopoly of the Catholic Church. Later "ethnic" churches appeared—22 were counted in Argentine alone (Read, Monterroso, and Johnson, 1969:82). There are Armenian, German, Slavic, Scandinavian, Dutch, Swiss, French, and Scotch churches, most of them with no more than a few hundred members, but a few are relatively large and are inclined to transcend ethnic boundaries and to evangelize Argentines.

The other source of diffusion is organized religious proselytism initiated mostly by established churches in North America and, to a much smaller extent, in Europe. By 1900 the Presbyterians, Methodists, and Baptists had been able to gain a definite foothold, at least in Brazil, where the total number of communicant members of all churches was 11,376—as opposed to 5,246 in the rest of South America. (Beach, 1900:225) In 1905 Mexico had 20,832 active Protestants, but the revolution impeded substantial growth for more than a decade. In 1916 there were 22,282 Protestants in Mexico, 10,442 in Central America, and 93,337 in South America. (Read, Monterroso, and Johnson, 1969: 41)

The expansion of Protestantism during the last half-century approximately has affected every country in Latin America. In 1967 the total number of active (communicant) Protestants in Latin America was reported to be 4,915,400. Among these, 3,313,200 were Brazilians, 441,700 Chileans, 429,900 Mexicans, and 249,500 Argentines, the remaining 281,100 being distributed over 13 countries excluding the Caribbean republics. (Read, Monterroso, and Johnson 1969:50) Since only communicants are included in these figures, the number of Latin Americans who either descend from Protestant families or were converted to the Protestant faith must exceed 10 million. Indeed, according to William Read and his colleagues, there may be 15 or 20 million. (Read, Monterroso, and Johnson, 1969:50)

The highly uneven distribution of Protestantism cannot be related to a single variable, but in some countries at least, there is a correlation between general culture change and growth of Protestantism. In Chile we found the heaviest concentrations of evangelical Protestants in areas whose social structure had been most strongly affected by industrialization and urbanization. In 1960 41.7 percent of all Protestants were concentrated in the two most heavily industrialized provinces of Chile—namely, Santiago and Concepción, which at the same time held 40.4 percent of the total population. (Willems, 1967b:271) In Brazil there is a marked contrast between the conservative northeast, containing 22.1 percent of the total population but no more than 9.2 percent of all Brazilian Protestants, and the eastern and southern states, which in 1960 held 85.7 percent of all Protestants and 70 percent of the total population. (Willems, 1967b:190–191) The relative strength of Protestantism in eastern and southern Brazil appears to derive from two circumstances: Most evangelical immigrants settled in the south, and the east contains the largest urban and industrial agglomeration of the country—São Paulo and its satellite cities. In 1960, in fact, 58.1 percent of the state's Protestants were living in this industrial area, although only 46.0 percent of the total population was located there. (Willems, 1967b:192)

It would seem that the changes attending rapid urbanization provide the sociocultural climate for the development of new religious creeds. A very large proportion of the urban population, particularly in the lower classes, consists of migrants and their immediate descendants, who had left behind them the tightly woven communities in which a change of religious affiliation would have met the sanctions of kinsfolk and landowners. On the other hand, the uprooted individual finds it difficult to orient himself in an improvised urban society. Emotional isolation and economic insecurity are intensified by social problems of staggering proportions. The religious sect appears to be one of several alternatives promising relief from the tribulations of life, and the most successful of these religious bodies are the ones that most effectively address the frustrations and aspirations of the underprivileged. The majority of these sects represent versions of Pentecostalism, or the belief in the descent of the Holy Spirit, Who temporarily possesses the faithful and bestows His "powers" on them. As a personal experience, available to all, it is mystical identification with the deity and a form of messianism that redeems here and now, rather than in an uncertain future. The Pentecostal sects are oriented toward the lower classes in ideology, religious teachings, ritual, and organization. Intellectual requirements are limited to reading the

Bible and religious tracts. The Holy Spirit comes to each individual, speaks and acts through him, and cures him of physical and mental ills. Spirit possession generates ecstatic euphoria and a feeling of power, in sharp contrast to the miseries of daily life and the political and economic impotence of the lower classes.

Equally important are the opportunities afforded to the convert to cooperate in the development of the sect whose egalitarian structure negates the principle of hierarchy, as well as clerical privilege and the rigors of social stratification of the larger society. In the extremely close solidarity of the sect, the convert finds the kind of moral and pragmatic support that appears to be rare in a haphazardly growing urban society.

If Protestantism as a whole grew by 95 percent from 1967, most of this rate must be attributed to the Pentecostal sects, whose communicant membership amounted to 63.3 percent of all active Protestants in Latin America. (Read, Monterroso, and Johnson, 1969:58) In Chile the proportion of Pentecostals stood at 81.3 percent in 1965, in El Salvador it was 73.7 percent; in Brazil the followers of Pentecostalism represented 68.5 percent of all evangelicals, and in Mexico they had reached 63.9 percent in 1965. Rapid Pentecostal growth has been reported from Argentina where in 1970 an estimated 50 percent of all Protestants belonged to various Pentecostal sects. (Read, Monterroso, and Johnson, 1969:90) Other countries, particularly Bolivia and Peru, reported much smaller proportions of Pentecostals, but relatively high growth rates seem to prevail almost everywhere.

Although the implantation of Protestantism in Latin America cannot be understood apart from other aspects of cultural change, particularly urbanization and industrialization, such changes fail to account for the highly uneven distribution of Protestant populations in different countries. An estimated 6.9 percent of the total population in Chile were practicing Protestants in 1960. At the same time, no more than 0.4 percent of all Colombians belonged to Protestant churches, and membership in Venezuela did not exceed 0.6 percent. The difference is not a reflection of different rates of sociocultural change, but perhaps such changes affected Chile much earlier than they did in either Colombia or Venezuela.

Protestantism was neither endogenous nor spontaneous. It was introduced by immigrants or implanted by missionaries, but organized proselytism appears to be a time-consuming task. Brazil and Chile were already intensively missionized in the 1800s, but Venezuela remained untouched by Protestantism until the early twentieth century. Furthermore, resistance to missionary endeavor was certainly stronger and longer lasting in some countries than in others. To the extent that resistance was (or still is) spontaneous, it might well be related to the corporate nature of the peasant community, which is far less receptive to extraneous influences than the open communities of eastern South America. Sometimes resistance took the form of prohibition of missionary activity by conservative governments. When Protestant congregations had already become permanent fixtures in Chilean towns, for example, no Protestant missions were allowed in Ecuador. These and perhaps other variables may account for the uneven development of Protestantism. Yet we are dealing with a process rather than a situation—the 67,101 Colombian Protestants represented no more than a tiny fraction of the total population in 1965, but that figure acquires a slightly different significance if we note that their numbers had more than doubled in only five years.

Two religious developments have affected Brazil to a far greater extent than Spanish America: Spiritualism and African cults. To be sure, religious cults of African origin have survived in various regions of Afro-America, but with the exception of the Caribbean islands, such survivals do not seem to play more than a limited role.

In contrast to the Protestants, the devotees of Spiritualism and African religions are virtually impossible to count because most of them declare to be Catholics and are registered as such by the census taker. In fact, these religions violate the Western pattern of mutual exclusivity of religious creeds and institutions, and the concept of pluralism suddenly acquires a somewhat different meaning. Thus we have not simultaneous but separate existence and reciprocal tolerance of groups adhering to differing norms and modes of behavior that are recognized as valid alternatives by society, but rather, groups of people professing beliefs and alternately engaging in forms of ritual behavior claimed by practitioners to be consistent but regarded by the society at large as mutually irreconcilable. Brazilian Spiritualism has been traced to the transfer of the teachings of Allan Kardec, but only since 1920 has Spiritualism assumed the proportions of a religious mass movement. In the 1930s Francisco Candido Xavier, a famous medium, reinterpreted and adapted Kardecism in nationalistic terms that were particularly meaningful to Brazilians. (Willems, 1966:218–219)

> Spiritualist sessions are attended by groups of faithful who number from five to one hundred. One or several of the participants are mediums who, at the ritual request of the leader receive disembodied spirits of various types. . . . The more "enlightened" spirits may offer so-called *passes* through the body of a medium, whose hands, touching head, shoulders and arms of a patient, are believed to com-

municate "beneficial fluids" facilitating the solution of physical, mental or moral problems. The therapeutic powers of a medium possessed by a spirit are comparable to those of a Pentecostalist who performs miraculous cures or is cured himself by temporarily partaking of the powers of the Holy Spirit. (Willems, 1966:209)

As Spiritualism grew, thousands of centers were integrated in federations. Twenty years ago there were 21 federations in Brazil, and most of them had joined the Brazilian Spiritualist Federation. (C. P. F. de Camargo, 1961:28) In the early 1960s a center of social assistance and evangelization, maintained in São Paulo City by the two largest regional federations, was sought by approximately 10,000 people every week. (C. P. F. de Camargo, 1961:28) The Brazilian census of 1960 counted 680,511 Spiritualists, but the actual number of people who occasionally or regularly seek the aid of mediums associated with Spiritualistic centers, is probably several times as high.

African cult forms, variously called *Macumba, Candomblé, Xangô*, or *Batuque* have been traced mostly to Dahomean and Yoruban ancestral forms. These regional designations cover relevant differences in areas of origin and in series of adaptive changes experienced by African religious beliefs and practices in Brazil. Many new deities were added to the African *orixás* or gods, and new and old ones were often identified with Catholic saints. In fact, effigies found in Bahia often carry the face of the saint on one side and that of the orixá on the other. Such religious syncretism on the folk level not only implies availability of supernatural resources of two diverse cultures, it also serves to disguise the practice of a religion that was rejected and often ruthlessly repressed by the ruling class. In Haiti Vodoun is a peasant religion, but Afro-Brazilian cults have required the anonymity of the city to survive and flourish. The *Candomblé* is one of several forms of organized worship carried out under the leadership of male or female priests (*pai* or *mãe de santo*) in buildings (*terreiros*) of unpretentious design and modest size, although some are well maintained and specially constructed with elaborate chapels and built-in seating arrangements for an audience. (Leacock and Leacock, 1972:47) The specialized personnel of the *Candomblé* includes a group of female mediums (*filhas do santo*) who are trained and initiated in the mysteries of the cult.

When all are properly arranged for the ceremony in the principal room of the *Terreiro* the *filhas do santo* in a circle, the *pai* and *mãe de santo* in the center, the drummers on one side, and the spectators in the back of the room—the *pai de santo* begins the *pade*, or the sacrifice to *Exu*. After this *despacho* come the songs and dances dedicated to various *orishás* [orixás]. These continue until late in night, the rhythm marked by the beat of the drums. It is a choreography hallucinating to the *filhas do santo*, with the total participation of the body—arms, hands, legs and head—in movements and contortions, rhythmic and violent, unceasing until the onslaught of the spasmodic manifestations and the final phases of the *queda no santo* (falling into the saint or trance). (Ramos, 1951:140–141)

One might be surprised that unlike many other traits of archaic or "primitive" folk cultures, African cults have not succumbed to the disintegrating influences of the modern city; thus they do not seem to be moving along toward extinction. Instead of vanishing, Afro-Brazilian religion has entered a phase of unprecedented growth. From obscure rituals of illiterate Negroes and former slaves, despised as manifestations of savagery by the society at large, it has blossomed into a highly differentiated, literate, and rather sophisticated religion, now found in all major urban centers of Brazil, from Belém in the north to Pôrto Alegre in the south. The uncountable devotees of African deities surely number in the hundreds of thousands. According to various estimates, the city of Salvador (Bahia), the traditional center of Afro-Brazilian religion, had between 500 and 600 cult centers in 1970. Belém in 1965 had more than 140 cult centers registered with the authorities. (Leacock and Leacock, 1972:45) There were, at the same time, an estimated 2600 men and women who considered themselves to be "mediums," and the Leacocks estimate the total number of committed believers in the Batuque to be greater than 10,000. (Leacock and Leacock, 1972:98)

Our present knowledge does not fully account for the success of Afro-Brazilian religion, but it is certainly not unrelated to the extremely high rates of internal migration. Without a continuous flow of people from the cities of the northeast to the northern and southern cities of Brazil, diffusion of African cult forms could hardly have taken place. As Afro-Brazilian religion spread, it showed an extraordinary capacity of adapting to and absorbing religious and magic elements that enhanced its credibility vis-à-vis the changing urban masses. Its alliance with folk Catholicism is close enough to allow worship to switch back and forth between African orixás and Catholic saints. In Belém, the curing techniques of the Batuque were found to be identical with "pajelança, the shamanistic tradition that has thrived in the Amazon Basin since the arrival of the first Europeans." (Leacock and Leacock, 1972:251)

Perhaps the most significant development of Afro-Brazilian religion was the emergence and rapid diffusion of Umbanda, a three-way syncretism associating African, Catholic, and Spiritualist elements in a loosely knit body of doctrine permitting unlimited local variations. (Bastide, 1960: 433ff.; C. P. F. de Camargo, 1961:36) Apparently, without assuming the characteristics of a schism, Umbanda originated in Rio de Janeiro and Guanabara State where it was reported to have about 30,000 centers in the late 1950s. (Bastide, 1960:33)

> Unlike the Spiritualist counterpart, the Umbanda leader appears to be a modern version of the shaman who competes with other shamans for control of the spirit world and those who believe in his powers. He is unlikely to surrender a fraction of his power to a federation, and if he does, it is usually external pressure or the impossibility of providing certain expected services which induces him to agree on an uneasy and precarious alliance with his competitors. There may be a local chief of police who loses no opportunity to arrest Umbanda leaders for "practicing medicine without a license" or for "breach of the peace." Experiences of this kind may convince the less influential Umbanda leaders of the advisability of joining a federation which has legal ways and means to protect them against high-handed police authorities. Nor is a local terreiro in a position to institute the kind of medical and social assistance which larger organizations can and do provide. The most effective and probably the largest organization of this sort is the Spiritualist Federation of Umbanda which claims to control 260 terreiros in São Paulo alone." (Willems, 1966:221)

Although the great success of Umbanda may lie in the belief that it is capable of curing all ills and solving all problems, its functions go well beyond these immediate objectives. The mediumistic abilities of the Spiritualists and Umbandistas confer a sense of power and achievement. A compensatory mechanism is put into motion when "meek public employees and humble domestic servants are suddenly transformed into vehicles of illuminated spirits, bearers of sublime messages." (C. P. F. de Camargo, 1961:125)

Whereas the Spiritualists proper seek the association of spirits that during their lifetime had achieved distinction and high status, the followers of Umbanda prefer to invoke the spirits of their lowly African and Indian ancestors. The spirits of slaves and of their former masters often appear in Umbanda sessions. Invariably, the audience learns that the spirits of the slaves have already reached the higher levels of perfection, while the masters are still tormented by the illusion of being incarnated— they carry heavy chains and need all the charity and patience of mediums and guides to take their first steps on the narrow path of spiritual ascent.

(C. P. F. de Camargo, 1961:125) The vindication of high status for the spirits of Indians and former slaves seems to be quite consistent with the desire to subvert the traditional social order and its value system. Since subversion cannot be carried out in reality, it is transferred to the spirit world, where the Indians and Africans occupy higher levels of perfection and the class of the masters is relegated to the lower levels. (Willems, 1966:230) In broader sense it may be said that Umbanda validates the Indian and African heritage of the lower social strata. (Bastide, 1960:230)

Originally Afro-Brazilian religion attracted only people of African descent, but as the number of practitioners and devotees grew, more and more people of diverse ethnic backgrounds joined the cult centers. In fact, Umbanda has acquired too many adherents of non-African descent to be regarded as a "Negro religion." In São Paulo, for example, "the whites attend, in large proportions, *the terreiros,* and even descendants of Italians, Syrians and Japanese seek in their practices the magic effectiveness which had not been unknown to them in their countries of origin." (C. P. F. de Camargo, 1961:35) Also in Belém, the African-derived religions have been found to draw members from the lower classes, regardless of race. (Leacock and Leacok, 1972:118)

Yet the lower classes are not what they were half a century ago. They have become increasingly literate and many practitioners of Afro-Brazilian religious cults are no longer satisfied with oral transmission of sacred lore. There is now what may be called an Afro-Brazilian theological literature of many hundreds of published items. Specialized stores in most major cities not only sell doctrinal treatises, but display in addition a wide variety of paraphernalia, including incense, herbs, amulets, effigies, and other items needed for the correct performance of religious rituals.

Finally, the clientele of Umbanda and the more orthodox cult forms is no longer exclusively of lower-class standing, at least in some cities. Virtually all students of Afro-Brazilian religion report the participation of middle-class people, although the proportion of such members is still mostly a matter of conjecture. At any rate, along with a change in the social composition of its clientle, Afro-Brazilian religion has gained the respect and the recognition of a larger segment of the society, and this has certainly contributed to the legalization of the centers and the removal of constant threats of harassment and persecution.

Allan Kardec's Spiritualistic gospel left its imprint all over the Western world, including Latin America; but nowhere did its diffusion approach to the extraordinary impact observed in Brazil. Apparently Argentina became a secondary center of publication and dissemination of Kardecist literature, and Kardecism has allegedly been flourishing in Mexico. (Kelly, 1965:2A) A folk version of Spiritualism, apparently unconnected with Kardec's teachings, has developed in Mexico, and in the mid-1950s Spiritualist centers were reported to exist from Torreon to Tehuantepec. (Kelly, 1965:3A)

Even the most superficial comparison reveals obvious similarities with Brazilian Spiritualism. Mexican folk Spiritualism is a somewhat nationalistic institution with a mestizo clientele of lower-class standing. Sessions are held in specially appointed *centros* or *templos*, and mediums are possessed by a variety of spirits, many representing mythological Indian ancestors. As in Brazil, the centers are attended by people seeking relief from all kinds of personal distress. (Kelly, 1965:8A–13A)

In many areas of Spanish America, the importation of African slaves was not large enough or consistent enough to prevent the Africans' total absorption into the population. It makes no sense to look for African survivals in Argentine, Uruguay, or Chile. Such cultural survivals have been reported, however, from a number of Caribbean and circum-Caribbean countries, although definite forms of African religion do not loom large among them except in Haiti. Where the Shango cult exists (as in Grenada), it is associated with Catholicism and Catholic saints. (M. G. Smith, 1965:6) The frequent occurrence of African cults has been reported from Cuba, but nowhere in the area has African religion found as much receptivity as in Haiti, where during the first 60 or so years of political independence it was virtually unhampered by the Catholic Church, which was in no condition to compete with Dahomean Vodoun. (Courlander, 1966:16–17)

Along with obvious similarities, there are three major differences between Afro-Haitian and Afro-Brazilian religions. In Brazil, African religion has been flourishing in the cities, whereas in Haiti (and in Cuba) it is primarily a peasant religion. In Brazil, African religion is practiced by a minority, but in Haiti its clientele encompasses virtually the entire peasantry. As a peasant religion, however, it has not diversified into more modern and sophisticated movements specially adapted to the vicissitudes of urban development.

Conclusions: common configuration and internal differentiation

To offer more than a descriptive account of Latin American culture, our inquiry was obliged to attempt to answer several fundamental questions. We did not assume the existence of a common Latin American culture but took it as a hypothesis to be tested. We began by comparing Brazil and Spanish America, but as the cultural process went beyond the formative phase, questions of regional adaptations and their conceivable impact on the cultural foundations became increasingly relevant. With the advent of political independence, the interaction between cultural evolution and national development had to be dealt with, and the problem of a common cultural identity grew in complexity with the emergence of a number of Hispano–American states.

The Portuguese and Spanish conquerors, it was emphasized, bore a common Iberian heritage molded by centuries of warfare against the Moors, by the religious fervor of the medieval Church, and by a polity characterized by patrimonial absolutism. The conquest itself shows differences as well as basic similarities between Spaniards and Portuguese. Spain and Portugal alike legitimized occupation and settlement through the institution of the land grant. Both created a privileged class of large landowners whose politico-economic position was enhanced and perpetuated by the transfer, from Iberia, of slavery and serfdom. The structure of the landed estate, one of the common denominators of Spanish and Portuguese America, weathered three centuries of colonial rule, survived the vicissitudes of political emancipation and revolutionary wars, and remained essentially intact until the Mexican Revolution.

The landed estate came to life in association with the patripotestal extended family and the kinship group, both transfers from Iberia. In Spanish and Portuguese America alike, the landed estates were owned by lineages rather than by families. Throughout the centuries the extended family and the landed estate grew on each other, and neither can be fully explained without the other. Contained within the structure of the landed estate also grew a dependent labor force, whose status became a major focus of tension and conflict among the historical power contenders of Latin America.

The rural labor force, whether servile or free, bore a subculture resembling that of the peasantry. It perpetuated African or Indian elements, usually in syncretistic association with Iberian traits. Lacking the centripetal attraction of landownership the family tended to be neither tightly structured nor extended, and "free" marital unions were (and still are) frequent.

The patrimonial state, embodied by the Spanish and Portuguese monarchs, was soon caught in a dilemma. To ensure the loyalty of the conquistadores and settlers it had to reward them with the spoils of the conquest —namely, land and labor. Land was granted and its Indian inhabitants entrusted to the grantees; slavery was legally instituted and the slave trade protected. Yet no matter how careful the Iberian kings were in granting privileges that might one day threaten their absolute rule, there was no way of avoiding the development of rural domains powerful enough to generate a tradition of noncompliance with the flow of royal decrees from Madrid and Lisbon.

The landowning, multifunctional family and kinship group was de facto or de jure in control of local politics. The Spanish policy of selling municipal offices to the highest bidder contributed to the firm entrenchment of local oligarchies, and many developed into miniature states within the state. Relation between the landowning kinship group and the patrimonial state were characterized by smoldering antagonisms and opposition, by competitive striving for power, and eventually by conflict that exploded into the wars for independence. This pattern of latent rebellion seems to lie at the roots of the revolutionary tradition born of these wars and their bloody aftermath.

The patrimonial state was autocratic by implication and so was its principal opponent—the seigneurial estate owner. In fact, he was an autocrat as head of his extended family, as boss of his labor force, as commander of his private army (if any), and as power contender in local politics. On the political level, connubial alliances with other extended families reinforced his position against competing power contenders, and uneasy compromises were apparent in cabildos and senados de camara, preempted as they were by a self-styled local aristocracy. As an autocrat, the seigneurial estate owner was not inclined to recognize the legitimacy of his competitors' political aspirations, nor was he willing to surrender all his power to the state. Thus existing political structures could be broken only by the use of force, and the stage was set for the dialectic interplay between autocracy and rebellion.

Another source of political anomie could be seen in the rather precarious control of the power holders over the Indian and slave populations. Indian uprisings were recurrent events, and bands of marauding runaways posed a perennial threat to the countryside wherever slavery had been implanted. And in addition to rebellious Indians and slaves, there was a growing mestizo population, rejected by colonial society for its spurious origin —a vast human resorvoir ready to be tapped by revolutionary leaders and a source of future caudillos.

The pattern of miscegenation emerging in Latin America was firmly anchored in Spanish and Portuguese customs. Interbreeding among the members of the three major racial stocks was universal and frequent enough to produce a large and steadily increasing population of mixed racial origin. The social classification of the mestizo was determined by apparent inconsistencies that cannot be understood without reference to family structure and political institutions. In Spanish America a white father could legitimize his mixed offspring and herewith remove the taint of *mestizaje*, and anyone whose *limpieza de sangre* was in doubt, could petition the king and be cleared, for a fee, by royal decree. The Portuguese, however, did without such elaborate legal instruments. As in Spanish America, racially mixed marriages were not unheard of, and the matrimonial bond itself removed racial taint, especially if the wife belonged to the native aristoc-racy. Prejudice and rejection was directed against those who had neither the protection of a wealthy father nor the resources to purchase a certificate of racial purity. Apparently, wealth was sufficient to pave the road to social ascent of the mestizo. And everywhere in Latin America political emanci-pation removed legal handicaps related to race, making upward mobility less difficult than before.

Miscegenation occurred (and still occurs) at two levels—within the do-main of the seigneurial estate (i.e., between the upper-class male and the lower-class female), and among the people of equal or nearly equal class status, particularly among the peasantry. Without capital and technical assets deriving from European cultural transfers, the peasantry had to rely on the resources made available by association with indigenous peoples. Many of the items of indigenous cultures absorbed by the peasantry came to them through marriage or consensual unions with Indian women.

It was among the peasantry that the greatest amount of racial and cul-tural hybridization took place. However, there appears to be a significant difference between the areas in which a sedentary Indian population sur-vived the decimating clash with the conquerors and the rest of Latin Amer-ica, where with few exceptions the indigenous peoples were exterminated or absorbed by the Iberian settlers. In the former type of area—Meso-america and the Andes—Iberian culture (mostly technology and religion) came to the Indian peasant community by imposition or by free choice. The initial blend crystallized behind the protective shield of the corporate community, whereas elsewhere selected elements of indigenous cultures were absorbed by open peasant communities that were basically Iberian. Brazil happens to be located in this area, but so are large sections of Span-ish America. At any rate, the outcome of the initial contact was a hybrid peasant culture, whether its bearers were Indians or mestizoes.

To grasp the cultural dimensions of the peasantry one must probe its relationships to the seigneurial estate and to the city. Often enough peas-ants were deprived of their holdings by estate owners, and this drove them into the economic and political orbit of the seigneurial estate or into areas of refuge. But coexistence of small holders and large estates was often feasi-ble. The peasant's ability to produce a salable surplus was determined by his relationship to the large estate on the one hand, and to the city on the other. More often than not the large estate showed little inclination to supply city markets with food; thus most urban populations had to rely on the agricultural production of small holders. In many regions of Latin America, however, the peasantry was barely able to rise above a precarious subsistence-level agriculture, not far removed from that of the tribal Indians.

Culture areas developing in traditional Latin America were either spontaneous adaptations achieved with predominantly local resources, as the Amazonian peasant culture and the pastoral cultures of the pampas or the llanos, or they resulted, like all plantation areas, from the transfer of entire cultural complexes. Whatever their characteristics, they did not coincide with political boundaries between Portuguese and Spanish America. On the contrary, none was exclusive to either region.

Urbanization was much slower in Brazil, than in Spanish America, and conquest and settlement showed little dependence on urban centers. The belated emergence of a mining industry in Brazil did much to speed up urbanization, but there remained a perceptible lag that did not begin to close until late in the nineteenth century.

Alleged differences in the physical structure between Spanish American and Brazilian cities were neither generic nor significant enough to justify separate categories. Whether Portuguese or Spanish American, the colonial city was a highly centralized structure; but socially it was a far cry from the two-class system often attributed to traditional Latin American society.

Among the different types of early urban development, the mining town stands out for its overall homogeneity. Within a global social structure said to be predominantly agrarian as well as rigid, the mining town anticipated the industrial city; its structure exhibited a high degree of instability, and as a center of conspicuous consumption, it commanded the agricultural resources of vast agricultural and pastoral areas. Being the continuous or sporadic place of residence of the surrounding rural patriciate, the city was largely controlled by the same extended families and kinship groups that dominated the countryside and the smaller towns. Perhaps more than any other single factor, the presence of the Catholic Church marked the colonial city. Much as it prevailed in the medieval city, it dominated the Latin American city through numerous churches and monasteries, religious orders and brotherhoods, and the celebration of religious fiestas dedicated to the patron saints of its parishes. More than any other cultural factor, Iberian Catholicism homogenized Latin America. At the folk level it compromised with indigenous and African beliefs and practices, and at higher levels it streamlined the intellectual elites, primarily through its educational institutions controlled by the Society of Jesus. The closest possible association with the state made it possible for the Church to monopolize institutionalized religion and to mold the Latin American mind until late in the nineteenth century.

To the cursory observer, political emancipation appears to be a sort of continental divide, throwing Spanish and Portuguese America on divergent courses of development. Any such divergences, however, turned out to be temporary and rather superficial. Brazil did not break up into a number of independent republics, although rebellion and caudillism repeatedly flared at local levels, but the dialectic interplay between autocracy and rebellion eventually came to be as pervasive in Brazil as in Spanish America.

Three centuries of relatively homogeneous evolution could not be reversed by political emancipation, which did little to alter the traditional social structure. In fact, certain developments of the nineteenth century reinforced rather than weakened cultural parallelism in Latin America. Ideological rejection of the Iberian heritage was accompanied by extensive borrowing of French, British, and North American philosophy, literature, art, educational systems, political constitutions, technology, and a life style that set the middle and upper classes even farther apart from the lower classes than they had been before. Many foreign models, particularly political constitutions, proved to be unadaptable without gross distortions reflecting an implicit decision of the ruling classes to prevent the structural changes demanded by the transfer of constitutional models.

The agrarian and mining basis of the Latin American economy not only persisted, but under the impact of the Industrial Revolution in Europe and later in North America, it entered a phase of unprecedented expansion. Coffee agriculture became a new source of wealth; sugar-producing areas multiplied, and wheat, beef, cocoa, and bananas expanded the domain of the seigneurial estate in regions previously unexploited. The mining sector was revitalized and greatly expanded as demands grew for silver, copper, guano, nitrate, tin, and oil.

The Industrial Revolution in Europe stimulated major cultural changes through the channels of international trade. All over Latin America urban enclaves of British merchants served as disseminators of new artifacts, new consumption habits, and a new style of living. Beginning in the middle of the nineteenth century, massive transfers of technology could be increasingly financed out of present and future income from the export trade. Again it was predominantly British capital and technical skills that created railway systems, steamboat lines, and modern port facilities. The infrastructure of the largest cities rapidly changed with the construction of gas and water works, sewers, trolley lines, and power plants. Built and supervised by British engineers and managers, who were later joined by other Europeans and Americans, these new establishments depended on the recruitment of domestic manpower. Thus a process of social differentiation (or division of labor) was set into motion that was to bring radical changes to the traditional structure of Latin American society.

Simultaneously, and also in connection with the development of international trade, the multiplication of banks and insurance companies, as well as the beginnings of a genuine industry, had similar differentiating effects on the urban social structure. European immigration, particularly to Argentina, Uruguay, and southern Brazil, accelerated the implantation of industries. In many cases the importers were also among the first industrial entrepreneurs; but the early social structure of industrial establishments, slowly developing from craft shops into mass-producing plants, often resembled the paternalistic familism of the agricultural estate. In spite of certain adjustment problems, industrial wage-earning had enough adaptive value to attract a landless rural proletariat that had been living on the edge of a fast-developing money economy.

Almost a century of expanding international trade created a substantial number of needs that could be satisfied only with imported artifacts, technical equipment, and food stuffs. Any disruption in the flow of imports was bound to stimulate domestic production of scarce commodities. This is exactly what happened when two world wars cut down on imports and the intervening worldwide depression sharply reduced income from diminishing exports. Four distinct phases of industrialization can be distinguished, but only three or four countries have reached the most highly differentiated technological phase in which industry commences to compete in international markets. Most Latin American countries are still in the first or second phase.

As industrialization proceeded and became an article of policy actively promoted by the state, international agencies, and private enterprise, the secondary nature of the process came to the fore, making it possible to transfer at once the most recent versions of technological and social inventions whose development had taken a century or more in Europe or North America. Along with desirable effects, there came about the undesirable and unforeseen chain reactions of secondary evolution. For example, Latin America became the scene of the almost explosive disintegration of the city and the vertiginous rate of urban growth. Uncontrolled and sudden expansion of urban areas, fed by internal migrations of unprecedented volume, generated shantytowns or squatter settlements in virtually all major cities. These settlements developed a way of life and their own cultural dynamics. Increasing occupational differentiation and a varying, but always substantial, structural mobility have been causing a series of changes in the former class structure. New upper, middle, and lower classes are said to exist, although the situation is far too fluid to permit us to assign definite class status to a number of occupational groups.

The rapid growth of the Latin American city is closely related to the population explosion that has affected almost all Latin American countries. At the root of the high natural increase rates lies the transfer of new scientific and technical resources that suddenly reduced mortality rates while birthrates continued high. The result has been a population growth that the economy is unable to absorb.

As urbanization proceeded, political power potentials shifted from the rural areas to the cities. No regime could hope to survive without relying on the urban areas, where an increasing proportion—often the majority—of the population was located. Marshaling political support required approaches different from those that had been used by seigneurial power holders, however. A variety of such approaches has been subsumed under the heading of *populismo*. The increasing social differentiation of urban society is reflected in a growing number of political parties and movements, many composed of people belonging to the same social class, and some advocating the total restructuring of the society by revolutionary means. In fact, the traditional pattern of rebellion has evolved into genuine revolutionary ideologies; revolution has occurred in Mexico, Bolivia, Cuba and until 1973 was being attempted in Chile through the constitutional means of the representative democracy. Urbanization and industrialization have produced new (mostly populist) power contenders who have been active in enlisting the support of large segments of Latin American society formerly excluded from political participation. The urban masses, and recently, their rural counterparts, have been intensively politicized; and to the extent that elections have been held, the number of qualified participant voters has grown substantially.

This sort of democratization is not synonymous with the diffusion of democracy in the North American sense; neither elections nor political parties are necessarily concerned with the maintenance or resurrection of representative democracy, which is merely one of several options open to victorious power contenders. The principle of autocracy is so deeply rooted in Latin American politics that its traces can easily be detected even in political structures modeled after the American or British institutions. Torn asunder by conflicting interests and incapable of solving such conflicts except by the use of physical coercion, the power contenders and their followers are typically forced into submission to the military, whose intervention is often actively sought as the only available alternative to civil war.

The mushrooming population all over Latin America, particularly the extraordinary growth of the cities, had to be matched by an expansion of food production. Extensive areas, formerly unexploited and scarcely known, were settled and brought under cultivation. Within the orbit of the big cities, peasants became farmers, and city-bound agricultural entrepreneurs, often of European or Japanese extraction, disseminated modern agricultural techniques. In some countries, agrarian reform contributed to the social and economic differentiation of the peasantry, and rural cooperatives as well as sindicatos begin to have an economic impact on traditional ways of life. The large estate itself began to develop from the technologically archaic, labor-intensive, family-run hacienda into the technologically modern, capital-intensive, corporation-owned plantation.

Large-scale internal migration, rapid urbanization, and industrialization are apparently affecting the traditional family structure in a way that fails to conform to current stereotypes. Available evidence indicates that the extended family, at least in the form of the personal kindred, has so far survived changes; but within the extended structure, the nuclear family has gained greater autonomy. At the same time, the position of the women has changed as educational opportunities and gainful employment have reduced controls formerly exercised by parents, male siblings, and spouses.

There is some evidence of the continuing viability of the extended family as an institution capable of providing valuable services to its members, in urban as well as in rural settings, in Spanish America as well as in Brazil. Its survival, including polygynous arrangements, seems to depend on the control, however limited, of economic resources.

However, the descent group, once the dominant form of kinship group on upper-class levels, seems to have given way to the kindred, whose composition is apparently geared more effectively to individual needs.

Of all the aspects of Latin American culture, none appears to reflect the social structure more faithfully than the educational system. In Spanish and Portuguese America alike, formal education was a class privilege, authoritarian, male oriented, and humanistic rather than pragmatic. Changes were intended to make formal education available to the lower classes and to women, and to fit the content of the educational process to the exigencies of an emerging industrial order. On the lower levels of the educational system, this meant reduction and eventual elimination of illiteracy, an objective that has been difficult to accomplish because of an extraordinary increase in members of the younger age groups. On the secondary level, change meant increasing differentiation and specialization of schools and a gradual moving away from the elitist principle limiting access to segments of the society that can defray the high cost of secondary education. Predictably, this trend has opened channels of upward mobility to the working class.

At the university level, the quest for change has been accompanied by controversy and conflict, often by violence. The students themselves have been active in changing the structure of the university, and the familiar interplay between authoritarianism and rebellion has generated frequent confrontations between student bodies and governments. However, student bodies are divided over what the modern university should be. Some demand participation in the governance of the institution, and expansion and modernization of its facilities; others look at the university as the training ground for revolutionary action that will remake the entire society. On the other hand, government policy has oscillated between extreme permissiveness and ruthless repression. The university systems of Latin America have expanded indeed, and enrollment figures have grown by leaps and bounds; but with rare exceptions, strikes, sporadic violence, and government repression have prevented the public university from offering education of the quality necessary to spur scientific and technological development. Whatever the shortcomings of the system, the multiplication of colleges, in capital cities as well as in many provincial towns, has made it possible for the university to serve as a channel of upward mobility.

Thus far our review of cultural changes has feasibly ignored the Catholic Church. This suggests the diminishing influence of an institution that once played a pivotal role in Latin America. Even today, however, the educational systems are either controlled by the Church or paralleled by educational structures owned and directed by religious orders. Not so long ago, the Church had a virtual monopoly over secondary education; but with the rapid expansion of public secondary school systems it has been losing ground in a number of countries. Nevertheless, the Church has been able to establish numerous universities, even though none of these institutions, whether secondary schools or colleges, have escaped the secularization of learning and scientific inquiry. All have to comply with secular legislation; technical and professional schools are undistinguishable from lay institutions, and there are not enough clergy to fill more than a small proportion of the teaching positions.

The scarcity of priests appears to be a major problem that has caused the Church to lose ground to competing religious bodies. In fact, in many areas the Church would not have been able to continue its religious services, limited as they were, without importing many foreign clerics. The multinational composition of the clergy, their allegiance to different religious orders, and their diverse cultural orientation, created as many problems as the additions to the priesthood solved. Because of its political alliance with the traditional upper class, the Catholic Church was bound to be criticized and beset by all the groups that felt the need for major reform or revolution, as the case might be. Thus factionalism within the Church, involving clergy and daity alike, was almost inevitable. In many cases, Church authority assumed a more progressive stance and initiated processes of guided change, but it was unable to stem the development of religious pluralism in many parts of Latin America.

Protestant denominationalism was implanted by European immigrants and, on a much larger scale, by Protestant missionaries. Within Brazil, Chile, Mexico, and perhaps Argentina, the dissemination of proselytic Protestantism appears to be related to industrialization and urbanization; but cross-national comparison shows widely differing rates of acceptance and rejection that cannot be explained in terms of those two variables alone. Of all Protestant bodies, the Pentecostal sects gained the greatest currency, suggesting that their emphasis on spirit possession and instant messianism, associated with a high degree of social solidarity, has met the needs of the lower classes to an extent unmatched by other creeds.

The presence of former slave populations from certain areas of West Africa seems to account for the survival of African cult forms in Brazil, Haiti, Cuba, and other parts of the West Indies. In Haiti, Vodoun fused with folk Catholicism and became a peasant religion. Syncretism with the Catholic cult of the saints also occurred in Brazil; but here African religion survived in the cities of the northeast and east, and its increasing differentiation somewhat reflects the growing heterogeneity of the urban lower classes. Far from succumbing to the secularizing influences of the modern city, African cults are thriving in many urban environments where they had formerly been unkown. Umbanda, a modernized and literate version of the African Candomblé and its counterparts, probably has more members than any of its parental groups. Umbanda also absorbed elements of Spiritualism, a European transplant that is very popular in Brazil. Like all African cults it is not felt by its practitioners to contradict Catholic doctrine.

No matter how different in some respects, Pentecostalism, African cults, and Spiritualism share a focal concern with spirit possession, and spirit possession is widely believed to have therapeutic value. Although the presence of Spiritualism and African religious survivals have been reported from certain areas of Spanish America, neither religious phenomenon gained as much currency there as in Brazil. Noteworthy is not only the relative ease with which these religious creeds spread, but also the people's desire and ability to reinterpret and work them into the fabric of national culture. It took no more than an initial effort of a handful of foreign missionaries to set into motion a widespread Pentecostal movement carried out by native missionaries. Spiritualism was nationalized by Francisco Candido Xavier and his followers, and African cults ceased to be the exclusive concern of blacks to become an integral piece of Brazilian folk religion shared by individuals of widely differing ethnic backgrounds.

The study of religious pluralism is consistent with our intention not to minimize processes of cultural differentiation within the common configuration of Latin American culture. Differences sometimes fall into categories, which may be conceived of as cultural types; these in turn may be homogeneously attached to geographical areas. The peasantry, the hacienda, the plantation, the corporate Indian community, the mining town, and the different social classes of the city are cultural types, and our own implicit typology is somewhat similar to the "typology of Latin American subcultures" proposed by Wagley and Harris. (Wagley and Harris, 1955: 428–451)

In contrast to these categories cutting across national borders, attempts have been made to arrange the Latin American nations into another kind of typology. Only two of these attempts can be mentioned here. One is based on the criterion of cultural orientation according to which Latin America "may be divided into countries of European origin or orientation, those of heavy Indo-mestizo population, and those with heavy Negro population; and these categories are not mutually exclusive." (Beals, 1953:329) Five countries—namely, Argentina, Uruguay, Chile, Costa Rica, and Santo Domingo belong to the first category; Ecuador, Colombia, Venezuela, Panama, Haiti, Cuba, and Brazil are assigned to the last type and all others belong to the group characterized by a "heavy Indo-mestizo population." Doubtlessly countries such as Mexico, Guatemala, Ecuador, Peru, and Bolivia have large Indian populations, constituting distinct subcultures some of which cut across national borderlines. But does this mean that the cultural orientation of whole nations like Mexico or Peru is influenced by its Indian population to the point of setting it apart from nations labeled "European" or "Euro-American"? There is no evidence that the Indian cultures have any bearing on national institutions. On the contrary, all sedentary Indian communities have changed under the westernizing influences of economic development, internal migration, and government policies intended to incorporate the Indians into the national society.

To attribute Indian orientation to countries with large mestizo population seems even more unreal. At least the urbanized mestizoes are known to rid themselves of any thing that could possibly be taken as vestiges of their Indian ancestry. And whatever the number of Indian elements preserved by rural mestizoes, their influence never goes beyond the boundaries of the region they inhabit. While certain Indian populations have so far preserved their cultural identity, no such assertion could be made concerning the Negro populations of Latin America. There are, as we have seen, survivals of religious cults, heavily mixed with Catholic components; food items, dances, musical style, drums, and a few more items could be added, but there is no full-fledged African culture in Latin America (with the possible exception of bush Negroes in Surinam), and even if there were, its influences would have little chance of rising above the folk level. The notion that the cultural orientations of such nations as Brazil or Cuba could be affected by "Negro" elements (whatever they may be) borders on the preposterous. As a matter of fact, the presence or absence of Indian, mestizo, or Negro populations seems to have no bearing on the cultural orientations observed at the national level.

Equally open to doubt is the assumption that the cultural orientation of some countries is "predominantly European" or "Euro-American." Heavy cultural borrowing from Europe has been going on continuously since the days of the conquest; *all* countries have been deeply involved in this process, and many European models are still distinguishable in custom and law, in the economy and polity, in literature and art. In addition, ethnic minorities that are not yet totally assimilated have preserved some cultural traits brought by their ancestors from Italy or Germany, from Poland or Great Britain; but none of these groups has been able to exert a decisive influence on the cultural orientation of the nation immigrated to. On the contrary, a rather stringent and at times fanatical nationalism has been at work to encourage assimilation and to disparage adherence to ethnic variants. At any rate, there does not seem to be any country in Latin America that has not succeeded in creating its own cultural identity and orientation, none of which could possibly be taken as "European."

The criterion of development has been frequently used to establish typologies of Latin American nations. (Purely economic typologies based on such indicators as gross national product, income per capita, and industrial production are omitted here because they present no more than a single aspect of any particular culture.) However, there has been at least one attempt to characterize development by combining economic indices such as per capita income, per capita consumption of electricity, cement, and newsprint, with data on urbanization, occupational structure, illiteracy, enrollment in schools and universities, newspaper circulation, number of radio sets, total seating capacity of movie theaters, number of doctors per 100,000 inhabitants, number of inhabitants per hospital bed, birth and death rates, and the ethnic composition of the population. (Vekemans and Segundo, 1963:88–89) On the basis of the aforementioned indices, the authors distinguish five groups or socioeconomic types of Latin American countries. Argentina, Chile, and Uruguay rank highest; and Haiti, Guatemala, Honduras, the Dominican Republic, Nicaragua, and El Salvador are at the bottom of the ladder. Brazil and Mexico are grouped together and occupy a middle position. The type next to the highest-ranking one is composed of Panama, Costa Rica, Venezuela, and Cuba.

Since the authors do not claim that their classification constitutes a *cultural* typology, they should not be criticized for not accomplishing something they never intended. Too many cultural elements are absent from their table of indicators, and similar figures do not necessarily express cultural affinities. Furthermore, a typology is presumably based on the assumption of relative stability. The statistical sources used to establish the Vekemans-Segundo socioeconomic typology go back to 1950 and before; but, the socioeconomic changes that have occurred in the last 25 years are so numerous and of such magnitude that if the attempted typology were revised today, it would look quite different.

If such typologies are difficult to establish, any endeavor to delineate cultural areas under conditions of massive and rapid change would be an exercise in futliity. Almost 40 years ago, Ralph Linton warned that applicability of the culture area concept is contingent on "static culture conditions" and that it "breaks down entirely" wherever population movements are in progress. (Linton, 1936:388) Population movements tend to destroy homogeneity implicit in the concept of culture area, exactly as they destroyed the homogeneity of pampas or the llanos. At present, no major region of Latin America appears to be stable and homogeneous enough to allow a meaningful application of the culture area concept.

But there remains the idea of national culture, which was occasionally referred to without explanation. Needless to say, in Latin America as elsewhere, each nation, claims its own cultural identity. In an era of intense nationalism, the obvious cultural unity of Ibero-America itself seems to call for a compensatory mechanism enhancing differences rather than similarities. Of course, the idea that a century and a half of independent existence should have produced a sequence of unique historical events in each country has indubitable validity. Each nation attaches specific meanings to the wars and revolutions in which it has been involved. Each nation has its statesmen, generals, heroes, martyrs, and villains, who are remembered with love, admiration, or shame. Each nation takes pride in a set of symbols that may be unknown or meaningless to all others. And presumably the people of each country adhere to modes of behavior by which they recognize themselves and their compatriots. The total of all these modes of thinking, acting, and feeling supposedly constitutes the national character of the Brazilians, for example, as distinct from those of the Argentines, Paraguayans, or Mexicans.

Unfortunately, national character research has failed to produce more than a few tentative results. Some Latin American writers have attempted national self-interpretations, but qualities they regard as unique are often shared by other Latin American nations. For example, according to some authors, Mexicans are disinclined to accept authority, which is looked on as arbitrary and capricious. "Thus the Mexican is a rebel and a would-be dictator, not a fanatical cog in a state machine." (Needler, 1971:159) This sentence seems to describe what we have called the dialectic interplay between autocracy and rebellion, seen in the perspective of the personality structure. It appears to be common to all of Latin America, as are many other traits that are regarded by particular nations as being components of their own unique cultural heritage. Indeed, it has been pointed out that traits allegedly unique in Latin America can be traced to the Mediterranean area of which Iberia is but a part. (Quigley, 1973:319ff.)

More relevant perhaps than such vague and somewhat naïve conjectures about national character seems to be the question of the role of revolution in generating more definite behavioral and institutional differences among the Latin American republics. Far more radical than the others, the Cuban Revolution perhaps marks the birth of a new species within the genus Latin America. It certainly appears that the almost total destruction of the traditional class structure, the elimination of the seigneurial estate and its corporate successors, and a remaking of the institutions reflecting class privileges and private power domains, are irreconcilably opposed to many basic characteristics by which we identify Latin American culture. On the other hand, authoritarianism and intense nationalism, inherent in the Castro regime, fit the general pattern. Whether rebellion, the traditional reaction to authoritarian rule, has in fact been eliminated remains to be seen.

Of course, socialism of one kind or another has been widespread in thought and in action, in political parties and in government programs. Some nations have carried out socialist changes, by revolutionary fiat or by legislation; others have been experimenting with legislative changes combining, for example, agrarian reform and the development of private industrial enterprise. Thus to the extent that genuinely revolutionary forces are at work in some countries, while others cling to more conservative approaches, one may expect increasing cultural differentiation among the Latin American republics.

Glossary

affinal Referring to relationships by marriage with a consanguine relative of a spouse or with the spouse of a consanguine relative.

agregado Resident farm hand; also tenant farmer or sharecropper.

anomie A state of sociocultural disorganization in which traditional norms of behavior have lost much of their regulating force and emergent norms are not yet generally recognized.

audiencia In Spanish America the advisory and judicial body subordinate to the viceroys.

bandeirismo In Brazil events relating to the colonial exploratory expeditions called *bandeiras* and organized to enslave Indians and to search for mineral wealth..

barragania In Spanish America, concubinage.

barrio In Spanish America a city district often coinciding with a parish.

caatinga Semiarid region of northeastern Brazil characterized by thorny, stunted vegetation.

cabalgada In medieval Spain a raiding party organized to move rapidly and to inflict damage on the enemy.

cacique Indian chieftain. In contemporary Latin America, a local political leader. The term frequently carries a derogatory meaning.

candomblé In Brazil a complex of religious rites whose original forms were introduced by African slaves. *Macumba, xangô, umbanda,* and *batuque* are regional variants of the *candomblé.*

capitania An administrative division of colonial Brazil.

capitão Portuguese colonial functionary in charge of a *capitania.* Full title was *capitão-mor.*

chacara A small farm in the vicinity of a town.

compadrazgo Ceremonial kinship tie between a person and the godfather of his child. In Portuguese, *compadrio.*

composición In colonial Spanish America an institution designed to legalize ownership of land that had been in the possession of the petitioner.

conjugal family See nuclear family.

consanguinal Related by blood or consanguinity.

coronel In Brazil the local political boss.

crystallization Series of changes resulting into adaptation and consolidation of Iberian culture in America.

encomienda In early colonial Spanish America, a royal grant by which a number of Indian families were entrusted to a Spaniard, the *encomendero,* who was entitled to exact tribute and labor services from these Indians.

estancia Usually a cattle ranch. In colonial Spanish America, *estancia, hacienda,* and *hato* were synonymous.

extended family Social group consisting of several interrelated nuclear families.

fazenda In Brazil a large agricultural or pastoral establishment.

finca In Spanish America a farm.

foreiro A leaseholder, usually of a rural property. In Spanish, *forero.*

gamonalismo In Spanish America a system of political control exercised by *gamonales* or political bosses.

hacienda In Spanish America a large landed estate.

hato In Spanish America a farm or cattle ranch.

inquilino In Spanish America a farmhand living on a *hacienda.*

kindred A group of relatives related through male and female lines.

ladino Member of the westernized upper class of certain areas of southern Mexico and Central America.

lavrador In Brazil anybody who cultivates the soil with his own hands. In some areas a sharecropper.

mayorazgo In Spanish America an entailed estate whose inheritance was limited to the eldest son of a family. In Brazil the institution was called *morgadio.*

mameluco On Brazil a person of mixed Portuguese and Indian parentage.

merced de tierra In colonial Spanish America a royal land grant.

mestizo In Spanish America a person of mixed Spanish and Indian ancestry.

municipio In most countries of Spanish America and in Brazil, a local administrative division roughly comparable to a county.

nuclear family Social group consisting of husband, wife, and their children.

patriarchal Referring to an extended family structure in which authority is vested in the eldest male.

patripotestal Referring to a family structure in which the authority is vested in the father or paternal grandfather.

polygyny Formal or consensual marriage of a man to more than one woman.

rancho In Venezuela a shanty in an urban squatter settlement.

reduction   Sociocultural process of selection by which certain Iberian cultural elements were accepted or rejected in America.

regidor   In Spanish America a member of a municipal council.

seigneurial   Of or having to do with the self-styled landholding aristocracy of Latin America.

sesmaria   In Brazil a land grant bestowed by the king or, later, by the imperial government.

sertão   In Brazil sparsely settled or uninhabited backland regions.

vecino   In colonial Spanish America a person classified as a Spanish citizen.

vereador   In Brazil a member of a municipal council.

Bibliography

ABRAMS, CHARLES *Man's Struggle for Shelter in an Urbanizing World.* Cambridge, Mass.: M.I.T. Press, 1964

ADAMS, D. W., AND A. E. HAVENS *The Place of Socio-Economic Research in Developing a Strategy of Change for Rural Communities: A Colombian Example.* Madison: Land Tenure Center of the University of Wisconsin. Mimeographed, n.d.

ADAMS, RICHARD N. *A Community in the Andes.* Seattle: University of Washington Press, 1959.

"Social Change in Guatemala and U.S. Policy," in Richard N. Adams, John P. Gilling, Allan R. Holmberg, Oscar Lewis, Richard Patch, and Charles Wagley, eds., *Social Change in Latin America Today.* New York: Vintage, 1961.

ADAMS, RICHARD NEWBOLD *The Second Sowing: Power and Secondary Development in Latin America.* San Francisco: Chandler, 1967.

Crucifixion by Power. Essays on Guatemalan National Social Structure, 1944–1966. Austin: University of Texas Press, 1970.

AGULLA, JUAN CARLOS *Eclipse de una Aristocracia.* Buenos Aires. Ediciones Libera, 1968.

ALBERTI, GIORGIO *Intervillage Systems and Development. A Study of Social Change in Highland Peru.* Ithaca, N.Y.: Cornell University Press, 1970

ALDEN, DAURIL *Royal Government in Colonial Brazil.* Berkeley and Los Angeles: University of California Press, 1968.

AMATO, PETER WALTER *An Analysis of the Changing Patterns of Elite Residential Areas in Bogotá, Colombia.* Dissertation Series. Ithaca, N.Y.: Cornell University Press, 1968

ANDERSON, CHARLES W. *Toward a Theory of Latin American Politics.* Nashville, Tenn.: Vanderbilt University, Graduate Center for Latin American Studies, Occasional Paper No. 2.

ANONYMOUS *El Desarrollo Económico de la República Argentina.* Buenos Aires: Ernesto Tornquist, 1920.

ARGENTINA, DIRECCION NACIONAL DE ESTADISTICA Y CENSOS *Informe Demográfico de la República Argentina, 1944–1954.* Buenos Aires, 1956.

ASTIZ, CARLOS A. "Introduction," in José Luiz de Imaz, *Los que Mandan.* Albany: State University of New York Press, 1970.

AZARA, FELIX DE *Viajes por la América Meridional,* 2 vols. Madrid: Calpe, 1923.

AZEVEDO, FERNANDO DE *A Cultura Brasileira.* Rio de Janeiro: Servico Gráfico do Instituto Brasileiro de Geografia e Estatística, 1943.

AZEVEDO, THALES DE "Indios, Brancos e Pretos no Brasil Colonial," *América Indígena,* 8, no. 2. Mexico City: Instituto Indigenista Interamericano, 1963.

BAER, WERNER *The Development of the Brazilian Steel Industry.* Nashville, Tenn.: Vanderbilt University Press, 1969.

"Import Substitution Industrialization in Latin America: Experiences and Interpretations," *Latin American Research Review,* 7, no. 1 (1972).

BAGÚ, SERGIO *Estructura Social de la Colonia.* Buenos Aires: Libreria el Ateneo Editorial, 1952.

BANCO CENTRAL DE VENEZUELA *Informe Económico 1970.* Caracas.

BARGALO, MODESTO *La Mineria y la Metalurgia en la América Española durante la Epoca Colonial.* Mexico City: Fondo de Cultura Económica, 1955.

BASTANI, TANUS JORGE *O Líbano e os Libaneses no Brasil.* Rio de Janeiro: C. Mendes Junior, 1945.

BASTIDE, ROGER "Religion and the Church in Brazil," in T. Lynn Smith and Alexander Marchant, eds., *Brazil: Portrait of Half a Continent.* New York: Dryden, 1951.

Les Religions Africaines au Brésil. Paris: Presses Universitaires de France, 1960.

BATESON, GREGORY "Culture Contact and Schismogenesis," *Man,* 35 (1935).

BEACH, HARLAN P., ET AL. *Protestant Mission in South America.* Chicago: Missionary Campaign Library, 1900.

BEALS, RALPH L. "Social Stratification in Latin America," *American Journal of Sociology,* 68 (1953).

"Social Stratification in Latin America," in Dwight B. Heath and Richard N. Adams, eds., *Contemporary Cultures and Societies in Latin America.* New York: Random House, 1965.

BELLO, JULIO *Memórias de un Senhor de Engenho.* Rio de Janeiro: Livraria José Olympio, 1948.

BEMDOC *Vial Proletária da Penha.* Rio de Janeiro: 1965.

BERLINCK, MANOEL TOSTA *The Structure of the Brazilian Family in the City of São Paulo.* Ithaca, N.Y.: Cornell University Press, 1969.

BIESANZ, JOHN, AND MAVIS BIESANZ *Costa Rican Life.* New York: Columbia University Press, 1944.

BLASIER, COLE "Studies of Social Revolution: Origins in Mexico, Bolivia and Cuba," *Latin American Research Review,* 2, no. 3 (1967).

BON ESPASANDIN, MARIO *Cantegrilos*. Montevideo: Editorial Alfa, 1963.

BOXER, C. R. *Race Relations in the Portuguese Colonial Empire, 1415–1825*. Oxford: Clarendon, 1963.

The Golden Age of Brazil, 1695–1750. Berkeley and Los Angeles: University of California Press, 1969.

BRANDÃO LOPES, JUAREZ RUBENS *Crisis do Brasil Arcáico*. São Paulo: Difusão Européia do Livro, 1961.

BRITO FIGUEIROA, FEDERICO *Historia Económica y Social de Venezuela*, vol. 1. Caracas: Universidad Central de Venezuela, 1966.

BROWNING, HARLEY L., AND WALTRAUT FEINDT "The Social and Economic Context of Migration to Monterrey, Mexico," in Francine F. Rabinovitz and Felicity M. Trueblood, eds., *Latin American Urban Research*, vol. 1. Beverly Hills, Calif.: Sage, 1971

BUARQUE DE HOLANDA, SÉRGIO *Raizes do Brasil*. Rio de Janeiro: Livraria José Olympio, 1948.

BUTTERWORTH, DOUGLAS S. "A Study of the Urbanization Process Among Mixtec Migrants from Tilantongo in Mexico City," in William Mangin, ed., *Peasants in Cities*. Boston: Houghton Mifflin, 1970.

CABRAL DE MONCADA, LUIS *O Casamento em Portugal na Idade Média*. Coimbra: Losada, 1922.

CAJA COLOMBIANA DE AHORROS *Memória del Primer Congreso Latinamericano del Ahorro*. Bogotá: Talleres Gráficos del Banco de la Republica, 1968.

CAMARGO, CÁNDIDO PROCÓPIO FERREIRA DE *Kardecismo e Umbanda*. São Paulo: Livraria Pioneira Editora, 1961.

CAMARGO, J. F. *A Cidade e o Campo*. São Paulo: Editora da Universidade de São Paulo, 1968.

CANCIAN, FRANK "Political and Religious Organization," in Robert Wauchope, ed., *Handbook of Middle American Indians*, vol. 6. Austin: University of Texas Press, 1967.

CANDIDO, ANTONIO "The Brazilian Family," in T. Lynn Smith and Alexander Marchant, eds., *Brazil: Portrait of Half a Continent*. New York: Dryden, 1951.

Os Parceiros do Rio Bonito. Rio de Janeiro: Livraria José Olympio Editora, 1964.

CARDONA GUTIERREZ, RAMIRO "Migración, Urbanización y Marginalidad," in Ramiro Cardona Gutierrez, ed., *Urbanización y Marginalidad*. Bogotá: Publicación de la Asociatión Colombiana de Faculdades de Medicina, 1968.

CASTRO, DICKEN *La Guadua*. Bogotá: Talleres Gráficos del Banco de la Republica, 1964.

CAVALCANTI, FLAVIO *Brasil em Dados*. Rio de Janeiro: Editoração de Índice; Banco de Dados, 1971.

CERECEDA, RAUL *Las Institutiones Políticas en América Latina*. Friburgo and Bogotá: Oficina Internacional de Investigaciones Sociales de FERES, 1961.

CHARDON, ROLAND E. "Changes in the Geographic Distribution of Population in Brazil, 1950–1960," in Erik N. Baklanoff, ed., *New Perspectives of Brazil*. Nashville, Tenn.: Vanderbilt University Press, 1966.

CHEVALIER, FRANÇOIS *Land and Society in Colonial Mexico*. Berkeley and Los Angeles: University of California Press, 1963.

CHUECA GOITIA, FERNANDO, AND LEOPOLD TORRES BALBAS *Plano de Ciudades Iberoamericanas y Filipinas*, vol. 1. Madrid: Instituto de Estudios de Administración Local, 1951.

COCHRAN, THOMAS C., AND RUBEN E. REINA *Enterpreneurship in Argentine Culture*. Philadelphia: University of Pennsylvania Press, 1962.

COLEMAN, WILLIAM J. M. *Latin American Catholicism*. New York: World Horizon Reports, Maryknoll Publications, 1958.

COLLIN-DELAVAUD, CLAUDE *Consecuencias de la Modernización de la Agricultura en las Haciendas de la Costa Norte del Perú.* Lima: Instituto de Estudios Peruanos, 1967.

COLOMBIA INFORMATION SERVICE *Colombia Today.* Newsletter published by Colombia Information Service.

CONI, EMILIO A. *El Gaucho: Argentina/Brasil/Uruguay.* Buenos Aires: Editorial Sudamericana, 1945.

CONJUNTURA ECONOMICA Vol. 25. Rio de Janeiro, 1971.

COSIO VILLEGAS, DANIEL, ed. *El Porfiriato: La Vida Económica. Historia Moderna de México,* vol. 7. México City: El Colegio de México, 1960.

COSTA PINTO, LUIS AGUIAR DE *Lutas de Famílias no Brasil.* São Paulo: Companhia Editora Nacional, 1949.

COTLER, JULIO *El Populismo Militar como Modelo de Desarrollo Nacional. El Caso Peruano.* Lima: Instituto de Estudios Peruanos, 1967.

Organizaciones Campesinas en el Perú. Lima: Instituto de Estudios Peruanos, 1968.

COURLANDER, HAROLD *Religion and Politics in Haiti: Vodoun in Haitian Culture.* Washington, D.C.: Institute for Cross-Cultural Research, 1966.

COUTU, ARTHUR J., AND RICHARD A. KING *The Agricultural Development of Peru.* New York: Praeger, 1969.

CRIADO DE VAL, M. *Fisionomia del Idioma Español.* Madrid: Aguilar, 1954.

CRIST, RAYMOND "Life on the Llanos of Venezuela," *Bulletin of the Geographic Society of Philadelphia,* 35 (1942).

"Geography and Caudillism: A Case Study," in Hugh M. Hamill, Jr., ed., *Dictatorship in Spanish America.* New York: Knopf, 1965

CRUZ, GUILLERMO FELIU *Santiago a Comienzos del Siglo XIX.* Santiago: Editorial Andrés Bello, 1970.

CUEVAS, MARCO ANTONIO *Análisis de Tres Areas Marginales de la Ciudad de Guatemala.* Guatemala City: Ministerio de Educación, 1965.

CZAJKA, WILLI Buenos Aires als Weltstadt; in Joachim H. Schultze, ed., *Zum Problem der Weltstadt.* Berlin: de Gruyter, 1959.

DA COSTA, P. AVELINO DE JESUS "População da Cidade da Bahia em 1775." Coimbra: *V. Colóquio Internacional de Estudos Luso-Brasileiros,* 1965.

DA CUNHA, EUCLIDES *Rebellion in the Backlands.* Chicago: University of Chicago Press, 1944.

DAVIS, KINGSLEY "Political Ambivalence in Latin America," *Journal of Legal and Political Sociology,* 1, nos. 1–2 (October 1942).

DEAN, WARREN *The Industrialization of São Paulo, 1880–1945.* Austin: University of Texas Press, 1969.

DE KADT, EMANUEL *Catholic Radicals in Brazil.* New York: Oxford University Press, 1970.

DELLA CAVA, RALPH *Miracle at Joaseiro.* New York: Columbia University Press, 1970.

DENTON, CHARLES F. *Patterns of Costa Rican Politics.* Boston: Allyn & Bacon, 1971.

DEPARTAMENTO DE ESTATÍSTICA DO ESTADO DE SÃO PAULO *Favelas de São Paulo.* Unpublished results of a census of shantytowns in the city of São Paulo. March–July 1968.

DESAL-CELAP (Centro para el Desarrollo Económico y Social de América Latina-Centro de Estudios Latinoamericanos de Población)

Encuesta sobre la Familia y la Fecundidad en Poblaciones Marginales del Gran Santiago, 1966–1967. Santiago: Desal-Celap, 1968.

DESCOLA, JEAN *La Vida Cotidiana en el Perú en Tiempos de los Españoles, 1710–1820.* Buenos Aires: Hachtte, 1962.

DIRECCION GENERAL DE ESTADISTICA *Aunário Estadístico de Venezuela.* Caracas: Dirección General de Estadística y Censos Nacionales, 1972.

DOZIER, CRAIG L. *Land Development and Colonization in Latin America.* New York: Praeger, 1969

DRAPER, THEODORE *Castroism: Theory and Practice.* New York: Praeger, 1965.

EASTON, DAVID "Political Anthropology," in Bernard Siegel, ed., *Biennial Review of Anthropology, 1959.* Stanford, Calif.: Stanford University Press, 1959.

ECLA (Economic Commission for Latin America) *The Process of Industrial Development in Latin America.* New York: United Nations, 1966.

"Industrial Development in Latin America," *Economic Bulletin for Latin America,* 14, no. 2 (1969).

EDWARDS, ALBERTO *La Fronda Aristocrática en Chile.* Santiago: Imprenta Nacional, 1928.

EGUIA RUIZ, CONSTANCIO *España y sus Misiones en los Paises del Plata.* Madrid: Ediciones Cultura Hispánica, 1953.

ENDREK, EMILIANO *El Mestizaje en Córdoba.* Córdoba: Universidad Nacional de Córdoba, 1966.

ERASMUS, CHARLES J. "The Occurrence and Disappearance of Reciprocal Farm Labor in Latin America," *Southwestern Journal of Anthropology,* 12 (1956).

"Upper Limits of Peasantry and Agrarian Reform: Bolivia, Venezuela and Mexico Compared," *Ethnology,* 6, no. 4 (1967a).

"Culture Change in Northwest Mexico," in Julian H. Steward, ed., *Contemporary Change in Traditional Societies.* Urbana: University of Illinois Press, 1967b.

ESPINOZA R., GUSTAVO, AND CARLOS MALPICA *El Problema de la Tierra.* Lima: Biblioteca Amauta, 1970.

FALS-BORDA, ORLANDO *Subversion and Social Change in Colombia.* New York: Columbia University Press, 1969.

FARIA, BENTO DE *Direito Comercial,* vol 1. Rio de Janeiro: Coelho Branco, 1947.

FASOLINO, NICOLAS "Una Institución del Clero Porteño en los Dias de la Colonia," *Academia Nacional de Historia, II Congreso Internacional de Historia de América,* vol. 3. Buenos Aires, 1938.

FERRAZ, PAULO MALTA "Como Vieram os Primeiros Colonos," in *Centenário de Blumenau.* Blumenau: Ediçã de Commissão de Festejos, 1950.

FERREIRA RODRIGUES, ALFREDO *Almanak Literário e Estatístico do Rio Grande do Sul para 1915.* Rio Grande: Pinto, 1915.

FERRER, ALDO *The Argentine Economy.* Berkeley and Los Angeles: University of California Press, 1967.

FIENUP, DARELL F., RUSSELL H. BRANNON, AND FRANK A. FENDER *The Agricultural Development of Argentina.* New York: Praeger, 1969.

FITZGIBBON, RUSSELL H. "Continuismo," in Hugh M. Hamill, Jr., ed., *Dictatorship in Latin America.* New York: Knopf, 1965.

FORMAN, SHEPARD, AND JOYCE F. RIEGELHAUPT "Market Place and Marketing System: Toward a Theory of Peasant Economic Integration," *Comparative Studies in Society and History,* 12, no. 2 (1970).

FOSTER, GEORGE N. *Empire's Children: The People of Tzintzuntzan.* Washington, D.C.: Institute of Social Anthropology, Smithsonian Institution, 1948.

Culture and Conquest: America's Spanish Heritage. New York: Wenner-Gren Foundation for Anthropological Research, 1960.

Traditional Cultures and the Impact of Technological Change. New York: Harper & Row, 1962.

FREYRE, GILBERTO *Ingleses no Brasil.* Rio de Janeiro: Livraria José Olympio, 1948.

FUNDAÇÃO IBGE *Brasil, Séries Estatísticas Retrospectivas.* Rio de Janeiro: Instituto Brasileiro de Estatística, 1970.

Anuário Estatístico do Basil, 1972. Rio de Janeiro: Instituto Brasileiro de Estatística, 1972.

FURTADO, CELSO *Economic Development of Latin America*. Cambridge: Cambridge University Press, 1970.

GANON, ISAAC *El Movimiento Estudantil en Uruguay*. Montevideo: Mimeographed. 1965.

GARCIA, ANTONIO *Perú: Una Reforma Agraria Autentica*. Lima: Institutó Nacional de Planificación, 1970.

GERMANI, GINO *Estructura Social de la Argentina*. Buenos Aires: Editorial Raigal, 1955.

"The Process of Urbanization in Argentina," *United Nations Economic and Social Council General*, E/CN 12/URB/LA/9, New York: September 1958.

GIBSON, CHARLES *Spain in America*. New York: Harper & Row, 1966.

"Spanish-Indian Institutions and Colonial Urbanism in New Spain," in Jorge Enrique Hardoy and Richard P. Schaedel, eds., *The Urbanization Process in America from Its Origins to the Present Day*. Buenos Aires: Editorial del Instituto Torcuato Di Tella, 1969.

GILLIN, JOHN "Tribes of the Guianas and the Left Amazon Tributaries," in Julian H. Steward, ed., *Handbook of South American Indians*. Washington, D.C.: Government Printing Office, 1948.

"Modern Latin American Culture," *Social Forces*, 25 (1946–1947).

GILMORE, ROBERT C. *Caudillism and Militarism in Venezuela, 1810–1910*. Athens: Ohio University Press, 1964.

GLADE, WILLIAM P., JR., AND CHARLES W. ANDERSON *The Political Economy of Mexico*. Madison: University of Wisconsin Press, 1968.

GONDRA, LUIS ROGUE *Historia Económica de la República Argentina*. Buenos Aires: Editorial Sudamericana, 1943.

GÓNGORA, MARIO *Origen de los Inquilinos de Chile Central*. Santiago: Universidad de Chile, 1960.

GOULART REIS FILHO, NESTOR *Evolução Urbana do Brasil*. São Paulo: Livraria Pioneira Editora, 1968.

GRAHAM, RICHARD *Britain and the Onset of Modernization in Brazil, 1850–1914*. Cambridge: Cambridge University Press, 1968.

GUARDA, GABRIEL *La Ciudad Chilena del Siglo XVIII*. Buenos Aires: Centro Editor de América Latina, 1968.

GUTIERREZ DE PINEDA, VIRGINIA *La Familia en Colombia*, vol. 1, Trasfondo Historico, Bogotá: Facultad de Sociologia, 1963.

Familia y Cultura en Colombia. Bogotá: Coediciones de Tercer Mundo y Departmento de Sociologia, Universidad Nacional de Colombia, 1968.

HAGEN, EVERETT E. *On the Theory of Social Change*. Homewood, Ill.: Dorsey, 1962.

HANKE, LEWIS *The Portuguese in Spanish America, with Special Reference to the Villa Real de Potosí*. n.d.

"Potosí: Suprema Ciudad del Auge," in Luis Capoche, ed., *Relación General de la Villa Imperial de Potosí*. Madrid: Atlas, 1959.

HARDOY, JORGE ENRIQUE "Dos Mil Años de Urbanización en América Latina," in Jorge Henrique Hardoy and Carlos Tobar, eds., *La Urbanización en América Latina*. Buenos Aires: Editorial del Instituto Torcuato di Tella, 1969.

HARING, CLARENCE HENRY *The Spanish Empire in America*. New York: Oxford University Press, 1947.

HAVIGHURST, ROBERT J., AND APARECIDA J. GOUVEIA *Brazilian Secondary Education and Socio-Economic Development*. New York: Praeger, 1969.

HAWTHORN, HARRY B., AND AUDREY ENGLE HAWTHORN "Stratification in a Latin American City," *Social Forces*, 27, no. 1 (1948).

HEATH, DWIGHT B., CHARLES J. ERASMUS, AND HANS C. BUECHLER *Land Reform and Social Revolution in Bolivia.* New York: Praeger, 1969.

HEATON, LOUISE E. *The Agricultural Development of Venezuela.* New York: Praeger, 1969.

HECHEN, JORGE "The Argentine Republic," in Oscar Handlin, ed., *The Positive Contribution by Immigrants.* Paris: UNESCO, 1955.

HERRMANN, LUCIA "Evolução da Estrutura Social de Guaratinguetá num Período de Trezentos Anos," *Revista de Administração,* 2, nos. 5–6. São Paulo: Universidad de São Paulo, 1948.

HERSKOVITS, MELVILLE, J. *Man and His Works.* New York: Knopf, 1948.

HEYDUK, DANIEL *Huayrapampa: Bolivian Highland Peasants and the New Social Order.* Ithaca, N.Y.: Cornell University Press, 1971.

HOETINK, H. *The Two Variants in Caribbean Race Relations.* New York: Oxford University Press, 1967.

HOLMBERG, ALLAN R. "Changing Community Attitudes and Values in Peru: A Case Study in Guided Change," in Richard N. Adams, John P. Gillin, Allan R. Holmberg, Oscar Lewis, Richard W. Patch, and Charles Wagley, eds., *Social Change in Latin America Today.* New York: Vintage, 1961.

HOLMBERG, ALLAN R., AND HENRY F. DOBYNS "The Cornell Program in Vicos, Peru," in Clifton R. Wharton, Jr., ed., *Subsistence Agriculture and Economic Development.* Chicago: Aldine, 1969.

HOUTART, FRANÇOIS, AND EMILE PIN *The Church and the Latin American Revolution.* New York: Sheed and Ward, 1965.

HUGHLETT, LLOYD J., ed. *Industrialization of Latin America.* New York: McGraw-Hill, 1946.

HUMBOLDT, ALEXANDER VON *Political Essay of the Kingdom of New Spain.* vol. 1, New York: Riley, 1811.

HUTCHINSON, BERTRAM *Mobilidade e Trabalho.* Rio de Janeiro: Centro Brasileiro de Pesquisas Educacionais,1960

"Social Mobility Rates in Buenos Aires, Montevideo and São Paulo: A Preliminary Comparison," *América Latina,* 5, no. 4 (1962).

"The Migrant Population of Urban Brazil," *América Latina,* 6, no. 2 (1963).

HUTCHINSON, HARRY WILLIAM *Village and Plantation Life in Northeastern Brazil.* Seattle: University of Washington Press, 1957.

IANNI, OCTAVIO *Crisis in Brazil.* New York: Columbia University Press, 1970.

IBGE (Instituto Brasileiro de Geografia e Estatística) *Sinopse Estatística do Brasil.* Rio de Janeiro: Conselho Nacional de Estatística, 1946.

Estado de São Paulo. Sinopse Preliminar do Censo Demográfico. Rio de Janeiro: Serviço Nacional de Recenseamento, 1962.

IMAZ, JOSÉ LUIS DE *Los que Mandan.* Albany: State University of New York Press, 1970.

IRELAND, ROWAN "The Church and Social Change," in Riordan Roett, ed., *Brazil in the Sixties.* Nashville, Tenn.: Vanderbilt University Press, 1972.

ITURRIAGA, JOSÉ E. *La Estructura Social y Cultural de México.* México City: Fondo de Cultura Económica, 1951.

JARAMILLO URIBE, JAIME "Esclavos y Señores en la Sociedad Colombiana del Siglo XVIII," in *Anuario Colombiano de Historia Social y de la Cultura,* 1, no. 1. Bogotá: Universidad Nacional de Colombia, Facultad de Filosofia y Letras, 1963a.

"Historia de Pereira, 1863–1963," in Luis Duque Gomes, Juan Friede, and Jaime Jaramillo Uribe, eds., *Historia de Pereira.* Pereira: Edición del Clube Rotario, 1936b.

"Mestizaje y Diferenciación Social en el Nuevo Reino de Granada en la Segunda Mitad del Siglo XVIII," *Anuario Colombiano de Historia Social y de la Cultura,*

2, no. 3. Bogotá: Universidad Nacional de Colombia, Facultad de Ciencias Humanas, 1965.

JOHNSON, JOHN J. *Political Change in Latin America*. Stanford, Calif.: Stanford University Press, 1958.

KELLEY, R. LYNN "The Role of the Venezuelan Senate," in Weston H. Agor, ed., *Latin American Legislatures: Their Role and Influence*. New York: Praeger, 1961.

KELLY, ISABEL "Mexican Spiritualism," in George M. Foster, ed., *Contemporary Latin American Culture: An Anthropological Sourcebook*. New York: Selected Academic Readings, 1965.

KING, JAMES F. "The Case of José Ponciano de Ayarza: A Document on Gracias al Sacar," *Hispanic American Historical Review*, 31 (1951).

KONETZKE, RICHARD *Die Indianerkulturen Altamerikas und die spanisch-portugiesische Kolonialherrschaft*. Frankfurt: Fischer, 1965.

"La Legislación Española y el Mestizaje en América," in *El Mestizaje en la Historia de Ibero-América*. Instituto Panamericano de Geografía e Historia. Mexico City: Comisión de Historia de Mexico, 1967.

KOTTAK, CONRAD PHILLIP "Kinship and Class in Brazil," *Ethnology*, 6, no. 4 (1967).

KUBLER, GEORGE A. "The Quechua in the Colonial World," in Julian H. Steward, ed., *Handbook of South American Indians*, vol. 2. Washington, D.C.: Government Printing Office, 1946

"Cities and Culture in the Colonial Period of Latin America," *Diogenes*, no. 47 (Fall 1964).

LAMBERT, JACQUES *Latin America: Social Structure and Political Institutions*. Berkeley and Los Angeles: University of California Press, 1967.

LA PRENSA Lima, December 26, 1970.

LAS SIETE PARTIDAS Translation and notes by Samuel Parson Scott, New York: Commerce Clearing House, 1931.

LATTES, ZULMA L. RECCHINI DE, AND ALFREDO E. LATTES *Migraciones en la Argentina*. Buenos Aires: Editorial de Instituto, 1969.

LAUTERBACH, ALBERT *Enterprise in Latin America*. Ithaca, N.Y.: Cornell University Press, 1966.

LEACOCK, SETH, AND RUTH LEACOCK *Spirits of the Deep. A Study of an Afro-Brazilian Cult*. Garden City, N.Y.: Doubleday, 1972.

LEEDS, ANTHONY "Brazil and the Myth of Francisco Julião," in Joseph Maier and Richard W. Weatherhead, eds., *Politics of Change in Latin America*. New York, Praeger, 1964.

"The Significant Variables Determining the Character of Squatter Settlements," *América Latina*, 12, no. 3 (1969).

LÉONS, MADELINE BARBARA "Stratification and Pluralism in the Bolivian Yungas," in Walter Goldschmidt and Harry Hoijer, eds., *The Social Anthropology of Latin America*. Los Angeles: Latin American Center, 1970.

LEWIS, OSCAR "The Culture of Poverty," in *La Vida*. New York: Random House, Vintage, 1966.

LINTON, RALPH *The Study of Man*. New York: Appleton, 1936.

LIPMAN, AARON *The Colombian Entrepreneur in Bogotá*. Coral Gables, Fla.: University of Miami Press, 1969.

LIPSET, SEYMOUR MARTIN "Values, Education and Entrepreneurship," in Seymour Martin Lipset and Aldo Solari, eds., *Elites in Latin America*. New York: Oxford University Press, 1967.

LITTLE, ARTHUR D., INC. *Industrial Development in Argentina*. Report to the Government of Argentina and the International Corporation Administration, 1961.

LOCKHART, JAMES *Spanish Peru 1522–1560*. Madison: University of Wisconsin Press, 1968.

MCALISTER, L. N. "Recent Research and Writings on the Role of the Military in Latin America," *Latin American Research Review*, 2, no. 1 (1966).

MCCOY, TERRY L. "Congress, the President, and Political Instability in Peru," in Weston H. Agor, ed., *Latin American Legislatures: Their Role and Influence*. New York: Praeger, 1971.

MCDONALD, RONALD H. *Party Systems and Elections in Latin America*. Chicago: Markham, 1971.

MACEDO, JOSÉ NORBERTO *Fazendas de Gado no Vale São Francisco*. Rio de Janeiro: Ministério da Agricultura, Serviço de Informação Agrícola, 1952.

MCGREEVY, WILLIAM PAUL *An Economic History of Colombia, 1845–1930*. Cambridge: Cambridge University Press, 1971.

MADDOX, JAMES G. *Technical Assistance by Religious Agencies in Latin America*. Chicago: University of Chicago Press, 1956.

MALLOY, JAMES M. *Bolivia: The Uncompleted Revolution*. Pittsburgh: University of Pittsburgh Press, 1970.

MANGIN, WILLIAM "Latin American Squatter Settlements: A Problem and a Solution," *Latin American Research Review*, 2, no. 3 (1967).

"Similarities and Differences Between Two Types of Peruvian Communities," in William Mangin, ed., *Peasants in Cities: Readings in the Anthropology of Urbanization*. Boston: Houghton Mifflin, 1970.

MANIFESTO DOS PIONEIROS DA EDUCAÇÃO NOVA São Paulo: Companhia Editora Nacional, 1932.

MANITZAS, NITA R. *Conflict, Consensus and the New Cuban Politics*. Nashville, Tenn.: Graduate Center for Latin American Studies, Vanderbilt University. Occasional Paper No. 7, 1971.

MARTINEZ, CARLOS *Santafé de Bogotá*. Buenos Aires: Centro Editor de America Latina, 1968.

MARTNER, DANIEL *Historia de Chile. Historia Económica*. Santiago: Barcello, 1929.

MATHIASON, JOHN R., AND JOHN D. POWELL "Participation and Efficacy: Aspects of Peasant Involvement in Political Mobilization," *Comparative Politics*, 4 (1972).

MATOS MAR, JOSÉ "Migration and Urbanization," in Philip Hauser, ed., *Urbanization in Latin America*. New York: United Nations, 1961.

Urbanización y Barriadas en América del Sud. Lima: Instituto de Estudios Peruanos, 1968.

La Tenencia de la Tierra en una Micro-Región de Costa Central. Lima: Instituto de Estudios Peruanos, 1969.

MAWE, JOHN *Travels in the Interior of Brazil*. Philadelphia: Carey; Boston: Wells and Lilly, 1916.

MECHAM, J. LLOYD *Church and State in Latin America*. Chapel Hill: University of North Carolina Press, 1934.

MENDOZA, DANIEL *El Llanero*. Buenos Aires: Editorial Venezuela, 1947.

METRAUX, ALFRED *La Civilisation Materièlle des Tribus Tupi-Guarani*. Paris: P. Geuthner, 1928.

MILLER, DELBERT C., EVA CHAMORRO GRECO, AND JUAN AGULLA *De la Industria al Poder*. Buenos Aires: Ediciones Libera, 1966.

MINTZ, SIDNEY W., AND ERIC R. WOLF "An Analysis of Ritual Co-Parenthood (Compadrazco)," *Southwestern Journal of Anthropology*, 6, no. 4 (1950).

MISHKIN, BERNARD "The Contemporary Quechua," in Julian Steward, ed., *Handbook of South American Indians. The Andean Civilizations*. Smithsonian Institution-Bureau of American Ethnology, Bulletin 143. Washington, D.C.; Government Printing Office, 1946.

MÖRNER, MAGNUS *Race Mixture in the History of Latin America*. Boston: Little, Brown, 1967.

MORSE, RICHARD M. "Some Themes of Brazilian History," *South Atlantic Quarterly*, 61, no. 2 (1962).

"Recent Research on Latin American Urbanization: A Selective Survey with Commentary," *Latin American Research Review*, 1 (Fall 1965).

MORSE, RICHARD M., ed. *The Bandeirantes*. New York: Knopf, 1965.

MOSK, SANFORD A. *Industrial Revolution in Mexico*. Berkeley and Los Angeles: University of California Press, 1954.

MYREN, DELBERT T. "The Rockefeller Foundation in Corn and Wheat," in Clifton R. Wharton, Jr., ed., *Subsistence Agricultures and Economic Development*. Chicago: Aldine, 1969.

NASH, MANNING *Machine Age Maya*. Chicago: University of Chicago Press, 1958.

NEEDLER, MARTIN C. *Anatomy of a Coup d'Etat*. Washington, D.C.: Institute for the Comparative Study of Political Systems, 1964.

"Politics and National Character: The Case of Mexico," *American Anthropologist*, 73 (1971)

NEGLIA, ANGELO, AND FABIO HERNANDEZ *Marginalidad, Población y Familia*. Bogotá: Instituto de Desarrollo de la Comunidad, 1970.

NICHOLLS, WILLIAM H. "The Agricultural Frontier in Modern Brazilian History: The State of Paraná, 1920–1965," in Merrill Rippy, ed., *Cultural Change in Brazil*. Muncie, Ind.: Ball State University Press, 1969.

NORDENSKIÖLD, ERLAND *The Ethnography of South America Seen from the Mojos in Bolivia*. Göteborg (Sweden): Comparative Ethnographical Studies, 5 (1924).

NORTH, LISA *Civil/Military Relations in Argentina, Chile and Peru*. Berkeley: University of California, Institute of International Studies, 1966.

OLIVEIRA MARTINS, JOAQUIM PEDRO *A History of Iberian Civilization*. New York: Oxford University Press, 1930.

OTS CAPDEQUI, JOSÉ MARIA *El Estado Español en las Indias*. Mexico City: El Colegio de México, 1941.

PARSONS, JAMES J. *Antioqueño Colonization in Western Colombia*. Berkeley and Los Angeles: University of California Press, 1968.

PATCH, RICHARD "Bolivia: The Restrained Revolution," *Annals of the American Academy of Political and Social Science*, March 1961.

PERLMUTTER, AMOS "The Praetorian State and the Praetorian Army: Toward a Taxonomy of Civil/Military Relations," *Comparative Politics*, 1, no. 3 (1969).

PETERSON, JOHN H. "Recent Research on Latin American University Students," *Latin American Research Review*, 5, no. 1 (1970).

PETRAS, JAMES *Political and Social Forces in Chilean Development*. Berkeley: University of California Press, 1969.

PICKLES, ALAN "Cassava in the Amazon Valley," *Proceedings of the Agricultural Society of Trinidad and Tobago*, 42, pt. 2 (1942).

PIKE, FREDERICK B., ed. *The Conflict Between Church and State in Latin America*. New York: Knopf, 1964.

PIN, EMILE *Elementos para una Sociologia del Catolicismo Latinoamericano*. Freiburg and Bogotá: Oficina Internacional de Investigaciones de Feres, 1963.

PINCHAS GEIGER, PEDRO *Evolução da Rede Urbana Brasileira*. Rio de Janeiro: Instituto Nacional de Estudos Pedagógicos, 1963.

PINEDA GIRALDO, ROBERT *Crecimiento Urbano. Causas y Consecuencias. Notas de Catedra*. Bogotá: Centro Inter-Americano de Vivienda y Planeamiento, 1969.

POBLETE, TRONCOSO MOISES *Condiciones de Vida y de Trabajo de la Población Indígena del Perú*. Geneva: Oficina International de Trabajo, 1938.

PORTES, ALEJANDRO *Cuatro Poblaciones: Informe Preliminar sobre Situación y Aspiraciones de Grupos Marginados en el Gran Santiago*. Santiago: 1969. Mimeographed.

PRADO JUNIOR, CAIO   *Formação do Brasil Contemporâneo*. São Paulo: Editora Brasiliana, 1963.

PREFEITURA MUNICIPAL DE SÃO PAULO   *Plano Urbanístico Básico*, vol. 1. *Desenvolvimento Físico e Socio-Cultural*, Mimeographed, 1968.

QUEIROZ, MARIA ISAURA   *Os Cangaceiros. Les Bandits d'Honeur Brésiliens*. Paris: Collections Archives, No. 34, 1968.

QUIGLEY, CARROLL   "Mexican National Character and Circum-Mediterranean Personality Structure," *American Anthropologist*, 75 (1973).

RAMA, CARLOS M.   *Las Clases Sociales en el Uruguay*. Montevideo: Ediciones Nuestro Tiempo, 1960.

Die Arbeiterbewegung in Lateinamerika. Berlin: Gehlen, 1967.

RAMIREZ, MUÑOZ HUMBERTO   *Sociologia Religiosa de Chile*. Santiago: Ediciones Paulinas, 1957.

RAMOS, ARTHUR   "The Negro in Brazil," in T. Lynn Smith and A. Marchant, eds., *Brazil, Portrait of Half a Continent*. New York: Dryden, 1951.

RANDLE, P. H.   *La Ciudad Pampeana*. Buenos Aires: Editorial Universitaria, 1969.

RAY, TALTON F.   *The Politics of the Barrios of Venezuela*. Berkeley and Los Angeles: University of California Press, 1969.

READ, WILLIAM R., M. MONTERROSO, AND HARMAN A. JOHNSON   *Latin American Church Growth*. Grand Rapids, Mich.: Eerdmans, 1969.

REBELLO DA SILVA, L. A.   *Memória sôbre a População e a Agricultura*. Lisbon: Losada, 1868.

REDFIELD, ROBERT   *The Folk Culture of Yucatán*. Chicago: University of Chicago Press, 1941.

REIS FILHO, NESTOR G.   *Quadro da Arquitetura no Brasil*. São Paulo: Editora Perspectiva, 1970.

REPÚBLICA DE VENEZUELA, MINISTÉRIO DE FOMENTO   *Octavo Censo General de Población*, vol. 12. Caracas: Dirección General de Estadística y Censos Nacionales, 1957.

RIBEIRO, FAVILA   *A Latifúndio na Conjuntura Urbana*. Fortaleza, Brazil: manuscript, n.d.

RIBEIRO, JOÃO   *História do Brasil*. Rio de Janeiro: Livraria Francisco Alves, 1935.

RIBEIRO, RENÉ   *Religião e Relações Raciais*. Rio de Janeiro: Ministério da Educação e Cultura, 1956.

RICARDO, CASSIANO   *Marcha para Oeste*. Rio de Janeiro: Livrria José Olympio, 1965.

RICHARDSON, M.   *San Pedro, Colombia*. New York: Holt, Rinehart & Winston, 1970.

RIOS, JOSÉ ARTHUR   "The Cities of Brazil," in T. Lynn Smith and Alexander Marchant, eds., *Brazil: Portrait of Half a Continent*. New York: Dryden, 1951.

Plano de Recuperação de Alagdos. Salvador: Mimeographed, 1969

RIPPY, J. FRED   *Latin America and the Industrial Age*. New York: Putnam, 1944.

RIVAROLA, D. M. AND G. HEISECKE   *Población, Urbanización y Recursos Humanos en el Paraguay*, 2nd ed. Asunción: Centro Paraguayo de Estudios Sociologicos, 1970.

RIVERA, JULIUS   *Latin America*. New York: Appleton, 1971.

ROCHA POMBO, JOSÉ FRANCISCO DA   *História do Brasil*, vol. 8. Rio de Janeiro: Benjamin Aguila, n.d.

ROETT, RIORDAN   "A Praetorian Army in Politics," in Riordan Roett, ed., *Brazil in the Sixties*. Nashville, Tenn.: Vanderbilt University Press, 1972

ROMANO DE TOBAR, MARGOT   "El Buenos Aires de los Villeros," *Nuevo Mundo*, no. 29 (1968).

ROMERO, EMILIO   *Historia Económica y Financera del Perú*. Lima: Torres Aguirre, 1937.

Historia Económica del Perú. Buenos Aires: Editorial Sudamericana, 1949.

ROSENBLAT, ANGEL. *La Población Indígena y el Mestizaje en América*, 2 vols. Buenos Aires: Editorial Nova, 1954.

ROSENZWEIG, FERNANDO "El Desarrollo Económico de México de 1877 a 1911," *Trimestre Económico*, 33 (1963).

ROYAL INSTITUTE OF INTERNATIONAL AFFAIRS *The Republics of South America*. New York: Oxford University Press, 1937.

RUDDLE, KENNETH, AND MUKHTAR HAMOUR, eds. *Statistical Abstracts of Latin America 1970*. Los Angeles: Latin American Center of the University of California, 1971.

RUDDLE, KENNETH, AND PHILIP GILLETTE, eds. *Latin American Political Statistics*. Los Angeles: Latin American Center of the University of California, 1971.

RUSSELL-WOOD, A. J. R. "Mobilidade Social na Bahia Colonial," *Revista Brasileira de Estudos Políticos*, 27. Belo Horizonte: Universidade Federal de Minas Gerais, 1969.

SAHLINS, MARSHALL D., AND ELMAN R. SERVICE *Evolution and Culture*. Ann Arbor: University of Michigan Press, 1960.

SALMON, LAWRENCE F. "A Perspective on the Resettlement of Squatters in Brazil," *América Latina*, 12 (1969).

SANCHEZ, CARLOS E., AND WALTER E. SCHULTHESS *Inmigración y Población en la Ciudad de Córdoba, 1947–1966*. Córdoba: Instituto de Economia y Finanzas, 1967.

SANDNER, GERHARD *Die Hauptstädte Zentralamerikas*. Heidelberg: Quelle & Meyer, 1969.

SANDOVAL, FERNANDO B. *La Industria del Azucar en Nueva España*. México City: Publicaciones del Instituto de Historia; 1st ser. no. 21, 1951.

SANTOS, PAULO T. "Inventário de Plantas dos Arquivos como Ponto de Partida do Estudo de Formação de Cidades," *V Colóquio Internacional de Estudos Luso-Brasileiros*. Coimbra: Gráfica de Coimbra, 1963.

SARFATTI, MAGALI *Spanish Bureaucratic-Patrimonialism in America*. Berkeley: Institute of International Studies, University of California, 1966.

SAUER, CARL O. "Cultivated Plants of South and Central America," in Julian H. Steward, ed., *Handbook of South American Indians*, vol. 6. Washington, D.C.: Government Printing Office, 1950.

SCHAEDEL, RICHARD P. "Land Reform Studies," *Latin American Research Review*, 1, no. 1 (1965).

SCHEMAN, RONALD L. "The Brazilian Law Student: Background, Habits, Attitudes," *Journal of Inter-American Studies*, 5 (1963).

SCHMIDT, CARLOS BORGES *O Milho e o Monjolo*. Rio de Janeiro: Ministério da Agricultura, Serviço de Informação Agrícola, 1967.

SCHUH, EDWARD *The Agricultural Development of Brazil*. New York: Praeger, 1970.

SCHWARTZ, STUART B. "Cities of Empire: Mexico and Bahia in the Sixteenth Century," *Journal of Inter-American Studies*, 2 (1969).

SCOBIE, JAMES R. *Argentina, A City and a Nation*, 2nd. ed. New York: Oxford University Press, 1971.

SECRETARIA DA AGRICULTURA, INDÚSTRIA E COMÉRCIO DO ESTADO DE SÃO PAULO *Estatística Industrial do Estado de São Paulo, Ano de 1935*. São Paulo: Tipografia Siqueira, 1937.

SEPÚLVEDA, ALBERTO "El Militarismo Desarrollista en América Latina," in Carlos Naudon, ed., *América 70*. Santiago: Ediciones Nueva Universidad, 1970.

SERVICE, ELMAN R. *Spanish/Guarany Relations in Early Colonial Paraguay*. Anthropological Paper, No. 9, Museum of Anthropology, University of Michigan. Ann Arbor: University of Michigan Press, 1954.

SILVERT, KALMAN "The Social Origins and Political Commitment of the Latin American University Student," presented to the Sixth World Congress of the International Political Science Association, Geneva, 1964.

SINGER, PAUL *Desenvolvimento Econômico e Evolução Urbana.* São Paulo: Companhia Editora Nacional, 1968.

SKIDMORE, THOMAS E. *Politics in Brazil, 1930–1964.* New York: Oxford University Press, 1967.

SMITH, M. G. *The Plural Society in the British West Indies.* Berkeley and Los Angeles: University of California Press, 1965.

SMITH, ROBERT S. "Medieval Agrarian Society in its Prime: 3, Spain," in M. M. Postan, ed., *The Cambridge Economic History of Europe,* vol. 1, 2nd ed. Cambridge: Cambridge University Press, 1966.

SMITH, T. LYNN *Brazil, People and Institutions.* Baton Rouge: Louisiana State University Press, 1963.

——— *Colombia. Social Structure and the Process of Development.* Gainesville: University of Florida Press, 1967.

——— "Studies of Colonization and Settlement," *Latin American Research Review,* 1, no. 1 (1969).

——— *Studies of Latin American Societies.* Garden City, N.Y.: Doubleday, 1970.

SOLARI, ALDO "Secondary Education and the Development of Elites," in Seymour Martin Lipset and Aldo Solari, eds., *Elites in Latin America.* New York: Oxford University Press, 1967.

SOLBERG, CARL *Immigration and Nationalisms Argentina and Chile, 1890–1914.* Austin: University of Texas Press, 1970.

SOUZA, BERNADINO JOSÉ DE *Ciclo de Carro de Bois no Brasil.* São Paulo: Companhia Editora Nacional, 1958.

SPRINGER, PHILIP B. "Social Sources of Political Behavior of Venezuelan Officers: An Exploratory Analysis," *Politico,* 30 (1965).

STADEN, HANS *The True History of His Captivity 1557.* New York: McBride, 1929.

STEGER, HANNS-ALBERT "Einige für das Verständnis des lateinamerikanischen Hochschulwesens wichtige historische und ökonomische Aspekte," in Hanns-Albert Steger, ed., *Grundzüge des Lateinamerikanischen Hochschulwesens.* Baden-Baden: Nomos Verlagsgesellschaft, 1965.

STEIN, STANLEY J. *The Brazilian Cotton Manufacture.* Cambridge, Mass.: Harvard University Press, 1957.

——— *Grandeza e Decadência do Café no Vale do Paraiba.* São Paulo: Editora Brasiliana, 1961.

STEIN, STANLEY J., AND BARBARA H. STEIN *The Colonial Heritage of Latin America.* New York: Oxford University Press, 1970.

STOLNITZ, GEORGE J. "The Revolution in Death Control in Nonindustrial Countries," *Annals of the American Academy of Political and Social Science,* 316 (1958).

STOVALL, ROLLO P. "Dominican Yuca Plays a Dual Role," in U.S. Office of Foreign Agricultural Relations, *Agriculture in the Americas,* vol. 7. Washington, D.C.: Government Printing Office, 1947.

STRICKON, ARNOLD "Class and Kinship in Argentina," in Dwight B. Heath and Richard N. Adams, eds., *Contemporary Cultures and Societies of Latin America.* New York: Random House, 1965.

STYCOS, J. M. *Family and Fertility in Puerto Rico.* New York: Columbia University Press, 1955.

TANNENBAUM, FRANK "Personal Government in Mexico," in Olen E. Leonard and Charles P. Loomis, eds., *Readings in Latin American Social Organization and Institutions.* East Lansing: Michigan State College Press, 1953.

TAYLOR, CARL C. *Rural Life in Argentina.* Baton Rouge: Louisiana State University Press, 1948.

TINNERMEIER, RONALD L. *New Land Settlement in the Eastern Lowlands of Colombia.* University of Wisconsin unpublished Ph.D. dissertation, 1964.

TISCHENDORF, ALFRED *Geat Britain and Mexico in the Era of Porfirio Dias*. Durham: Duke University Press, 1961.

TORMO, LEANDRO *Historia de la Iglesia en América Latina*, vol. I. *La Evangelización de la América Latina*. Bogotá: Oficina Internacional de Investigaciones Sociales de FERES, 1962.

TORRES, ANTÔNIO *As Razões da Inconfidência*. Belo Horizonte: Editora Itatiaia Limitada, 1957.

TURNER, JOHN C. "Barriers and Channels for Housing Development in Modernizing Countries," in William Mangin, ed., *Peasants in Cities*. Boston: Houghton Mifflin, 1970.

UNESCO *World Survey of Education: Secondary Level*. Paris: United Nations, 1961.

UNITED NATIONS *Statistical Yearbook 1971*. New York: United Nations, 1972.

UNITED NATIONS *Demographic Yearbook 1972*. New York: United Nations, 1973.

UNITED NATIONS FOOD AND AGRICULTURAL ORGANIZATION *Coffee in Latin America. I. Colombia and El Salvador*. New York: United Nations, 1958.

UNIVERSIDAD DE CHILE *La Población del Gran Santiago*. Santiago: Instituto de Economia, 1959.

USANDIZAGA, ELSA, AND EUGENE A. HAVENS *Tres Barrios de Invasión*. Bogotá, Ediciones Tercer Mundo, 1966.

VALDES, ERNESTO GARZON "Die Universitätsreform von Cordoba-Argentinien (1918)," in Hanns-Albert Steger, ed., *Grundzüge des Lateinamerikanischen Hochschulwesens*. Baden-Baden: Nomos Verlagsgesellschaft, 1965.

VALDIVIA PONCE, OSCAR *Migración Interna a la Metropoli*. Lima: Imprenta de la Universidad Nacional Mayor de San Marcos, 1970.

VALLENILLA LANZ, LAUREANO *Cesarismo Democrático*. Caracas: Tipográfia Garrid, 1961.

VALLIER, IVAN "Religious Elites: Differentiations and Developments in Roman Catholicism," in Seymour Martin Lipset and Aldo Solari, eds., *Elites in Latin America*. New York: Oxford University Press, 1967.

VALVERDE, ORLANDO, AND CATHARINA VERGOLINO DIAS *A Rodovia Belém-Brasília*. Rio de Janeiro: Instituto Brasileiro de Geografia, 1967.

VASQUEZ DE ESPINOSA, ANTONIO *Compendium and Description of the West Indies* (translated by Charles Upson Clark). Smithsonian Miscellaneous Collection, vol. 102. Washington, D.C.: Smithsonian Institution, 1942.

VEKEMANS, ROGER, AND J. L. SEGUNDO "Essay of a Socio-Economic Typology of the Latin American Countries," in Egbert de Vries and José Medina Echavarria, eds., *Social Aspects of Economic Development in Latin America*, vol. 1. Paris. UNESCO, 1963.

VELIZ, CLAUDIO, ed. *The Politics of Conformity in Latin America*. London, New York: Oxford University Press, 1967.

VENEZIAN, EDUARDO L., AND WILLIAM K. GAMBLE *The Agricultural Development of Mexico*. New York: Praeger, 1969.

VIANNA, OLIVEIRA *Instituições Políticas Brasileiras*, vol. 1. Rio de Janeiro: Livraria José Olympio, 1949.

Populações Meridionais do Brasil, vol. 2. Rio de Janeiro: Livraria José Olympio, 1952.

VILAÇA, MARCOS V., AND ROBERT C. DE ALBUQUERQUE *Coronel, Coroneis*. Rio de Janeiro: Tempo Brasileiro, 1965.

VILLALOBOS, R. SERGIO *El Comercio y la Crisis Colonial*. Santiago: Ediciones de la Universidad de Chile, 1968.

VILLEGAS, DANIEL COSIO "The Mexican Left," in Joseph Maier and Richard W. Weatherhead, eds., *Politics of Change in Latin America*. New York: Praeger, 1964.

VILLELA, ANNIBAL VILLANOVA, AND WILSON SUZIGAN *Política do Governo e Crescimento da Economia Brasileira. 1889–1945.* Rio de Janeiro: Instituto de Planejamento Econômico e Social, Instituto de Pesquisas, 1973.

VIOTTI COSTA, EMÍLIA "Cotia e Itapecerica da Serra, Subúrbios Agrícolas," in Aroldo de Azevedo, ed., *A Cidade de São Paulo*, vol. 4. São Paulo: Companhia Editora Nacional, 1958.

VOGT, EVON Z. *The Zinacantecos of Mexico.* New York: Holt, Rinehart & Winston, 1970.

VOLLMER, GÜNTER *Bevölkerungspolitik and Bevölkerungsstruktur im Vizekönigreich Peru zu Ende der Kolonialzeit (1741–1821).* Berlin: Gehlen, 1967.

VON MARTIUS, CARL F. P. *Zur Ethnographie Amerikas.* Leipzig: Fleischer, 1867.

VON SPIX, J. B., AND C. F. P. VON MARTIUS *Travels in Brazil in the Years 1817–1820*, 2 vols. London: Longmans, 1824.

WAGLEY, CHARLES *Introduction to Brazil.* New York: Columbia University Press, 1963.

Amazon Town: A Study of Man in the Tropics. New York: Knopf, 1964.

The Latin American Tradition. New York: Columbia University Press, 1968.

WAGLEY, CHARLES, AND MARVIN HARRIS "A Typology of Latin American Subcultures," *American Anthropologist*, 57 (1955).

WALKER, KENNETH N. "Political Socialization in Universities," in Seymour Martin Lipset and Aldo Solari, eds., *Elites in Latin America.* New York: Oxford University Press, 1967.

WEBER, MAX *Grundriss der Sozialökonomik*, vol. 3. *Wirtschaft und Gesellschaft*, 2 vols. Tübingen: Mohr, 1925.

WEST, ROBERT C. *The Mining Community in Northern New Spain: The Parral Mining District.* Berkeley and Los Angeles: University of California Press, 1949.

WHETTEN, NATHAN L. *The Role of the Ejido in Mexican Land Reform.* Madison: Land Tenure Center, University of Wisconsin, 1963.

WHIFFEN, THOMAS *The North-West Amazonas.* London: Constable, 1915.

WHITE, LESLIE A. *The Evolution of Culture.* New York: McGraw-Hill, 1959.

WHITTEN, NORMAN E., JR. *Class, Kinship, and Power in an Ecuadorian Town.* Stanford, Calif: Stanford University Press, 1965.

WILDENMANN, RUDOLF "Politische Stellung and Kontrolle des Militärs," in René König, ed., *Beiträge zur Militärsoziologie.* Köln and Opladen: Westdeutscher Verlag, 1968.

WILHELMY, HERBERT *Südamerika im Spiegel seiner Städte.* Hamburg: De Gruyter, 1952.

WILLEMS, EMILIO *A Aculturação dos Alemães no Brasil.* São Paulo: Companhia Editora Nacional, 1946.

Buzios Island. A Caiçara Community of Southern Brazil. Monographs of the American Ethnological Society, No. 20. New York: The Society, 1952a.

"Caboclo Cultures of Southern Brazil," in Sol Tax, ed., *Acculturation in the Americas. Proceedings of the 29th International Congress of Americanists*, vol. 2. Chicago: 1952b.

"The Structure of the Brazilian Family," *Social Forces*, 31 (1953).

Uma Vila Brasileira: Tradiçao e Transiçao. Sao Paulo: Difusao Européia do Livro, 1961.

"Religious Mass Movements and Social Change in Brazil," in Eric N. Baklanoff, ed., *New Perspectives of Brazil.* Nashville, Tenn.: Vanderbilt University Press, 1966.

"A Classe Alta Chilena," *América Latina*, 10, no. 2 (1967a).

Followers of the New Faith: Culture Change and Rise of Protestantism in Brazil and Chile. Nashville, Tenn.: Vanderbilt University Press, 1967b.

"Culture Change and the Rise of Protestantism in Brazil and Chile," in S. N.

Eisenstadt, ed., *The Protestant Ethic and Modernization. A Comparative View.* New York: Basic Books, 1968.

"Social Differentiation in Colonial Brazil," *Comparative Studies in Society and History,* 12, no. 1 (January 1970a).

"Peasantry and City: Cultural Persistence and Change in Historical Perspective: A European Case," *American Anthropologist,* 72, no. 3 (June 1970b).

"The Rise of a Rural Middle Class in a Frontier Society," in Riordan Roett, ed., *Brasil in the Sixties.* Nashville, Tenn.: Vanderbilt University Press, 1972.

WOLF, ERIC R. "Types of Latin American Peasantry: A Preliminary Discussion," *American Anthropologist,* 57, no. 3 (1955). Quotation on p. 131 reproduced by permission of the American Anthropological Association.

Sons of the Shaking Earth. Chicago: University of Chicago Press, 1959.

Peasant Wars of the Twentieth Century. New York: Harper & Row, 1969.

WOLF, ERIC, AND EDWARD C. HANSEN "Caudillo Politics: A Structural Analysis," *Comparative Studies in Society and History,* 9, no. 2 (January 1967).

The Human Condition in Latin America. New York: Oxford University Press, 1972.

WOLF, ERIC R., AND SIDNEY W. MINTZ "Haciendas and Plantations in Middle America and the Antilles," *Social and Ecoonmic Studies,* 6 (1957).

WRIGHT, MARIE ROBINSON *The New Brazil,* 2nd ed. Philadelphia: Barrie, 1907.

ZEA, LEOPOLDO *The Latin American Mind.* Norman: University of Oklahoma Press, 1963.

Index